FOUR MIDDLE ENGLISH
MYSTERY CYCLES

Four Middle English Mystery Cycles

TEXTUAL, CONTEXTUAL, AND CRITICAL INTERPRETATIONS

MARTIN STEVENS

PRINCETON UNIVERSITY PRESS
PRINCETON, NEW JERSEY

Copyright © 1987 by Princeton University Press
Published by Princeton University Press, 41 William Street,
Princeton, New Jersey 08540
In the United Kingdom: Princeton University Press,
Guildford, Surrey

Publication of this book has been aided by a grant from the
Paul Mellon Fund of Princeton University Press
This book has been composed in Linotron Baskerville

Clothbound editions of Princeton University Press books
are printed on acid-free paper, and binding materials are
chosen for strength and durability. Paperbacks, although satisfactory
for personal collections, are not usually suitable for library rebinding

Printed in the United States of America by
Princeton University Press
Princeton, New Jersey

For Rose

And ek the pure wyse of hire mevyng
Shewed wel that men myght in hire gesse
Honour, estat, and wommanly noblesse.

CONTENTS

ILLUSTRATIONS

PREFACE

THIS book is the product of some twenty years of graduate teaching as well as the interest of an adult lifetime in the medieval drama. I believe that the Corpus Christi play was the root of the native dramatic tradition. It is primarily from the religious theater of the Middle Ages that the later English stage, especially that of the High Renaissance, gained its sense of time and space and, therefore, its dramatic form—one that is, in many respects, the antithesis of the classical drama. I perceive that this debt was the product of a world view more than a direct influence. Shakespeare, as is widely speculated, may have seen the Coventry plays. But what he knew about the *theatrum mundi* of the Middle Ages probably came less from being a spectator than it did from the absorption of the environment in which the drama was bred. He and other playwrights did inherit a stage that accommodated all the varieties of medieval drama, and they lived in a world that was influenced by a uniform salvation history, based on the Bible and its multiple interpreters and reflected in the liturgy, the art, and the social context of the late Middle Ages. This book argues that the English mystery cycles, as the first popular plays of a culture in which playcraft is of signal importance, were major works of dramatic art, each exploring its metaphysical universe in its own unique way.

The book is necessary, I believe, because it insists on recognizing the cycle form as a generic entity. As I hope to demonstrate, the Corpus Christi play has too often been represented to modern readers in partial or anthologized form. Most undergraduate students of literature receive their introduction to the medieval drama—and often make their only acquaintance with it—from a reading either of the Second Shepherds' Play or of an anthology of pageants put together from the several cycles. The graduate survey of Middle English literature is likely to repeat this practice, and the result is that the cycle as a literary form remains a much neglected genre of medieval literature. In fact, the great Corpus Christi cycles were among the most interesting and important literary texts of the late Middle Ages. They reflect the intellectual, spiritual, social, and aesthetic currents of their time as fully as the great works of the fourteenth century did, and they deserve to be seen whole as the finished works of art that they were. My hope is that this book will urge its readers to regard the cycles in this light.

The debt I owe to scholars who have written about the cycles and their contexts is too great to enumerate specifically here. My notes will single out a good many of them, but I am sure that there are others whose works influenced me profoundly if indirectly. One of this group needs, however, to be mentioned—not because I was his student (which I was not) and not because I have become his disciple (to the contrary, I have been his adversary). He is D. W. Robertson, Jr. In the small social world of medievalists, I have never met him, and so I have not been able to thank him in person. But I want him to know that I consider his *Preface to Chaucer* the most profound, even if sometimes the most obstinate, book in literary criticism that has been written in the last generation of medieval scholarship. I am not a Robertsonian, but I have learned more from the founder of that putative school than from many others whose doctrines I blindly accept.

My many graduate students, from the first time I taught the medieval drama at Ohio State to my present seminar at the City University of New York Graduate Center, have helped to create a forum that has brought the drama to life for me. I thank them deeply. Some have gone on to put their own work on record. Among the latter I want especially to acknowledge Lawrence Clopper, whose contributions to the scholarship on the Chester cycle have become indispensable, as my discussion of that cycle will demonstrate.

Some parts of this book in earlier form have been the subject of lectures and papers at various universities and conferences.

A version of the Introduction was read at the Middle English Section of the MLA in 1983. Earlier versions of the York chapter were presented as part of the Fifteenth-Century Symposium at Regensburg, West Germany, in 1982, and later at the always hospitable Medieval House at Rochester (under the auspices of Thomas Hahn) and the Medieval Seminar at the University of Pennsylvania. It was also the subject of a lecture before my home away from home, the Columbia University Medieval Seminar, where I have the good fortune from month to month to enjoy the wit and to profit from the learning of Robert Hanning, Howard Schless, and Joan Ferrante, among many other friends and associates. Parts of the Wakefield chapter were twice the basis of papers I read at what is always the liveliest medieval conference of the year at Western Michigan University of Kalamazoo, Michigan, where Clifford Davidson has repeatedly been my gracious and generous host.

There are several scholars without whose steady influence I simply would not have become a student of the medieval drama. The first is Arnold Williams, my mentor and dissertation director. His book, *The Characterization of Pilate in the Towneley Plays*, is still a model of responsible and, I think, right-minded dramatic criticism thirty-five years after its publication. It has guided my thinking beyond my power to specify. And Arnold himself, as scholar and teacher, has taught me that Chaucer's Clerk was by no means the only practitioner who did his job gladly. Arthur C. Cawley, with whom I have collaborated on the text of the new Wakefield edition for more years than either of us will comfortably admit, has been during our long association my good friend and unofficial teacher. Whatever is controversial in this book, I am sure he has warned me at one time or another to say more cautiously. If I did not always listen, I did hear—and I hope that the resonances of his wisdom and his scholarly good sense echo frequently in what I have written between these covers.

I am grateful as well to several scholars who generously made available to me substantial and exciting papers prior to their publication: Kathleen Ashley, Michael Bristol, Richard

Emmerson, C. Clifford Flanigan, Gordon Kipling, and especially my colleague Pamela Sheingorn, whose work in iconography has been an inspiration to me and who read my chapter on N-Town at a time when her enthusiasm fired me on to finish the book. My very special thanks go to the readers of my manuscript for Princeton University Press, David Bevington and Del Kolve. My gratitude to them for their objectivity (especially at times when I argue with them) and their generous wise counsel, to say nothing of their good opinion, is boundless. They are of course free of blame for any blemishes in this book. These are entirely the result of my blindness or carelessness.

Princeton University Press has put at my disposal its superb expertise, and I am immensely grateful for all the help and the courtesies that have been extended to me from the first day that Marjorie Sherwood, then the Literature Editor, received my manuscript. I owe deep gratitude to Robert Brown, her successor, to Marilyn Campbell, Senior Editor, and Diane Grobman for her meticulous and knowledgeable copy editing of the manuscript. I also wish to extend my thanks to the Henry E. Huntington Library and Art Gallery, the British Library, and the Galleria Sabauda in Turin for allowing me to reproduce the manuscript pages and paintings that make up the illustrations of this book. In addition, I wish to acknowledge my gratitude to *Speculum* and *Comparative Drama* for allowing me to reproduce parts of my articles on the Wakefield cycle.

Much of the final research behind this book was made possible by a senior summer fellowship grant from the UCLA Center for Medieval and Renaissance Studies. I am grateful to Fredi Chiappelli, Director of the Center, and to his staff for allowing me to use the resources of the UCLA campus as well as to Professors Daniel Calder, Robert Kinsman, and Michael Allen for their help and abundant hospitality. The Huntington Library, as usual, allowed me access to its rich resources, including the Towneley and Chester manuscripts. I wish to thank especially Mary Robertson, the Curator of Manuscripts, for her patient help, and the many scholars whose presence around the garden cafeteria's tables provide the society and good fellowship to restore sanity after hours of lonesome research in the stacks and reading rooms. I am also grateful to the National Endowment for the Humanities for the award of a travel-to-collections grant that allowed me to study manuscript stage directions in various research libraries in Great Britain. A second summer in California, devoted to writing, was made possible by Donald R. Howard's kind efforts to have me designated as a Stanford visiting research scholar. For all of these opportunities, I express my heartfelt thanks.

This book was written during a period when most of my time was taken up with college administration. To allow me the time to write during a half-year sabbatical, I am deeply grateful to President Joel Segall and former Provost Philip Austin of Baruch College of the City University of New York, as well as to my good friend Robert McDermott who took over for me as Acting Dean during that time. I also wish to express my gratitude to Paul LeClerc, who, from his first day as the incumbent Provost at Baruch College, has given his support to my scholarly pursuits. To my secretary, Connie Terrero, who managed somehow always to straighten out all the mistakes I continually made in filing my computer copy and who nursed this book through all its stages of composition—what more can I say that I have not said in two previous books? Whatever it might be, it would not be enough.

Much of this book reflects a deep personal need to understand the tone and temperament of the late Middle Ages, which resemble in some ways our own times at least in their quest for spiritual satisfaction. I learned to make these connections and to arrive at a liminal understanding of late medieval piety from my friends and counselors, James Hinchey, Honora Nolty, and Dennis Corrado.

Finally I want to thank my wife, Rose Zimbardo, for her presence in the center of my life. She has demanded for years that I write this book. As my best and toughest critic, she has listened with unaccountable patience and good humor to my compulsive reading and rereading aloud of rough drafts. She was strong enough to interrupt my self-satisfied performances when sound and sense went wrong. And she guided me over the years to demand more of myself than I had been willing to give. She is, without any doubt, the one critic whose approval I sought incessantly as I wrote this book.

TEXTUAL NOTE

FOR the reader's convenience, I have cited the primary texts by *page* and line numbers rather than by *play* and line numbers throughout. The prevailing practice of referring to play or pageant numbers can be confusing or inconvenient because these numbers are not uniformly or clearly identified in the available editions. In one instance—that of the N-Town cycle—there is good reason, as I will show, to reject the manuscript's pageant numbering altogether. For example, the reference 329/105 cites page 329, line 105 of the cycle text under consideration.

Also for the convenience of the reader, I have punctuated quotations and standardized capitalization for the N-Town cycle. The K. S. Block edition, still the only full reliable text available, lacks punctuation except for periods at the end of stanzas.

I have relied on the following editions, full citations of which may be found in the Bibliography:

York: Richard Beadle, ed., *The York Plays.*
Wakefield: George England and A. W. Pollard, eds., *The Towneley Plays,* for all plays except those known as the Wakefield Group (i.e. Plays 2, 3, 12, 13, 16, and 21). For these I rely on A. C. Cawley's edition, *The Wakefield Pageants in the Towneley Cycle.* References to this edition are identified by the prefix "Caw."
N-Town   K. S. Block, ed., *Ludus Coventriae; or, The Plaie Called Corpus Christi.*
Chester: R. M. Lumiansky and David Mills, eds., *The Chester Mystery Cycle.*

References to editions other than these are contained in full bibliographic entries in the notes.

FOUR MIDDLE ENGLISH
MYSTERY CYCLES

INTRODUCTION

THIS book undertakes to develop a comprehensive study of the four extant complete Middle English mystery cycles. It does so at a time in the genesis of medieval drama scholarship when all of the plays have either been, or are in the process of being, reedited and when the records of the early English drama are being collected as part of a major scholarly enterprise.[1] Its principal contentions are that the cycles deserve to be read as self-standing and individual works of literature, that they must be studied in the context of the manuscripts that have transmitted them, and that the text must be seen as an entity separate from the cycle's performance history.

To put this study into perspective, it will be helpful to trace the progress of medieval drama scholarship since its inception nearly two hundred years ago. It was at the turn of the nineteenth century that the cycle manuscripts first captured the attention of the learned world and that the earliest editions of single medieval mystery plays were printed. The first full edition of a medieval cycle, that of the Towneley plays by the Surtees Society, was published in 1836. By 1841, a second cycle, Chester, was published in an edition by Thomas Wright with the Shakespeare Society, and by the early part of the twentieth century, all four of the modern cycles had appeared in schol-

---

[1] Of the four extant complete cycles, two have been newly edited: Richard Beadle, ed., *The York Plays*, (London: Edward Arnold, 1982); and Robert M. Lumiansky and David Mills, eds., *The Chester Mystery Cycle* (London: Oxford University Press, 1974). The two others are in the process of being reedited: Stephen Spector is at work on the N-Town manuscript; and A. C. Cawley and I are editing Huntington MS HM 1 of the Wakefield plays (also known as the Towneley cycle). Both are projected for publication by the EETS. The dramatic records are being published by the REED project (Records of the Early English Drama) at the University of Toronto.

3

arly editions.[2] Indeed, in the case of two cycles, Wakefield (Towneley) and Chester, reeditings were by that time already in print.[3]

Alongside full editions of individual cycles, there also appeared what might be called synoptic versions of the mystery cycle in anthologized editions. The earliest of the latter was John Payne Collier's modest edition of *Five Miracle Plays, or Scriptural Dramas* in 1836 (the same year that saw the publication of the first complete cycle). Before the end of the century, several other such volumes appeared, including especially the anthology *English Miracle Plays, Moralities, and Interludes*, edited by Alfred W. Pollard in 1890, and thereafter brought through eight editions and subsequent reprintings; and a projected three-volume edition (the third volume of commentary never saw the light of day) by John M. Manly, entitled *Specimens of the Pre-Shakespearean Drama*, which was first published by Athenaeum Press in 1897 and held sway long enough to be republished as a Dover edition as late as 1967. Yet another major anthology was published on this side of the Atlantic in 1924 by Houghton Mifflin, entitled *Chief Pre-Shakespearean Dramas*, edited by Joseph Quincy Adams, then supervisor of research at the Folger Shakespeare Memorial Library.

The anthology clearly served the purpose in the early years of literary scholarship of acquainting students with a large segment of the early English drama. The subtitle of the Adams collection makes this purpose clear: *A Selection of Plays Illustrating the History of the English Drama from Its Origin Down to Shakespeare*, a course of study that the editor says was invited by the Riverside Press as a companion volume to Neilson's *Chief Eliz-*

[2] See Joseph Hunter, ed., *The Towneley Mysteries* (London: J. Nichols and Son, 1836); George England and A. W. Pollard, eds., *The Towneley Plays* (London: Oxford University Press, 1897); Lucy Toulmin Smith, *York Plays* (Oxford: Clarendon Press, 1885); K. S. Block, ed., *Ludus Conventriae; or, The Plaie Called Corpus Christi* (London: Oxford University Press, 1922); Thomas Wright, ed., *The Chester Plays* (London: Shakespeare Society Publications, 1843, 1847; reprinted, 1853); Hermann Deimling and J. Matthews, eds., *The Chester Plays* (London: Oxford University Press, 1892, 1916).

[3] The Deimling-Matthews edition of *The Chester Plays* and the England-Pollard edition of *The Towneley Plays*.

abethan Dramatists. The school anthology usually began with excerpts from the Latin church drama (with side-by-side translation), followed by a synoptic cycle and representative samples of saints' plays, moralities, interludes, folk plays, school plays, and other forms of sixteenth-century drama. The mystery cycles thus became subsumed under the heading of the "medieval drama," and most students were undoubtedly introduced to them in the form of what John Manly called "the artificial cycle." Manly goes so far as to apologize for putting "pageants together from various sources," but he felt that no serious objection should be raised against this procedure given "the heterogeneous character of the cycles themselves and their complex inter-relations" (p. viii). While that justification might in retrospect be sufficient reason to object to the process in the first place, the texts in these school editions were in general well edited and considerably easier to master than the early editions of complete cycles. They were usually accompanied by headnotes and, at least in Adams's edition, by glossarial footnotes.[4] In recent years, the school edition has been elevated to very high quality indeed. Perhaps the best examples of the newer version of the school edition are A. C. Cawley's superbly glossed Everyman edition, *Everyman and Medieval Miracle Plays*, which includes a synoptic cycle and the morality play *Everyman*; and David Bevington's masterful anthology of the *Medieval Drama*, which in terms of scholarly apparatus can only be described as state of the art. Bevington not only expands the coverage of the Adams text that his anthology replaces, but he also undertakes quite deliberately to remove the study of the medieval drama from the anti-Catholic and "Protestant Whig-Liberal biases common to men" of Adams's generation.[5] As a result, the Bevington volume has none of the shortcomings of its predecessor. It prints selections in

---

[4] For the modern reader perhaps the most disconcerting editorial practice was the bowdlerizing of passages; see, for example, Adams's ellipses throughout the text of *Mankind* with such remarks as "omitted because of obscenity" or "the language is unprintable" (*Chief Pre-Shakespearean Dramas*, p. 307).

[5] See David Bevington, ed., *Medieval Drama* (Boston: Houghton Mifflin, 1975), p. xiii.

full, and in its annotations it treats its subject with the serious scholarly respect that the individual texts deserve. The edition is in every sense the best, most scholarly anthology of the medieval drama ever published.

Most readers of the medieval drama are aware of the contents of a typical "artificial cycle." The Manly version can serve as an example here. It begins with the Norwich Creation and Fall and then moves on to the N-Town Lamech, the Wakefield Noah, the Brome Abraham and Isaac, the Wakefield Isaac, the Wakefield Jacob, the Chester Balaam and Balaak, the N-Town Annunciation and Conception, the Coventry Nativity and Slaughter of the Innocents, the Wakefield Second Shepherds, the York Resurrection, the Chester Antichrist, and the York Judgment. Clearly the selections in this cycle are based on arbitrary choice, as is true of all the other collections as well. The Manly "specimens" seem to focus on the Old Testament, and they contain not a single episode from the Passion sequence, which is usually regarded as the heart of the cycle. Whatever the reason for the individual choices, it is clear that Manly wished his artificial cycle to be a composite of as many source manuscripts as possible. And therein lies what appears to be the sole reason for anthologizing the early drama: The volume was to give the reader a taste of the range of the medieval drama. The course for which the book was used was unquestionably designed to present a progressive history of the drama. It mattered little what the individual specimens were— they were really seen as interchangeable—so long as the major types of the drama could be seen as part of a developing genre that culminated in the plays of Shakespeare.

As laudable as the purpose of the early anthology was in an age that gave emphasis to the accumulation and ordering of historical facts, it nevertheless had a decidedly negative influence on the way the medieval drama came to be studied. The central idea of the anthology was to isolate parts—in effect, to highlight individual pageants—and not to be concerned with whole works of dramatic literature, the cycles themselves. No other major work of medieval literature, not even the Arthurian romances, received such isolated, "artificial" treatment. The anthologies, in fact, became so popular that not until very recently have there been reasonably priced editions of condensed single cycles, and even now such volumes are hard to come by. For the typical student reader, the cycle was therefore not a palpable literary work, and even the scholarship devoted to the medieval drama tended to put emphasis on individual episodes and on lateral analysis (the comparison and contrast of various versions of the same pageant). While such studies are, of course, in themselves of great value, they are also limited in what they tell about the medieval mystery play. An analogy with the Gospels comes to mind. The study of synoptic cycles is no doubt similar to reading a synoptic text of the Gospels. While a complete synoptic version of Mark, Matthew, and Luke would provide a more detailed text of the life and the wisdom of Jesus, we could not know from such a version that Mark lacks the Infancy Gospel, that Matthew consistently pictures Jesus as the new Moses, or that Luke puts primary emphasis on the forgiveness of Christ. An equally distorted and, I believe, unthinkable parallel would be an anthology of the story of Arthur from a patchwork of Chrétien, Geoffrey of Monmouth, Wace, Layamon, the Alliterative *Morte*, the Stanzaic *Morte*, and Malory.

Texts are more readily available in recent times, and scholarly editions of complete cycles with helpful apparatus are now replacing the old standards. One would hope, therefore, that students are being introduced to the Corpus Christi cycles in the same way as to the other genres of literature—by an integrated and representative sampling of the major works. But even under the better prevailing circumstances, the likelihood is that the anthology approach is still dominant. So also, unfortunately, is the critical framework within which we read the Corpus Christi drama. While numerous excellent book-length studies of the drama have appeared over the years, only few of them, notably Arnold Williams's *Characterization of Pilate in the Towneley Plays* and Peter W. Travis's *Dramatic Design in the Chester Cycle* have responded to the cycles as individual works of art.[6] In fact, one pioneering volume of criticism, *Drama and Religion in the English Mystery Plays*, by Eleanor Prosser, takes as its underlying notion that "an entire mystery cycle should not be considered as one play."[7] In keeping with this view, Prosser proceeds to analyze individual pageants without any regard to their dramatic contexts and determines as most successful those episodes in which repentance is a major theme. Her selection of repentance doctrine as the central theme of all the cycles is purely arbitrary. As for the cycles themselves, Prosser, as implicitly so many others who have written about the medieval drama, forms her critical assumptions on a false base: that the cycles were folk art that lacked a controlling plan and that they were, in effect, accretions of so many independent street-corner plays. This critical assumption, as I shall show, is not only wrong, but it also rests on the dubious premise that the texts and performances of the cycles were interchangeable.[8]

The approach of singling out individual pageants for their artistic success, often without any reference to the cycle as a whole or to other pageants within it, has been a dominant form of criticism in the journal literature especially since World War II. The Wakefield Second Shepherds play has no doubt been

---

[6] Among other studies that have focused on single cycles are F. M. Salter's *Mediaeval Drama in Chester* (Toronto: University of Toronto Press, 1955); Timothy Fry's article "The Unity of the *Ludus Coventriae*," *Studies in Philology* 48 (1951), 527–570; John Gardner's *Construction of the Wakefield Cycle* (Carbondale and Edwardsville: Southern Illinois University Press, 1974); Richard J. Collier's *Poetry and Drama in the York Corpus Christi Play* (Hamden, Conn.: Archon Books, 1978); and Jeffrey Helterman's *Symbolic Action in the Plays of the Wakefield Master* (Athens: University of Georgia Press, 1981).

[7] Published by Stanford University Press, 1961 (p. 54).

[8] The notion that a literature that was performed before a listening audience was likely to be more loosely organized than a work addressed to a reader is widely held by many scholars; see, for example, Edmond Faral, *Les arts poétiques du XIIe et du XIIIe siècles* (Paris: Librairie H. Champion, 1924), p. 199. While the view that listeners are likely to pick up fewer organizational clues than readers is undoubtedly right, it need not follow that a writer, even if he intentionally sets out to address listeners would therefore not attempt to order his work as fully and intricately as he felt necessary. The act of composition is finally a literary act—one at work very clearly in the manuscripts of the Corpus Christi cycles.

the most popular subject of such studies, which resemble most nearly in strategy and focus the many readings of individual Canterbury tales. I hasten to add my awareness that certainly not all critical studies focusing on single plays are oblivious to the full context of their subjects, and some, of course, which explicate passages or allusions in the text, do not need to extend beyond the scene or pageant in question. But a good many either have an extremely vague sense of where to draw dramatic boundaries or else follow a doctrine similar to Prosser's, which denies the existence of a whole beyond the part. Some, indeed, go further and find that unity is really a modern idea, imposed upon medieval works by ingenious critics, a view that has received serious attention by at least one thoughtful scholar.[9] This view has its proponents among drama critics as well.

The two books justly admired as the outstanding contributions to scholarly criticism of the Middle English Corpus Christi plays—those by V. A. Kolve and Rosemary Woolf—unfortunately contribute as well to the slighting of the cycle as the literary form within which pageants must be seen to exist. Kolve's book, *The Play Called Corpus Christi*, has had such a powerful influence on the interpretation of the mystery plays that no serious study, my own certainly included, can proceed without reference to it and profit from it. Kolve begins on the assumption that the cycles are basically alike not only in coverage but also in outlook and approach. His interest is to find the common ground upon which the cycles rest—their treatment of time and place, their use of play and game, their sense of the comic, and their representation of good and evil. Thus, for example, he extrapolates the character type of "the natural man"—the individual who is distinctly human, severed from God, and whose most striking trait is his "exuberant vitality" (p. 210). This character is, by definition, a follower, a doer who

---

[9] Arthur K. Moore, "Medieval English Literature and the Question of Unity," in *Contestable Concepts of Literary Theory* (Baton Rouge: Louisiana State University Press, 1973), pp. 126–154.

9

lacks "inner direction and a capacity for private judgment." He is, as one might expect, everywhere in the drama, and Kolve summons examples from each cycle: Cain's Garcio in Wakefield, the Torturers in the Cornish cycle, the persons addressed in the rants of the York Pilate or the Wakefield Herod, the Knights guarding the sepulcher in N-Town. It is, of course, useful to recognize this type, especially in any postulations about the playwright's view of the fallen condition of man, but the category does not serve to differentiate one playwright's treatment of the type from the other's. Kolve's book presents generic, not textual, criticism. In fact, his analysis of the cycles is directly traceable to his belief in an abstract cycle form, a "protocycle" or, as he calls it, "the generic thing-in-itself" (p. 51). The Kolve approach, therefore, indirectly provides a theoretic reinforcement of the artificial cycles in the anthologies. Both divert attention from the true cycle, the whole text of the separate Corpus Christi plays.

In a curious way, Rosemary Woolf's penetrating book of interpretation, *The English Mystery Plays*, leads to the same effect even though its method of analysis and focus is diametrically opposed to Kolve's type of generic criticism. If Kolve's book provides synthesis, Woolf's gives analysis. She, too, in the main disregards cycles. Her interest is in episodes—the pageants or groupings of pageants in the cycles—and on the basis of a chapter-by-chapter enumeration, she actually builds her own sweeping Corpus Christi cycle, the ultimate superstructure that includes every incident ever put into any vernacular enactment. In the main section of the book, her discussion of "The Plays" from the four cycles (and sometimes also from Continental models, moralities, and noncycle Biblical plays) focuses on characters, thematic considerations, styles, and dramatic approaches. For example, in her discussion of the Passion, she considers all the characters under general headings of types who appear in all of the pageants. She shows how one Judas or Christ differs from another, or how those cycles which have a Procula differ from those which do not. While this method does certainly highlight the different approaches of the different cycles, one never obtains the view of a sustained action or characterization within a whole cycle. If, for example, we come to realize from her discussion that Annas and Caiaphas are more fully developed and interesting characters in the Wakefield cycle than in any of the others, we do not know from what she says how those characters in the Passion are integrated within a whole view of salvation history that this particular cycle gives. In essence, the analysis by Woolf is lateral. It gives far greater insight into how the segments in each of the cycles differ from one another than into how they contribute to the substance or dramatic approach of the cycle of which they are a part.

It is in response to the larger textual and critical context I have reviewed that this book seeks to make its statement. The approach to the Corpus Christi cycles here offered focuses on the cycle as a whole work of dramatic literature. I want to examine, within the covers of one book, the four extant Corpus Christi cycles as individual dramatic works, each with its own interpretation of salvation history, each exercising its own options in developing the familiar material drawn from a wide variety of such sources as sermons, Gospel harmonies, liturgical plays, and the Scriptures themselves. While I will, where necessary, single out individual pageants, the object of my concentration (as, for example, on the York Entry into Jerusalem or the Chester Coming of Antichrist) will be on the integration of the part into the whole, of viewing pageants as part of the larger concerns of the cycle. My approach does not, of course, obviate lateral readings of pageants, but these again will be done as a way of reinforcing the unique purpose of a whole cycle. My purpose is to show that the Corpus Christi cycles are not so many interchangeable structures built to carry out the same function, but carefully constructed frameworks that, like cathedrals, have about them a unique beauty and understanding not only of the subject that they all have more or less in common but also of the way in which they make that subject come alive in each of their dramatic settings. I am, in short, interested in the cycles as major works of dramatic art in the same way as critics are now wont to see Chaucer's *Canterbury Tales* or Gower's *Confessio Amantis* or Malory's Arthurian cycle as sustained works of narrative art. Throughout, my readings of the cycles put emphasis on the dramatic design, the effort of the playwrights to use their available tools in order to bring forward a dramatic vision of their subject. In every instance, moreover, I am concerned with the way in which the historical subject is integrated with the social context of the late Middle Ages. The cycles are the first major plays of the native dramatic tradition; they form the core of the "modern" drama of their time.

My study of the cycles is based first and foremost on the surviving manuscripts. Each chapter includes a close scrutiny of what is now known about those manuscripts, and it then reinterprets the evidence so that a reasonable conclusion can be formed about the origin, the nature, and the function of the text, as differentiated from the performance and its history. The confusion of those two entities—text and performance— has long added to the confusion about the history of the cycles. There is no doubt that the cycles, in one form or another, date back in some locations—certainly in York and probably in Chester—to the late fourteenth century. But it is also certain that we do not possess a single manuscript of a cycle that goes back to that early period. In fact, recent scholarship has established that not a single Corpus Christi cycle manuscript can be dated prior to the last third of the fifteenth century. Whether, therefore, those manuscripts reflect the form or the performance of those cycles a century earlier is open to question.

My general conclusion is that not only are we in the dark about the nature and the style of the cycles as they were performed prior to (or, for that matter, after) the existence of their manuscripts, but that more than likely no prior compendiums of plays existed. I see the history of the cycles in roughly the following manner: I think that the early cycles arose out of the liturgical procession of Corpus Christi, probably in the middle of the fourteenth century. Since we know that craft guilds took part in that procession, it seems reasonable to conclude that gradually as the Host was carried through the streets of various municipalities, the craft guilds began to display representations of Biblical scenes that were germane to their occupations or their patron saints. In turn, these representations—whether merely images or actual tableaux is open for speculation—became animated, first in tableaux vivants and later plays with speeches or with entire texts.[10] The records of York, which are the most copious we possess, show that by 1415 there existed in that city a complete descriptive list of all the pageants that were then included in the dramatic procession. (Whether that procession was the same or separate from the civic liturgical procession is a matter of scholarly debate.) There is good reason to believe that this list existed in lieu of a text, for if a composite text actually existed, there would have been no need for the list in the first place. It was only when the craft guilds formally undertook to write up their pageants that texts began to exist, and these were likely to be what the records consistently refer to as the "regynalls," or originals, in other words the texts devised and held by the craft guilds themselves. The effort to register plays did not come until a good deal later. At least one manuscript, that of York, is clearly a register, the function of which seems to have been to record the pageants into a "city book" for the archives. Other manuscripts are compilations of a different sort. In Chester they are antiquarian books. In Wakefield and the location known as N-Town, they are literary texts in which every effort is made to assemble a whole, continuous cycle. I believe that the literary/dramatic unity of the cycles dates to a period, whether still in the "regynall" stage or at the time of the extant compilation, when a conscious effort

---

[10] While this view of the genesis of the Corpus Christi drama is but one of several theories, I find it the most plausible. Others have held that the Corpus Christi drama had its origin in the Latin plays of the church (see E. K. Chambers, *The Mediaeval Stage*, 2 vols. [Oxford: Clarendon Press, 1903], 2:69) or in the vernacular cycles (see Rosemary Woolf, *The English Mystery Plays* [London: Routledge and Kegan Paul, 1972], pp. 54–76) or a combination of Latin liturgical plays and vernacular cycles (see O. B. Hardison, *Christian Rite and Christian Drama in the Middle Ages* [Baltimore: Johns Hopkins University Press, 1965]).

was made by the guilds to design a unit under the guidance of an author/reviser. The Wakefield Master is the best known of this hypothetical group.

It is a mistake to assume that the extant manuscripts were used as play texts for the performance. We know as a matter of fact that the York manuscript existed *independently* of the performance of the plays, and we can reasonably conclude that in the other localities text and performance were similarly distinct. The temptation, therefore, to derive critical conclusions about the manuscript by drawing on the circumstances of performance should be avoided. It is better to look upon the manuscripts as the fullest, most developed form of the individual cycles and not as the record of what was actually performed. There is no way of knowing whether the performance of the plays regularly, or even singularly, included all of the pageants. We know, in fact, that one contemplated performance at York, the one in 1535, would not have included such vitally important plays as Noah, the Annunciation, the Shepherds, Christ Led to Calvary, Jesus' Appearance before Mary Magdalene, and the Incredulity of Thomas, because the supporting guilds did not contribute the required pageant money, as agreed upon, to the Common Chamber.[11] The only way, therefore, that we can know what the full York play was really like is to consult the manuscript. The unity of the cycle is, therefore, finally a literary matter. It results from the author/reviser's effort to put a play together on the subject of salvation history from the Creation to Doomsday.

I need to make another point about the history of the Corpus Christi cycles. Perhaps as a result of the ready availability of generic criticism, most historical approaches have assumed that the Corpus Christi cycles are all substantially alike and that they reflect not only similar conditions of performance but also roughly the same circumstances of historical development.

---

[11] See Alexandra F. Johnston and Margaret Dorrell (Rogerson), eds., *York: Records of the Early English Drama*, 2 vols. (Toronto: University of Toronto Press, 1979), 1: 256–261.

The case history of York has been the unwritten model upon which this history was collected. In fact, York is quite different from all the other cycles both quantitatively and qualitatively. York is singular because it is "city" rather than "town" drama. It reflects in its approach, its theatricality, and its organization the identity of its locale and its makers: the guilds. No other cycle is so episodic in its divisions or so self-conscious of its place. On the other hand, Wakefield is decidedly a late spinoff from the York cycle. However, it is a different play—one that reflects the ethos of a manorial seat and a provincial market town much more readily than the ethos of an archdiocesan center. N-Town, in turn, is another late amalgam, a cycle for which the pageant-wagon mode of performance is at best a remnant. And Chester may well reflect the view of its dominant abbey, as a play that was revised into its present tight and uniform structure by a playwright who was responding to the leading theological issues of his time. It is wrong, I think, to assume that the dramatic circumstances for each of these cycles were the same. Not every one of the cycles, for example, has tyrants clearing their path through the crowd as they mount the stage with their stereotypic rants. This is a mark of the "city" play in which street drama is a fact of the play's genesis. To assume that all tyrants entered thus is to mistake the history and development of all cycles on the basis of what happened in the case of one.

Finally, a word needs to be said about the unity of the individual cycles. I do not wish to propose that this unity is always or even predominantly thematic, though I do believe that each cycle has its own voice and its own point of view. A cycle may be unified by its setting, as I believe the York cycle was. It may be unified by its authorial voice and point of view, its versatile and sophisticated display of language that in itself becomes its dominant subject, as I believe the Wakefield cycle was. It may be unified by its way of juxtaposing the main actions, by finding new macrostructures within which to weave together the main strands of the play, as I believe the N-Town cycle was. Or it may be unified by its concern, philosophically and technically, with its sense of endings, as I believe the Chester cycle was.

In the chapters that follow, I will expand upon these several unities as means of reading each of the cycles whole. I do not intend to suggest that these are the only bases for overall interpretations of the cycles, but I do insist that each must be read as a work that has its own demonstrable and unique artistic coherence.

ONE

The York Cycle: City as Stage

THE York plays present a special problem for those who find thematic or structural unity in the medieval Corpus Christi cycles. The difficulty is that the play in York, perhaps because it was staged from the outset in what was then a large regional city, was more nearly a communal enterprise than any other extant English cycle. One senses in reading the manuscript of the plays and the copious municipal records from York that the cycle itself is a corporate work, and not so markedly as the other cycles the work of an individual consciousness. In part one gets that feeling because the documents themselves are testimony to the civic enterprise of nurturing and preserving the play. In York it was not enough to have a Corpus Christi play; it was necessary in addition to have a civic record of that play. The existence of a trove of municipal documents in addition to an official copy of the Corpus Christi play is not simply an accident of history; it is a reflection of the York civic temperament that placed a premium on the preservation of the city's institutions and insisted on the recognition of its longstanding and honored corporate identity. The Corpus Christi play there was no mere popular entertainment, no ordinary annual festive occasion; it was the city's proud and solemn celebration of itself.

We are fortunate in possessing those civic records and doubly fortunate in having newly available a magnificently edited scholarly compilation of all the entries that touched on dramatic, ceremonial, and minstrel performances in York before 1642. These volumes, edited by Alexandra F. Johnston and Margaret Dorrell (Rogerson) under the title *York: Records of Early English Drama* (hereafter *REED: York*), provide the fullest documentary evidence available for any medieval dramatic work or activity, documenting in effect the history of the Corpus Christi play at York for its lifetime of some two hundred years, from circa 1376, when the play seems already to have been in existence, possibly for some time, to 1569, the date of its last performance. The dramatic records come from three major sources: the city itself (by far the most informative and voluminous source), the craft guilds (comprised mostly of the copious records from the Merchant Adventurers and the much more limited records of the Bakers), and the religious guilds and hospitals (though these records, especially of the Corpus Christi Guild, are primarily concerned with the Corpus Christi procession).[1] It would be redundant to describe those records here, since Johnston and Rogerson give an excellent summary of their contents and nature in the introduction of their edition (see *REED: York*, pp. xvii–xli). Suffice it to say that the records give a cumulative picture of the procedures and activities connected with the Corpus Christi plays. They include civic and guild ordinances and regulations; complaints and arbitrations of conflicts; records of fines, expenditures, and payments relating to the Corpus Christi plays; proclamations; and sundry descriptions and observations of activities relating to the plays, including remarks about the decorum of the spectators during performances.

With so much available information, one might expect that we can now produce a quite complete account of the York Corpus Christi performance over the course of its history. Unfortunately, however, that is not the case. As Johnston and Rogerson themselves observe,

The York records offer the familiar paradox of all collections of records. Although they are voluminous, they are also fragmentary, presenting some practices in tedious

---

[1] For a discussion, see Alexandra F. Johnston, "The Guild of Corpus Christi and the Procession of Corpus Christi in York," *Mediaeval Studies* 38 (1976): 372–384.

repetition while mentioning others only once, leaving room for speculation. (P. xv)

For example, the records tell very little about the performances themselves and virtually nothing about the manner of the accumulation of texts. Thus, while we are favored in our study of the York play with copious external evidence, we need to bear in mind that the records often fail to answer the most fundamental questions.

They do tell a great deal about the tone and the atmosphere of dramatic activity in the city. When, therefore, we seek to know what place the play held in the city's self-esteem, we have a valuable guide at hand. It is clear that from the time in 1396 when Richard II transformed the city into a county in its own right, the Corpus Christi play draws increasing official attention in the records. The earliest of the municipal books, the York *A/Y Memorandum Book*, already makes clear that the play is the ceremonial highlight in the annual calendar. Its performance is manifestly the culmination of a yearlong prescribed routine that is supervised by the city government, a mercantile oligarchy that consisted of the mayor, the aldermen, the council of twenty-four (later expanded into the common council), and such officers as the city clerk, the chamberlains, sheriffs, bailiffs, and bridgemasters. The preparation of next year's play began shortly after the current performance when many of the craft and trade guilds appointed their new pageant masters,[2] and the guild carried on with its preparations always under the watchful eye and the scrupulous guidance of the city, highlighted by the stately moment of the delivery of the "billet," which was either a play description or an approved script.[3]

[2] See, for example, the entry concerning the Curriers in the *A/Y Memorandum Book* in 1424; *REED: York*, p. 40. Among the Mercers, which was York's largest and most influential trade guild, the pageant masters were chosen annually ("with þe assent of þe ffelship") on the Friday after Midsummer Day (24 June); see Alexandra F. Johnston and Margaret Dorrell (Rogerson), "The York Mercers and Their Pageant of Doomsday," *Leeds Studies in English*, n.s. 6 (1972): 12.

[3] Richard Beadle assumes that the "billets" contained the description of the pageants from the 1415 *Ordo Paginarum*; see *The York Plays* (London: Edward

The conveyance of this document was indeed ceremonious: Six of the mayor's sergeants-at-arms, most likely constituting the elite of the city's police force, brought the billets to each of the participating guilds during the first or second week in Lent, as specified in the first full description of the plays, the well-known *Ordo Paginarum* copied by the city clerk, Roger Burton, in the *A/Y Memorandum Book* (the Latin phrase for "billets" is *sedule paginarum*; see *REED: York*, p. 17). The city was clearly in charge. And the play, in its official eyes, brought it glitter and glory, as attested in the following words addressed to the Goldsmiths concerning their performance of the Herod pageant, which was to be presented "in the more lavish manner which is seemly for the praise of the city" ("honestiori modo quo decet in laudem ciuitatis"; see *REED: York*, p. 48). Moreover, the city itself was the official host of the play; its banner depicting the municipal arms was displayed at each of the assigned stations of performance (*REED: York*, p. 12). Every official document made clear that the York city fathers were deeply committed to the perpetuation of the play, which was consistently acknowledged for the glory and profit that it brought to the whole community.

This reverence for the play was, however, not shared by all of its producers, especially those guilds which faced financial difficulty. It is common knowledge that such guilds over the years sought to reduce their responsibilities in the sponsorship and support of their assigned pageants. Had it not been for the corporation and its insistent agenda of maintaining the Corpus Christi play in its accustomed form, many of the pageants at York would surely have died an early death. Just how successful the city was in maintaining the play can be seen by a com-

---

Arnold, 1982), p. 24. I have interpreted the word to mean "actors' parts"; see Martin Stevens, "The Johnston-Rogerson Edition of the York Records: An Initial Reading," in *Proceedings of the First Colloquium, REED*, ed. JoAnna Dutka (Toronto: Records of the Early English Drama, 1979), pp. 162–164. Possibly the nature of the billets changed over the years so that in the early period they were descriptions and in the later period parts copied out of the official register for the purpose of having the city control the production.

parative analysis of the famous *Ordo Paginarum* of 1415 and the manuscript itself, which dates to a period of at least fifty years later, though possibly as much as seventy-five to a hundred years later, as I shall show later in this chapter. By my count, forty-three of the pageants retained their original primary guild sponsorship, and those pageants which underwent change usually involved the shifting of guilds from primary to secondary responsibility. The records, moreover, confirm that in most instances this sponsorship persisted to the very end. However, the few instances in which guilds could not maintain their assignments are particularly instructive, and they give evidence of the durability of the play as a whole.

Consider, for example, the case of the "Saucemakers" (i.e. Sausagemakers). We encounter their name in the records for the first time in 1417,[4] as a result of a petition for relief in the financing of their play, the Hanging of Judas, which no doubt was assigned to the Saucemakers because a string of sausages could be used to represent Judas's entrails when his body, according to an entry from 1432, "burst in the middle" ("crepuit medius"; *REED: York*, p. 48). The Saucemakers complained that they could no longer support the pageant ("Salsarij ipsi paginam ipsam diucius sustinere non valebunt"; *REED: York*, p. 31) unless they received additional support from those who sold candles and who had traditionally helped to sustain the pageant. In particular, the Saucemakers asked for an assessment of all sellers of candles, even those, like the Skinners, who had lately taken up the practice of selling candles and who were not contributors to their pageant. The mayor thereupon agreed that all those who sold Paris candles by retail would thereafter contribute every third penny to the maintenance of the Saucemakers' pageant. Somewhat later, another mayor decreed that all those who sold mustard or other sauces be included in this order. With their new arrangement, the Sauce-

---

[4] The name "Sausmakers" also appears in the second list of pageant assignments that follows immediately after Burton's *Ordo* in the *A/Y Memorandum Book*. This list cannot be dated with any certainty, but it was more than likely compiled no earlier than 1417.

makers managed to continue their sponsorship of the pageant for some years, though they apparently quarreled with other crafts over its support. As a result, the mayor with the advice of the council combined the following five plays into one: the Condemnation of Jesus Christ ("pagina condempnacionis Iesu christi"; *REED: York*, p. 48); the Hanging of Judas (formerly the Saucemakers' play); Pilate's Condemnation of Jesus (the Tilemakers' play); the Flagellation (the pageant of the Turners, Hayresters, and Bollers); and the Playing of Dice for Jesus' Garment (the Millers' play). The new, combined play was to be produced by the joint effort and financial support of the Saucemakers and the Tilemakers, with specified contributions from the other crafts. Because of the joint sponsorship, none of the guilds was any longer known as full proprietor of the pageant and the several sponsoring guilds were therefore forbidden to "place any signs, arms or insignia upon the aforesaid pageant, except only the arms of this honourable city" ("Et quod nulla quatuor arcium predictarum ponat aliqua signa arma vel insignia super paginam predictam nisi tantum arma huius honorabil⟨..⟩ ciuitatis"; *REED: York*, p. 49). Probably by sharing the expanded pageant, the poor Saucemakers obtained some financial relief, but it is worth noting that they paid the price of no longer sponsoring a pageant by themselves.

And apparently things became worse over the years, for when we next encounter their name in the records, as late as 1515, the Saucemakers are no longer the coproducers of the Condemnation pageant; rather they have become contributors together with the Millers to what is now deemed the "Tilehouse[r]z" (i.e. Tilemakers'?) pageant. In the next three years, their fortunes apparently declined even further (or possibly they fought with the Millers), but they were now enjoined to contribute together with the Whitechaundlers (once more the old familiar candlemakers) to the Girdlers' pageant (see *REED: York*, p. 217). This story of the decline of the Saucemakers, no doubt linked to their economic hard times, gives a good glimpse into the process of play sponsorship in York and the strong role played by the mayor in maintaining the play of Corpus Christi. It is interesting to note that the surviving manuscript still contains the Hanging of Judas episode, though it seems to have been merged at some time with the Remorse of Judas, which was sponsored by the Cooks and Waterleaders. The Saucemakers, alas, are expunged from history; their name subsequently appears nowhere in the register. Their instance discloses that while sponsorships could change, the play itself, with the persistent guidance and management of the city, remained.

I have included this lengthy illustration to cite the usefulness of the records in tracing the fortunes of guild sponsorships. Many other crafts, over the years, petitioned for help, most often for financial reasons, though sometimes for other reasons as well. The Masons, to cite one example, became disenchanted over their play of Fergus (the name of the man who attacked the bier of Mary and whose arm came off and stuck to the bier), for several reasons. First, its performance attracted noise, laughter, and violence. Second, its episode was apocryphal. Third, the pageant often could not be put on because its turn for performance came in darkness (see *REED: York*, pp. 47–48). The Fergus play was one of the very few, if not the only one, that eventually was dropped from the cycle, but even it (with all the trouble it caused) managed to stay around long enough to be enacted again in 1476. This exception shows how durable the play of York was. Like the government itself, the play was an outward sign of the persistence of institutions in the city. True, the play was finally abandoned, but its demise was imposed by a harsh diocesan administration that was determined to quash all attempts at resistance. The records made clear that if York had had its way, the plays would have continued for a long time to come.

Collectively the guilds were strongly supportive of their government since in so many respects they really were the essential substance of that government. The most common way of becoming a freeman in the city—the first requirement for a potential officeholder—was to finish an apprenticeship in one of the crafts or trades. The regular ladder of promotion for the potential officeholder was the assumption of an accounting office like bridge- or muremaster, then election to chamberlain, then advancement to the council of twenty-four, and, finally, for the most successful, to alderman—a position that would automatically lead to at least one term as mayor. The records attest that aldermen attained the "freedom of the city" at a mean age of twenty-four, came onto the council of twenty-four at age forty-one, and served as aldermen between the ages of forty-six and sixty-seven. The sixteenth-century records show a total of 106 aldermen. Of these, 60 were merchants, 10 were drapers, 4 were haberdashers, 6 were lawyers and gentlemen, 4 were goldsmiths, 4 tailors and hosiers, 3 pewterers, and 15 more came from other craft guilds.[5] These statistics show that the government of York was composed essentially of guildsmen and that, with an established ladder of achievement, it was composed of persons who, at the pinnacle of decision making, were elder statesmen with a lifetime of experience in running the affairs of the guilds and the city. The system encouraged the maintenance of institutions and of established processes. Its governing class undoubtedly saw little distinction between their lives as guildsmen and their lives as civic officials. The Corpus Christi play was thus a self-perpetuating civic institution.

It had to be that in order to have survived for the long period

[5] See D. M. Palliser, *Tudor York* (Oxford: Oxford University Press, 1979), pp. 71, 88. Urban historians have done much in uncovering demographic information from the York civic records, including the Memorandum Books, the House Books, the Freemen's Register, the collections of wills, rent rolls, and the chamberlain's rolls and books, among others. Palliser's book is extremely useful as background for anyone interested in the historical setting of the York plays. So also is P. M. Tillott's volume on the City of York in *The Victoria History of the County of York* (Oxford: Oxford University Press, 1961). Two articles of special interest for their interpretation of the records are J. N. Bartlett, "The Expansion and Decline of York in the Later Middle Ages," *Economic History Review*, 2d ser. 12 (1959): 17–33; and R. B. Dobson, "Admission to the Freedom of the City of York in the Later Middle Ages," *Economic History Review*, 2d ser. 26 (1973): 1–22. Also extremely useful are sundry published papers in the series of the Borthwick Institute of Historical Research, University of York.

of its existence. In fact, a close look at the economic history of York shows that during the lifetime of the plays, the fortunes of the city steadily declined, and the maintenance of the plays was a genuine hardship for its sponsors. When the plays were inaugurated, probably some time in the 1360s or 1370s, York was the largest provincial city in England. Estimates of its population vary, in part because the Freemen's Register during the fourteenth century failed "to record the names of those whose title to the franchise rested on birth or patrimony,"[6] but it was probably in the neighborhood of 15,000. By the mid-sixteenth century, when the plays entered their demise, the population had shrunk to 8,000 people, and York, while still among the half-dozen largest provincial cities in England, was considerably smaller than Norwich, Bristol, Exeter, Salisbury, and possibly Newcastle.[7] At its high point, York was the foremost northern center in religion and administration, and it was a focal point for social life, industry, and the distribution of goods. Its early prosperity rested on all these diverse activities. At the close of the fourteenth century wool was the leading product of York's considerable international trade, and its cloth trades in general were thriving. J. N. Bartlett reports,

> The most striking development occurred in the clothmaking industry and the York crafts making cloth shared in the growth of English industry which virtually priced foreign cloth out of the English market and created a substantial demand for English cloth in the Baltic, Gascony, and Flanders. Between 1331 and 1371 there was a sixteen-fold increase in the number of weavers, fullers, shearmen, dyers and tapiters becoming freemen of York, and the percentage of new freemen in these clothmaking crafts rose from two to fifteen per cent.[8]

[6] Dobson, "Admission to the Freedom of the City," p. 8.

[7] W. G. Hoskins, *Local History in England*, 2d ed. (London: Longmans, 1972), p. 238; and Palliser, *Tudor York*, p. 202.

[8] Bartlett, "Expansion and Decline of York," p. 23.

The merchants, always the most prosperous guild in York, also benefited greatly from this period of expansion in the cloth trades. York merchants were men of consequence in international trade (two were among the aldermen appointed by the Company of the Staple at Calais), and they were the ranking wool traders in the city of Hull. At the same time, all the other trades and crafts prospered as well, so that the city reached its apogee in influence and population between the years 1391 and 1421. Notably, these are the early years of the Corpus Christi pageants and procession, and much of our information about the nature of the cycle, especially Burton's list of 1415, comes from this period. Hence, the York cycle in its general character reflects the prosperity of the city, especially in its wide involvement of guilds from virtually all areas of trade and manufacture.

Most historians agree that York's golden prosperity came to an end in the mid-fifteenth century. Many causes were at work behind this reversal, but among the more important was the gradual replacement of the larger cities by small provincial towns in the West Riding—Wakefield among them—which could produce cloth at much lower cost and which traded directly with London. The result was a dramatic decline in the numbers of craftsmen among the clothmaking guilds. Bartlett shows that the combined numbers of weavers, fullers, shearmen, and dyers fell from a total of 430 in the first half of the century to 331 in the second half. The Weavers, in particular, suffered during this period, which Palliser calls a "catastrophic depression,"[9] with the result that their annual fee farm was reduced by half in 1478 and was totally remitted eight years later.[10] There were clearly other causes behind the depression, such as the competition of the Hanseatic League, which reduced the influence and activity of the York merchants, the heavy inflation of the sixteenth century, and the dissolution of the church and the consequent demise of trades that depended

---

[9] Palliser, *Tudor York*, p. 41.
[10] Ibid., p. 30.

largely on work commissioned by the church, like that of the acclaimed York glaziers. It must be emphasized that while some of these problems were endemic to York itself, most operated on the industry and prosperity of England at large. The economic plight of Coventry, for example, was every bit as severe as that of York during a comparable period.[11]

The survival of the Corpus Christi plays during such a stark period of economic depression is truly remarkable. For it was during the worst times that the city seemed to take the most trouble to perpetuate its plays. With the advent of the House Books in 1476, the city increased considerably its already prominent activity in record keeping, an effort that is noticeable as well in the writing of the York manuscript. The iteration of the city's rules and regulations shows a deep concern over the proper management of the dramatic festival, as in the order, at the very beginning of the House Books, against tripling by actors: "no plaier þat shall plaie in þe saide Corpus christi plaie be conducte and Reteyned to plaie but Twise on þe day of þe saide playe And þat he or thay so plaing plaie not ouere twise þe saide day" (*REED: York*, p. 109). What needs to be realized, then, in coming to terms with the York plays is that their composition (whether in some "prehistoric" form or the one that survives in the manuscript—a distinction that may not be very great) reflects the halcyon days of medieval York, and the bulk of the records describing their performance reflects the times of the city's drawn-out and catastrophic depression. The whole of the survival of the York performance during this period is a reflection of the city's dogged determination to remain stable even in the face of what must have been wrenching turns of its collective fortune.

I have observed that the York cycle differs in character from the other extant cycles and that this difference is in large part the result of its place of origin. No other cycle comes from what

[11] See the classic study by Charles Phythian-Adams, *Desolation of a City: Coventry and the Urban Crisis of the Late Middle Ages* (Cambridge: Cambridge University Press, 1979).

one might perceive, somewhat in advance of its time, as a "metropolitan" city. There is a habit of lumping in one category all Corpus Christi plays and of not considering seriously the differences that exist among the individual cycles in this category. One point to note, for example, is the fact that two cycles—Wakefield and N-Town—are virtually devoid of references to craft guilds. Certainly neither one uses the names of crafts as running titles for its pageants. Another point is that only York consistently divides its material into short episodes, probably to accommodate its diverse crafts, while the drift in all the other cycles is to combine material into expanded pageants. The Creation plays are a good example. In the York cycle, the Creation is divided into six very brief pageants to accommodate the crafts of the Barkers, Plasterers, Cardmakers, Fullers, Coopers, and Armourers. In contrast, Chester combines this material into two pageants, with the second extending into the story of Cain and Abel. Wakefield has one play for the whole Creation (including the Fall of Lucifer), though the Temptation and Expulsion scenes are missing from the manuscript. N-Town has no significant break until the Noah pageant, and a case can even be made that all the Old Testament plays are a single dramatic segment. I believe that the difference in construction between York, on the one hand, and the remaining cycles, on the other, has to do with their time and place of origin respectively. The York cycle is medieval "city drama"; the other three are more nearly town or provincial drama, thus reflecting a more compact act of composition. Each of the three develops a distinct voice and structure; at least two of the cycles—N-Town and Wakefield—have patched together material borrowed from other sources, including certainly in the case of Wakefield the York cycle. The distinction between York and Wakefield is historically demonstrable. Wakefield is, in a sense, a clone of the York cycle, even as the city comes late to imitate York's erstwhile prosperity.[12] York pioneered; Wake-

---

[12] I am not suggesting that the two cycles were once identical, a thesis developed years ago by Marie Lyle, *The Original Identity of the York and Towneley Plays*

field adapted. If the Wakefield cycle is more nearly a projection of an individual consciousness, the reason is its provincial and derivative origin.

Medieval city drama, both in its manner of production and its dramatic content, presented to its spectators a mirror of their lives and their environment. The York cycle derives its unity from its multifaceted view of the city and its inhabitants. Thus, for example, the trade symbolism in the York plays is no mere comic byproduct of the dramatic presentation but a vital part of its motivation and meaning. Modern sophistication often makes fun of the quaintness and artlessness of medieval playcraft: the Bakers' making the Last Supper, the Shipwrights' building Noah's Ark, the Couchers' preparing Procula's bed, the Saucemakers' displaying Judas's entrails. The fact is that the trade or the craft was defined by what it did, and the demonstration of its ware or its skill as part of the anachronism of playcraft linked the performer with the play and created a larger meaning for the performance. The linkage helped to incorporate the city's ordinary purpose—its daily ritual of work and human intercourse—into the play action and thus into the grand design of salvation history. There can be little doubt that the Armourers chose (or were assigned) the play of the Expulsion because the Archangel Michael is its principal character, and traditionally he was depicted in medieval art as wearing armor while wielding a huge sword to bar Adam and Eve from Paradise. The Angel in the parallel Chester scene describes his function in words (as the York Angel does not): "Our swordes of fyer shall bee there bonne" (31/422). Here then is an instance of positive association between the handicraft and God's dominion. The play not only endowed the craft of the Ar-

---

(Minneapolis: University of Minnesota Press, 1919). The likelihood is that Wakefield was not large enough to organize a cycle of its own until well after the mid-fifteenth century. Hence when it was ready to form a cycle, it had many sources from which to draw, including the York plays, which were performed a mere thirty miles away and which were probably well known to Wakefielders. The production of a new cycle under those circumstances is likely to be an adaptation or an assemblage.

29

mourers with an elevated mythology but it also brought the Creation into the familiar setting of the City of York. Some have argued that such trade symbolism simply serves the practical purpose of providing the guild with a showcase in which to display its product or its skill. While, of course, it does that, and thus adds to the immediate interest of the spectators for whom the association would serve as what Brecht called an "alienation device" by making the playcraft a self-conscious allusion, that would not have been its primary purpose or function. It is worth noting that often the trade symbolism does not elevate. Take, for example, the Pinners, makers of pins, fish-hooks, mousetraps, and other small metallic objects, who put on the Crucifixion play. Clearly, they were associated in some way with the nailing process itself and perhaps also with the boring of holes into the Cross, an action that provides a gruesome tug-of-war game by the torturers to pull Jesus' hands and feet in preparation for the nailing. Obviously, the Pinners are not elevated by this association. But the action itself is brought into the present; the Pinners of York demonstrate their human culpability in the death of Christ, which, by extension belongs to all persons. Guilds are part of the York power structure; they also reflect all human enterprise and government. By allowing them to be incorporated into salvation history, York, the city, becomes a *theatrum mundi*.

York is, of course, not the only cycle that developed trade symbolism, but in the others—particularly Chester and Coventry—there are only vestiges of the practice, and in no cycle is the trade or craft guild so prominent a theatrical factor as it clearly is in York. The City of York as an official entity was really a creation of its many trade and craft guilds, including the powerful Mercers (after 1581, the Merchant Adventurers) with their great timbered hall on the Foss. Apart from the Mercers, and the two other large trade guilds—the Drapers and the Haberdashers (later combined with the Feltmakers and Cappers)—some sixty to seventy craft guilds flourished in the city during the sixteenth century, a complement that "compared closely to the sixty crafts of London in 1531 and greatly ex-

30

ceeded those of most provincial towns."[13] The number of guilds mentioned in the rubrics of the York Register is fifty-nine, and the Burton List of 1415, a much edited and annotated text over the years, numbers by my count a total of ninety-three crafts that were in one or another way associated with the Corpus Christi play in the course of much of its lifetime.[14] These numbers alone attest to the multiplicity of skills and the range of technology and dramatic properties that made up the *mise en scène* of the York Corpus Christi play. While we cannot estimate the specific nature of the performance, we can infer that it must have been something of an extravaganza—surely a show such as no provincial city in England, especially in the early years of the York cycle, could produce. When we add to these impressive numbers the fact that every person admitted to the freedom of the city had to join a trade or craft guild as the first step of York citizenship,[15] we can see that the official city and the guilds were really one inseparable entity, and that the Corpus Christi play was their most ambitious and acclaimed public enterprise of festive display.

Some scholars have questioned the overall importance and influence of trade symbolism in the assignment of plays to various guilds by the city. Richard Beadle, the editor of the most recent edition of *The York Plays*, offers the following opinion in his introduction: "In the majority of cases, however, no obvious

---

[13] See Palliser, *Tudor York*, p. 151. It is difficult, if not impossible, to draw up a definitive list of guilds for the period of the plays. Many guilds combined with others, some disappeared, and some changed their specialty in response to economic circumstances.

[14] The list has been edited twice in recent years; see Martin Stevens and Margaret Dorrell (Rogerson), eds., "The *Ordo Paginarum* Gathering of the York *A/Y Memorandum Book*," *Modern Philology* 72 (1974): 45–59; and *REED: York*, pp. 16–24. See also the article by Peter Meredith, "The *Ordo Paginarum* and the Development of the York Tilemakers' Pageant," *Leeds Studies in English*, n.s. 11 (1980): 59–73. My count includes interlineated additions by later hands, though not multiple references like those to the Masons. It excludes simple translations like "Glouers" for "Gaunters."

[15] Palliser, *Tudor York*, pp. 151–152.

correspondence is to be seen between the activity of the gild and the subject matter of the play, and the reason for the assignment—if indeed it was not arbitrary—must be sought elsewhere."[16] While I agree that there were other reasons for assigning the plays (for example, the connection of a guild with a patron saint, like the Barbers' traditional association with Saint John the Baptist), Beadle is mistaken in his estimate of the extent to which trade symbolism played an obvious role in the various York pageants. In a study of the subject, Alan D. Justice concludes that in a majority of instances (twenty-nine by his count of the registered plays) trade symbolism played a discernible role, and he concludes that "the importance of trade symbolism to both the text and the performance of the York cycle suggests that the relationship was deeper and more intimate than has heretofore been thought."[17] In fact, Justice is too conservative in his estimate, since his list of pageants with no apparent trade symbolism contains a number of instances wherein a connection between the sponsoring craft and the subject matter of the play is easily inferable. For example, the Coopers, makers of barrels, are the right craft to make the Tree of Paradise; the Pewterers to supply household items for the domestic scene between Joseph and Mary; and the Tile-thatchers to build a house (with a leaky roof, as shall be seen) for the Nativity—and all of these crafts are part of the excluded list in Justice's study. A careful critical reading of the York plays clearly demands the making of inferences regarding the ways in which the products or activities of the sponsoring crafts related to the subject matter of the pageants. And while in some cases there will not be any trade symbolism since numbers of crafts had changes in assignments in the course of the performance history of the cycle, there nevertheless is a sound basis for taking the relationship of the trade and the play as a fundamental fact of the character of the York plays.

That there are some instances in which the trade symbolism

---

[16] Beadle, *The York Plays*, p. 30.

[17] Justice, "Trade Symbolism in the York Cycle," *Theatre Journal* 31 (1979): 58.

goes far beyond the obvious is a fact well worth illustrating. Justice gives an instructive example: the case of the Marshals' sponsorship of the Flight into Egypt. The obvious relationship is in the provision of a horse by the Marshals, who shod horses and provided veterinary services, to carry Mary out of Bethlehem at the end of the play (Joseph tells Mary, "And yf þou can ille ride / Haue and halde þe faste by þe mane," 165/205–206). As Justice points out, this dialogue suggests that one of the Marshals walking with the pageant actually brought a saddled horse along for use to convey Mary down the street to the next station. In such a scene the association of York with Bethlehem is made a vivid dramatic reality. But the association of guild and play does not end there. Justice calls attention to the fact that "unless specifically sent for, marshals were prohibited by their own rules from frequenting inns to drum up business among travellers."[18] This exclusion from the world of privileged wayfaring would certainly allow a further, subtle association between craft and performers.

A final observation is necessary about the correspondence between the sponsoring crafts and the list of pageants. Historically there may be some significance in the fact that the Mercers are the sponsors of the last guild in the procession of plays. One could justify that placement solely on the basis of the lavish requirements for the enactment of a credible Doomsday performance.[19] But their assignment to the last place may also hold significance because the *end* of a procession was, in fact, the place of greatest honor. Since the Mercers were always last, this placement may well reflect the earliest circumstances of the dramatic procession, possibly reaching back to a time when the

[18] Ibid., p. 51.

[19] We know in fact that the Mercers spent a good deal of money on their pageant over the years. In 1449/1450 alone they paid a certain Thomas Steynour 13s. 4d. for "steynyng of þe clothes of oure pageand," i.e. for the painting of ornamental designs on the backdrops. The Mercers were the richest guild in York, and their records give ample proof that they took great pains in presenting their pageant. For a detailed discussion of the Mercers' pageant, see Johnston and Dorrell, "Mercers' Pageant of Doomsday," pp. 11–35.

civic religious procession preceded the dramatic procession and no doubt influenced its organization. Significantly various other important sponsors are placed near the end of the procession, including the mayor, who had charge of the Coronation play until 1463;[20] the Weavers and their Assumption pageant, which sometimes was used for occasions other than the performance of the Corpus Christi play (see *REED: York*, p. 149); the Drapers and their play of the Death of the Virgin; and the influential and prosperous Tailors and their pageant of the Ascension. The end of the dramatic procession was certainly dominated by some of the more powerful trade and craft guilds in York to help give a climactic close to the play and, not so incidentally, to bring recognition and honor to their guilds. In a very general sense the dramatic procession reflects the hierarchical parade order associated with the solemn Corpus Christi procession, and that fact, too, provides the proper atmosphere for bringing the play to a close.

In the foregoing discussion I have tried to demonstrate the distinctiveness of the York cycle as a corporate civic entertainment that to a large extent took itself as the object, if not the subject, of performance. To understand fully how this play evolved as a work of dramatic literature, one must take a look at the York manuscript.

THE text of the York plays (British Library MS Additional 35290) survives in a single complete manuscript of 268 vellum leaves. According to Anthony G. Petti, its main hand is in *secretaria hybrida formata*, while the names of characters are written in *hybrid anglicana* (possibly by a different scribe). Petti dates the hand as "late fifteenth century."[21] Two special features of the manuscript are worthy of note. First, it is truly a register in the sense that each pageant is entered separately. Breaks between plays always occur after deliberate spacing varying from

---

[20] See Margaret Dorrell (Rogerson), "The Mayor of York and the Coronation Pageant," *Leeds Studies in English*, n.s. 5 (1971): 35–45.

[21] Petti, *English Literary Hands from Chaucer to Dryden* (London: Edward Arnold, 1977), p. 12.

half a page (as at the end of the Barkers' pageant of the Fall of the Angels; see f. 4)[22] to nearly ten full pages, pricked and ruled for insertion of text (as at the end of the Curriers' play of the Transfiguration; see ff. 106–110v). New plays always begin at the top of a leaf, whether recto or verso. The large spaces left are clearly for the registry of plays that had been omitted at the time that the register was compiled or of plays that had since been added (thus, for example, the space after f. 100 is reserved for the text of the Ironmongers, whose name is inserted in the usual form at the top of f. 106v together with almost a verbatim copy of the description of their play from the 1415 list by Roger Burton).

The second notable feature of the York manuscript is its generally attractive appearance. It is not a true luxury manuscript, yet its vellum is of good grade, and the hand, when executed at its best (see ff. 116, 126, 132, 176v, etc.), is handsome and readable. The rubrication is, unfortunately, incomplete: Large initial capitals are absent throughout the manuscript, and rhyme markers exist only from ff. 9v to 113v and ff. 164 to 174. The rubricator seems to have had a much less sure hand than the scribe; at times his work is extremely untidy (see, for example, f. 112). The most noteworthy feature is the transcription of six songs accompanying the Weavers' pageant of the Assumption. John Stevens describes this notation as follows:

> The music of the songs is well-written in a professional hand accustomed to writing music. The scribe, perhaps one of the cantors of the cathedral, fully understood the notation he was using, with its complicated system of ligatures and coloured notes.

---

[22] I adopt the foliation used by Beadle in his edition (see *The York Plays*, p. 14). The MS itself has two foliations: the first, which was used by L. T. Smith in her 1885 edition, now canceled; and the second, which is the current British Library foliation. The latter, however, does not number the many blank pages. For a facsimile of the manuscript, see Richard Beadle and Peter Meredith, eds., *The York Play: A Facsimile of British Library MS Additional 35290* (Leeds: University of Leeds, 1983).

Stevens adds that the style of this notation is similar to that found in late-fifteenth-century manuscripts, and he observes in particular that the black and red notation, which was "gradually being replaced both in England and on the Continent, continued in use . . . until the early years of the sixteenth century."[23]

Two important conclusions need to be drawn from this information. The first is that the York manuscript was truly the official text owned by the city and, on the basis of marginalia as well as entries that appeared in the civic records, we know that it was used as a true register. In the later years of the cycle's performance this very manuscript was held by the city clerk, and provision was made for him to check what was being performed against what was recorded in the book. The city chamberlains' books tell, for example, that the first station was regularly reserved for the city clerk where he "kept" (held?) the "Registre." Here is the entry for 1536 (the first recorded): "In primis the ffyrst place at Trenytie yaites where as the Comon Clerke kepys the Registre wherefore that place goith free" (*REED: York*, p. 263; the entry is repeated almost verbatim in 1541 and 1554). Later the manuscript is referred to as the "Cite booke," and a call for unregistered plays is inserted in the House Books: "Item that [the] suche pageantz as be not registred in the Cite booke shall be called in to be registred by discrecion of my lord mayor" (*REED: York*, p. 324). A second call of the same kind dated 1566 is of special interest because it is confirmed by a notation in the York manuscript and thus provides incontrovertible evidence that the manuscript is indeed the "Cite booke" to which reference has been made. Here is the entry in full:

> Aggreed that the Pageantes of Corpus christi suche as be not allready Registred shalbe with all convenyent spede be fayre wrytten by Iohn Clerke in the [bo] old Registre yerof viz. of Vyntenors the Archetricline / of thyron mongars /

[23] John Stevens, "The Music of Play XLV: The Assumption of the Virgin," in *The York Plays*, ed. Beadle, appendix 1, p. 466.

Marie Magdalene wasshyng the Lordes feete &c. of the Tylars the lattr part of their pageant / Of the Labrors the Purificacion of our lady & [of] the Cappers to be examined with the Register & reformed / And Iohn Clerke or oyer taking peyne to be honestly recompensed for there peyne (*REED: York*, p. 351)

The text of the Purification play was copied into the manuscript shortly after this entry was made. On folio 74, in the proper space for the insertion of the play, there was insufficient room for its text to appear; consequently the scribe (John Clerke, who was attached to the office of the common clerk) entered it in the register in a vacant space much later in the manuscript, between the Supper at Emmaus and the Incredulity of Thomas, on folios 227v through 234. To orient the reader he inserted the following note in the manuscript where the Purification should have appeared:

Hatmakers Maysons and Laborers / purificacio Marie / the Laborers is assigned to bryng furth this pagyant / It is entryd in the Latter end of this booke / next after the Sledmen or / palmers and it begynnyth (by the preest) All myghty god in heven / so hye[24]

This confirmation of the entry in the House Book makes clear not only that the extant manuscript was the official register but also that plays were entered into it almost at the very end of the cycle's performance life.

The second notable fact about the manuscript has to do with its appearance. Even though it was used as the official book by the common clerk at the first station to check out the performance against the text, it was never used as an official script. It was written as an archival text, and considerable care was taken to make it an attractive book. It no doubt had "literary" value for the city—more so than any of the other municipal records, which are written in paper manuscripts in the customary una-

[24] See Beadle and Meredith, *York Facsimile*, f. 74; cf. Beadle, *The York Plays*, p. 436.

dorned secretary hand. But the desire for a beautiful book wherein to preserve the municipal play was not so dominant that it kept John Clerke from making notes in the text or the margins to update the performance. Frequent annotations in the manuscript bear out this point: for example, "Nota quia non concordat" and "novo addicio facto" (f. 114) or "this matter is newly mayde whereof / we haue no coppy" (f. 44). Thus, while the extant manuscript is clearly an official text, it is also meant to be read and admired as a work of apparent literary value. The fact that the missing plays were to be "fair written" is in itself an indication of the care that was taken in the upkeep of the "booke."

The late entry of the Purification play, as well as that of the Fullers of Adam and Eve in Eden (Play 4, which was not entered in the "booke" until 1557–1559),[25] is sufficient evidence that for many years the plays themselves were performed *without* reference to the manuscript. In the case of the Fullers' play, we are dealing with a pageant that had been part of the performed cycle from at least the time of the Burton List of 1415, the description of which exactly matches the text in the register, to the time that the text was finally entered into the manuscript in 1559 when the city chamberlains' books show that John Clerke was paid 12d. "for entryng in the Regyster the Regynall of the pagyaunt pertenyng to Craft of ffullars which was never before Regestred" (*REED: York*, p. 330). We therefore know that the play text for the performances was held by the individual guilds all along and that the manuscript is the city's effort to bring the whole cycle together as a literary text. The individual copy of the guild was called the "regynall" (i.e. "original"); the "Cite booke" was called the "register" (a distinction that I shall return to examine in the chapter on the Chester plays), and the "register" was clearly a quite literal compilation of the guilds' "regynalls." We have, of course, no way of knowing whether the whole text of the "regynalls" was actually performed—there is some legitimate doubt that the actors in the

[25] See Beadle, *The York Plays*, pp. 418–419.

fifteenth century could actually read their parts—but it is clear that what was transcribed in the register did not always match the performance. John Clerke's notes in the manuscript document at least some of the aberrations in the late years of the cycle's performance.[26]

THE relation of text to performance in York has long been a difficult problem in York scholarship. The interpretation I have offered in the preceding discussion makes clear that there was no central text from which the performance was drawn. And since the individual guilds apparently each had their own regynalls to guide their productions, we are obliged to question the extent to which the surviving register is a unified whole. It seems evident that its text is basically a composite of all the distinct regynalls of the York guilds. Can we then assume that the cycle has a common author or redactor? And if so, when and how did he manage to provide the continuity and thematic unity that modern critics have found in the cycle? It seems clear that the person(s) who collected the material for the register did little more than collect texts and "fair write" them. We know this in part from the work that was performed in the addition of the unregistered plays. A good illustration is the aforementioned Fullers' pageant of Adam and Eve in Eden, which in style and content exactly fits into the slot that was left for it. There is no reason to assume that the plays that surround it, which were there from the time that the register was compiled, were edited rather than simply transcribed.

We know also from other passages that the York Register copied its exemplars with remarkable fidelity. The manuscript pageants of the plays of Herod and the Magi furnish an instructive example. Modern editions have varied in the treatment of the two pageants: They were edited as separate plays

---

[26] John Clerke worked in or for the office of the common clerk from 1538/ 1539 until the end of his life in 1580. He is responsible for most of the marginalia in the MS. For a full discussion, see Peter Meredith, "John Clerke's Hand in the York Register," *Leeds Studies in English*, n.s., 12 (1981): 245–271.

by Lucy T. Smith[27] but were combined by Richard Beadle in the latest edition of the cycle. In the manuscript there are two distinct plays, the first of which is the Masons' play of Herod, occupying folios 62v through 66. The second, the Goldsmiths' Magi, follows after three blank pages and occupies folios 68 through 73v. In itself there is nothing remarkable about that division, but a question must be raised by the fact that a lengthy scene (the visit by the Magi to Herod's court) occurs verbatim in the two plays (cf. ff. 63v–66 and ff. 69–71v). Beadle's explanation of this duplication is persuasive: It stems from the order for the Goldsmiths and Masons to combine the two pageants into one, according to an entry in the *A/Y Memorandum Book* in 1432. Because both guilds were involved in producing the scene between Herod and the Magi, they obviously both needed a copy of the text of that scene, and that is why it is duplicated in their regynalls. The copyist of the register thus accepted verbatim the two texts, including the duplication. A true editor or redactor would undoubtedly have combined the two plays into one to get rid of the duplication, which makes sense in terms of performance but which interferes with the reader's understanding of the text.[28] The register thus gives primary emphasis, here as elsewhere, to making an exact record of what was performed.

Unfortunately, no early regynall survives, and hence the relationship of the regynalls to the register can now only be inferred from the evidence that we do have. There is, however, one extant mid-sixteenth-century regynall of a York pageant,

[27] L. T. Smith, *York Plays* (1885; reprint ed., New York: Russell and Russell, 1963).

[28] For Beadle's discussion of this complicated editorial problem, see *The York Plays*, pp. 429–434. Whether he is right about recombining the play is an open question. I believe that he made the wrong editorial decision. He should have maintained the two pageants even though the scene in question would then be duplicated. There is no evidence that the Goldsmiths ever went back to the *status quo ante* 1432 and presented the combined play. To the contrary, the Herod and the Magi pageants, as Beadle himself notes, very clearly are still separate plays as late as 1561 when the Herod pageant was performed by the Minstrels; see *REED: York*, p. 334.

the Scriveners' manuscript of the Incredulity of Thomas, which casts some interesting light on that relationship. The Scriveners' regynall, known as the Sykes manuscript and now in the Yorkshire Museum, York, is an independent text though it is closely related to and often identical with the copy of the play in the register. Its editor, A. C. Cawley, believes that "neither text is likely to have been copied from the other, since each has a verse that is not found in the other, and each has a number of satisfactory readings where the other is corrupt." He thinks, moreover, that both may be descended from a text "of the play which had already deviated from the original text in some particulars." The text itself seems to have been a prompt copy, since it was stitched into a leather wrapper and "folded lengthwise down the middle, as though one of its users made a practice of carrying it in the pocket."[29] In light of the foregoing discussion, it seems clear that the Sykes manuscript was a copy of an earlier regynall that probably itself was a copy of yet an earlier text (the Scriveners after all would have had little trouble making clean copies of their play). That earlier text, removed by two generations from the Sykes manuscript, could well have been the source of the play in the register. The Scriveners' play was still performed in the mid-sixteenth century—the latest evidence for its performance is 1554—and hence, in this one instance we do have an example of a text that was used as the play book for a performance. What it proves is that for a half century at least (i.e. from the time that the register was copied in the late fifteenth century to the estimated mid-sixteenth-century date of the Sykes manusript) and possibly for the lifetime of the play, dating back to its composition (which I believe to have occurred in the second quarter of the fourteenth century), the text of the play underwent no substantive change, though of course its performance might have. It also proves that at least one guild, but probably all of them,

---

[29] A. C. Cawley, "The Sykes MS of the York Scriveners' Play," *Leeds Studies in English and Kindred Languages* 7–8 (1952), see esp. pp. 45–48.

used the regynall as the play text throughout the lifetime of the Corpus Christi cycle.

Yet despite the fact that the evidence establishes the York manuscript as being the compilation of independent regynalls sponsored by the separate guilds, there is an unmistakable continuity in large segments if not in the whole cycle. For a long time now, York scholarship has identified various individual authors or redactors of portions of the cycle by such exotic names as the "Great Dramatist," the "Great Metrist," the "Passion Playwright of York," and the "York Realist."[30] There is no strong need to review that scholarship here, since much of it, as Jesse Byers Reese has shown in a rigorous article,[31] is based on impressionistic conclusions. However, there is something to be said for the "feel" that most readers experience in finding that continuity, and several studies deserve singling out for isolating significant details that document that continuity.

The first of these has to do with the relationship of the York cycle and the Middle English poem *The Northern Passion*. As

[30] Charles Mills Gayley noted several stages of composition in York, and he coined the names the "Passion Playwright of York" and the "Realist" (presumably the same person); see *Plays of Our Forefathers and Some of the Traditions upon Which They Were Founded* (1907; reprint ed., New York: Biblo and Tannen, 1968), p. 158. W. W. Greg follows Gayley's "stages" and adopts the terms the "Great Metrist" and the "Great Dramatist"; see "Bibliographical and Textual Problems of the English Miracle Plays," *Library*, 3d ser. 5 (1914): 289–291. See also E. K. Chambers, *English Literature at the Close of the Middle Ages* (Oxford: Clarendon Press, 1945), pp. 29–33.

[31] Reese shows that thirteen plays in the York cycle are written in true alliterative verse, a form that is based on stress rather than meter and that is part of the native poetic tradition shared by *Piers Plowman* and *Sir Gawain and the Green Knight*; see pageants 1, 11, 16, 26, 28, 29, 30, 31, 32, 33, 36, 44, and 45. He demonstrates that the labels used by Greg and others are wholly inadequate since they fail to take the alliterative system into account; for example, the so-called Great Metrist writes plays in both the metrical and alliterative stress modes; and he finds, moreover, that the Great Dramatist, who according to Greg was not a metrist, used exactly the same metrical style as the Great Metrist! See Reese, "Alliterative Verse in the York Cycle," *Modern Philology* 48 (1951): 646–647. It should be noted that Reese is uncertain whether the stressed alliterative verse is the work of one author.

long ago as 1911, Frances Foster observed that the influence of *The Northern Passion* on the York cycle was pervasive "in determining the sequence of events" in most of the plays dealing with the Passion, particularly pageants 26 through 29, 32 through 36, and 38. Noting the work of William A. Craigie, who ten years earlier had already shown the influence of the Middle English *Gospel of Nicodemus* on the York cycle, she concludes that "the *Northern Passion* and *The Gospel of Nicodemus* would appear to supply the basis for whole plays, the sources being used to supplement each other." She goes on to say that "the English playwright [note the singular] appears to have followed the line of least resistance: in constructing these scriptural plays he turned naturally enough to English paraphrases of the scriptural stories already in meter—obviously a much easier method than one which involved translation."[32] Any theory about the evolution and growth of the York play text obviously has to take this influence into account.

The second study, a classic article by J. W. Robinson, documents the similarity in style and the use of detail in several of the York Passion plays written by the playwright whom Gayley (at times) named the "York Realist." The plays in question are all largely written in the stressed alliterative line identified by Reese, and they are all based on *The Northern Passion*. Robinson observes that the playwright is, therefore, "not to be credited with any fundamental structural work." What he is responsible for is an "all-pervading realism" (later in the article redefined as naturalism) that highlights "a biting portrayal of worldliness" and focuses on small but compelling details, such as Her-

---

[32] See Frances A. Foster, "The Mystery Plays and the Northern Passion," *Modern Language Notes* 26 (1911): 171. The Craigie study, "The *Gospel of Nicodemus* and the *York Mystery Plays*," appeared in *An English Miscellany Presented to Dr. Furnivall* (Oxford: Clarendon Press, 1901), pp. 52–61. In an important follow-up article, Frances H. Miller found numerous additional parallels leading her to conclude that "there is practically nothing in the Passion group of York" that cannot be found in either *The Northern Passion* or *The Gospel of Nicodemus*; see "The Northern Passion and the Mysteries," *Modern Language Notes* 34 (1919): 88–92.

od's concern with wrinkles in his clothes or the Messenger's effort to warm the water in which Pilate will wash his hands. That realism, according to Robinson, is also responsible for purposeful repetition, like the various retirements and arousals of tyrants, thus "working out the events of the Passion story in their natural sequence and logical detail" and providing the plays with an unmistakable identity. Robinson believes that the emphasis on process of behavior rather than separate actions establishes a difference between the plays of the Realist and other medieval Passion plays similar to "the difference between Richardson's and Fielding's novels."[33] The importance of this study is its attention to the unique details that identify the work of a playwright that others before Robinson had sensed to exist but not documented. Clearly, the work of this playwright must be accounted for in any theory about the composition of the manuscript.

The studies by Foster and Robinson lead inevitably to the conclusion that a large part of the cycle—the whole of the Passion and some of the later plays—was subjected to at least one major editing, and possibly two. The redactor who relied upon *The Northern Passion* material might have been the original author of the cycle. If that was the case, then at some early point the several guilds of York who sponsored pageants for the dramatic procession apparently hired a writer to provide individual regynalls for each of them. If, on the other hand, they already had individual texts, then *The Northern Passion* material must have been the result of a second editing. And if we are persuaded, further, that the contributions of the York Realist

---

[33] See J. W. Robinson, "The Art of the York Realist," *Modern Philology* 60 (1963): 241–251. A more recent article by Clifford Davidson attempts to place the York Realist's work into the contexts of late-medieval nominalism and affective piety as well as the iconography of the northern painters. While Davidson provides some solid and interesting parallels, I am not convinced that he has shown the York treatment to be more keyed to "immediate present reality" than the plays of the other cycles, particularly those of N-Town. See Clifford Davidson, "The Realism of the York Realist and the York Passion," *Speculum* 50 (1975): 271–283.

are distinct from all other writing in the cycle, as Robinson believes, then there had to have been a second editing of the eight pageants to which he contributed. Whichever the case, it is clear that the York cycle at an early stage was the work of at least one author/redactor who gave coherence to the separate regynalls that made up the cycle. This was the source of whatever dramatic, thematic, metrical, stylistic, or linguistic unity that is found in the extant cycle.[34]

The important point is that it was clearly possible for a collection of separate regynalls to be welded into larger dramatic designs. It was even possible for a single dramatist to have written the entire cycle of some fifty regynalls in a play unified by a central intelligence. Unfortunately, the otherwise copious York records tell nothing about the actual first composition of the regynalls nor about subsequent editings. I find it difficult to believe that a single writer could have been commissioned by a large number of unrelated guilds, and yet the incorporation of *The Northern Passion* material is much more plausibly the result of one writer's choice than the choice of a group of disparate guilds.

Scholars have thus far failed to recognize that it was this early stage in the evolution of the York cycle that was the true date of composition. Much emphasis has been given to the dating of the manuscript, and lately the consensus has formed that it was written in the latter third of the fifteenth century, with the implication that this was also the date when the plays in their pres-

---

[34] Apart from the studies already mentioned, numerous others have found unity in the York cycle. Effie McKinnon has taken what is perhaps the broadest view of the question; she finds that the salvation of mankind itself is the "theme running throughout all of the plays and giving to the cycle a comprehensive and artistic unity" that transcends the arbitrary divisions of pageants; see McKinnon, "Notes on the Dramatic Structure of the York Cycle," *Studies in Philology* 28 (1931): 438. Others find the design to be restricted, as Robinson did, to segments of the cycle; see, for example, Clifford Davidson, "After the Fall: Design in the Old Testament Plays in the York Cycle," *Mediaevalia* 1 (1975): 1–24. Still others find a link between pageants to exist in consistent characterizations, as does Robert Brawer in "The Characterization of Pilate in the York Cycle Play," *Studies in Philology* 69 (1972): 289–303.

ent form originated. As I have shown, that conclusion is wrong, for the manuscript simply copied the play texts held by the guilds, and therefore the date of composition that we should be concerned about is that of the regynalls.

We are aided in inferring that date by several facts. The first is the *a quo* date of the surviving register—in other words the earliest possible date when the register could have been copied from the regynalls. That date is in dispute by those who have carefully studied the manuscript evidence against that of the records, but it is safe to say that the most convincing *a quo* date is 1462, a date that marks the time when the mayor was no longer responsible for bringing forth the Coronation play (no. 46), which had been assigned to him in Burton's *ordo* of 1415. After 1462 (though the exact year could have been any year up to 1468) the Ostlers took over the responsibility for the play. Since the manuscript attributes the play to the Ostlers (in the hand of the main scribe and rubricator), it had to have been copied after this shift in sponsorship had taken place. The evidence for other proposed *a quo* dates, specifically 1482 and 1485, is considerably more circumstantial.[35] Hence, while it is safe to say that the manuscript could not have existed before 1462, it was possible for it to have been copied just prior to 1501 when the first station of the Corpus Christi plays was for the first time called the "Common Clerk's station," where the

[35] Margaret Dorrell (Rogerson) has argued for these dates on the basis of changes that occurred in the Carpenters' sponsorship of the Resurrection play and in the apparent demise of the Linenweavers' play of Fergus; see "The Butchers', Saddlers', and Carpenters' Pageants: Misreadings of the York *Ordo*," *English Language Notes* 13 (1975): 1–4; and idem, "External Evidence for Dating the York Register," *REED Newsletter* 2 (1976): 4–5. Richard Beadle and Peter Meredith proposed the 1462 *a quo* date. They also challenged the conclusions drawn in Dorrell's argument concerning the evidence involving the Fergus play, though they have not refuted the argument she advanced concerning the Carpenters. Their view is that the *ad quem* date for the register is 1477, but the evidence they offer regarding the scribe's intentions in leaving blank spaces for missing plays is highly circumstantial; see Beadle and Meredith, "Further External Evidence for Dating the York Register (BL Additional MS 35290)," *Leeds Studies in English*, n.s. 11 (1980): 51–55.

register was kept and checked against the performance. But whatever the date of the register might have been, the important one for us was that of the regynalls.

If the *a quo* date for the manuscript was some time between 1462 and 1468, and if, further, the manuscript was copied from the regynalls then the *ad quem* date for the latter had to be 1468. How much earlier did these regynalls come into being? To deduce their *a quo* date we need to go back to the Burton *Ordo* of 1415. Scholars agree that there would have been no need for the detailed description of that list if there had been a written text for the plays.[36] Moreover, we need to note that in the earliest years of the York plays, and until at least 1426, the plays processed through the streets of York on the same day that the civic liturgical procession took place. This meant that on the single day set aside for performance, only a part of the time could have been dedicated to the plays. The mayor, who was an important spectator of the play, was a participant, together with the aldermen and all the leaders of the parish clergy, in the liturgical procession. Time was consequently available for no more than a civic riding of tableaux vivants intermingled with perhaps a few speeches that would have been delivered at the various stops or stations.[37] We know that in the year 1426 a Franciscan friar named William Melton proposed to the people of York that henceforth the play should be played on one day of the feast and the procession on the other ("ad hoc populum ciuitatis inducebat vt ludus ille fiat in vna die & processio in die altera"; see *REED: York*, p. 43), and the com-

[36] See Beadle, *The York Plays*, p. 24.

[37] For a full reconstruction of the dramatic procession prior to 1426, see my article, "The York Cycle: From Procession to Play," *Leeds Studies in English*, n.s. 6 (1972): 37–62. On the basis of discoveries made since the publication of that article, I am no longer sure that the dramatic and religious processions were one and the same in the early years. However, they did undeniably take place on the same day, and therefore my account of the performance stands very much as recorded. For a similar account of the early years of the play, see Alan H. Nelson, *The Medieval English Stage* (Chicago: University of Chicago Press, 1974), pp. 42–45.

mon council agreed to institute that arrangement.[38] If the foregoing is sufficiently specific about grounds for ruling out the existence of a text for the York plays (and I think it is), then a provisional *a quo* for the regynalls is 1426. At a point after 1426, therefore, the conditions were ripe for the expansion of the civic riding into a series of full-fledged plays. I believe the composition of the regynalls can be moved forward to a date after 1432.

The significance of that date has already been discussed in

[38] An extended argument has been offered by Alexandra F. Johnston that, despite the elaborate decision made by the common council and the citizens of York in 1426, the procession and play were not assigned to separate days until 1468. The argument is based on a close examination of the York records between 1426 and 1476. Although the evidence is scanty, Johnston found what she believed to be references to the performance of the play taking place on Corpus Christi Day until 1468. Actually not one of these references is to a performance per se; rather the allusion is to something associated with the play—for example, an entry in the chamberlains' books listing the "expense in festo corporis christi" (see *REED: York*, p. 65). That phrase does not describe a specific day; rather it refers generically to the "feast," which at the time began on the eve of its vigil, Wednesday, and did not end until the subsequent Monday. "Expense in corporis christi" simply means "expenses accrued during the feast of Corpus Christi"; it in no way describes a specific day of performance. For the procession, on the other hand, the day of Corpus Christi is always specified; we have phrases like "in festo eiusdem corporis christi" or on "Corpus Christi Day." I interpret these references to mean that the City of York, indeed, lived up to its resolve of 1426: The procession now did take place *alone* on Corpus Christi Day, when according to Friar Melton, the citizens should go to Mass or attend religious offices. The play, on the other hand, was to have been moved to the vigil of the feast, in other words, the preceding Wednesday. Nothing in the records says that this solemn resolution was not followed. The vigil, after all, is part of the feast, and the references culled by Johnston never refer directly to a performance where a specified date would have been expected. Even the evidence for 1468, where she allegedly finds reason to believe that the two functions took place on separate days, does not give more than the customary phrase "in festo corporis christi." The probability is that the play continued to be done on the vigil of the feast and the procession on Corpus Christi Day until 1468 when, for whatever reason, the procession was moved to the day after Corpus Christi and, one assumes, the play to the day of Corpus Christi (see *REED: York*, p. 109). See Johnston, "The Procession and the Play of Corpus Christi in York after 1426," *Leeds Studies in English*, n.s. 7 (1973): 55–62.

connection with the Masons and the Goldsmiths. It was in 1432 that the Magi play described in Burton's list was expanded and divided between the Masons who now performed Herod, and the Goldsmiths who retained the play dealing with the Magi. The register contains the two plays with a shared scene that is repeated in the text. This play came to the register from the regynalls of the Masons and the Goldsmiths. While it is possible that these regynalls might have been a revision of an earlier written text, that would only have been possible if there indeed had been a written text before 1432, and I have already shown the unlikelihood of that circumstance.

It is therefore possible to date the composition of the York plays in the period between 1432 and 1468. If that date is correct, then the York plays are almost certainly the oldest of the English Corpus Christi cycles. A date of composition in the early 1440s would seem in keeping with our knowledge of the state of literacy in the city of York. It was in 1449 when the manuscript of the Creed play, written in English, was bequeathed to the Corpus Christi Guild by William Revetour, its owner (listed under receipts in the Corpus Christi Account Rolls: "Et de vno libro anglicano continente [blank] paginas de instrucione & informacione fidei christiane vulgariter vocate Crede Playe / per dominum Willelmum Revetour"; *REED: York*, p. 78). Hence we know of the existence of at least one other text of a York play in the vernacular by midcentury. Moreover, it was a time in York when private libraries included a good many English titles, especially of devotional books. The same William Revetour, a York chaplain, owned a copy of *The Prick of Conscience*; a legend of saints in English; "a book in English treating the Bible," which is assumed to be a translation of Peter Comestor's *Historia Scholastica*; and numerous others, including a Latin Bible with images.[39] Records give evidence of other great collections of private citizens, the most notable of

[39] Joann H. Moran, "Education and Learning in the City of York, 1300–1560," Borthwick Papers, no. 55, Borthwick Institute of Historical Research, University of York, 1979, p. 30.

which is that of John Dautre, who at his death in 1458 left a magnificent library that included, among other books, a romance of Alexander and another of the Trojan War, a copy of Bonaventure's *Meditations*, and several grammar books, primers, and books of devotion.[40] York was a center of learning with several ecclesiastical libraries and with known private collections that are traceable to the period in question. Certainly by the second quarter of the fifteenth century, the city had the resources among both the ecclesiastical and the lay communities to write the York plays.

I have demonstrated that the York cycle grew in performance as a corporate activity and that gradually the guilds obtained written texts for their plays. Its unity as a cycle stems in large part from the city's interest in self-celebration, including especially the efforts by the guilds to incorporate themselves in the dramatic representation of salvation history. This theme is one that undoubtedly became prominent in later revisions, as redactors, like *The Northern Passion* editor or the York Realist, set to work in giving ever more coherence to the plays as a unified cycle. I want now to look specifically at what I consider to be the central unifying strand in the cycle: the self-conscious concern of the York plays with the city itself.

ALMOST literally at the center of the York cycle, both physically and dramatically, is the Skinners' pageant of Jesus' Entry into Jerusalem. It is the twenty-fifth play in a collection of forty-eight, and it marks the end of the Ministry and the beginning of the Passion. By all odds it is the most developed Entry into Jerusalem play in the medieval drama, and, more than any other pageant, it puts in the foreground York's obsession with civic ceremony and self-celebration, for nowhere else is the issue of any play so directly the processional pageant, the very mode of performance that the York cycle enacts for its audience, than in this pivotal dramatic episode. Indirectly, the play imitates a civic procession resembling the annual civic liturgical

[40] Ibid., p. 31.

procession of Corpus Christi, in which the city officials as well as the parish clergy "entered" the city with the Host, the Body of Christ. This event was, of course, the core of the civic celebration of Corpus Christi, and it is thought by many (myself included) to have been the germ of the Corpus Christi play itself. Directly, it imitated the royal entry ceremony, which came to be a highly developed genre of civic procession in York. In both frames of reference, the Skinners' play served the ultimate function of highlighting the corporate community of York. It focused attention on the cycle itself and on the occasion of its performance and thus caused the city to become identified with the dramatic subject being enacted. In short, it transformed the city into the stage of the cycle. And in the broadest terms, it mirrored the soul of its creation—the civic processional—which, in the words of one critic, "affirmed corporate entity [and] manifested the complexity and ideal stability of urban society."[41] The Skinners' pageant of the Entry into Jerusalem is thus the ultimate York play.

When Jesus enters Jerusalem, he also enters York. He comes, of course, in a dramatized procession that itself is an imitation of the event that, at the time when the play was written, was the central festivity of the Corpus Christi feast—the carrying of the Host through the streets of York. The drama reminds us of the historical reality of Jesus, and it gives us a present-day setting within which to understand what the York play calls his "rawnsom" (205/9, compare 219/525). It is, then, in the Skinners' play that we find the core significance of the York cycle, the dramatization of the meaning of the feast of Corpus Christi. In it religious and dramatic processions merge, and the city is led to a reenactment and commemoration of the Passion in the spirit that was prescribed by the bull of Urban IV that established the feast: "We rejoice with pious weeping and weep with devout jubilation, happy in our lament and sad in our joy" ("gaudemus pie lacrimantes et lacrimamus devote gaudentes,

[41] David Mills, "Religious Drama and Civic Ceremonial," in *The Revels History of Drama in England*, vol. I, *Medieval Drama* (London: Methuen, 1983), p. 156.

letas habendo lacrimas et letitiam lacrimantem"). As V. A. Kolve has shown, the joyful celebration of the Holy Sacrament was the object of the Corpus Christi Feast; the day was set aside not only to reflect upon the sorrow of the Cross but also upon the joy of the Resurrection.[42] Both, of course, are contained in the meaning of the Host.

At the same time that the procession of the Entry into Jerusalem imitates the civic liturgical procession, it also mirrors another kind of procession, the royal entry. York throughout the Middle Ages was noted for its splendid civic shows with which it greeted visiting royalty. The prescribed route of the royal entry processional was, interestingly, very much the same as that of the Corpus Christi play, and when, therefore, Jesus is greeted in the course of the Skinners' pageant with the accustomed royal entry ceremony as the King of Kings in the streets of York, the spectators saw him take possession of their city much as they had secular kings and queens. There was no more powerful a link to be found between present-day York and historic Jerusalem than this dramatic setting provided. Indeed, the setting of the Skinners' play puts a whole new focus on everything that has transpired and everything that will yet transpire in the cycle. The Passion is taking place here and now. The characters are Yorkshire people. The place is York. And yet the spectators in the streets gradually recognize that they are really in Jerusalem.

To understand just how close the parallels are between the agenda of the royal entry ceremony and the action of the play, let us take a closer look at both. The royal entry ceremony had a long history in medieval England at the time that the York plays were written. Extending back to the thirteenth century, it developed over the years not only to celebrate visits of royalty, but also coronations, births, marriages, political events (like the restoration of rights by Richard III to the citizens of London in 1392), and victorious returns from war, which eventually be-

[42] V. A. Kolve, *The Play Called Corpus Christi* (Stanford: Stanford University Press, 1966), pp. 44–49.

came expanded into "triumphs."[43] Customarily, royal entries involved the greeting of the royal personage outside of town by a carefully prescribed delegation of town officials, the subsequent ceremonial ride into the city proper, welcoming speeches by persons enacting legendary heroes of the city spoken at set points along the itinerary and usually given on elaborate pageants, the giving of gifts to the visitor, and the ending of the ceremonial ride before a palace or a cathedral. By the second quarter of the fifteenth century, descriptive or celebratory verses came to be written for or about these triumphs, as for example on the occasion of the return of Henry VI from Paris in 1432 and the 1445 royal entry of Margaret of Anjou into London.[44] Although we have no precisely contemporary analogue of such a "show" from York, two vivid accounts survive of Henry VII's entry into the city in 1486. It would be in-

[43] The best available history of the royal entry is that of Robert Withington in *English Pageantry*, 2 vols. (Cambridge: Harvard University Press, 1918), 1:124–197. An interesting recent account, concentrating on French pageants, can be found in Alan E. Knight's *Aspects of Genre in Late Medieval French Drama* (Manchester: Manchester University Press, 1983), pp. 117–140. The definitive history and interpretation of the civic triumph is now being written by Gordon Kipling, who generously allowed me to read several finished chapters of his manuscript. Professor Kipling corrects the old impression, advanced mostly by E. K. Chambers and Robert Withington, that civic triumphs were essentially spectacles that put a great deal of emphasis upon trade symbolism. His examination of the four pageants in the 1392 entry of Richard III into London has led Kipling to see an allegorical scenario that is like the one that I am proposing for the Entry into Jerusalem pageant in the York cycle. He shows that "long before European cities began decorating their streets with pageantry, they imagined themselves transformed into another Zion, a celestial Jerusalem, whenever a king made his ceremonial entry."

[44] John Lydgate's role in the 1432 triumph has long been questioned. It is now generally agreed that he did not write the triumph for Henry VI. In addition, Gordon Kipling has shown that Lydgate is not the author of the triumph for Margaret of Anjou in 1445. It was principally on the basis of that putative authorship that a recent argument has been made for his having written the N-Town cycle; see Gail McMurray Gibson, "Bury St. Edmunds, Lydgate, and the N-Town Cycle," *Speculum* 56 (1981): 82. For Kipling's argument, see "The London Pageants for Margaret of Anjou: A Medieval Script Restored," *Medieval English Theatre* 4 (1982): 5–27.

structive to examine that entry in the context of the Skinners' play.

The triumph of Henry VII was a way for the City of York to embrace the new monarch, who was not a welcome replacement for Richard III in the eyes of York citizens. Richard was a true patron of the city, and its leading citizens were fiercely loyal to him. Under the circumstances, the official city needed to do all in its power to mask its former loyalties and to greet the new king with a strong show of tribute. In consequence, the city spent sixty-six pounds, a very princely sum, to greet Henry VII; "along his route was presented a series of pageants and speeches, all stressing his virtues and his hereditary right, and culminating in a representation of Our Lady, promising her son's aid for the King."[45] The two surviving documents describing this memorable occasion are first, an official account of the processional greeting and a text of the "speeches" in the York House Book (see *REED: York*, pp. 146–152); and second, an independent account, apparently by an eyewitness, of the event together with a transcript of the "speeches," in Cotton MS Julius B.xii (ff. 8b–21b).[46] From a composite reading of these accounts, we learn that Henry VII, dressed in a gown of gold cloth furred with ermine, was met by the city's two sheriffs at Tadcaster, some ten miles away from York and the outermost extremity of the "franchise." The sheriffs brought twenty horses to help conduct the king into the city. At Bilburgh Cross, about five miles from the city, the king was met by the common council, the city clerk, the chamberlains, and many of the inhabitants of the city (apparently all dressed in red livery). Then, either two or three miles from the city (depending on the account), the mayor, the aldermen, and still more citizens, probably the most privileged, all on horseback, waited to meet the king and his entourage. Finally, a half-mile outside the city gate, the king was greeted by all the orders of friars, the prior,

---

[45] Palliser, *Tudor York*, p. 43.

[46] For a transcription as well as commentary, see A. H. Smith, "A York Pageant, 1486," *London Mediaeval Studies* 1 (1937–1939): 382–398.

and the brothers of Saint Trinity's, the abbot of Saint Mary's with his convent, the canons of Saint Leonard's, and "the general procession of al the parisshe churches of the saide citie" together with a great number of ordinary citizens on foot—men, women, and children—who lined the road, shouting "King Henry, King Henry." The ceremony of greeting along the road was clearly done in rank order, as York was accustomed to do in its civic processions.

At the city gate, apparently Micklegate (which also was traditionally the place from which civic processions and the Corpus Christi play itself began), the king was met by the first of the ceremonial pageants, a scene representing Heaven, the angels, and a world full of trees and flowers. This might have been the pageant of the Tanners for the Creation play in the York cycle; provision is made for its storage throughout the York records (see the Bridgemasters' Account Rolls; and *REED: York*, passim). In the midst of this world, a rich red rose was contrived to pop up when Henry looked upon the scene, followed by a white rose, and all the other flowers were then made to bow to the roses. Thereafter, a crown descended from a cloud and covered the roses. Then (in some manner not specified) a city with citizens appeared and from its midst the founder of York, King Ebrauk, stepped forward to hand the keys of the city to the king and to read or recite a speech, the gist of which is that York greets him, submits to his royal power, and begs for his favor.

The entourage then proceeded along Micklegate, which was bedecked with cloths that hung from houses on both sides of the street so that no gaps showed between them, and a device was rigged up to spew forth rose water that fell, if the weather was fair, before the lords, but—in cautious restraint—not before the king. The procession moved forward to the foot of Ouse Bridge, where it was met by another pageant "garnysshede with shippes, and botes in every side" (Cotton MS Julius B.xii, f. 11a).[47] One is tempted to equate this pageant with

[47] The House Book description does not mention this pageant. It was clearly

55

that of the Shipwrights' play of Noah. If that is so, the order of pageants is reflective of the Corpus Christi cycle itself, and the association of the two civic shows becomes a matter for common recognition. The significance of the ships, we are told, was to recall the king's landing in England at Milford Haven.

The next stop for the procession was the middle of Ouse Bridge where it encountered a pageant (probably borrowed from the Goldsmiths who did Herod and the Magi in the Corpus Christi cycle), featuring a royal throne. Six kings, the previous Henrys, thereupon appeared, and as Henry VII watched, they handed a scepter to yet another king, Solomon, who in turn passed the scepter, signifying wisdom and justice, to Henry VII while reciting a speech of welcome and petition.[48] After crossing the bridge, the procession moved on to the corner of Ousegate and Coneygate (the route is still identical with that of the Corpus Christi play and procession), where a hailstorm of sweetmeats, made by the craft of "cumfettes," showered the lords (but, again, not the king). Next, as the procession turned into Coneygate, and moved up to the Common Hall, it was met by a pageant in the form of a castle (perhaps the Pilate pageant of the Tapiters). In front of it appeared King David handing King Henry a sword of victory, and in the company of citizens dressed in white and green, signifying truth and heartfelt affection, David gave his speech of welcome and submission.[49] The last processional station was the pageant of "Our Lady," standing at the end of Stonegate near the Minster, to which King Henry retired at the end of the civic festivities. She stood on what Cotton MS Julius B.xii identified as the "paiaunt of theassumptoun," which is manifestly the pageant of the Weavers from the Corpus Christi play. We are told that she ascended in this pageant up to Heaven, with angel song (we recall

---

situated on the Micklegate side of Ouse Bridge, which is referred to as "the hider ende."

[48] The pageant of the Henrys is not mentioned in Cotton MS Julius B.xii. Solomon's speech, however, appears there, with an additional stanza.

[49] The David pageant appears out of place in the Cotton MS Julius B.xii account, where it comes last.

the musical notations accompanying the Weavers' pageant in the York Register), and she welcomed King Henry in behalf of her Son, because, as she put it, "this citie is a place of my pleasing."

With this summary in mind, we are now in a position to understand the full civic context of the Skinners' Entry into Jerusalem. But before we examine the play as entry ceremony, let us recall the Biblical passages upon which it draws. The principal ultimate source for the York Entry episode is the Gospel of Saint Matthew, though it also draws on Luke. The synoptic Gospels perceive the life of Christ as something of a pilgrimage, and his ministry is one that gains its strength from the grass roots from which it grew. In a very real sense, the whole of the ministry is seen by Saint Luke, for example, as an inevitable journey to Jerusalem (see Luke 13:23), the malevolent city that represents the epitome of the earthly, where moneylenders are in the Temple and Pharisees confuse God's power with Caesar's. The inevitability of the Passion being played out in Jerusalem is recognized by Jesus himself, who asserts shortly before his arrival, "it cannot be that a prophet perish outside Jerusalem" (Luke 13:33). The city then was conceived as the main site of corruption, and the Entry was portrayed at once as the end of the road for Jesus and the liberation of the citizens. The Biblical context is obviously different from the civic. The triumph in this instance is one of the spirit, not the corporate body, and thus the play reaches out for a higher meaning and a deeper truth than the civic ceremony. If in the royal entry the object was to impress King Henry with the splendor and good will of the city (for the purpose ultimately of seeking his support), the implicit purpose of the play is quite the opposite—to associate York with the old Jerusalem, a place of corruption and injustice, the city in which Jesus was to undergo the Passion. The Skinners' play of the Entry must put one in mind of a different York from that which furnishes the self-congratulatory festival. It must make known that York, like all earthly cities and like all civilization, is in need of renewal. The vicarious enactment of the death of Jesus within its corporate boundaries will perform that renewal. We must therefore apply to our comparison of play and civic ceremony an ironic perspective.

The entourage of Jesus and his Twelve Disciples is notable from the beginning by its contrast to the rich royal entry procession. Instead of being met by twenty white horses at the outermost point of greeting, Jesus will encounter his host riding an ass, and he himself has made the arrangement to obtain that lowly beast of burden. In the beginning of the play, he stands with Peter and Philip, instructing them to "vnbynde" the ass with her foal and to bring them to him, so that he can ride into the city as the prophecy of Isaiah has declared (compare Isaiah 62:11 and Matthew 21:5). The setting is just outside Jerusalem/York, in Bethpage (207/88), which in the constricted geography of the play corresponds to Tadcaster. He instructs the two disciples to go "vnto ȝone castell þat is ȝou agayne," (205/15), that is, that is plainly visible from where they stand, and the ride itself will be brief, a mere "space" (206/23), or more precisely, "a mile," as we learn later (210/196).

In this entry, Jesus obviously plans his own triumph. When Peter and Philip enter the town, they make straight for the common pasture, and they decide that since the beasts that graze there belong to the city (Philip says, "the beestis are comen"; 207/57), they need not ask permission to fetch the ass. However, they are surprised by the Porter, who challenges them because he does not recognize them as townsmen (they appear "withoute leverie"; 207/65). The Porter is one of several splendid minor characterizations in the York cycle (compare the Beadle in the Pilate pageants),[50] who as ordinary man lives the life of a true Christian. He is, indeed, the bedrock citizen of York, drawn by the playwright on the model of those in the audience to whom the play is meant to appeal. He allows them to borrow the animal (the contrast with the twenty white

---

[50] Kathleen Ashley has written a compelling analysis of the Beadle's role in a paper, read at the MLA Convention in 1982, entitled "Pilate's Courteous Beadle and the Audience of the York Cycle," which she kindly made available to me.

horses becomes all the more compelling as this scene is played out), and he arranges as well, after hearing for whom the ass is intended—"Jesus, of Jewes kyng" (207/80)—to go

> To the chiffe of þe Jewes, þat þei may sone
> Assemble same to his metyng.
>
> (208/94–95)

The chief of the Jews are, of course, the York Aldermen, who are also called "the citezens . . . of þis cyté," and who, he is sure, will want to come and "mete þat free" (208/103–105). The Aldermen are characterized as sympathetic to Jesus and eager for his new laws, even at the expense of their own (here the Skinners may be flattering their oligarchs!):

> In oure tempill if he prechid
> Agaynste þe pepull that leued wrong,
> And also new lawes if he teched
> Agaynste oure lawis we vsed so lang,
> And saide pleynlye
> The olde schall waste, þe new schall gang,
> þat we schall see.
>
> (209/141–147)

They resolve to meet him as their king and to "honnoure [him] as we wele awe / worthely tyll oure citee" (210/184–185). Clearly they have in mind the royal entry in a manner similar to that which greeted English kings as they came to York. Since Jesus is "Kyng of Juuys" (211/223), they discuss his "genolagye," consisting of Jesse, David, and Solomon, as well as "his modir kynne" (211/240–242), a list suggesting a row of pageants that an audience familiar with York triumphs can easily picture. Thereupon we see the Aldermen assemble to form the greeting party:

> Go we þan with processioun
> To mete þat comely as vs awe,
> With braunches, floures and vnysoune.
> With myghtfull songes her on a rawe

> Our childir schall
> Go synge before, þat men may knawe.
>   (212/260–266)

We must bear in mind that the Skinners' play was enacted in the streets of York. The procession of Aldermen thus looks very like the real thing, as it advances in the opposite direction of the play proper, toward Micklegate and implicitly out on the road to Tadcaster.

Meanwhile the ass is delivered to Jesus, and a cloth is spread for him on the animal's back, in keeping with Saint Matthew: "And they brought the ass and the colt, laid their cloaks on them, and made him sit thereon" (21:7; compare 212/275). This is the scene in which the Skinners associate their craft with the play, for they are makers of furred garments, and they are particularly associated with the making of civic ceremonial costumes. The trade symbolism is, therefore, a prominent feature in the play. We can assume that the actors playing the Aldermen were splendidly bedecked for their procession. It is also likely that, as in the Gospels, the Skinners strewed the way for Jesus with furred gowns. The Skinners, in any case, obtrude prominently upon their own performance.

As Jesus and his party now advance "vnto ȝone cyté ȝe se so nere" (212/283), the dramatic moment of meeting is highlighted with the two processions advancing toward each other. At this point the play creates its own audience, the spectators who stand to cheer the entry of the king. In its midst (this is no doubt the *real* audience of the play) stand four characters: the Pauper, the Blind Man (Cecus), the Cripple (Claudus), and the Man Stunted from Birth (Zaccheus). Amid the cheering, Jesus is drawn to them, and he performs his miracles, bringing sight to the Blind Man and straightening the legs of the Cripple. He also speaks with the rich publican Zaccheus, who has found a sycamore tree to climb from which to see Jesus amid the throng and to catch his attention. In these characters, the playwright manages to personalize the waiting crowd, and to associate the stage audience ("oure pepill same thurgh strete and gatte";

216/402) with the street audience of the Corpus Christi play. The privileged spectators are thus the lame, the halt, the blind, and the poor, whom Jesus has, true to his role, brought forward from the York crowd with compassion.

The moment of the meeting is at hand. As Jesus and his entourage move with the stream of the Corpus Christi play, they suddenly stop, and Jesus exclaims:

> Petir, take þis asse me fro
> And lede it where þou are it toke.
> I murne, I sigh, I wepe also
> Jerusalem on þe to loke.
> And so may þou rewe
> þat euere þou þi kyng forsuke
> And was vntrewe.
>
> (217/468–474)

With this foreboding (echoing Luke 19:41–44) of what his entry into Jerusalem will mean, we somberly look forward to the Passion amid the street celebration simulated by the play. The counterpoint of voices is unmistakable, and York itself, so closely associated with this dramatic entry, must have shuddered at the prospect. Now the moment of climax is here: The two groups meet amid cheering from the crowd, and each of the Aldermen comes forward to give formal greeting in a string of stanzas in which every sentence begins with "Hayll."

When the Skinners' pageant is thus read in the context of the ceremonial procession that it mirrors, it becomes a central scene in the cycle. We have seen that the entry ceremony itself mirrors the Corpus Christi cycle in its clear progression from the Creation setting of the first pageant to the Assumption scene of the last. With that correspondence as background, and further with the processional and counterprocessional movements within the play as a point of parallelism to the street drama that contains them, the Skinners' pageant becomes a microcosm of not only the ceremonial triumphs of the city but also of the Corpus Christi procession and cycle proper. It links the City of York profoundly with the subject of the Passion, and it allows the spectators to assess the meaning of civic ceremonial in its most timeless sense. It is in the Skinners' play that the City of York emerges as the focus of the Corpus Christi cycle.

WHILE procession is manifestly the subject of the York Skinners' play, it is also in the foreground as a mode of dramatic representation throughout the cycle. In reading the York play from beginning to end, one has the feeling that the city setting dominates the entire dramatic movement. Somehow it is impossible in the context of the York social setting not to associate the advancement of the action—from Old Testament, to Nativity, Ministry, Passion, Appearances, and Doom—with the advancement of the pageants through the city from outer perimeter, appropriately Holy Trinity (which was always the first station and rightly the place in which the trinitarian God should first appear), past the Common Hall (where the magistrates sat), and ultimately to the Pavement (the invariable last station, the site also of public punishments, with its Biblical echo of the place where Pilate handed over the condemned Jesus to the vengeful crowd at the sixth hour to be crucified; see John 18:13–16). As I remarked in my analysis of the Skinners' play, the dramatic-processional route leads steadily inward into the city, so that the death of Jesus and his Resurrection are placed in the heart of York.

I realize, of course, that in practice the play did not work that way at all. The stations were stopping places for the pageants, with the result that the Creation play as well as the Conspiracy and the Resurrection, and all the others, played at each of the stations, and no episode became identified with a place per se in actual performance. What I am talking about is more a feeling about the dramatic movement than a demonstrable correspondence between text and performance. The feeling is what is registered by civic processions like the liturgical procession of Corpus Christi or the royal entry, with their clearly defined locus of beginning and ending. It is also what is registered by a reading of the text, wherein the presence of York is so strong that one cannot dissociate the Via Crucis from Stonegate and Petergate. The Skinners' play seen in this context is the gateway to a strictly York Passion, and the association of Jerusalem with York is thereby made inevitable. No other cycle has precisely this quality.

The York cycle might well be called the first city play in the English drama. The fact that it is also so dominantly a play produced by and for the trade guilds of the city makes it uniquely a forerunner of a mode of drama with which it is rarely associated otherwise, the "City Comedy" of the Renaissance.[51] It is true that there are few overt marks of resemblance between the York cycle and, say, *Eastward Ho*, the collaborative play of Chapman, Marston and Jonson, performed in 1605; yet at base both plays are concerned with the new urban life of tradesmen. The difference lies essentially in the subject matter and the mode—*Eastward Ho* comments directly on the aspirations and follies of bourgeois life, whereas the York cycle makes such comments only indirectly. But at a deeper level, both plays are concerned fundamentally with a new, critical look at the city setting, and both place a mirror of the city before their audiences. It is important, of course, to remember that the York cycle is about the life of Christ; but one cannot forget that it is also about the life of York.

Before we take a closer look at procession (or more broadly, the journey motif, including wayfaring and pilgrimage) in the York cycle, we must linger for a moment to consider the place that city drama, with its own peculiar form of journey, occupied within the framework of medieval literature. The major genres of that literature in greater or lesser degree all focused on journey: the quest of romance, the epic voyage, the trek of exile, the pilgrimage, or the dreamer's flight aloft. Moreover, all of these narrative modes usually focus on the outward journey. The emphasis is either on departure or on the journey, in-

---

[51] For a definition of this term, see Brian Gibbons, *Jacobean City Comedy*, 2d ed. (London: Methuen, 1980), pp. 1–17.

cluding its destination, but rarely on return.[52] Note, for example, the masterworks of the fourteenth century: *The Divine Comedy, The Decameron*, and *The Canterbury Tales*. Each chronicles departure from the earthly city of sin, corruption, or affliction, and, metaphorically, if not directly, it transports us to a place of spiritual peace. Interestingly, the Corpus Christi play, as yet another genre of wayfaring, reverses the direction of the journey. In its vision of the world, the earthly city suddenly becomes the focus of interest, and wayfaring is, of course, enacted in the form of procession. I maintain that this new drama not only makes a significant about-face in its direction of travel but that it also constitutes a revolutionary transformation in cultural perspective. For the popular religious drama in England, as in other European cultures, is the first true bourgeois genre. The reversal of the ubiquitous route is, I believe, a change in perspective toward the earthly and heavenly cities. By making the city the destination rather than the place of departure, the drama reflects a whole new view toward urban culture, of which the Corpus Christi play is the first authentic literature. Moreover, by allowing the road to travel into the bustle of earthly life, the festive drama of the Middle Ages makes room for a new understanding of the road to salvation: It takes into account the commerce of daily life as a necessary context within which to comprehend the peace and tranquillity of the new life. The plays, in their festive role, function to transform the earthly city into the heavenly. If annually, we condemn Christ in the marketplace of York, we also see him rise anew and bring to the city an awareness of his presence in its midst.

The history of the metaphor of wayfaring is, of course, traceable to Saint Augustine, who taught us to see life as a journey to the heavenly city. In more general terms, that journey is also a pilgrimage of thought that became an integral part of the conceptual design that governed the world view of the Middle

[52] See Donald R. Howard, *The Idea of the Canterbury Tales* (Berkeley and Los Angeles: University of California Press, 1976), pp. 28–30.

Ages. The very notion of procession—which is, of course, the origin of the popular religious drama—depends on that conceptual design. The procession is an *Imitatio Christi*; the Corpus Christi procession in particular, since it does not commemorate a specific historical event, celebrates the whole of salvation history, thus, in effect, enacting the substance of Augustine's *City of God*. The Corpus Christi cycles, as an outgrowth of that procession, are therefore mimetic reenactments of man, and even the incarnated God, as earthly wayfarer traveling through the span of salvation history.

The processional journey that led inward into the city was, in effect, a vicarious pilgrimage. Like all of the highest pilgrimages, its goal was the visitation of Jerusalem, which, in the mimetic mode of drama, the host city had become. Possibly the drama gained its popularity with the decline of pilgrimages in the late Middle Ages, but whatever the reason for its growth it certainly served as a perfect surrogate for those who could not undertake the real journey to the shrines in Jerusalem or the other pilgrim centers. Surrogate pilgrimages were, actually, very popular in the Middle Ages. As Donald Howard explains,

> The Jerusalem Pilgrimage was the pilgrimage of pilgrimages: others were types and shadows of it, for Jerusalem was at the center of the world (it is regularly pictured there in maps of the period), it was the ground the Lord had walked upon, and it was symbol of the Heavenly City. Other pilgrimages were therefore in some sense substitutes. At the furthest remove, it was possible to make a substitute pilgrimage by crawling about a cathedral labyrinth, and it was possible to make a pilgrimage by proxy, hiring a pilgrim to travel in one's place. Implicit in the institution itself was the conception of a vicarious pilgrimage.[53]

[53] Donald R. Howard, *Writers and Pilgrims: Medieval Pilgrimage Narratives and Their Posterity* (Berkeley and Los Angeles: University of California Press, 1980), p. 12.

While I am not aware that the drama ever served officially as a substitute for a real pilgrimage, it certainly had all the necessary ingredients that vicarious pilgrims sought.

Audiences could, in any case, experience a vicarious bonding with the Holy Land by retracing the steps of Jesus through the Ministry and especially the Passion and thereby reenliven their faith. In a sense, they walked the pilgrimage of Jesus through their own streets, both in their empathetic relationship with the actors and in their street-side mimesis of the crowds that witnessed and condemned Jesus. The spectator drawn into the "crowd" witnessing the York Crucifixion, standing in the company of the actor playing the part of a ruthless Pilate (328/231), must have felt at this chilling moment that he really was in Jerusalem at the very source of his religion. If, as Victor and Edith Turner report, "the pilgrim centers and ways . . . can be regarded as a complex surrogate for the journey to . . . the heartland of faith,"[54] then certainly the cycle play, which converted a local city like York into Jerusalem must have become a mimed pilgrimage at a time when real pilgrimages were no longer common or accessible experiences to many persons who might formerly have sought out distant shrines in sundry lands.

The impulse of the drama is toward mimed visitation of the holy—an impulse that is traceable to its earliest form, the *quaem quaeritis* trope, within the Easter liturgy. Visitation (whether directed toward the sepulcher or the *praesepe*), is, in itself, a form of journey reminiscent of pilgrimage—an attempt to walk upon the holy ground, to become incorporated in sacred history, and to experience the source of the Christian faith. Nothing is more central to Christian rite and Christian drama than the processional walk of the three Marys through the nave or choir up to the ubiquitous sepulcher where the dialogue with the Angel took place. Procession is woven into the very fabric of the early church drama. Discovery was almost invariably the

[54] Victor Turner and Edith Turner, *Image and Pilgrimage in Christian Culture* (New York: Columbia University Press, 1978), p. 6.

consequence of movement from one place to another, and therefore the church itself became a *platea* of the universe, and the drama consisted of the journey from one *sedes* to another. Thus, whether the play was centered on Bethlehem or Golgotha or Emmaus, the action required its participants to move through the *platea* to a *sedes*. Movement in the church served at once to animate it as the conceptual heavenly city and to mime the life of Christ, which was itself a journey. The medieval drama from its very beginning was construed as a visitation—a seasonal commemoration of the sacred events that gave structure to the liturgical calendar. Insofar as it recreated sacred space within the heavenly arches of the cathedral it was, from the outset, a form of pilgrimage for its participants.

But, as ritual drama, the *visitatio*, especially in its earliest forms, had a limited audience, and that audience was composed essentially of the initiated. Its effect as surrogate pilgrimage, thus, was restricted to small numbers of the monastic community, and in the course of years, became increasingly remote from the public at large. As Clifford Flanigan has said, the liturgy itself, as early as the Carolingian era, was "no longer genuinely communal."[55] As reactualization of sacred history it reached primarily the clergy, and with its ever more elaborate adornments, neither the liturgy nor the drama that sprung from it could "be the center of popular medieval piety."[56] It was, therefore, the growth of that drama in the popular arena—the streets and marketplaces of medieval cities—that gave wide currency to the reenactment of the Jerusalem pilgrimage. Essential to this transformation is the emphasis that the popular drama gave to the Via Crucis, which within Christendom is the paradigm for pilgrimage.[57] The church, as has

[55] I am quoting from an unpublished paper on the relationship of the medieval liturgy to the cycle plays. The paper was read at the International Congress of Medieval Studies in Kalamazoo in 1982. Mr. Flanigan has kindly made a copy of his important paper available to me.

[56] Ibid.

[57] Turner and Turner, *Image and Pilgrimage*, p. 6.

been pointed out by Glynne Wickham,[58] could clearly not give emphasis to dramatic representations of the Crucifixion except in highly symbolic rites like the *Depositio* and *Elevatio*, and thus as substance for "realistic" enactment it had to await a more secular stage. In the mystery cycles of England, the Crucifixion became the climactic scene, and the dramatic movement focused upon it.

In essence one can say that the York cycle in its very makeup is built upon the dramaturgy of the Latin church drama. With its relatively short episodes and the requirement of movement from dramatic station to station, it replicates the *sedes* and *platea* stage. While it is true that the wagon journey through the streets does not always take on dramatic significance, one gains the impression that movement in the York play is at least in part the outcome of its staging. Take, for example, the plays of Joseph's Trouble about Mary, the Nativity, the Shepherds, Herod, and the Magi—a dramatic cluster in which the action is noticeably continuous when pictured as street drama. The play of Joseph's Trouble about Mary is a short domestic drama put on by the Founders and Pewterers, who no doubt built the replica of a sitting room, together with entryway for this play, and who decorated the room with everyday household objects, like candlesticks, vases, and plates—articles they made as part of their handicraft. While the major part of the play is concerned with Joseph's response to the Virgin Birth, it ends with Joseph and Mary setting out on their way to Bethlehem. Here is an instance where the dramatic action and the logistics of York playcraft exactly coincide, for as Joseph and Mary exit from the pageant stage, they undertake their required journey to the next station as well as to their dramatic destination, Bethlehem.

With the arrival of the Tilethatchers' wagon, the station is transformed into Bethlehem. Joseph and Mary (now played by new actors) enter walking in search of a place to stay. The pag-

[58] Glynne Wickham, *Early English Stages, 1300 to 1660*, 3 vols. (London: Routledge and Kegan Paul, 1959–1981), 1:315–316.

eant scene is apparently a thatched cottage made by the Tile-thatchers. The stations (or more accurately, stages) of the York cycle are remarkably adaptable. In the course of the day, they present a veritable panorama of salvation history. Sometimes they become *sedes*, as happens when Joseph and Mary enter the cottage. Sometimes, as in the following scene, they are merely wayside stops for action that processes without need of a wagon through the streets. The *platea* is therefore the ever-present road on which history processes before the spectator's eyes. It is, in the largest theatrical sense, a ubiquitous stage. All the streets—indeed the whole route of the play through the city of York—become the *platea* of a *theatrum mundi*.

The play that follows the Tilethatchers' is that of the Chandlers concerning the Shepherds. This play, as I have suggested elsewhere,[59] needs no pageant wagon, since it is enacted on the *platea* from beginning to end. It concerns the Shepherds' seeking the Christ Child with the help of the bright star guiding them along the way (note the association with the trade of the Chandlers). In this instance both Burton's list and a marginal note in the register confirm that at one point the Tilethatchers' play of the Nativity must have been used in conjunction with the Chandlers' play.[60] The description in the *Ordo* of the Tile-thatchers' play ends with the following words: "And the angel speaking to the shepherds and to the players in the pageant which follows" ("et angelus loquens pastoribus et ludentibus in pagina sequente"; *REED: York*, p. 18). This can mean only that the Nativity scene of the Tilethatchers' pageant remained behind to wait for the Shepherds at each station, thus providing a joint set. We see then a second instance in which street procession leads to the *sedes* of a pageant wagon. The subsequent plays by the Masons and Goldsmiths similarly alternate *platea* scenes on the streets of York with set pageants, like Herod's

---

[59] M. Stevens, "From Procession to Play," p. 50.

[60] Richard Beadle argues that the evidence linking the two plays occurred late in the development of the York text. However, there is no reason to rule out such a linking from the performance that would have antedated the change in the register (see *The York Plays*, pp. 425–427).

castle and again the nativity stable (though now a new model, sponsored by the Goldsmiths). The clustering of plays is not adequately defined by the text, but it seems virtually unavoidable in performance. And once we are able to picture how the pageants might have clustered, we will also become aware of the specific use to which the streets of the city were put in representing the *platea* action of the text.

From the foregoing illustrations we can see that journey is not only the mode of the play's performance through the streets of the city but it is also a major subject of its dramatic action. Almost every pageant from the Creation on is concerned with movement, replicating the *platea* concept of the liturgical stage. Individual plays and pageant wagons contribute to this dynamic so that the press to move forward becomes an essential feature of mimesis between play and stage. It is hard to know whether the almost ubiquitous journey motif in the York cycle was the result or the cause of its staging, but it is clear that the pageant stage is one that is functionally in motion much of the time. From the very beginning God's presence, in almost classic Boethian terms, is at the still center of the universe. He creates the firmament, which he declares "sal nough[t] moue" (55/41). The fruit on the tree, he bids, "shuld hynge stylle" (68/145), as does the star at the Nativity, which, according to prophecy, "owte of the eest shulde stabely stande" (136/62), a phrase that is repeated to describe the infant Jesus in the Purification play when Simeon bids him farewell as "starne stabylyst" (160/455). Stillness and stability in the York cycle are repeatedly associated with God's world.

In stark contrast, man is constantly in motion once he has disobeyed God's commandment. The great regret of Adam and Eve is that they ever approached the Tree in Paradise— "þat euyr we neghed it nere" (71/65), a phrase that haunts the action as warning throughout the Creation plays (see 63/68, 73; 64/92; 65/38). Man's travail begins when Adam leaves the stable enclosure of Paradise. Now a wayfarer, the York Adam commences the journey of mankind with the lament, "On grounde mon I never gladde gange, / withowten glee" (73/

161–162). Significantly, before he walks away from the stations of performance in the streets and the marketplace of York, he picks up a wholly uncanonical tree that he resolves to carry: "This tree vnto me will I ta" (73/165). With those words the first Adam strikes out figuratively as wayfarer on the Via Crucis.

The journey of exile, in one form or another, thereafter becomes a main theme in the Old Testament plays: the *Sacrificium Cayme and Abell*, the Flood, Abraham and Isaac, and Moses and Pharaoh. The play of Cain and Abel takes place primarily in the *platea*. The two brothers, as we meet them, are walking toward the sacrifice (see 75/43, 46, 57), which probably would have taken place on the Glovers' pageant wagon, though we cannot be certain about the staging of this scene because it is missing from the manuscript. We do know that the play picks up again (in a sixteenth-century addition) with the scene between Cain and his servant Brewbarret, followed by the dialogue between the Angel and Cain. The Angel dooms Cain to be an outlaw for all eternity:

> Thou shalle be waferyng here and þere
> þis day.
> In bittir bale nowe art þou boune,
> Out-castyn shal þou be for care.
> (77/112–115)

At the end of the play, therefore, we see Cain wandering off in his role as outcast from God's created world (see 78/124–125), a scene that complements that of Adam as pilgrim carrying the Cross. The stage is now set for the metaphysical journey of the earthly exile among all those who serve or defy God.

That theme is developed in the remaining Old Testament plays. In the Shipwrights' pageant, the Building of the Ark, God addresses Noah as "stabill in stede and stalle" (79/34) and prepares this one obedient man to ride out the storm—he and his sons and their wives "away sall wynne" (79/32)—a journey that is, of course, the subject of the Fishers' and Mariners' pageant that follows. The Abraham and Isaac pageant continues the journey motif: Here father and son lead forth their ass on

the three-day journey (93/89) to Mount Moriah with its figu-
rative foreshadowing of the Via Crucis. And the final play of
the group, about Moses and Pharaoh, prepares for the quintessential journey in the Old Testament, the Exodus from
Egypt. At the end of the play, Moses says,

> For at oure will now sall we wende,
> In lande of lykyng for to lende.
>   (109/361–362)

With the parting of the waves and the subsequent drowning of
the Egyptians, the stage is now set for the commencement of
the New Testament plays. The much abridged treatment of
the Old Testament narrative by the York cycle is, in sum, a pre-
dominant *platea* action that moves irrepressibly in its street
pageantry toward the birth of Christ.

Apart from their concern with the pilgrimage of man, the
Old Testament plays establish an overall setting for the cycle.
The playwright asks in the fashion of Chorus in *Henry V* that
the spectators allow their "imaginary forces" to work and make
of their own wooden O's, "ciphers to this great acompt." God
creates an imaginary mise en scène for the *theatrum mundi*, one
that will govern the spectator's vision throughout the subsequent action:

> Here vndernethe me nowe a nexile I neuen,
> Whilke ile sall be erthe. Now all be at ones
> Erthe haly, and helle, þis hegheste be heuen.
>   (49/25–27)

Those who are "stabill in thoghte" (50/30) will enjoy the best of
what earth can offer, namely Paradise, which God creates as
the "wonnyng" for Adam and Eve (62/1–7). But after the Expulsion, Paradise is of course sealed off, and all that remains of
what is now called *middilerth* (69/167) are two locations: the
town and the wilderness. Both clearly are places of unrest and
exile. The wilderness is seemingly any undefined place that
serves explicitly as setting for those who must wander about or

travel. Abraham leads Isaac "to wildirnesse" (93/98) for the sacrifice; God bids Moses to lead the Israelites to the wilderness (103/125, 105/209) for their Exodus. The wilderness is the open *platea* of the countryside: it is where Joseph takes a walk (123/239), where Jesus goes to be tempted by the Devil (187/33). While it is an important site for exile, it is not really the focus of man's *peregrinatio*. The site for that is the earthly city, Cain's abode, and thus the very place wherein the plays are performed. It is the purpose of the play to transform as annual renewal rite the earthly city into the heavenly, to make York finally at the play of Doom the gateway to the New Jerusalem.

The presence of the city becomes more and more important as we enter the life of Christ. A good illustration of the merging of form and content to render a cityscape occurs in the Tile-thatchers' play of the Nativity. When the play begins, the "journey" is already over; it took place after the conclusion of the preceding pageant of Joseph's Trouble about Mary. In dramaturgical terms, the street scene would have shown Mary and Joseph walking through the crowded streets of York (Bethlehem) and coming upon the pageant wagon of the Tilers that had already been stationed up ahead. Its *sedes*, as we have seen, would have consisted simply of the Nativity stable, with leaky roof and collapsed walls—a jocular trade symbol of the Tile-thatchers, from whom one might expect a roof that is weatherproof. As the two are scouting for a place to stay overnight, Joseph complains:

> Lorde, graunte vs gode herberow þis nyght
> Within þis wone.
>
> For we haue sought bothe vppe and doune
> Thurgh diuerse stretis in pis cité.
> So mekill pepull is comen to towne
> þat we can nowhare herbered be,
>   þer is slike prees;
> Forsuthe I can no socoure see,
>   but belde vs with þere bestes.

And yf we here all nyght abide
We schall be stormed in þis steede,
þe walles are doune on ilke a side,
þe ruffe is rayued aboven oure hede.

(125/6–18)

Stage and text blend beautifully here. Joseph and Mary are, of course, pictured as a poor Yorkshire couple, just arrived in the city, which is inordinately crowded (one is tempted to say, for the feast), and they are forced to stay overnight in a broken-down stable. The scene is, in general, true to its historical source; but it also puts one in mind of the present time where the crowded city street is lined with spectators, and the audience consequently becomes part of the dramatic setting. The Holy Family is thus put into the midst of the poverty of York-shire. Heat, we are told a bit later, must come from the ox and the ass; light, miraculously, from the star of the Nativity. The city, insofar as it has been rendered a stage, is cold and inhospitable. Jesus is born in its midst; he has for now become a son of York, neglected by the populace, which is in fact blind to his presence, and neglected (by extension) even by the Tilethatchers, who, if they had done their job, should have placed a good roof over his head.

It is, of course, a commonplace that in all the medieval cycles raving tyrants come onto the scene by clearing away the crowds. In actual fact, that is primarily a scene found in the York cycle (and, on the inspiration of York, in the Wakefield cycle). Here the street locale is once more contributory to the dramaturgy of the cycle. We see it, interestingly, in the entrance of Satan, the first ranting tyrant who clears his path through a crowd in a busy thoroughfare. The scene occurs ironically in the wilderness of the Temptation play, where in terms of the dramatic narrative no crowd is expected. Here, as in various other scenes, the York plays are self-referential, calling our attention to their mode of performance, and thus highlighting their city setting. Satan clears away the spectators at York:

> Make rome belyve, and late me gang!
> Who makis here all þis þrang?
>
> For sithen the firste tyme þat I fell
> For my pride fro heuen to hell,
> Euere haue I mustered me emell
> emonge mannekynde.
> (186/1–2, 7–10)

This moment comes at the beginning of the Ministry plays. It is the first appearance that Satan makes since the Fall, giving us fair warning that the time of Christ's trial is at hand. Most significantly, it allows us to apprehend the spirit of Satan within the crowded street corners of the city and to look with fear at York itself wherein he seemingly has found shelter.

We have seen that Jesus enters York with great ceremony and that his reception by the Aldermen is jubilant and festive. That, of course, is not to be his reception hereafter by the worldly rulers of the city in their grim administrative roles. The Conspiracy to Take Jesus is the very next play, and from Christ's capture to the Crucifixion the spectator is caught up in a whirl of cruelty that seems to have no end. The Jerusalem that Christ entered amid the joy of celebration has turned into an urban nightmare of treachery, abuse, injustice, torture, and utter disorder. Among the ranting tyrants, no one is seemingly in charge, and Jesus is shunted back and forth in the open streets. The York cycle is unique in the emphasis it gives to the indecision of the rulers, to their drunkenness, to the repeated cruel shuttling of Jesus through the streets, to the swift meting out of justice. The whole extended action of the accusations and trials takes place in one night so that a seemingly preordained Crucifixion can take place before the Sabbath. Even before we enter the Via Dolorosa, with its dramatic Stations of the Cross, we are hurtled through the streets of York, which are at this point the chief nexus of the dramatic action.

The York trial of Jesus is, despite the pageant divisions of the extant register, one extended play that takes the street as *platea* and tyrants' halls as the recurrent *sedes* of the action. I count a total of seventeen scenes between the beginning of the Cutlers' pageant of the Conspiracy (no. 26) and the Tilemakers' pageant of the Second Trial before Pilate (no. 33), in which Pilate renders his judgment. There are, in this span, four trials—one each before Caiaphas and Herod and two before Pilate—and recurrent scenes in which Jesus is bound and scourged while being led from one temporal judge to another. The tyrants' *sedes* is always the same: a hall with an antechamber. It is night-time, the tyrant is about to go to bed, has a drink, falls asleep, and is awakened by the clamor of the soldiers who approach a beadle or porter to obtain a trial for Jesus. The stage before us, no matter how the play might have been played, is a repeated series of entrances and exits, and much of the action takes place directly on the street. Procession seems an indispensable part of Jesus' agony from the beginning of his capture. It extends, of course, to the Via Crucis proper, where the entire action is in the *platea*.

The plays of the appearances reinforce the subject I have been discussing, for not only are they in themselves concerned with *peregrinatio* but they trace the genesis of the Jerusalem journey. In them, Jesus himself is hailed as "sir pilgrime" (364/145), foreshadowing the role that will be assigned to the Apostles. When enlightenment comes to the pilgrims at Emmaus, they understand that their new mission is to spread the Word, to bring the "good news"; as the second of the pilgrims on the road to Emmaus says, "Go we to Jerusaleme þes tydingis to telle" (365/188). Here, in a phrase, the play reveals its own purpose, for it, too, is spreading the Word in the Jerusalem it has created. The Pilgrims' play makes this point dramatically at the very end with one of those jocular reminders of playcraft which fuses the world of the play with the world of the spectator:

> Here may we notte melle more at þis tyde,
> For prossesse of plaies that precis in plight
> (365/191–192)

When Christ, in the Ascension, announces that "Nowe is my jornay brought till ende" (376/153), Peter resolves for the company to return once more to "Jerusalem," and as we return yet again to the heart of the city we await the descent of the Son for the last time to render his doom (410/177–178). We have reached the end of the journey and the play.

THROUGHOUT this chapter, I have emphasized the importance of the social setting to an understanding of the York plays. I have argued that the city of York itself, in all its complexity, is really the subject of the cycle. York, we have seen, is a major city—a provincial capital, a regional if not international trade center, as well as the seat of an archdiocese—and to the extent that the cycle implicitly reflected life in the city and brought into conjunction its diverse and unrelated institutions, it is a more highly charged instrument of social criticism than any of the other cycles. I say this in full knowledge that the Wakefield cycle is usually held up for its pungent criticism of the power of landlords and the courts, especially in the plays of the Wakefield Master, which have been justly admired for their social commentary. Yet, in essence, the Wakefield plays reflect the interests of a manor, not a city. Their most biting commentary occurs in essentially rural and agricultural plays, the *Mactatio Abel* and the two Shepherds' plays, as I shall show. There is very little of the sense of the discretely urban scene in that cycle, even though guilds seem to have been involved in the performance of at least some of the pageants. But the York plays are unmistakably "big city," and because they are so much concerned with the urban life and landscape, I want to conclude this chapter with some observations of the social criticism that is inherent in them.

As I shall show in my consideration of the N-Town cycle, scholars have long been aware of the use of anachronism in the Corpus Christi plays as a conscious device by which to bring the historical past into the present. In placing the life of Jesus into the social setting of the late Middle Ages—by means of theat-

77

rical tools like contemporary language, costume, sets, and stage props—the playwrights highlighted the important points of contact between the times of sacred history and what was present time to them. In the eyes of most modern critics, the significance of this use of anachronism lay in the light that the similitude between historical and present times could shed on the spectators' (and our) understanding of the life of Jesus and the meaning of his teachings. For example, the anachronistic dramatization of Jesus and the Doctors in the Temple as a scene between a contemporary student (a "clergeon") and his masters would clarify just how much courage and intelligence was required of Jesus to demonstrate to the secular world the nature of his wisdom. Viewed in this contemporary context, the scene provided a potent interpretation of the power structure that Jesus had to confront to bring forth his New Law. It was the device of anachronism that brought late-medieval popular piety, especially as taught by the translation of Pseudo-Bonaventure, into focus and familiarity. By this means the common person of the Middle Ages could learn more directly how to empathize with Christ and to understand the enormous significance of his sacrifice for mankind. Anachronism made the life of Christ relevant.

But what the critics have thus far not emphasized is the fact that anachronism is a two-way mirror. They have concentrated on the benefit that a view through the perspective of the present lent to the audience's perception of the past. The reverse view is equally possible and, I hope to show, enlightening. We can look by means of the anachronistic perspective through the past into the present. We can, for example, see in the episode with the Doctors a disposition by the playwright to examine the wisdom of those in the present-day power structure who represent institutional learning. If Jesus appears as a contemporary gifted student, who in the eyes of the playwright and in the dominant cultural perspective brought a whole new critical understanding to the meaning of God's commandments, then it is the student who is, in fact, teaching the stodgy establishment, and it is the latter that is being examined critically for the way in which it carries on its mission. Most significantly, this way of reading or viewing the anachronistic interpretation brings a new understanding to what it means to live the life of a Christian in the fifteenth century. Seen in this light, the Corpus Christi cycles are a powerful critical instrument. They are, one might say, a medium of subversion; they give, in the language of anthropologists, an antistructural interpretation of the existing social order.

I have shown that the York cycle was the product of the joint planning and preparation of the guilds and the city government. In its long lifetime, the cycle was undoubtedly one of the most admired and glittering symbols of the unity and continuity of the city. It provided a showcase for the city's industry, faith, and devotion; it also gave a focus for its most festive holiday celebration. It brought commerce to the city, and it was sufficiently admired to be borrowed in large part by at least one other town in the province. It is no wonder that throughout the cycle's history, the city government gave it its unstinting support and insisted, as I have shown, on being prominently identified with the performance. In terms of the contribution that the play made to civic pride, it was then a very positive institution that added significantly to York's status as *the* important city of the northern counties. Speaking about both the Corpus Christi procession and the play, Mervyn James has pointed out that "as a symbolic system" they expressed "wholeness," both in their linkage of episodes to cover the spectrum of sacred history and in their grouping of occupational guilds to produce the cycle. He finds in the Eucharistic conception of "body" a metaphor that also described a particular view of society—the "social body." Corpus Christi was, in his view, the occasion when "specialized roles and differences of function and status are dissolved into a simple membership of a social body."[61] Applied to medieval York, the metaphor describes well the sense

[61] Mervyn James, "Ritual, Drama and Social Body in the Late Medieval English Town," *Past and Present*, no. 98 (1983): 6, 11, 15–16.

of wholeness that the procession and play brought to the community.

But the festive events, in their high cost and their persistent demand for expense of energy and time, were also cause for division and isolation. To some extent that was, ironically, an outcome of the social wholeness built into the Corpus Christi celebrations. James sees this opposite tendency as part of a "typical Lévi-Straussian mythological contradiction: social wholeness vs. social differentiation" (note the infinite potential for division of the Eucharist wherein the part becomes the whole). Speaking about the Corpus Christi procession, he puts the matter as follows:

> Yet the opposite emphasis, that of social differentiation, with its stress on the segmented occupational roles in the urban community, and its vertical structure of status and authority, is if anything even more emphatically spelt out, as the gilds file past in the due order and precedence laid down by authority, the procession culminating in the representatives of the magistry and their head, the mayor, whose place is next to the Corpus Christi.[62]

The fact is that the individual guilds often competed with one another either for priority in status or for reducing their share for the maintenance of a pageant. The York civic records are full of ordinances and resolutions to solve such grievances, and often the only entries for a whole year have to do with disorder or strife among the guilds. In 1419, for example, we find three consecutive items detailing the following:

> The Skinners' complaining that the Carpenters and Cordwainers attacked them in the Corpus Christi procession and destroyed their torches with Carlisle axes (amid other enormities: "alia enormia");
> The Tilers' and Plasterers' petitioning for a reduction of support to the Masons for the maintenance of their pageant. (The conflict was apparently over the assessment

[62] Ibid., p. 11.

of those tilers and plasterers who did not work with stone and who were, therefore, not directly allied to the masons.)

The Sailors' and Fishmongers' disputing the share that each was to contribute to the playing of the Noah pageant.

(REED: York, pp. 32–34)

Here we see the interests of the guild, in terms of prestige or material welfare, overshadow the interests of the city. Since it was usually the mayor and sometimes also the aldermen who served as arbiters in such disputes, and since the city was called upon to maintain the peace among the guilds, there were bound to be smoldering discontents among many with the city administrators. Much of the Corpus Christi festivity, therefore, was not at all the outcome of cooperation and harmony. The guilds were united and yet divided in the fulfillment of their civic obligations.

Add to this picture of guild competition the fact that for some one hundred and fifty years the Corpus Christi play was maintained during periods of severe economic decline and depression, and it is clear that there were aggravated causes for the expression of discontent (directly or indirectly) against the power structure of the city. And there was cause also to look askance at the power of the king and the state in the regulation of York's affairs, though the cause for discontent in that sphere was not so great during the times that the plays were written as during the reign of Henry VII, who was not friendly toward York. Finally, there was good reason for the unhappiness of the ordinary freeman in York with the ecclesiastical authorities. This latter area of conflict is of sufficient importance to deserve a closer look.

Apart from its numerous parish churches, York was the site of a great many religious houses, and of course of Saint Peter's, the great cathedral, which also served as administrative center of the archdiocese. These religious houses all enjoyed "liberties" or exemptions from the city, and thus, within the precincts of York, there were numerous districts that controlled their own trade and even actively competed with the guilds. Craftsmen who lived in the districts of the Minster, Saint Mary's Abbey, Saint Leonard's Hospital, or in any of the seven priories in the city, did not need to take up the freedom of the city, were not obliged to join guilds, and were free to buy and sell without regard to city regulations. Resentment against not only the inhabitants of these districts but also against the religious houses was therefore widespread. It was, in general, not based on anticlericalism, but on the unfair economic competition that the system of liberties fostered, and it was the underlying cause of the riots recorded in June 1381, and of numerous other altercations, including no doubt the instance when "two sheriffs' sergeants drew blood in an affray at the Minster gates, and the chapter imposed a penance on them," but the city forbade the men to perform it.[63] With so much of a presence in the city, the church also became an oppressive power in the lives of many citizens through its variety of courts, which held jurisdiction over all persons guilty of moral infractions, including heresy. (The Summoner in *The Canterbury Tales* gives insight into the power of the ecclesiastical courts and the opportunities for church officers to enrich themselves through bribes.) The causes for conflict between the city and the church were clearly many, including the privilege of the archbishop to sponsor the renowned Lammas fair in July, during which he had full jurisdiction over the city, empowering him even to hang thieves.[64] These facts must be kept in mind as part of the social context within which the York plays were performed.

The Corpus Christi cycles have rarely been looked at as festive "Carnival" plays. I would like to propose that we regard the York cycle, in its overall dramatic impact, precisely as such a form. The Carnival approach is now being applied broadly to the popular theater of the Elizabethan period, and much that relates directly to that theater also relates, perhaps even more

[63] See Palliser, *Tudor York*, p. 234; and Dobson, "Admission to the Freedom of the City," p. 13.

[64] Palliser, *Tudor York*, p. 182.

cogently, to the Corpus Christi plays of the Middle Ages. Mikhail Bakhtin has been influential in formulating the critical perspective that links the popular drama with Carnival. He has said, "Carnival is not a spectacle seen by the people; they live in it, and everyone participates because its very idea embraces all the people."[65] Enlarging upon this idea, Michael D. Bristol has written,

The participatory masquerades of Carnival permit people to "put on" new social roles, to borrow the clothing and identity of someone else, and to adopt the language and manners—even the social position—of another. The festive liberty of physical involvement in the street pageantry of Carnival transforms and deconstructs the "truth already established" by official ideology. The chaotic disarray produced by this arrangement is symbolically subversive of harmonious order; it is also pragmatically threatening and potentially mutinous. The experience of the participants, in contrast to that of detached observers, is the experience of social solidarity and cohesion; participatory masquerade promotes a feeling of communal integrity and of the rough equality of the subjects who perform together.[66]

[65] Mikhail Bakhtin, *Rabelais and His World*, trans. Helene Iswolsky (Cambridge: MIT Press, 1968), p. 7.

[66] Michael Bristol, "Carnival and the Institutions of Theater in Elizabethan England," *ELH* 50 (1983): 643. Bristol has shown in a paper read at the MLA Convention in 1982 that there are two contrasting theoretical models for the understanding of Carnival structure. One is traceable to Durkheim; the other, indirectly to Marx. The Durkheim school, known also as "the 'safety valve' or 'morning after' theory of social catharsis," views society as essentially benign and sees in Carnival a reconstitutive act. This, for example, is the view adopted by C. L. Barber in *Shakespeare's Festive Comedy* (Princeton: Princeton University Press, 1959). The other school, the Marxist, adopted by Bristol in his essay on the Elizabethan theater, sees Carnival as a "vehicle of plebeian social protest and resistance to the dominant ideology and its institutional constraints." These views are expressed in the MLA paper, "The Battle of Carnival and Lent: The Structural Rhythm of *King Lear*," pp. 2–3. I am grateful to Mr. Bristol for making his incisive paper available to me. For a more extended discussion, see his

This description of how a Carnival street festival works is also a perfect summary of the dramatic impact of the York cycle in its performance during the late Middle Ages. One need only bear in mind the ordinary resentments that citizens of York felt against the governing power structures—civil and religious—and one can see that the Corpus Christi cycle is the obvious choice in which that anger could be constructively vented. How better to express—consciously or unconsciously—bitterness over the misuse of power by the ecclesiastical establishment than to represent Annas and Caiaphas, the brutal judges of Christ, as contemporary bishops who had the power to condemn heretics? How better to make York aware of its daily misuse of power, in whatever sphere, than to let it be "entered" by Jesus as its temporary king? Seen in this light, the Corpus Christi play becomes a powerful commentary on the way corporate York lived its life. For a day in the festive midsummer season, it was occupied by a Carnival king, who was Jesus himself, and the ordinary as well as extraordinary injustices of civic life were exposed by the reenactment of his experience in the setting of the contemporary city. Jesus, as Carnival king, reigned spiritually in York as he had in Jerusalem, and he was again crucified. Even the least sensitive of observers and participants would not fail to perceive the devastating analogy.

The study of folk festivals and games has attracted the interest of numerous historians in recent years. Many of them have turned to the findings of anthropologists like Arnold Van Gennep to gain a clearer understanding of the nature of folk customs and of everyday life in general based on systematic and exhaustive studies of public records. Some of these same historians have turned as well to the structuralist orientation of Bakhtin and others to interpret the evidence. Of particular interest to students of the Middle English Corpus Christi plays is

book *Carnival and Theatre: Plebeian Culture and the Structure of Authority in Renaissance England* (London: Methuen, 1985). My own argument adopts the perspective of Marx and Bakhtin in the analysis of the process, but it sees the end result—the cleansing and reconstituting of the social order—according to Durkheim's model.

the work of Natalie Z. Davis that has focused on the playacting societies known as Abbeys of Misrule in sixteenth-century French villages and cities.[67] Such societies were not exactly similar to the sponsors of the urban mystery cycles in England, and they certainly did not plan their festivities along with city governments. Rather they were informally organized (though they could consist of craft guilds and confraternities). Their object was to put on a Carnival of some sort that mocked the real life of the community. The themes of these Carnivals were many—they could address "power, jurisdiction, youth, misrule, pleasure, folly, even madness."[68] In the urban centers of sixteenth-century France, the Abbeys of Misrule were usually professional or neighborhood organizations, and unlike the abbeys of the villages that addressed mostly domestic matters, the urban groups concerned themselves with issues of politics and government.

> Those Judges of Misrule, that company of Princes, Patriarchs and Bishops were more likely to direct their barbs at the powerful than was the young village Abbot. It was not the domestic disorder of the governing families that was criticized, but rather their political misrule. And this was an important channel for criticism in those oligarchical cities, where even rather substantial artisans and merchants had little, if any, chance to make political decisions.[69]

In general, the issues addressed by the Abbeys of Misrule in French cities were much more specific and immediate than anything that one might construe as veiled criticism of the power structure in the York mystery plays. Yet the very impulse to build such institutionalized criticism into the social structure of the city is of interest to those who wish to study the Corpus Christi cycles as organs of social protest. Turning to the

[67] Natalie Zeman Davis, "The Reasons for Misrule: Youth Groups and Charivaris in Sixteenth-Century France," *Past and Present* no. 50 (1971): 41–75.

[68] Ibid., p. 43.

[69] Ibid., p. 67.

Mardi Gras revels at Rouen, Davis shows the range of political criticism and commentary that such revels might contain:

> One year they dramatized the venality of specific magistrates who had demanded a large sum from a pleader instead of the modest hare he offered them; the judges claimed their wives did not like to eat game. The Mardi Gras parade of 1540 was less personal, the political observation more general and veiled. We hold up "a Socratic mirror" to the world, said the Abbot. Business was so bad that the procession began with an elaborate funeral for Merchandise, followed by a float bearing Hope in a laughing and joyous mask. Another float bore a king, the pope, the emperor and a fool playing catch with the globe of the world: "Tiens-cy; Baille-ca, Ris-t'en, Mosque-t'en." There was also a procession of Old Testament prophets uttering prophetic riddles with reference to current political responsibility for pauperization and religious troubles.[70]

The sweep of criticism in these Carnival shows was obviously wide, and the targets were easily recognizable. In Davis's view, the criticism itself was intended to "destroy-and-renew political life in Mikhail Bakhtin's sense, but not to lead directly to further political action."[71]

Obviously, the York plays, while resembling the French Carnival festivities as instruments of criticism, were not designed to render topical commentary. Nor are they properly to be classified with feasts of "misrule," since they are designed to show the most exemplary rule that any community could achieve. They depart then from the festival tradition of enacting the rule of a mock king, and they are not meant to be grotesque parodies of the city government or ruling classes. Rather they reverse the view of Carnival: They allow the spectator to view true kingship while exposing the political rulers of "this" world (in Jerusalem or in York) as the corruption or even

[70] Ibid., p. 68.
[71] Ibid., p. 69.

the parodies of that standard. Their criticism is therefore much more sweeping than that of the Abbeys of Misrule.

The issues they address are as broad as the categories of venality and mortal sin. They extend from the exposure of the domineering wife in the person of Noah's *uxor* (a subject that in France was treated extensively in charivaris, or mock serenades to newly married couples)[72] to the characterization of the businessman in the person of Simon of Cyrene (who is too occupied with the world to suffer for others) or perhaps of Armiger (who, in the play of the Remorse of Judas, is too blind to know that he is buying title to Calvary, the mortgage of which is being held by Pilate). The sweep of the critical attack is as broad as society—it fixes not merely on the powerful but on the actors themselves. For in every instance that a craftsman builds a product for our admiration and diverts attention from its use—be it the couch on which Procula dreams of the Devil, the pins that are used to wedge the Cross, the purple coat that is put on Christ to mock his kingship—the play is critical of those who put industry above humanity, skill above compassion. The play is meant to revitalize the humanity of the city, to bring a new sense of charity to all who take part in the civic life of York.

[72] Ibid., p. 65.

TWO

The Wakefield Cycle:
The Playwright as Poet

WE HAVE seen that the York cycle developed over the years as a corporate enterprise. As civic pageantry it apparently started in improvisational performance, gradually became recorded in a series of texts by the performing guilds, and eventually was compiled by the city fathers into a register, or a permanent, unified text that functioned both as official source and archival record. The whole play, in process and product, was a municipal enterprise of self-examination and self-celebration, and the York cycle as a whole was the first true "city play" in the history of the English drama.

The Wakefield cycle (if that is, indeed, the proper name for the collection of plays that survive in the Towneley volume of mystery plays now held by the Huntington Library, MS HM 1) presents a very different case. Here we have a cycle that was quite clearly written and compiled for a much smaller community, which through commercial growth had at a certain point in its history become sufficiently prosperous to sponsor a Corpus Christi play. It was consequently built from scratch. The text, if it did not precede the performance, was at least coeval with it. In the Wakefield cycle then, we preserve more nearly a product than the record of a process, and the product we retain seems to have been the work of a single, guiding intelligence from the very beginning. While it has been customary to regard the well-known "Wakefield Master" in the same light as the "York Realist," or whatever name we wish to bestow upon that particular contributor to the York cycle, a strong case can be made for the Wakefield Master to have been the principal compiler and the guiding intelligence of the Wakefield cycle.

My argument is admittedly circumstantial. It is based on a reinterpretation of the Wakefield stanza, and it depends fundamentally on how authorship—that is, the invention and even the disposition and elocution of a narrative—functioned as creative acts in the Middle Ages. If I am right that in the plays of the Towneley manuscript we have a fully evolved text rather than the gradual compilation of a performance (that is to say, a text like that of York for which the expectation of growth was a built-in condition of its very existence), then the so-called Wakefield cycle is a model of mystery cycles quite different from that of York. While this second generation of English cycles was not exactly cut out of whole cloth—it was more nearly a patchwork of many fabrics—it was, from the beginning, the work of a compiler, and to the extent that he worked with a design of his own choice, the cycle is primarily a literary original and not an anthology edited for a reasonably uniform style and conceptual design. I am convinced that the Wakefield Master wrote his Shepherds play twice precisely because he was a poet, who, like Langland, needed to explore alternative possibilities, not because they were already there (in acting versions) but because they were provocative options. Any text that gives such a choice is, by its very nature, literary. It is addressed to a reader (who might, of course, be a theatrical director), and it invites that reader to choose one play over the other, or, at very least, to allow the one to resonate against the other. (The Second Shepherds' Play is entitled simply *alia eorundum*, "another of the same.") But whatever the choice, the very fact that there are two shepherds' plays creates a redundancy rich in potential reader response. I believe that of the other extant cycles, N-Town is very much like the plays of the Towneley manuscript, while Chester, as I shall show, is a mixture: It is at once a consciously wrought literary product and the consummation of a developing performance. In the four extant cycles, we have then what may well be perceived in overview as three different models of text and performance.

Without, for the time, differentiating between York and Wakefield as "city drama" and "town" or "manorial drama" respectively, I do want to linger for a moment on the contrast between the two collections as early examples of process and product-directed texts. The point I have made about the performance orientation of York against the literary orientation of Wakefield is nowhere better supported than in their two manuscripts. The York manuscript (British Library MS Additional 35290) is unmistakably a register. It has running titles naming the sponsoring guild throughout the volume at the top of each leaf. The purpose of these titles, as Beadle and Meredith have observed in their excellent facsimile volume, was to allow "any user of the manuscript . . . to find his way quickly and easily around a large compilation of short units."[1] The York manuscript is clearly a collection, and it has an official stamp about it. Most important, as we have already seen, it leaves numerous blank pages at the end of pageants, indicating the compiler's intent to leave space for changes or additions. The York manuscript is truly put together as an open-ended compendium that could serve the city as an ongoing, adaptable record of changes in performance. The numerous marginalia, especially those by John Clerke, give indisputable evidence that in fact changes of performance, while not always integrated with the existing text, were carefully noted. They will indicate, for example, "here wantes a pece newly mayd for saynt John Baptiste" (f. 92v) or "this matter is newly mayd & devysed wherof we haue no coppy regystred" (f. 94) or, more generally, "nota quia non concordat / novo addicio facto" (f. 114). The many notes, in fact, make clear that the copy we have of the York plays, while still a register was unable to keep up with the performance changes that took place in the play.

The Towneley manuscript, in contrast, is a finished book. It contains no running titles, and except for one puzzling blank

[1] Richard Beadle and Peter Meredith, *The York Play: A Facsimile of British Library MS Additional 35290* (Leeds: University of Leeds, 1983), p. xxvii.

page (f. 20),[2] its text runs continuously from beginning to end. Plays follow in close succession, one upon the other, so that often handsome titles conjoin explicits and incipits on the same page (see figure 1). The ornamentation of the manuscript, moreover, is more lavish than that of any other extant cycle. The handsome strap-work initials are clearly decorative (see figure 2); they are designed for the admiration of readers and viewers, not surely for the eyes of the practical-minded town clerk whose interest in the manuscript is solely to check it against the performance of the plays. I do not mean to suggest that the Towneley manuscript is a luxury volume; it is too uneven and unimpressive for that designation. But it is also not simply a book designed for ordinary record keeping and maintenance. It contains, above all, a continuous text. There is no apparent hesitation in its execution. It was meant to bring us a finite text, one that moved in steady progression from Creation to Doomsday with very little marginal comment and virtually no recognition that it had any connection with an ongoing, annual performance. Interestingly, the marginalia, unlike that of the York manuscript, is chiefly concerned with regulation or official examination of the text. Most of it must come from the period when the mystery cycles were under scrutiny by the archbishop of York, who had jurisdiction over Wakefield. We find several anti-Marian notations, as in the Second Shepherds' play where "lady" is crossed out and "lord" written above in the phrase "oure lady hym saue" (134/553) or the passage in which

[2] More than likely this folio was left blank to leave room for the eventual finishing of Play 7 (the *Processus Prophetarum*), which stops *in medias res* at the bottom of f. 19v. The top of f. 20v carries an erasure that is still visible of the title "Incipit Pharao" (in red), thus showing the intention by the scribe originally to begin the next play, that of Pharaoh and the Departure of the Israelites, at that point. He probably had second thoughts, not knowing how large the lacuna of his copy text was at the end of the Prophets play, and he decided instead to begin the next play on f. 21, the place that it now occupies in the MS. For a discussion of this lacuna, see A. C. Cawley and Martin Stevens, eds., *The Towneley Cycle: A Facsimile of Huntington MS HM 1* (Leeds: University of Leeds, 1976), p. xiii. Also see Martin Stevens, "The Missing Parts of the Towneley Cycle," *Speculum* 45 (1970): 255.

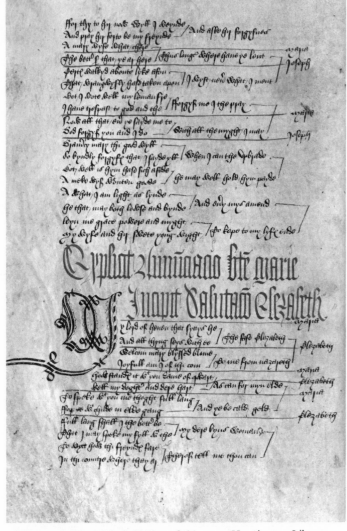

FIGURE 1. The Wakefield Plays, f. 31 verso, Huntington Library
HM 1. (Courtesy the Henry E. Huntington Library and Art Gallery)

FIGURE 2. The Wakefield Plays, f. 67 recto, Huntington Library HM 1. (Courtesy the Henry E. Huntington Library and Art Gallery)

Joseph describes how the Son was to have descended from the heavens "in a madyn for to light" (183/59) with the remark "no maters ben as sade [said]" cryptically noted in the margin. There are also obvious passages of censorship, such as the stanza describing the seven sacraments in the play of *Johannes Baptista* crossed out in red (200–201/193–200) and marked "corected and not playd." But nowhere in the entire manuscript do we find the kind of notations about discrepancies of performance and text that John Clerke and other commentators left in the York volume. All this would suggest that the Towneley manuscript was probably not intended to be a register, as is usually surmised,[3] but rather something like a presentation copy of the play for the safekeeping of the lord of the manor or some other eminent person. All signs are that the compiler set out to produce a book of literary value rather than an official municipal register.

[3] The argument that the text is a register is perhaps best stated by A. C. Cawley, *The Wakefield Pageants in the Towneley Cycle* (Manchester: Manchester University Press, 1958), p. xii. It is based principally on the fact that the manuscript was almost certainly copied from individual texts of different pageants and that the corrections in it were probably "made by a municipal authority in an effort to counter Reformist objections" (p. xiii). Neither of these conditions, however, necessarily supports the theory that the manuscript was designed as a municipal register as opposed simply to a collected volume of the cycle prepared for another purpose. The extant dramatic records of the Wakefield Burgess Court, as I shall show, are extremely sparse and they are late, even for this late cycle of plays. They refer only once, in an entry now dated 1559, to a "regynall of Corpus Xty play," which was to have been brought to the Burgess Court by a certain Gyles Dolleffe. That "regynall" was almost certainly the Towneley MS, which at that date might still have been part of the Wakefield Manor Library from which Dolleffe, who is identified as bailiff of Kirgate in the court records (see J. W. Walker, *Wakefield: Its History and People* [Wakefield: West Yorkshire Printing Company, 1934], p. 133), was to fetch it. The order would make sense in light of the fact that the Wakefield Manor had been handed over by royal charter to the Duchy of Lancaster during the preceding year, on 15 April 1558 (see ibid., pp. 104–105). If the book had originally been deposited in the private library of the Lord of Wakefield Manor at his home in Sandal Castle, it would have been logical for it to have been called in, perhaps even for the first time by the Burgess Court, as a way of ascertaining its existence and its authority. Whatever the reason for the entry, the term "regynall," as we have seen, is not a synonym of "register." Rather it refers to the "original" book or play.

Although I am persuaded that the plays of the Towneley manuscript were performed at Wakefield, that conclusion is not universally accepted. It was, in fact, recently challenged by several commentators at a scholarly symposium.[4] The principal reasons for the challenge are apparently the absence of external records that link the plays with Wakefield and the fact that, although the name Wakefield occurs twice in the titles of the manuscript, there is no absolute and unmistakable attribution of the manuscript to the West Riding city. Since my argument is at least partially based on the assumption that the plays came from Wakefield at a relatively late period—late enough to qualify as a second-generation cycle—it is important before I proceed further to review the evidence relating to the cycle's provenance.

THE first full edition of the Wakefield cycle came out in 1836 under the title, *The Towneley Mysteries*, and the preface of that volume, written by Joseph Hunter, ascribed the plays to Woodkirk, a village about four miles north of Wakefield, where in the Middle Ages, there had been a "cell" of Augustinian canons. The site was associated with two annual fairs where presumably the plays were performed. The editor tells us that this ascription was based on genuine tradition.[5] Whatever the source of that tradition might have been, I have been able to trace it back only some twenty years, specifically to Francis Douce, who in the catalog of the first sale of the manuscript in 1814, claims that the manuscript formerly belonged to the "Abbey of Widkirk."[6] Unhappily there were three things

---

[4] The session—"Were the Towneley Plays Wakefield Plays?"—was part of the program of the International Congress of Medieval Studies at Western Michigan University in Kalamazoo, Michigan, in May 1984. The name Wakefield is now widely accepted by editors and critics; see, for example, David Bevington's consistent use of the name in *Medieval Drama* (Boston: Houghton Mifflin, 1975).

[5] Joseph Hunter, ed., *The Towneley Mysteries* (London: J. Nichols and Son, 1836), pp. viii–ix.

[6] See Francis Douce, *Bibliotheca Townleiana: A Catalogue of the Curious and Extensive Library of the Late John Towneley, Esq.*, part I (London: R. H. Evans, 1814), p. 45.

wrong with this ascription: first, there is no such place as Wid-kirk;[7] second, there never was an Abbey of Widkirk; and finally no evidence exists to link the manuscript with an abbey. Douce himself, realizing that the ascription was apparently wrong, of-fered a new place of ownership, the "Abbey of Whalley," in his edition of the *Juditium* for the Roxburghe Club eight years later. He is as silent about the evidence for this ascription as for the former, but in fairness to him, it should be noted that he as-cribed performance, not ownership, to the two abbeys.[8] The Surtees editor seems to prefer the earlier ascription to the later, mainly because he found that he could substitute Woodkirk, a real place, for the fictitious Widkirk. But about Douce's ascrip-tion, all he could say was, "On what foundation either of these suppositions rests we are not informed." So much for "genuine tradition."

After the Surtees edition, the next important milestone in the editorial history of the Towneley manuscript was Lucy Toulmin Smith's edition of the *York Plays* in 1885, which re-vealed that five Towneley pageants were nearly identical to their counterparts in the York cycle. She published the parallel texts of the plays in question in her edition. Smith used only the name Towneley and made no attempt to find a place of per-formance for the cycle.

The next edition of the Towneley manuscript was published by the Early English Text Society in 1897. George England transcribed the text (under Dr. Furnivall's superintendence), and Alfred W. Pollard wrote a modest introduction that plain-tively calls for "some learned professor, or at any rate . . . an ed-

[7] I am aware of Walter W. Skeat's letter to the *Atheneum*, which argues that Widkirk is simply an older name for Woodkirk and is, therefore, one and the same place. However, Skeat gives no documentary evidence that the two names are, in fact, interchangeable, and he bases his argument on remote cognates that he found for *wudu* in Old High German, Old Icelandic, and Old Irish; see "The Locality of 'The Towneley Plays,' " *Atheneum*, 2 December 1893, p. 779. Skeat notwithstanding, there is consequently no evidence that a town of Widkirk ever existed.

[8] Francis Douce, ed., *Juditium* (London: Roxburghe Club, 1822).

itor of really wide reading experience" to study the problems posed by *The Towneley Plays*, so named by him in the title of the edition. Observing sensibly that "texts are far more important than introductions," Pollard simply quotes the introduction of the Surtees edition, which he considered of "real value" and which, he says, "has not yet been superseded." So, in essence, his ascription is to Woodkirk, though later in his preface he adds the following caution: "But we are bound to remember that the connection with Woodkirk is a mere tradition, and that it is quite possible that the whole cycle belongs to Wakefield, which is the only place with which it is authoritatively connected."[9]

The definitive case for Wakefield was made the year after the publication of the EETS edition by Matthew Peacock, headmaster of the Queen Elisabeth Grammar School at Wakefield. Peacock was the first to summarize the not inconsiderable internal evidence that associates the manuscript with the location: the reference to Wakefield "at the commencement of the first play (on the 'Creation')"; the several guild ascriptions (which associated the cycle with civic craft guilds, not an abbey); the title of the third play, the *Processus Noe cum filiis*, to which the name "Wakefeld" is added; the reference to place allusions within the play, like "gudeboure at the quarell hede" where Cain asks to be buried—a site associated since the Middle Ages with Wakefield and its grammar school, which in fact was built of stones mined from the quarry; and the several allusions in the Talents play to "this town," identifying the locale as a town, though not specifically Wakefield. Peacock, speaking of the state of scholarship in his time, laments: "It would have been more in accordance with the great classical authors . . . to name the plays themselves after the place where they were acted."[10]

---

[9] George England and A. W. Pollard, eds., *The Towneley Plays* (London: Oxford University Press, 1897), p. xxviii.

[10] Matthew Peacock, "Towneley, Widkirk, or Wakefield Plays?" *Yorkshire Archaeological Journal* 15 (1898–1899): 95 and passim. Peacock published another

Despite this lament, the name Towneley prevails as the name of the cycle in virtually all scholarly books and articles up to World War II and beyond. Interestingly, as late as 1983, the MLA International Bibliography still lists the name Towneley as its entry word and would ignore Wakefield altogether except that two of six entries under Towneley used Wakefield in the title. Two additional facts from the early scholarship in this century need to be noted. First, Charles Mills Gayley, in *Plays of Our Forefathers* (1907), was the first to single out the work of the Wakefield Master and to name him. Gayley's discussion opened a new area of concern, and it identified as an important segment within the cycle what was subsequently to be named the "Wakefield Group" of the Towneley cycle, especially in the work of Frank Cady, Millicent Carey, and most importantly A. C. Cawley.[11] The Wakefield Group as a segment within the cycle seems to recognize that at least some of the plays can definitely be attributed to Wakefield. Cawley puts it as follows: "The homogeneity of the pageants and parts of pageants written in the Wakefield nine-line stanza allows us to infer that *all* of them have associations with the Wakefield area" (p. xv). Altogether, he counts fourteen plays (those with Wakefield references and/or the Wakefield stanza) which "are connected, directly or indirectly, with Wakefield and its neighborhood" (p. xvi). I will return to a discussion of the Wakefield plays and the manuscript evidence in a moment.

The second important development was the discovery of external evidence that proved the existence of performances in Wakefield during the late Middle Ages. J. W. Walker, Wakefield's foremost historian, announced in the inaugural lecture in 1914 to the Wakefield Historical Society, "Wakefield Town Life in the Fifteenth and Sixteenth Centuries," that he had

---

article on the same subject with similar coverage under the title, "The Wakefield Mysteries," in *Anglia* 24 (1901–1904): 509–524.

[11] See Frank W. Cady, "The Wakefield Group in Towneley," *Journal of JEGP English and German Philology* 11 (1912): 244–262; Millicent Carey, *The Wakefield Group in the Towneley Cycle* (Baltimore: Johns Hopkins University Press, 1930); and Cawley, *Wakefield Pageants*, esp. pp. xvii–xx.

found several documents from the Wakefield Burgess Court for the years 1533, 1554, 1556, and 1579, of which he had made transcriptions twenty-three years before from the originals that were then in the collection of W. H. Battie-Wrightson at Cusworth Park in Doncaster. Two of these entries, those dated by Walker as 1554 and 1556, made specific reference to the "regenall and the performance of the Corpus Christi play at Wakefield."[12] In addition, Walker found a document in the York Diocesan Records at Saint Anthony's Hall in York that forbids the playing of any play in Wakefield in the year 1576 that tends "to the maintenaunce of superstition and idolatrie." According to the document, word had reached the commissioners at York that "a plaie commonlie called Corpus Christi plaie" was to have been performed in the town of Wakefield that year at Whitsuntide. On the basis of this evidence and the articles of Matthew Peacock, Walker says that "there can be no doubt that [the plays of the Towneley manuscript] were written for a Wakefield audience and were represented in Wakefield."[13] He accepts the Huntington manuscript as the register and refers to the contents as "The Wakefield, or as they were wrongly called, Towneley Plays" (p. 139). Regrettably, the Burgess Court Rolls have been lost since the time that Walker borrowed them from the Battie-Wrightson archives in Doncaster, though a photocopy of the original document bearing entries 1 to 30 of the 1554(?) roll does exist. In addition, there is a copy of the 1556 roll in the handwriting of Battie-Wrightson, but this copy includes only the first of a series of references to the performance of plays. These copies have turned out to be im-

[12] All four entries were originally published by J. W. Walker, "The Burgess Court, Wakefield: 1533, 1554, 1556, and 1579," *Yorkshire Archaeological Society Record Series* 74 (1929): 16–32. A slightly corrected version of the 1554 and 1556 entries appears in Cawley, *Wakefield Pageants*, appendix, 1.124.

[13] Walker, *Wakefield History*, p. 138. The York Commissioners' Instructions from the Diocesan records at St. Anthony's Hall were reprinted in Walker's two-volume edition of *Wakefield: Its History and People* (1939), 1:156. (The one-volume edition does not include them.) It is also reprinted in Cawley, *Wakefield Pageants*, see appendix, 1.125.

portant documents inasmuch as they vary from Walker's text in several details, and they give reason to believe that Walker's transcriptions and interpretations are not always accurate. The most critical error he made seems to have been the dating of the second of the Burgess Court Rolls, which he placed in the year 1554 when actually, according to incontrovertible internal evidence, that roll could not have been dated prior to 1559. The loss of the original records together with the questionable transcriptions by Walker have given rise to much of the uncertainty that is expressed of late by various scholars about the Wakefield provenance.[14] While I share the distress over the loss of the originals, I do not believe that the errors made by Walker are of any such magnitude as to cast significant doubt on the contents of the Burgess Court records as we have them nor to cause a reassessment of the history of the plays. The likelihood is that with the redating of the putative 1554 entry and the independent testimony of the Battie-Wrightson transcription of the entry for 1556, we probably have a very accurate idea of what those two documents—and they are the only ones relevant to the plays—actually said.[15]

[14] The spadework in uncovering the evidence here summarized was done by Jean Forrester and reported in a privately printed mimeographed edition entitled "Wakefield Mystery Plays and the Burgess Court Records: A New Discovery," published by Harold Speak and Jean Forrester, Ossett, Yorkshire, 1974. For a full scholarly discussion, see A. C. Cawley and Jean Forrester, "The Corpus Christi Play of Wakefield: A New Look at the Wakefield Burgess Court Records," *Leeds Studies in English*, n.s. 8 (1975): 108–116 (followed by three appendixes and facsimiles).

[15] I disagree, for example, with the strong conclusion drawn by Professor Alexandra Johnston at the 1983 Kalamazoo session, as quoted in the announcement of the 1985 Toronto Towneley Cycle in *The Medieval and Renaissance Drama Society Newsletter* (December 1984): "The authenticity of much of the external evidence has been so severely questioned that only one external reference to the biblical play in Wakefield, the 1576 prohibition, can be accepted as reliable." I would say to the contrary that the 1556 entry, with its corroborating text in the hand of Battie-Wrightson, now establishes all the more surely that the city of Wakefield had a Corpus Christi play that was performed in its streets. It is true that Walker's text of the lost portion of the 1556 text is left unconfirmed. Why Battie-Wrightson did not copy these dramatic entries remains a puzzle.

After the time of the Walker discovery the issue of the plays' ascription to Wakefield was widely accepted, as shown by E. K. Chambers's authoritative statement: "I think we may now safely regard the plays in the Towneley MS. as a Wakefield cycle."[16] Is it right to say then that, except for recent doubts raised by the Walker transcriptions, the Wakefield provenance has been accepted as established and that it no longer needs justification? Not quite.

The questions that have been raised direct attention particularly to the nature of the Wakefield identifications in the manuscript. The first to raise a query about this matter was Louis Wann in an important article describing the Towneley manuscript.[17] The question he raised had to do with the two references to Wakefield in the manuscript—one at the beginning of the first play in the title: "In dei nomine amen. Assit Principio, Sancta Maria, Meo. Wakefeld"; and one at the beginning of the third pageant: "processus Noe cum filiis. Wakefeld." About these headings he posed the following question:

> How shall we explain the appearance of the name "Wakefield" as a part of the title of *two* plays only? If the entire cycle of plays was produced at Wakefield, why are these two alone—and these not in consecutive order—designated as "Wakefield" plays? Does not the mention of Wakefield in the case of these two plays establish a pre-

---

Yet, there can be little doubt that they did exist in a version similar to that originally copied by Walker. Those who argue that those entries are not genuine would have to make a case for Walker's inventing them. I find no basis for such a dramatic conclusion, and in any case, even if the missing entries had been made up, we still have enough basis from the internal evidence to know that Wakefield had a play. Finally, it is true that the earliest documented date for the play in Wakefield must be moved from 1554 to 1556, but even that change of two years is surely not so great as to cause severe questioning of the external evidence, sparse as it is now and as it has been all along.

[16] E. K. Chambers, *English Literature at the Close of the Middle Ages* (Oxford: Clarendon Press, 1945), p. 35.

[17] Louis Wann, "A New Examination of the Manuscript of the Towneley Plays," *PMLA* 63 (1928): 137–152.

sumption that the others were *not connected with Wakefield*? (pp. 151–152)

Wann's question seems to have haunted Wakefield/Towneley scholarship, and it has often been repeated in one form or another. It is, for example, cited by A. C. Cawley in his introduction and thus adds a note of caution to the ascription of the cycle to Wakefield. It also appears in the introduction to Martial Rose's translation and acting version of the cycle (which was prepared for a performance at Bretton Hall College in Wakefield in 1958). Rose is troubled particularly by the appearance of the name "Wakefeld" in the title of the Noah play, a reference that he would explain as coinciding with the first of the set of plays in the manuscript written by the Wakefield Master. So despite the performance at the site and the daring title of the edition—*The Wakefield Mystery Plays*—Rose is not entirely convinced by his own argument. Curiously, he resurrects a theory that virtually everyone else had dropped: the notion advanced by Francis Douce (on the rebound from his Abbey of Widkirk suggestion) that the plays might have had a connection with the Abbey of Whalley in Lancashire. The connection that Rose draws concentrates more on authorship than place of performance, advancing the argument that the Wakefield Master might have been a monk in the abbey.[18]

To my knowledge, no one since Rose has raised any new or resurrected any old theories about the provenance of the plays or the early transmission of the manuscript. The question then becomes, do we now have sufficient perspective on the matter to determine with some certainty what the provenance was of the plays collected in the Towneley manuscript (i.e. Huntington HM 1)? My sense is that, with some further thought about the problem, we do. I should like now to show why I regard the plays as Wakefield plays and why I believe the attribution should no longer be made with any hesitation.

The basis for the hesitation all along has been the issue raised

[18] See Martial Rose, ed., *The Wakefield Mystery Plays* (London: Evans Brothers, 1961), pp. 11–14.

by Wann about the titles. In particular, the problem has been with the interpretation of the first of them. Does the title "In dei nomine amen. Assit Principio, Sancta Maria, Meo. Wakefeld" introduce the entire collection or simply the first play? E. K. Chambers, in *English Literature at the Close of the Middle Ages*, offered the opinion that "on the face of it, [it] looks like a title to the whole collection" (p. 34), a view that in A. C. Cawley's mind "has much to recommend it." Cawley leaves the question with this observation: If the title on folio 1 "refers to the whole manuscript the localization of the cycle is not in any doubt" (p. xvi). This is to say that the crucial point in the attribution of the cycle is the first reference to Wakefield, not the second in the title of the Noah play.

A new examination of that first title will, I think, show that it indeed does apply to the whole cycle and not to the single pageant of the Creation. Let us examine it (see figure 3). By comparing it with other titles, in this manuscript and in others, we will see that both in format and in content it serves a function different from the labeling of a single unit within the larger work. Take the format first. While, unmistakably, the title was done by the person who supplied the rubrics throughout the manuscript, it differs significantly from all the other titles in the manuscript. Each of the others is either a single name or a short phrase naming the central episode of the pageant (e.g. "Incipit Salutacio Elezabeth," see figure 1), and customarily that title is preceded by the title word "Incipit" or by "Sequitur." While there is no complete uniformity in the titles of the manuscript—a fact that is emphasized by the use of "Wakefeld" in the title of the Noah play (see figure 4)—there is a remarkable similarity of form in the titles, and all of them are truly descriptive. Now, when we look at the Latin words before Play 1, we have nothing to suggest that they introduce a play or, for that matter, that they are a title. The scribe is asking for assistance from the Holy Virgin to guide the beginning of his work (the sort of prayer that most writers understand very well!). It is, in fact, the only time in the whole manuscript that the scribe speaks in *propria persona*. Neither in form nor in con-

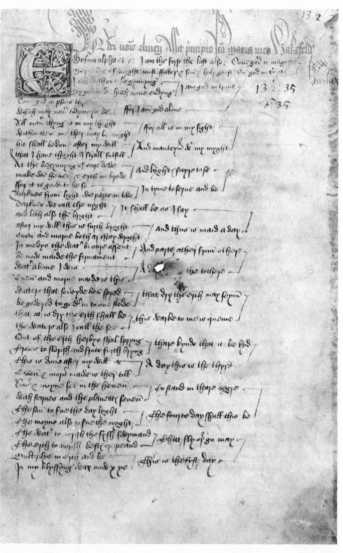

FIGURE 3. The Wakefield Plays, f. 1 recto, Huntington Library HM 1.
(Courtesy the Henry E. Huntington Library and Art Gallery)

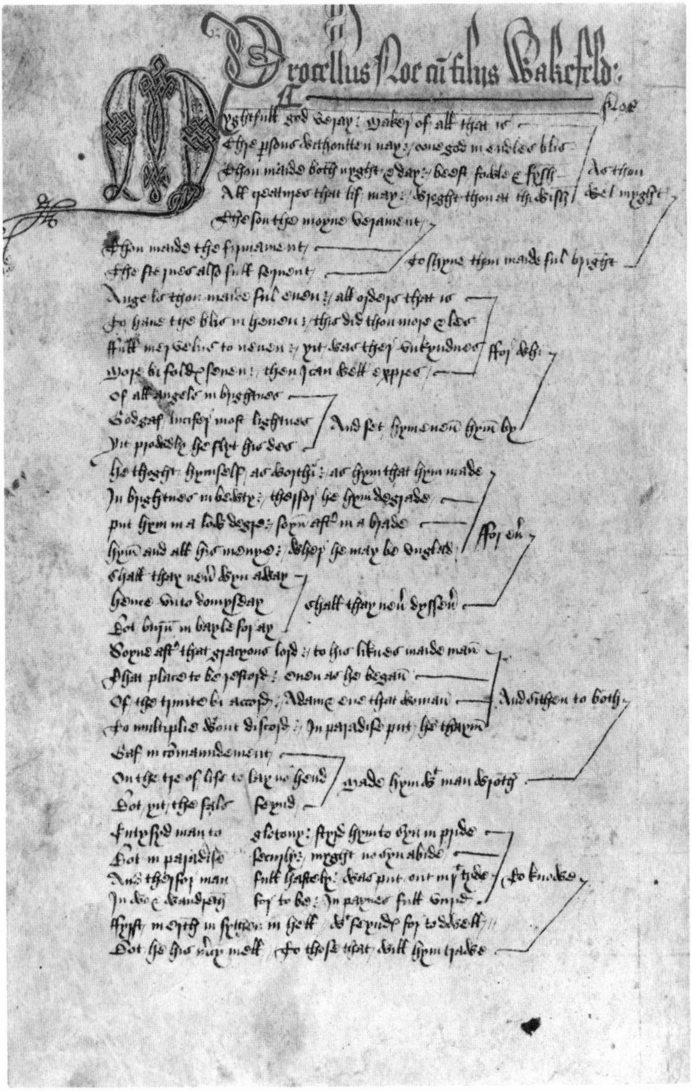

Processus Noe cum filiis. Wakefeld.

FIGURE 4. The Wakefield Plays, f. 7 verso, Huntington Library HM 1. (Courtesy the Henry E. Huntington Library and Art Gallery) tent does it even remotely function as a title for the Creation pageant.

Interestingly, practice in other manuscripts can cast some further light on the opening title of the extant manuscript—I say "extant" because at one point it was not an opening title. I have shown elsewhere that the Towneley manuscript once contained a complete set of banns, which of course preceded the opening of the Creation play.[19] In this respect, as in some others, the Towneley manuscript is similar to that of N-Town, though the two also differ significantly. N-Town has no pageant titles at all—in fact, I believe that the reviser who was responsible for the extant manuscript version set out to combine erstwhile pageants into larger units. Thus the manuscript, like Towneley, is continuous, with only occasional gaps between pageants and no clearly planned blank pages. In this feature, both manuscripts differ significantly from that of the York plays, which, as we have seen, is in design and format more obviously a register. For a manuscript like N-Town or Towneley, it therefore makes sense to have a single title. N-Town, in fact, has such a title, though in a different hand and not at all ornamental, "The Plaie called Corpus Christi." This title, however, occurs before the banns and not at the beginning of the first play. If the parallel holds, then Towneley would have had a general descriptive title on the first page of the banns that are now missing. The beginning of Play 1, on the extant first folio (see figure 3), is thus more nearly an invocation than a descriptive title, and as such it resembles in form the scribal "ceremony" of both the York and the N-Town manuscripts: a Latin phrase celebrating beginnings—beginnings that have to do with the creative act rather than the content of the work (see figure 5 for the York plays' opening). In Towneley, that phrase is cast in the form of a prayer; in the other two manuscripts, it is a variation of God's self-characterization from the Apocalypse of St. John (1:8): "Ego sum alpha et omega, principium et finis, dicit Dominus Deus: qui est, et qui erat, et qui venturus

[19] M. Stevens, "The Missing Parts," p. 257.

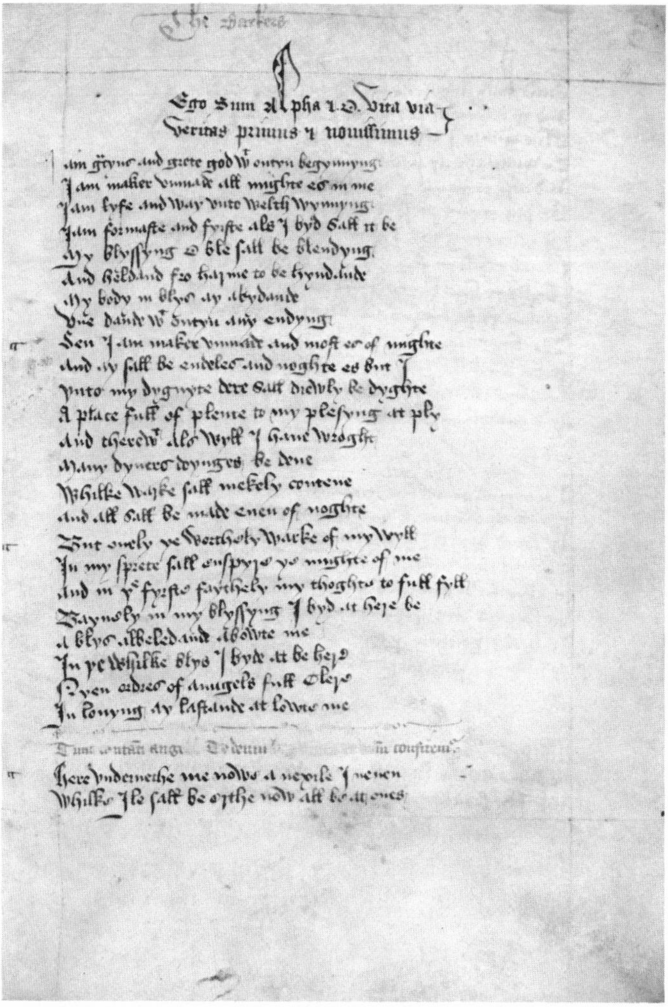

The Barkers

Ego sum Alpha et O vita via
Veritas primus et nouissimus

I am gracyus and grete god withoutyn begynnyng
I am maker vnmade all mighte es in me
I am lyfe and way vnto welth wynnyng
I am formaste and fyrste als I byd sall it be
My blyssyng o ble sall be blendyng
And heldand fro harme to be hyndande
My body in blys ay abydande
Vnendande withoutyn any endyng
Sen I am maker vnmade and moste es of mighte
And ay sall be endeles and noghte es but I
Vnto my dygnyte dere sall diewly be dyghte
A place full of plente to my plesyng at ply
And therewith also will I haue wroght
Many dyuers doynges be-dene
Whilke warke sall mekely contene
And all sall be made euen of noghte
But onely ye worthely warke of my wyll
In my sprete sall enspyre ye mighte of me
And in ye fyrste faythely my thoghts to full fyll
Baynely in my blyssyng I byd at here be
A blys al beledand abowte me
In ye whilke blys I byde at be here
Nyen ordres of aungels full clere
In louyng ay lastande at lowte me

Tunc cantant angeli Te deum laudamus te dominum confitemur

Here vnderneth me nowe a nexile I neuen
Whilke ile sall be erthe now all be at ones

FIGURE 5. The York Plays, f. 1 recto, Additional Ms. 35290.
(Courtesy the British Library)

est, omnipotens." Underlined and set apart as the phrase is in York and N-Town, it occurs as an extratextual statement recorded by the scribe/rubricator to let God's words stand as silent revelation to the reader of the significance of the work that is to follow: God will reveal his presence and purpose from beginning to end in the book for which it is an invocation. In this sense, all three manuscripts that are contemporary to performances in the late Middle Ages begin with a scribal incantation, which appropriately enough, with their emphasis on "in principio," relate the making of the book to the making of the universe.

Yet another point needs to be made about the Towneley rubric on folio 1. Manuscripts of works other than cycles seem to have the option of allowing a general title to replace that of the first unit or division of the work. A case in point occurs in the manuscripts of the *Troilus* that uniformly omit titles or incipits for the prologue to book 1. And, in fact, modern editions, including those of Root and Robinson that put the general invocation into the introduction to book 1, seriously misread the manuscripts. The double sorrow of which the narrator speaks applies to everything that follows and not specifically to the action of book 1. There is no separate prologue for book 1; the existing prologue is to the entire book. The title at the conclusion of the opening invocation in Root's edition, "Explicit Prohemium Primi Libri," appears in only one bad manuscript, and it is therefore misleading. The point I am making is that the scribe does not give titles for that opening invocation. The general title thus subsumes the title for the first book. The situation on the opening page of the Towneley manuscript is exactly parallel.

The foregoing discussion leaves as yet unexplained the appearance of Wakefield in the title of the Noah play. How might that allusion be explained? In one of two ways: either that the scribe copied it from the text of the Wakefield Master's contributions, which, in terms of original contributions began with the Noah play; or that the scribe was searching for a set pattern of titles. Thus, when he titled Play 2, the first true unit title in the manuscript, he decided to say "Mactacio Abel, Secunda Pagina" (see figure 6). When he came to the next pageant, the Noah, he dropped the numbering and put in "Wakefeld." In Play 4, the Play of Abraham, he used "Sequitur" for the first time as his title word, and in Play 8, he shifts to "Incipit." The point is that the Wakefield scribe is as inconsistent as most medieval scribes about the format of titles. Note, for example, that York, which conventionally gives only the name of the sponsoring guild as the title, is also inconsistent about its titles when it copies at a later time from independent "origenalls"—precisely the method I have postulated for the compiling of the Towneley manuscript (see, for example, the Armourers' play entitled "The Origenall Perteynyng to þe Crafte of the Armourrers"; figure 7).

We need to acknowledge that for an anonymous Middle English literary manuscript, the Towneley manuscript is unusually well endowed with evidence of provenance. Would that N-Town had given as much information! With the additional external evidence uncovered by Walker, and confirmed by the Battie-Wrightson transcription, I am frankly surprised in retrospect that scholars have not been bolder about stating the case for Wakefield. I find it surprising that a medieval manuscript that mentions the same place name twice in its titles and that, furthermore, has recognizable local allusions closely connected with that name should have caused the editors of the first two editions so much puzzlement and led them to identify the manuscript with another place. If, as I hope, the foregoing has reiterated the strength of the case for Wakefield as the home of the Towneley cycle, we are ready now to examine the historical circumstances that seemed to have given rise to the cycle.

I HAVE on several occasions referred to the Wakefield cycle as "second generation." That term is, I believe, an accurate representation of the process by which the mystery plays came to the West Riding in the course of the fifteenth century. My argument will be that the Wakefield cycle is, in effect, built upon

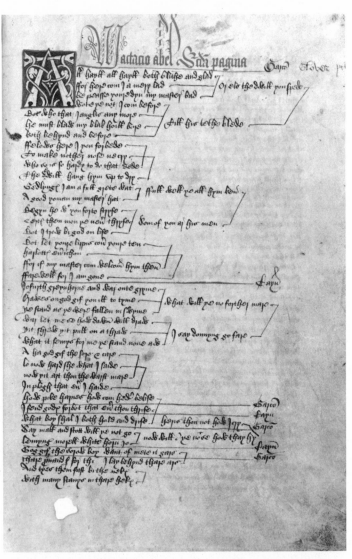

FIGURE 6. The Wakefield Plays, f. 3 recto, Huntington Library HM 1.
(Courtesy the Henry E. Huntington Library and Art Gallery)

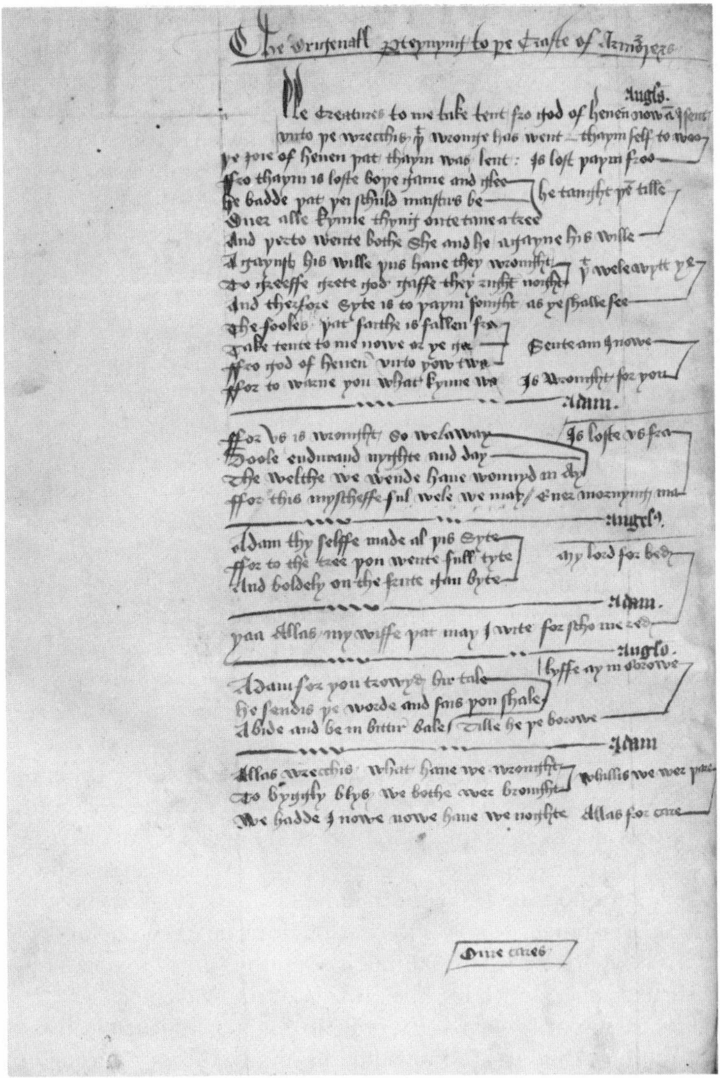

FIGURE 7. The York Plays, f. 16 verso, Additional Ms. 35290.
(Courtesy the British Library)

already existing plays, borrowed from nearby communities, especially the city of York, when economic and demographic conditions in the western county permitted the development of a cycle and its attendant festivities. It is known, of course, that at least five plays in the Wakefield cycle are nearly identical in content and even phrasing with five in the extant York cycle. All the evidence—internal and external—shows that Wakefield borrowed those plays from York, and not vice versa. External to the plays are the records showing that York clearly did support a cycle performance (even if not yet recorded in a text) as early as the latter quarter of the fourteenth century, which was the time of York's greatest prosperity in the Middle Ages. Wakefield in contrast developed, as I shall show, into a commercial hub, especially in the wool trade after the mid-fifteenth century. Before that time, it could not have supported a cycle of mystery plays. As for the internal evidence, it would be difficult to argue that the more polished, expanded versions of at least some of the Wakefield plays were the earlier of the two. Of special significance is the fact that the Wakefield Judgment play, which is one of the five, was expanded significantly and brilliantly by the Wakefield Master in his characteristic style and meter. If the borrowing had been in the other direction, one would have to explain the anomaly of the play's losing its best parts, including the role of Tutivillus, in the process.

The argument that the Wakefield plays are second generation is at odds with most explanations thus far offered about the development of the cycle. It was fashionable, from the very first, to assume that the Wakefield plays grew much in the same manner and time frame as the plays at York. This argument was, of course, simply inferential, since no records survive from a period earlier than mid-sixteenth century to ascertain the existence, much less the growth, of the Wakefield cycle. It was based partly on analogy, built no doubt on the unvoiced assumption that at a certain time in literary history all major towns or cities in England set out to create cycles. Though details of this putative history have been widely challenged, little has been written to refute the notion that cycles in one form or another arose simultaneously as part of the evolution of the vernacular religious drama. Even such an enlightened scholar as Woolf speaks of the northern dramatists as if they were indistinguishable:

> If there were London plays from about the middle of the fourteenth century onwards, the northern cycles could not have escaped their influence. Because the plays have been lost this influence cannot be investigated; but it is reasonable to suppose that the northern dramatists did not slavishly imitate the drama of the metropolis, that they were aware of the complex traditions that lay behind it, and that working within these traditions they designed their own form of cyclical play.[20]

This view assumes an ineluctable historical progress: The basic germ of the drama was swept northward where so many undifferentiated dramatists allowed it to grow into an indigenous form (everywhere much the same) of what is, by inference, the ubiquitous play.

This view of a general growth of the drama has dominated historical scholarship from the beginning of the modern era. It is true that dates have been slightly adjusted to conform more nearly with the facts; we are now more ready to locate the birth of the cycles as we have them in the fifteenth rather than the fourteenth century.[21] But the notion that cycles grew in relatively similar stages over the years to match the growth and interest of the communities that sponsored them is still very much an unwritten premise of our published scholarship. What is usually envisioned is a period of gestation during which a primitive cycle gradually became complex through a series of comprehensive revisions. The first stage is represented as consisting mostly of couplets and quatrains, and the

---

[20] Rosemary Woolf, *The English Mystery Plays* (London: Routledge and Kegan Paul, 1972), pp. 58–59.

[21] See, for example, the enlightened discussion on this point by Stanley Kahrl in *Traditions of Medieval English Drama* (London: Hutchinson University Library, 1974), chap. 1.

notorious tail-rhyme stanza of the metrical romances. This stage was marked by simplicity and plain-spoken devotion. It was followed by a reviser who wrote in more complex structures, perhaps in rime couée or the Northern Septenar stanza, and whose outlook was more worldly because he was attentive to contemporary texts from which he might borrow passages or techniques. The last stage burst forth with unbridled realism, in the work of "real" poets who were given names like the York Realist (clearly a compliment!) or the Wakefield Master. This is the scheme essentially proposed by A. W. Pollard in his introduction to *The Towneley Plays*:

> I think we may fairly regard this Towneley cycle as built up in at least three distinct stages. In the first of these we find the simple religious tone which we naturally assign to the beginning of the cyclical religious drama, the majority of them being written in one of the favourite metres of the fourteenth-century romances which were already going out of fashion in Chaucer's day. In the second stage we have the introduction by some playwright, who brought the knowledge of them from elsewhere, of at least five— possibly seven or eight—of the plays which were acted at York, and the composition of some others in the same style. In the third stage a writer of genuine dramatic power, whose humour was unchecked by any respect for conventionality, wrote, especially for this cycle, the plays in the 9-line stanza which form its backbone, and added here and there to others. Taken together, the three stages probably cover something like half a century, ending about 1410.[22]

Remarkably this scheme looks almost exactly the same as that posited by W. W. Greg for the York cycle. Greg also conjures up three stages (he calls them "layers"—the other favorite word is "strata"), of which the first was "a simple didactic cycle

---

[22] England and Pollard, *Towneley Plays*, pp. xxvii–xxviii.

carefully composed in elaborate stanzas and withal rather dull." The second introduced all the humor that we still find in the cycle, and it is the work of "the only great metrist who devoted his talents to the English religious drama as we know it." The last and crowning stage was produced by "a very remarkable though uneven writer . . . [who] is a real dramatist" and to whom we owe the masterly portrait of Pilate. The date of this writer is "hardly earlier than 1400"; a conclusion that would make him a contemporary of Pollard's poet with "genuine dramatic power."[23] These two sketches sound almost as if they were burlesque accounts of the Darwinian thesis that O. B. Hardison so effectively exposed. They are, unhappily, dead serious, and they show that the conception of literary history that ruled the early scholarship on the cycles was every bit as flawed by the evolutionary analogy as was the treatment addressed by Hardison of the liturgical drama. Even the notion that the cycles were essentially one model, undifferentiated in time and purpose, is similar to the conception that controlled the early historical accounts of the church drama. The whole matter would not be of great relevance to the present day were it not for the fact that the Pollard/Greg perspective still inspires criticism. Here, for example, are the opening sentences of a very recent book, otherwise a valuable study, about the work of the Wakefield Master:

> The outstanding playwright of the Middle Ages probably began his work at Wakefield as a play-doctor. His was the last of at least three different hands that composed the cycle.

[23] W. W. Greg, "Bibliographic and Textual Problems of the English Miracle Cycles," *Library*, 3d ser. 5 (1914): 290–291. A. P. Rossiter offers an amusing assessment of the Greg-type of stratification: "Criticism is confused by the discoveries of recent researchers that all four of the English cycles (Chester, York, Wakefield, and N-Town) have been extensively revised, never completely; so what one reads by nature's light is a kind of palimpsest with geologic 'intrusions' of varying date and intention"; see *English Drama from Early Times to the Elizabethans* (London: Hutchinson University Library, 1950, p. 72.

The passage is, of course, footnoted to Pollard.[24]

The history of Wakefield makes clear that this three-stage concept is manifestly unacceptable. The Pollard / Greg models assume that cycles grew over time in performance and that periodically they were put back in the shop, so to speak, for an overhaul by a reviser who would improve the text for the next run of twenty or thirty years. At York the process did not exactly work that way, though it probably came closer to Greg's layers than Towneley could have to Pollard's stages. To understand why the model could not have worked in Wakefield, we need to look at some demographics. M. G. Frampton has shown that Wakefield in the fourteenth century was simply too poor and too sparsely populated to support a major cycle, even in stage one. For example, the poll-tax records for 1379 indicate that the adult population of the town of Wakefield numbered a mere 315 (as compared with Beverley, for example, which seemingly did support a cycle, with a figure of 2,663). All signs indicate to Frampton that we must look to the reign of Henry VI (between the years 1422 and 1460) for the beginning of the cycle and the work of the Wakefield Master.[25] Other studies confirm Frampton's conclusion, and if anything, prompt the positing of an even later date. It is, for example, a fact that York reached the depth of its economic depression in the fifteenth century in the decade between 1457 and 1467, due mainly to the disastrous failure of the port of Hull as an export center, and that the distribution of cloth passed "out of the hands of York merchants . . . [to] that of the merchants and clothiers of Wakefield and Halifax" who transported their wool overland (perhaps on the Watling Street mentioned in the *Iudicium*?) directly to London for export.[26] By the 1470s, two-thirds of all the cloth made in Yorkshire came from the Aire

---

[24] See Jeffrey Helterman, *Symbolic Action in the Plays of the Wakefield Master* (Athens: University of Georgia Press, 1981), p. 1.

[25] Mendal G. Frampton, "The Date of the Flourishing of the Wakefield Master," *PMLA* 50 (1935): 651–660.

[26] See J. M. Bartlett, "The Expansion and Decline of York in the Later Middle Ages," *Economic History Review*, 2d ser. 12 (1959): 29–30.

and Calder valleys (the districts of Leeds and Wakefield respectively), and it was probably not until the turn of the sixteenth century that the new-found prosperity occasioned by the enormous rise in the manufacture and trade of wool manifested itself in Wakefield.[27] It was probably then the latter third of the century during which the town would have had sufficient resources and people as well as occasion for civic pride to begin a Corpus Christi cycle.

The other reason for assigning a late date to the Wakefield cycle has to do with the manuscript. Most scholars are agreed that the Towneley manuscript seems to have been copied with remarkable fidelity and that its "copyist was faithfully reproducing the peculiarities of independent source manuscripts."[28] The general sequence of recording independent pageant manuscripts into a book seems to have been the process at work at York as well. And if that is the right scenario for Wakefield, then there could have been only one reviser / compiler, and that person would have given shape to the material that was copied into the extant Towneley manuscript. If, in fact, there was no intervening manuscript between the individual pageant copies and the scribe's exemplar, then the reviser / compiler (who must have been the Wakefield Master since he clearly added material to already existing plays, as witness the transformation of the York Judgment play to the Wakefield *Iudicium*) must have done his writing, revising, rewriting, and compiling on the copies that ultimately went to the scribe. This step clearly rules out the Pollard scenario, and it allows us to think of the Wakefield Master as the Wakefield Author.

Given this process of composition, the date of the manuscript becomes a point of some importance, since it records what is the first true compilation of the Wakefield cycle. It serves at the very least as the logical *ad quem* date for the cycle.

[27] For a full discussion, see W. G. Rimmer, "The Evolution of Leeds," in *The Early Modern Town*, ed. Peter Clark (London: Longmans and Open University Press, 1976), pp. 273–291.

[28] See Cawley, *Wakefield Pageants*, p. xii; and Martin Stevens, "The Accuracy of the Towneley Scribe," *Huntington Library Quarterly* 22 (1958): 1-9.

Recent paleographic research has shown that the initials of plays 1 and 2 (ff. 1 and 3) are almost identical with capitals in printed books dated 1499 and 1506, while the strap-work initials of other plays suggest a date not earlier than 1500.[29] It should be observed that at least some of the strap-work initials were made prior to the copying of the text, as in figure 8, where the descender clearly determines the uneven left-hand margin of the page, and that fact rules out the possibility of a later insertion of the capitals in spaces left for that purpose. In consequence the general date of the capitals can be accepted as a date for the copying of the manuscript as a whole. It is therefore fair to conclude that the Wakefield cycle came into being some time in the last third of the fifteenth century, and if the process involved the compiling of pageants from other sources, as I believe to have been the case, the likelihood is that the cycle was not compiled until very shortly before it was "fair-written" into the extant manuscript—in other words, very nearly at the turn of the century.

There is, as already noted, no documentary evidence to tell how the Wakefield cycle came into being. Many have speculated on the point but none has ventured as credible a scenario as Arnold Williams, whose book on the characterization of Pilate in the Wakefield plays still ranks among the most persuasive critical studies done on any of the English cycles to date. Williams argues that the Towneley cycle presents a uniquely conceived and consistently executed "evil" Pilate, one who is an overwhelming presence in the cycle and who meets every requirement of a complexly drawn dramatic character. In this consistency and complexity, he is quite unlike any other Pilate in the English medieval drama, including the York Pilate, who appears in one clearly borrowed pageant, that of the Resurrection, where, however, his role is used by the Wakefield play-

[29] The research on the date and provenance of the capitals in the Towneley MS was carried out by S. I. Doyle, Keeper of Rare Books and Reader in Bibliography at the University of Durham, and by D. M. Rogers of the Bodleian Library, Oxford. For the full argument, see Cawley and Stevens, *Towneley Cycle*, pp. ix, xv–xvi.

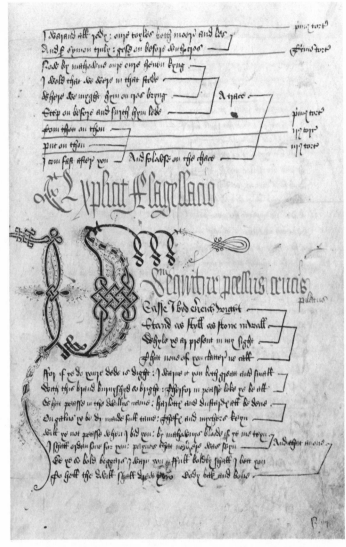

FIGURE 8. The Wakefield Plays, f. 84 recto, Huntington Library
HM 1. (Courtesy the Henry E. Huntington Library and Art Gallery)

wright to reinforce his overall interpretation. The unmistakable dramatic continuity of the evil Pilate in Towneley raises inevitably the fundamental question with which we have been grappling: How is it possible for what appears to be a patchwork cycle, with so many apparent strata, to be so unified? Williams shows in detail that the character of Pilate appears in virtually every major metrical form within the cycle: quatrains, octaves, the Wakefield nine-liners, Northern Septenars, seven-line and thirteen-line stanzas, and even rime couée (though in the latter only briefly and in that stanza form Pilate is uncharacteristically tame). He concludes, "The structure of the passion group, the consistency of characterization, the numerous anticipations and motivations—all point to a single author working according to a definite plan." Here is Williams's speculation of how that sort of authorship occurred:

> About 1420 the city authorities of Wakefield, which was rapidly becoming a commercial center of importance, decided to inaugurate a cycle of plays. Everything we know about the authorship of medieval drama indicates that a cycle so initiated would be a patchwork, based on some existing cycle or cycles of plays, which would then be more or less edited and interpolated to form a new cycle. This individual, struck with the dramatic validity of one or more plays containing a villainous Pilate, decides that the character of Pilate in the cycle which he is putting together shall be that of a villain. He therefore chooses only plays or parts of plays which present Pilate in this light. Perhaps he removes sections suggesting a kindlier Pilate, revises and edits all into reasonable conformity to his dominating conception.[30]

The date in Williams's speculation is, of course, too early, but the scenario he describes is in all respects quite possible. The single compiler or the group he conjectures might, of course,

---

[30] Arnold Williams, *The Characterization of Pilate in the Towneley Plays* (East Lansing: Michigan State University Press, 1950), pp. 72–73 and passim.

first have gathered the plays—perhaps each craft guild did its own searching among its counterparts in other cities[31]—and after all potential performing groups and all dramatic subjects had been found, either the newly collected patchwork cycle was performed or it was handed to a "literary man," one would think a monk or perhaps another kind of cleric like a chantry priest,[32] who then composed the book. If that was the scenario, we cannot of course know what influence the book ever had on the performance. All indications, as I have shown, are that the book was not used as an acting text or script, and that, in fact, the marginalia occurred only to show what was being censored after the 1550s, when the cycle was carefully scrutinized by the diocese. I suspect that the performance, however it was done, was guided by the scripts that the compiler used to develop his composite volume, though even if that did happen, we can of course not be sure that what was actually performed was the text that we retain.

The source of a very large part of the Wakefield play must have been individual pageants from the York cycle. However this borrowing took place, we can be certain that it was not from the York Register directly. Internal textual evidence supports that conclusion. One passage, for example, from the Towneley *Extraccio Animarum* reads as follows:

> SATHAN. Goddys son! nay, then myght thou be glad,
> For no catell *thurt the crave*;

---

[31] It is possible that Wakefield guilds actually obtained plays from their counterparts in York and elsewhere. Since only four guilds are mentioned in the Towneley MS (Barkers, Glovers, Listers, and Fishers), and all reference to them is written in later hands or at least hands different from that of the main scribe and rubricator and, therefore, are not part of the main text, we cannot know who actually performed the Wakefield plays when they were first performed. One discrepancy in guild names does occur: The York pageant of the Departure of the Israelites was performed by the Glovers, whereas the Wakefield play contains in the margin the name "Litsters pagonn" and again "lyster" in another hand halfway down the first page. Here the surface evidence would argue against a passing on of texts from one guild chapter to another.

[32] For a discussion of the authorship problem, See Rose, *Wakefield Mystery Plays*, pp. 12–14.

> Bot thou has lyffyd ay lyke a lad,
> In sorrow, and as a sympill *knaue*.
>> (301/255–258; italics added)

The York Register renders these lines:

> SATTAN. God sonne? þanne schulde þou be ful gladde,
> Aftir no catel *þus þe I telle*!
> But þou has leued ay like a ladde,
> And in sorowe a symple *braide*.
>> (339/241–245; italics added)

Here, quite apart from the fact that the Towneley version is better metrically, more accurate in rhyme, and more meaningful in sense, the York text, in the hand of John Clerke strikes out the italicized words and replaces them, curiously, with the Towneley readings: i.e. *þus þe I telle* is replaced by "neyd thowe crave" (242), and the last line is corrected with interlining to "And in sorowe *as* a symple *knave*" (245). It is clear that in this instance Towneley could not have copied from the York Register. The likelihood is that it copied the correct version from the York Saddlers' original copy and that John Clerke, who found the York meaning incomprehensible, corrected it from the same source or from a performance of the play based on that source. It follows, therefore, that the extant versions of the five nearly identical York and Towneley plays are not directly related, a point that should be borne in mind in any cross-analytical study. This fact may also help to explain differences in pairs of plays from the two cycles that are not so close in their verbal and narrative correspondences, as for example the Wakefield *Oblacio Magorum* and its York counterpart, the Magi play of the Goldsmiths. Here clearly the Towneley version must have originally been taken from the York pageant and then been revised (as the Goldsmiths' regynall itself might have been). The parallels in various portions of the two plays are too close, especially in phraseology, to allow another explanation. Here, for example, is the Angel's speech to the Kings in side-by-side juxtaposition from the two cycles:

Wakefield	York
Syr curtes kyngys, to me take tent,	Nowe curtayse kynges, to me take tent,
And turne by tyme or ye be tenyd;	And turne betyme or ȝe be tenyd,
From God his self thus am I sent	Fro God hymselfe þus am I sent
To warne you, as youre faythfull freynd,	To warne yow als youre faithfull frende.
How Herode kyng has malyce ment,	Herowde the king has malise ment
And shapys with shame you for to sheynd;	And shappis with shame yow for to shende,
And so that ye no harmes hent,	And for þat ȝe non harmes shulde hente,
By othere ways God wyll ye weynd	Be othir waies God will ye wende
Into youre awne cuntre;	Euen to youre awne contré.
And if ye ask hym boyn,	And yf ȝe aske hym bone,
For this dede that ye haue done,	Youre beelde ay will he be,
Youre beyld ay wyll he be.	For þis þat ȝe haue done.
(159/595–606)	(148/369–380)

What this isolated parallel passage shows, and there are many more from this pageant as well as from others, is that the Wakefield compilation probably borrowed the bulk of its plays from the already thriving mystery cycle at York. In her close study of the parallel passages of the two cycles, Marie C. Lyle showed that only nine of the thirty-two plays in the Towneley manuscript contained no instances of significant parallel phraseology, and of these nine, one was the late *Suspencio Iude*, an apparent intruder in the cycle, and another the *Processus Talentorum* of which an early York play did seem to exist though it was abandoned before the register was copied.[33] The

---

[33] Lyle's premise that the York and Wakefield plays were once identical has generally not been accepted by scholars. The only notable exception is Hardin

other seven plays may well have been borrowed from other relatively nearby cycles (e.g. Beverley, Hull, King's Lynn, Newcastle upon Tyne, or Norwich), or they were changed so radically in revision that they no longer bore any clear traces of their York origin.

As I proceed now to examine the role of the Wakefield Master as contributor and likely the only important reviser and compiler of the Wakefield cycle, it is necessary to remember the nature of authorship in the Middle Ages. I shall argue that the Wakefield Master was, in fact, the author of the Wakefield cycle. For reasons not entirely clear to me, revisers and redactors have persistently been spoken of in the development of the vernacular religious drama, but never authors. This may be the result of the fact that we know none of the playwrights by name. Yet in all respects they were authors, writers, playwrights, or whatever designation properly gives them credit for their creative and, in medieval terms, original work. No one would suggest that Chaucer was a reviser or a redactor because he took works by Boccaccio, Petrarch, Jacobus de Varagine, Dante, Machaut, Froissart, and countless other sources and revised and adapted them to his own purposes. In fact, his literary performance depended on his wide frame of reference in the world of letters, and in *The Canterbury Tales* he undertook as a major purpose to test what he had garnered from books against the experience of "modern" life in the late fourteenth

---

Craig, who went so far as to devote a chapter to what he called the "York-Wakefield" plays; see *English Religious Drama of the Middle Ages* (Oxford: Clarendon Press, 1955), chap. 6. Lyle, a student of Craig, wrote her dissertation largely to refute theories that accounted for the York-Wakefield similarities, e.g. the notion that they stemmed from a common liturgical source; see Frank Cady, "The Liturgical Basis of the Towneley Plays," *PMLA* 24 (1909): 416–463. But there is no evidence that there ever was what Lyle called "a parent cycle," and whatever external evidence there is rules that hypothesis out altogether. Nevertheless, Lyle did some creditable analytical work in showing the close correspondences in the two cycles, and her study is still very much worth referring to in that context; see *The Original Identity of the York and Towneley Plays* (Minneapolis: University of Minnesota Press, 1919).

century. Robert B. Burlin has written about this Chaucerian process:

> Authoritatively, he may cite a proverb or scriptural text, or he may reproduce an entire book—in translation (*Melibeus*), adaptation (*Troilus*), or in summary abstract (the *Somnium* in the *Parliament of Fowls*). But the material comes from the written page and usually from the remote past; it constitutes a vicarious acquaintance with another man's conscious reshaping of his own apprehension of reality, as, for example, when Chanticleer's men of "auctoritee" are defined as transmitters of what they "han wel founden by experience" . . . All of Chaucer's major works depend structurally on this opposition: of what the speaker has read against what he experiences in a dream; of the old books that he scrupulously follows against the experience of the narrator in reproducing them.[34]

In *The Canterbury Tales*, for example, Chaucer directly tests the *auctoritee* of the romance of antiquity by translating and adapting Boccaccio's *Teseide* as a vehicle for the Knight's storytelling performance against the *experience* of common folk who lived in contemporary Oxford (contrived as that wonderful story may be). The point is that he allows romance to be read in the framework of contemporary fabliau. I suggest that the Wakefield author does much the same type of thing. He, too, adapts and reshapes his sources—be they the York plays, or *The Northern Passion* from which in large part the York plays derived their Passion narrative, or even ultimately the Old and New Testaments. He was as much an author as Chaucer or Shakespeare or Dryden or Anouilh in reshaping a literary text into the sphere of his own experience and consciousness. The Wakefield Master is not a mere redactor, he is a playwright-poet of extraordinary genius.

How then did he reshape his auctoritee to his experience?

---

[34] Robert B. Burlin, *Chaucerian Fiction* (Princeton: Princeton University Press, 1977), p. 6.

He made a city play into one that fits the setting and the nuances of the manor. It must be remembered that Wakefield was not York, and what the Wakefield Master did was to make his cycle indigenous to his setting and responsive to his image of the people who inhabited that setting. Economically, Wakefield was a manorial seat and the chief town in the riding during the time that the plays were collected and performed. But even as a commercial hub it was always under seigneurial control, and its government in no way resembled the trade oligarchy of York with its mayor, aldermen, and common council. The manor court, whose rolls are still intact, was the chief juridical body, presided over by the steward and empowered to hear every kind of civil and criminal case that touched upon the manor.

> No detail of agricultural life was too insignificant to come before the court and be presented to the jurors, such as the keeping of unringed swine, their escape into the lord's woods or into other men's fields, or into the streets of the town, the neglect to scour ditches, or breaches of the pinfold laws.[35]

True, the town also had a burgess court, but that was a body restricted to suits brought by freemen. Wakefield was very much a county seat, run by landed gentry. W. G. Rimmer sums up the differences with York as follows:

> The town did not trail behind York and Beverley on the same path; it took a different course. Whereas the production and marketing of cloth took place mainly *within* York, the spinners and weavers of the Calder lived in rural hamlets and homesteads. Indeed, the argument that steep tolls repelled traders from Wakefield, thereby sending them to nearby small free-trade towns, is bereft of meaning *unless* most of the cloth sold at Wakefield was made in outlying villages.[36]

[35] Walker, *Wakefield History*, p. 77.
[36] Rimmer, Evolution of Leeds," p. 278.

While Rimmer argues that the tolls were not the cause of Wakefield's commercial downfall in the late sixteenth and early seventeenth centuries, there is no doubt that the lord of the manor set burdensome market tolls that impoverished trade by driving away foreigners and merchants from other parts of Yorkshire. All this helps to set the stage for the Wakefield plays.

The Wakefield author was not particularly interested in the commerce of the region, but he did make his cycle a mirror of the mean-spiritedness of both lords and vassals. If any tone dominates in the cycle, and especially in the plays that have traditionally been ascribed to the Wakefield Master, it is one of discordance, of the poor crying out about injustices, of farmers bewailing their poverty, of courts tyranizing one and all. Life, as the Wakefield author sees it, is miserable and mean in Yorkshire. If any place needs the return of Jesus, it is that bereft countryside and its churlish, crabbed, lying, and thieving inhabitants. He is as hard on lords (especially in their roles as rulers and judges) as he is on vassals, male and female. The evil Pilate is indigenous to this landscape. While, of course, the playwright is not oblivious to goodness in his "natural men" (the strength of Noah, the generosity of the Shepherds, the compassion of Joseph), mostly that quality is obscured until the force of God directly invigorates it (the Shepherds, Joseph, Noah's wife are basically distrustful people at the start). The vision is not exactly Bosch-like—it is not quite grotesque enough for that—but the distortions that the Wakefield author sees are not unrelated in mood and tone to what Bosch sees in the quasi-human figures that are so prominent in his world view.

I have shown that the York Entry into Jerusalem is central to the cycle's self-perception as city drama. If a single play can equally capture the perspective of the Wakefield cycle, it is probably the *Mactacio Abel*. It is in this play, after the more or less traditional opening of the now fragmentary Creation play that establishes the "authority" of the Biblical vision, that the Wakefield playwright sets his stage as dictated by his perception of the Wakefield "experience." If as audience we are to

127

perceive the real meaning of the coming of Christ, then we can do no better, in the playwright's view, than to visualize it and understand it in the midst of that stark manorial setting. We are in the field. A loud, cantankerous, foul-mouthed servant, the Garcio named Pikeharnes (the name means thief), comes forward preparing for the entrance of his master, a "good" yeoman but ominously one to avoid engaging in dispute. Yet the audience need not be told all this for, as Garcio says, "Som of you ar his men" (10/20). This broad burlesque entrance of the truly powerful—the conventional swaggering tyrant who comes in with a rant clearing a path for himself—does two things: It establishes that servants are in tone interchangeable with their masters, and it identifies at least a part of the audience with the brotherhood of Cain. The play, as Helterman has pointed out, focuses from the first "on the criminal rather than the victim."[37] It gives us from the start a "field of blood" on which the Crucifixion is the ultimate painful, though necessary, salvific event. Because life is so brutal and mean, the event of the Resurrection will be that much more glorious and inspiring.

I am, of course, suggesting that the *Mactatio Abel* must be read as a typological forecast, a kind of map for the full dramatic action to unfold before us. While I will save for the next chapter a more systematic analysis of the function of typology as a dramatic form, we do need that important perspective as a way of understanding the Wakefield author's blueprint for the cycle. The play, after all, is called the *Mactacio Abel*, not as in York the *Sacrificium Cayme et Abell*. The emphasis is on murder. Abel is the quintessential good shepherd, who is, of course, both a figural and a social presence. He reminds Wakefielders of the importance of their agrarian and commercial economy, and he is, in his social role, a precursor of the other Shepherds of the Wakefield plays, with a foreboding of all the hardships that we hear recited in their litanies within the opening passages of the two Shepherds' plays. Yet the play also focuses on

[37] Helterman, *Symbolic Action*, p. 26.

another socioeconomic situation of moment in late-fifteenth-century Yorkshire: the festering rivalry between the tenant farmer and the sheep raiser.[38] The anger of Cain reflects a social dislocation: The plowman had become in many ways a symbol of agrarian poverty, and therefore the Wakefield Cain, when he vents his ire at Abel, is surely speaking with an economic resentment that his "men" in the audience shared:

> Go grese thi shepe vnder the toute,
> For that is the moste lefe.

Or,

> How that I tend, rek the neuer a deill,
> Bot tend thi skabbid shepe wele;
> For if thou to my teynd tent take,
> It bese the wars for thi sake.
> (Caw. 2/64–65; Caw. 7/247–250)

Cain tells Abel, If I prosper in my sacrifice, it is all the worse for you—and so it is in the fierce agricultural economy of Wakefield.

Not that Cain should be regarded as a sympathetic figure for his deprivation. To the contrary. He functions almost as an icon of the dispossessed man who fails to share his worldly goods and who lacks charity. He is the archetypal "bad" Plowman, the opposite figure to Langland's Piers or to the Parson's brother in *The Canterbury Tales*. He and his Garcio remind us of the two plowmen in the famous picture from the Luttrell Psalter (see figure 9), except that those two at least work together and Cain is not left to "both hold and drife"; Caw. 2/39).[39] The discord in Cain's world is everywhere; even the plow team is

---

[38] For a discussion of the influence of the cloth trade on the rural economy of England in the fifteenth century, see E. F. Jacob, *The Fifteenth Century: 1399–1485* (Oxford: Oxford University Press, 1961), pp. 367–370.

[39] The covered forehead in the picture is typically a feature in the representation of Cain. For an interesting discussion of the Luttrell illumination and the Wakefield *Mactacio Abel*, see W. O. Hassall, *The Holkham Bible Picture Book* (London: Dropmore Press, 1954), 66–67.

FIGURE 9. The Luttrell Psalter, f. 170 recto, Additional Ms. 42130.
(Courtesy the British Library)

disobedient. There is no charity there, and everything is reduced to its lowest and meanest significance, even to the point of Cain's search for a sheaf too small for God to "wipe his ars withall" (Caw. 7/238). That sort of scatological profanity occurs only in this play, but it defines for the audience just how much mankind as seen in its localized setting needs salvation.

The Wakefield author depicts mortal sin in the world of his own habitat, in "Gudeboure at the quarell hede" (Caw. 10/367) and later, Horbury and Watling Street, extending from the heart of town to the surrounding villages. His characters speak "Yorkshire"; they project an indigenous, homely proverbial wisdom, usually concerned with food and work: "ther is a podyng in the pot" (Caw. 11/386); "cold rost is at my masteres hame" (Caw. 12/422); "ill-spon weft ay comes foule out" (Caw. 12/436). This is no place for the outsider, the intruder who speaks with a "Sothren tothe"; it is a down-home drama that insistently asks the audience to bring Jesus into its midst.

IN the foregoing discussion, I have not made an effort to identify the canon of the Wakefield Master. Since he is not generally regarded as the compiler of the Towneley cycle, his work has traditionally been identified as that which is written in the peculiar nine-line Wakefield stanza. This means that six entire plays are attributed to him as well as parts of several others for which he clearly served as reviser. Scholars have rightly insisted that the Wakefield Master was "invented" to account for the re-markable stanzas that bear his signature; to find his work in other stanza forms is to stretch the evidence beyond objectivity. Arnold Williams puts the point as follows: "Either the Master wrote the well-known nine-line stanza, with easily recognizable variations, or he wrote a number of stanzaic forms. If the latter, then we had better abandon altogether the task of fixing his canon on the basis of stanzaic form, for qualities so incapable of objective measurement as tone, style, raciness, vividness, proverbiality can never afford adequate criteria for attribu-tion."[40] It is important, I think, to reexamine the Williams premise, first by inquiring into the form of the so-called nine-line stanza and then to see whether, in fact, "objective measure-ment" is possible in fixing the Wakefield Master's canon. At the very least one must establish what the core of his work is. Only when that is done, can one surmise further about his overall substantive contribution to the cycle.

The first point to note is that the Wakefield stanza, as we have it in all available editions, is an editorial interpretation. A quick glance at the scholarly editions of the Wakefield plays shows that all but one—the Surtees edition of 1836, which made no stanzaic divisions of any kind,[41]—print the stanza as a nine-line unit. We owe that nine-line stanza to the Early Eng-lish Text Society edition by George England and Alfred W. Pollard, published in 1897 and still the standard text for the entire Towneley cycle.[42] In that edition, the two halves of the first four long lines are separated by slanting strokes (but no other marks of punctuation) to highlight the internal or central rhyme. Later, the edition of *The Wakefield Pageants* by A. C. Cawley, now the standard text for the plays attributed to the Wakefield Master, omits the slanting strokes and adds standard punctuation where necessary, thus providing greater coher-ence but minimizing, in visual terms, the rhyme and the end-

[40] Williams, *Chracterization of Pilate*, p. 63.

[41] See Hunter, *Towneley Mysteries*, passim.

[42] A new edition, for the EETS, is now being prepared by A. C. Cawley and myself.

ings of the first half-lines in the *frons* of the stanza. Except for this minor deviation the Wakefield stanza has been uniformly edited as a nine-line unit.

Before taking a closer look at the edited stanza, I need to make some rather general observations about stanzaic poetry. I believe that all stanzas are primarily designed for the eye of the reader. While it is true that stanzas may add regularity to the aural structure of a long poem—surely the closing alexandrine of the Spenserian stanza works that way—it is equally true that good poets as a general rule do not allow themselves to be read aloud in a string of equal units, particularly when those units are measured out in invariable rhythms and end rhymes. Even in such a measurable unit as the rhyme royal stanza with its noticeable closure, Chaucer manages at times to enjamb his stanzas and thus to allow the ear to hear continuities that the visual format of the stanza inherently denies. The same can be said of much of Shakespeare's dramatic poetry. Without the text in front of us we would, I am sure, have trouble recognizing that Romeo and Juliet meet within a sonnet. And we would have that problem even if the actors chose to punctuate the quatrains and closing couplet emphatically with appropriate variations in intonation and juncture. So also with the stanzas of the Wakefield cycle. I defy anyone to "hear" the nine-line stanza of the Wakefield Master when his plays are performed by professional actors. All this is to say that the format of the stanza is a literary concern. In the case of the Wakefield Master, the modern-day editor has had a choice in how to print that stanza, and he chose (perhaps at the insistence of his publisher because of the need to save space), for better or for worse, the nine-line design that may well have influenced certain aesthetic responses and inaccurate perceptions as a direct result of the visual impact that it has had.

What are the characteristics of this editorial stanza? Perhaps the best way to answer that question is to look at a reasonably typical example of it. The following, from the *Processus Noe*, qualifies as such:

Noe. Behold to the heuen! The cateractes all,
Thai ar open full euen, grete and small,
And the planettys seuen left has thare stall.
Thise thoners and levyn downe gar fall
Full stout
Both halles and bowers,
Castels and towres.
Full sharp ar thise showers
That renys aboute.

(Caw. 23/343–351)

The rhyme scheme of this stanza, first described by Alfred W.
Pollard in the introduction of the EETS edition, is generally
represented as $\frac{aaaa}{bbbb}$cdddc.[43] The a-rhyme in this schema is, of
course, the internal or central one in the first four lines (*heuen,*
euen, seuen, levyn), a rhyme that is somewhat obscured in the
run-on line of the Cawley edition. The b-rhyme serves as end
rhyme for the first four lines, which critics conventionally call
the *frons.* The c-rhyme is introduced in a one-stress (or, more
rarely, a two-stress) "bob," a type of line that also occurs in *Sir
Gawain and the Green Knight,* in numerous minstrel romances,
carols, other dramatic stanzas of the Towneley, York, and N-
Town cycles, and, of course, in Chaucer's *Sir Thopas.*[44] The
bob-line, in turn, rhymes with the last line of the stanza, sometimes inaccurately referred to as the "tag." The d-rhyme is composed of the middle three lines in the *cauda* section, a structural
term that refers to the five supposed "short" lines with which
the stanza ends. In actual fact, the *cauda* lines, with the exception of the bob, usually consist of two stresses with a variable
number of unstressed syllables, the same length as the half-

[43] See England and Pollard, *Towneley Plays,* p. xxii. The stanza has also been
described by among others, Charles Davidson, "Studies in the English Mystery
Plays," *Transactions of the Connecticut Academy of Arts and Sciences* 9 (1892): 125–
297; Cady, "Wakefield Group," pp. 244–262; Oscar Cargill, "The Authorship
of the Secunda Pastorum," *PMLA* 41 (1926): 810–831; Carey, *Wakefield Group,*
pp. 217–230; and Cawley, *Wakefield Pageants* pp. 127–129.

[44] For a table of some forty poems, see E. G. Stanley, "The Use of Bob-Lines
in *Sir Thopas,*" *Neuphilologische Mitteilungen* 73 (1972): 422–425.

lines of the *frons*. Thus, whether the stanza consists of "long" and "short" lines depends on our interpretation of the *frons*. If we see the *frons* as modern editors have, we have a pattern of four "long" lines each consisting of four stresses. In the usual edited version, the *cauda*, with its short lines, stands in notable contrast to the *frons* and indeed serves visually as a kind of tail.

Seen critically, this stanza is said to be an effective "dramatic medium"[45] because it allows for exposition in the opening "discursive section" and rapid dialogue or epigrammatic conclusions (the latter conceived as not unlike those of the Petrarchan sonnet) in the *cauda*, or tail section. As one critic, E. Catherine Dunn, puts it, commenting specifically on the "hayll"-stanzas in the *Secunda Pastorum*, "the division of the stanza occurs in such a way that a 'grand' style appears in the first four or five lines and colloquial speech in the final four."[46] I believe that this widely accepted view of the Wakefield stanza as a unique vehicle for dramatic representation is conditioned almost entirely by the shape that editors have given that stanza, and it has, finally, very little basis in reality. To clarify this point we need to take a close look at stanzaic forms in the Towneley manuscript.

The Wakefield stanza appears in three distinct formats within the Towneley manuscript. Of these, two record the *frons* in run-on lines, similar to the form reproduced in modern editions, but the stanzas differ in their treatment of the *cauda*. Another presents the *frons* in eight lines. The writing of the *frons* in four run-on lines is by far the preferred form of the scribe; in fact, it occurs in all but three Wakefield stanzas within the manuscript. Let us look at the three models separately.

Format A: This format is well illustrated by the second stanza of the *Prima Pastorum* at the top of folio 33a (see figure 10). The following is a diplomatic transcription:

> Thus this warld as I say: farys on ylk syde
> For after oure play: com sorows vnryde

[45] Carey, *Wakefield Group*, p. 502.

[46] E. Catherine Dunn, "The Literary Style of the Towneley Plays," *American Benedictine Review* 20 (1969): 502.

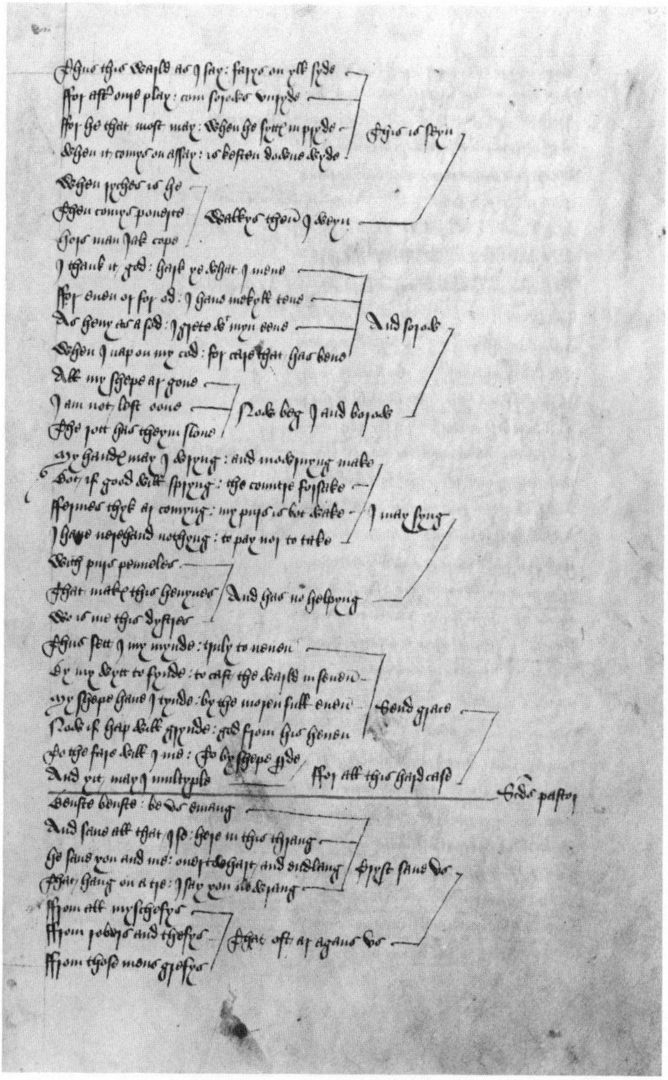

FIGURE 10. The Wakefield Plays, f. 33 recto, Huntington Library
HM 1. (Courtesy the Henry E. Huntington Library and Art Gallery)

> For he that most may: when he syttys in pryde
>   This is seyn
> When it comys on assay: is kesten downe wyde
> When ryches is he
> Then comys pouerte   Walkys then I weyn
> Hors-man Iak Cope
>
>   (Cf. Caw. 29/10–18)

The *frons* is written in four run-on lines with internal rhyme. To separate the half-lines, the scribe inserts a metrical mark in the form of a colon (:), an obelus (÷), or a colon followed by a slanting stroke (:/). The first four lines are grouped together by a rhyme marker that consists of a vertical line to the right of the *frons* and four parallel connecting lines that extend to the rhyme words. The bob appears to the right of the vertical line of the rhyme marker and is roughly on a level with the third long verse of the *frons*. The *cauda* in Format A is written in three separate lines directly after the *frons* and grouped together by another rhyme marker similar to the one of the *frons*. The last line appears to the right of the rhyme marker in the right-hand margin.

Format B: The diplomatic transcription of the following stanza from the *Magnus Herodes*, folio 55a, illustrates this format (see figure 11):

> Herode the heynd kyng: by grace of Mahowne
> Of Iury sourmontyng: sternly with crowne
> On lyfe that ar lyfyng: in towre and in towne
>   At his bydyng
> Gracyus you gretyng: commaundys you be bowne
> Luf hym with lewte // drede hym that doughty
> He chargys you be redy // lowly at his lykyng
>
>   (Cf. Caw. 64/10–18)

The *frons* and the bob in this model are rendered in exactly the same way as in Format A. The *cauda*, however, is written in run-on lines, more or less as follows: The first two verses of the *d*-rhyme are written on one line and separated by double slanting

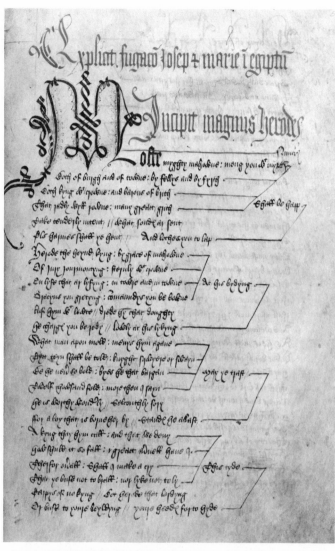

FIGURE 11. The Wakefield Plays, f. 55 recto, Huntington Library
HM 1. (Courtesy the Henry E. Huntington Library and Art Gallery)

strokes (//). The last *d*-rhyme and the last verse are run together and separated by double (//) or triple slanting strokes (///). The vertical rhyme marker of the bob extends to the end-rhyme of the last verse. We should note that Format B occurs much more frequently in all of the plays than Format A; in the *Processus Noe* alone it occurs in forty-five manuscript stanzas out of a total of sixty-two. Format A seems to be the preferred form when there are changes of speaker in the *cauda*, but that is by no means the sole reason for its use. I can find no systematic justification for the use of one pattern over the other.

Format C: The following stanza from the *Mactacio Abel*, folio 7a, again in diplomatic transcription, illustrates Format C (see figure 12):

Com downe yit in the dwillys way
And angre me no more
And take yond plogh I say
And weynd the furth fast before
And I shall if I may
Tech the another lore
I warn the lad for ay   That thou greue me noght
Fro now furth euermore
For bi codys sydys if thou do
I shall hang the apon this plo   By hym that me dere boght
With this rope lo lad lo

(Cf. Caw. 12–13/450–462)

As already noted, this format occurs very rarely in the manuscript, by my count a mere three times (once in the stanza from the *Mactacio Abel* and twice in the *Conspiracio*; see 223/600–612 and 224/626–638). In this pattern, the *frons* is written as eight lines with interlocking rhyme brackets, the *cauda* (not including the last line of the stanza) appears as three lines, and the bob and last line, connected by rhyme brackets, are written to the right, in the pattern of Format A.

As is evident from these scribal variants of the stanza, the editor must exercise choice in the format he wishes to adopt. To date, all editors have reproduced Format A, the one in which

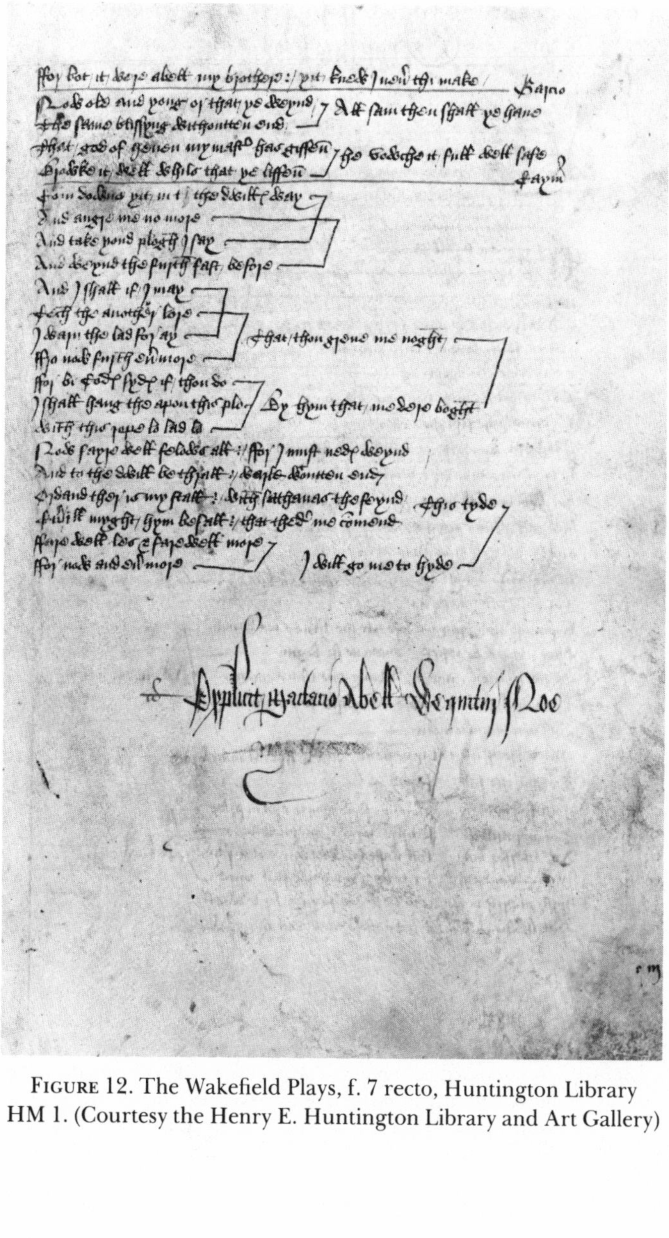

FIGURE 12. The Wakefield Plays, f. 7 recto, Huntington Library
HM 1. (Courtesy the Henry E. Huntington Library and Art Gallery)

the *frons* is compressed into four lines and the *cauda* appears in its long form. The editors have, of course, interpreted the bob as the fifth line and the last verse as the ninth line, though in the manuscript these lines appear to the right of the main stanza.[47]

The compression by modern editors of the *frons* into four lines with internal rhyme (a feature shared by Formats A and B) at first sight makes very good sense. The strongest support in the manuscript for this way of writing the stanza is the overwhelming frequency of its occurrence. It is, after all, the only format ever used for the *frons* in any of the five plays (2, 12, 13, 16, 21) written exclusively in the Wakefield stanza. Yet, this editorial decision prompts a number of questions that raise some doubt about its wisdom.

We must ask, to begin, whether there is any significance in the fact that the first Wakefield stanza in the entire manuscript appears in Format C, the long form rejected by all the editors. Interestingly, this first instance of the Wakefield stanza occurs just prior to the last stanza of the *Mactacio Abel*, which, in omitting one line from the *cauda*, is a variant of the typical Wakefield stanza. This latter stanza, from folio 7a, is written in the compressed format as follows (see figure 12):

Now fayre well felows all:/ for I must nedys weynd
And to the dwill be thrall:/ warld withoutten end
Ordand ther is my stall:/ with Sathanas the feynd   this tyde
Euer ill myght hym befall:/ that theder me commend
Fare well les and fare well more
For now and euer more   I will go me to hyde
(Cf. Caw. 13/463–470)[48]

---

[47] The placement of the bob-line and tail-rhymes to the right of the main verse is fairly common practice in Middle English manuscripts; see Stanley, "Use of Bob-Lines," p. 420.

[48] The two most authoritative editions of the *Mactacio Abel* (by the EETS and by A. C. Cawley) differ in their rendering of this stanza. EETS, no doubt on the influence of the long format of the preceding Wakefield stanza, writes it out in the long form as well. Cawley prints it with internal rhyme in the *frons*, thus following the manuscript.

This instance, despite the missing *cauda* line and the absence of rhyme markers for the *frons*, is the first in the manuscript of the typical representation of the Wakefield stanza. With a turn of the folio, we find the beginning of the Noah play in which the *frons* is written consistently in the compressed style of Formats A and B. The two closing stanzas of the *Mactacio Abel* may thus well stand as a result of experimentation in recording a particular verse form that the scribe knew to occur in his exemplar often thereafter.[49] I would venture the hypothesis that he rejected the long form because it took up too much space. After all, the Towneley manuscript is written on vellum, and we know that the scribe conserves space elsewhere, as in the recording of cross-rhyming octaves (a point to which I shall return momentarily) and the peculiar attempt to write the first full page of the *Annunciacio* (f. 28b) in two columns. The choice of the compressed form may have been suggested by his customary treatment of rime couée, in which the third and sixth lines were bracketed to the left of the main stanza as on folio la. Perhaps after pondering over the variations in the form of the last two stanzas of Play 2, the scribe chose to write the Wakefield Master's thereafter in the space-saving format with the compressed *frons*.

Another noteworthy point about the long format of the first Wakefield stanza is its establishment of what constitutes a full line in the *frons*. Modern interpretations have, with very few exceptions, projected the view that the full line of the *frons* consists of four stresses and internal rhyme, as we have seen. Indeed, the stanza is considered unique precisely for the length of the lines and the use of central rhymes in the *frons*. It is customarily spoken of as a nine-line stanza,[50] and nothing quite like it has been found anywhere in Middle English literature

[49] It is clear that the scribe copied from an exemplar. Note, for example, his crossing out of the line "Yit of thise kirkchaterars" prior to "David in his sawtere says thus" on folio 125a (see 376/292), anticipating its occurrence four lines later, at the beginning of the subsequent stanza. Such errors could only have resulted from copying a written text.

[50] See, for example, Cawley, *Wakefield Pageants*, p. 127.

because scholars have persisted in regarding the *frons* as containing four rather than eight self-standing lines. If we were to recognize the four-line *frons* as a scribal and editorial accommodation, we would be able to relate the Wakefield stanza to a good many other thirteeners, which, though they differ in the length of their lines, are the same in basic rhyme scheme (see the *Castle of Perseverance* stanza and the various thirteeners of the N-Town cycle).[51] The point that is indisputable in light of the initial instance of the Wakefield stanza in the manuscript is that the poet regarded the *a*-line of the *frons* not as a half-line but as a full verse, capable of standing alone. Thus, even if the scribe prefers to combine the *a*- and *b*-verses, by his logic and by the poet's, they were not construed as half-lines. It follows, therefore, that the Wakefield stanza is conceptually, if not scribally, a thirteener.

Another very important question to ask about the nine-line format has to do with the meaning of the symbols used as line separators (the colon, obelus, slanting strokes, etc.) in the Wakefield stanza. Are they meant to stand for a momentary pause or are they marks of convenience to signal the end of a line? The consistent use of those marks throughout the manuscript—especially the colon, which occurs by far most often in this function—is to separate two full lines that, for scribal reasons, are compressed into one. And this practice applies not just to the *frons* or *cauda* of the Wakefield stanza, but to all kinds of metrical forms including couplets, cross-rhyming quatrains and octaves, opening lines of tail-rhyme stanzas, and the Northern Septenar stanza. Unfortunately, the EETS edition is weakest precisely in its treatment of stanza forms, and probably for this reason the full significance of the line separation marks has been obscured to modern readers. Take, for example, the cross-rhyming quatrain or octave, a form that has particular relevance to the Wakefield stanza because that is the pattern of its *frons*. The first play written entirely in cross-rhyming octaves is the *Abraham*. Folio 14a (see figure 7) gives an excel-

---

[51] For a discussion of the latter, see Stephen Spector's unpublished Yale dissertation, "The Genesis of the N-Town Cycle," 1973.

lent illustration of the scribe's experimentation in recording this stanza. The folio begins with the first line (see 43/93) of the second quatrain of an octave here recorded in four separate lines (the first quatrain is compressed into two lines on the bottom of the preceding folio, 13b). The second four lines on 14a are the beginning of a new octave (43/97–104). But while, in this stanza, the first quatrain is written out in its long form, the second is compressed. The scribe on this page, and the preceding, is experimenting for the first (and last) time in the manuscript with the use of internal rhyme brackets as line separators. He persists in this practice until he is half-way down folio 14a. Thereafter, he uses the colon and slanting stroke, the double slanting stroke, and the colon combined with the double slanting stroke internally to separate the *a*- and *b*-lines in the compressed octave, similar to the treatment of the *frons* of the Wakefield stanza. What we see on this manuscript page, therefore, is a clear instance of the scribe's experimentation in rendering the cross-rhyming octave and seeking what appears to be the most economic format. He seems to use the long form only when speeches begin within a line or with a *b*-line, probably because the speaker identification would otherwise have to be wedged into the middle of a line. For our purpose, the significance of this folio is its variety of scribal forms for what is clearly one stanza: the eight-line cross-rhyming octave that is transcribed throughout the pageant by England and Pollard in its long form. One is led to ask on the basis of the practice here, Why is the same stanzaic unit compressed into four lines in the Wakefield *frons*? The EETS edition is obviously inconsistent in its interpretation of the line separators used throughout the manuscript.

The inconsistency becomes more prominent as we progress through the manuscript. Except for the compressed format in the Wakefield *frons*, the editors of the EETS edition always disregard the line separators and print couplets, quatrains, and octaves in their long forms up to Play 18.[52] Thereafter, their

---

[52] I disregard here their confusion in treating the Northern Septenar stanza, borrowed from the York cycle, in Play 8. In this instance they usually print an

practice becomes increasingly erratic. In Play 18, they depart twice from the long format and unaccountably print two quatrains in compressed form with internal rhyme (see 188/57–58, 67–68). They also include a footnote that acknowledges for the first time the manuscript practice of writing two lines as one with central rhyme, a point they had regularly disregarded heretofore (see p. 193, n. 1). Thereafter, especially in Plays 22 through 30, they resort indifferently to the long and to the compressed format, sometimes following the manuscript variations exactly (see 267/309–312 on f. 87b and 269/361–364 on f. 88a) and sometimes not (see their treatment of f. 98a, 294–296/49–102).[53] While the editorial practice of recording cross-rhyming quatrains thus becomes totally bizarre in the England-Pollard edition, we do have a clue as to its origin. It so happens that exactly the same bizarre pattern occurs in the Surtees edition published in 1836. It is clear that beginning with Play 18 the EETS editors used the Surtees edition as their copy text.[54] Whatever their reason for doing this, we have ample justification for questioning the metrical forms throughout their edition—and that questioning must include their rendering of the Wakefield stanza, which, after all, in its nine-line form originated in modern print with this edition.

One last question to be asked about the so-called internal rhyme and long line of the Wakefield *frons* concerns the editorial treatment of the *cauda*. If it is proper to follow the manuscript by printing the *frons* as run-on long lines, what justification is there for printing the *cauda* consistently and invariably

---

octave preceding a cross-rhyming quatrain, and each is numbered separately as a stanza. Actually, of course, the octave and quatrain belong together as a twelve-line stanza, a format correctly rendered in the L. T. Smith edition of the *York Plays* (1885; reprint ed., New York: Russell and Russell, 1963).

[53] There are two more footnotes in the EETS edition, on pages 296 and 339, which suddenly intrude to describe the MS practice of compressing two lines into one and to indicate that the slanting stroke used by the editors as line separators do not appear in the MS.

[54] For further discussion of this point, see my article on "The Manuscript of the Towneley Plays: Its History and Editions," *Publications of the Bibliographic Society of America* 67 (1973): 243–244.

as separate and independent lines? If editorial logic tells us that the line separators in the *frons* of the stanza serve to indicate that a line is run-on, what logic accounts for the opposite interpretation of these marks, when they are used in the *cauda*? No editor had ever rendered the Wakefield *cauda* as run-on, even though, as I have already shown, by far the more prevalent practice in the manuscript is to write the *cauda* in that form. In light of this inconsistency, we have further justification for regarding the nine-line Wakefield stanza as the result of arbitrary scribal or editorial choice and not as an organic structure chosen for its formal design by the poet.

IT is now time to look at the Wakefield stanza as a thirteener, a possibility that has been advanced by others before me. For example, A. C. Cawley, who chose the nine-line stanza for his edition of the Wakefield plays, nevertheless observes that "it is possible to regard the Wakefield stanza as one of thirteen verses rhyming *a b a b a b a b c d d d c*" on the model of its first appearance in the *Mactacio Abel*.[55] Charles Mills Gayley, long before Cawley, goes so far as to print an example of the Master's stanza in thirteen lines, calling it a modification of the York *Mortificacio and Conspiracio* stanzas, but he soon reclaims the nine-line stanza because it has been so "preserved in manuscript and print."[56] To my knowledge, only one other scholar, E. K. Chambers in *English Literature at the Close of the Middle Ages*, has identified the Wakefield Master's stanza as a thirteener. Interestingly he takes the point for granted, never troubling to explain his departure from received opinion. Quoting stanzas in their thirteen-line format, he describes the metrical features of the Wakefield Master's work as follows:

His contribution consists in the main of five plays, all written in a characteristic metre of his own. This too has a

[55] Cawley, *Wakefield Pageants*, p. 127.

[56] Charles Mills Gayley, *Plays of Our Forefathers and Some of the Traditions upon Which They Were Founded* (1907; reprint ed., New York: Biblo and Tannen, 1968), p. 163 and passim.

"bob" in it. Its technical description is $ababab ab_2 c_1 dddc_2$. The two-stressed lines give it an exceptional rapidity of movement. There is a good deal of alliteration, but this does not fall with such regularity on the stressed syllables as to constitute an alliterative metre, comparable to that of the York realist. The rhythm, however, is markedly ana-paestic, and may even be called *plus-quam* anapaestic, since a stressed syllable often carries with it more than two un-stressed ones.[57]

Chambers's description provides an excellent start for a new consideration of how the thirteen-line stanza functions as a metrical and literary unit.

First, because I believe that the stanza is a visual form (essen-tially addressed to a reader, not a hearer), we need to have a graphic image of it as a thirteener. What follows are two stan-zas, the first a single speech, the second an example of frequent and quick interchange among three speakers (eight speeches to a stanza is, by my count, the most dialogue occurring in any single Wakefield stanza):

> NOE. Myghtfull God veray,
> Maker of all that is,
> Thre persons withoutten nay,
> Oone God in endles blis,
> Thou maide both nyght and day,
> Beest, fowle, and fysh;
> All creatures that lif may
> Wroght thou at thi wish,
> As thou wel myght.
> The son, the moyne, verament,
> Thou maide; the firmament;
> The sternes also full feruent,
> To shyne thou maide ful bright.
>   (Cf. Caw. 14/1–9)

---

[57] Chambers, *English Literature*, p. 37.

1 Pastor.	Breke outt youre voce!
	Let se as ye yelp!
3 Pastor.	I may not for the pose,
	Bot I haue help.
2 Pastor.	A, thy hart is in thy hose!
1 Pastor.	Now, in payn of a skelp,
	This sang thou not lose!
3 Pastor.	Thou art an yll qwelp
	For angre!
2 Pastor.	Go to now—begyn!
1 Pastor.	He lyst not well ryn.
3 Pastor.	God lett vs neuer blyn;
	Take at my sangre.
	(Cf. Caw. 40/422–430)

In both of these examples, we can see immediately that there is very little difference in scansion or narrative function between the *frons* and *cauda*. The first example is no more discursive in the eight lines preceding the bob than it is in the four lines following it. The second example is as full of rapid-fire exchange in what is conventionally called the *frons* as in the *cauda*. And these are not isolated examples. The Wakefield playwright, in my reading of him, simply makes no systematic distinctions in his use of what have been considered the two major parts of his stanza. The remarkable point about this stanza in its long form is that all lines but one, the fifth—which is a one- or two-foot bob—are of equal length. It is true that especially in some of the later plays in the cycle, the Wakefield playwright is capable of writing longer lines (particularly by adding unstressed syllables). But that does not in any way alter the fact that the basic unit of his stanza is a two-stress, relatively short line, which is exactly the same in its metrical dimensions whether it appears in the *frons* or the *cauda*. The only variable part of the stanza is the bob, and this device, which originated in the minstrel romances, is one that the Wakefield Master handles with remarkable skill, especially in its rhythmic potential, by allowing it to enjamb with what precedes or follows. Indeed, enjambment is

147

TABLE 1
Changes of Speaker in the Five Plays of the Wakefield Master

Line #	N	PP	SP	MH	Col	Total # Speakers	% Speake
1a (1)	28	35	48	16	34	161	24.2
1b (2)	—	1	—	—	5	6	1.0
2a (3)	14	16	26	10	11	77	11.5
2b (4)	3	9	4	1	6	23	3.4
3a (5)	17	16	27	11	21	92	13.9
3b (6)	2	5	4	2	7	20	3.0
4a (7)	9	7	21	11	17	65	9.8
4b (8)	6	5	4	1	9	25	3.8
5 (9)	1	8	14	4	3	30	4.5
6 (10)	8	5	16	4	12	43	6.5
7 (11)	4	8	16	2	13	45	6.8
8 (12)	14	13	19	11	13	70	10.6
9 (13)	—	—	2	2	3	7	1.0
Total # Speakers	106	128	201	75	154	664	
Total # Lines	558	502	754	513	450	2,777	
	(806)	(724)	(1,088)	(741)	(650)	(4,009)	
% Speaker	19%	25.5%	26.7%	14.6%	34.2%	23.9%	
to Lines	(13%)	(17.7%)	(18.5%)	(10.1%)	(23.7%)	(16.6%)	

one of the more important devices by which the Wakefield Master provides variety in a stanza that otherwise could easily lead to jog-trot monotony.

Since in a play, dialogue is an essential ingredient, and since, moreover, dialogue—that is, change of speakers—provides one of the significant demarcations for rhythmic units, it may be of some interest to examine the frequency with which speeches begin at various points in the Wakefield stanza. Table 1 summarizes this information for the five plays written entirely in the Master's stanza. The numbering in the left-hand column is that of the nine-line format, with the thirteen-line numbering following in parentheses.

A closer look at this table will clear away a good many misconceptions about the dramatic and metrical qualities of the Wakefield stanza. First, it shows that the part of the stanza called the *frons* is, in fact, the unit used most consistently and most frequently for dialogue. Altogether, 70.6 percent of all speaker changes occur in the *frons* section of the stanza (or, in the first eight lines of the thirteen-line model). The one- or two-stress bob, moreover, is very rarely used for a short response—in the whole corpus of the five plays, the bob is a self-contained speech a mere six times. It begins speeches a total of only thirty times, and when it does, it is most frequently the first line of a speech that comprises the whole of the tail-rhyme section. The last line is likewise used rarely to begin a speech; it occurs only seven times in this function out of a total of 664 speeches. Hence neither the bob nor the "tag" serves a special dramatic purpose in enhancing the playwright's use of rapid, short dialogue. Nor are the traditional *b*-lines of the *frons* used for that purpose. Only 11.2 percent of all changes of speaker occur in the *b*-lines, and, indeed, the preferred places for changes of speaker are, in order, the 1*a*-line, the 3*a*-line, the 2*a*-line, and the eighth line in the conventional nine-line stanza (the first, fifth, third, and twelfth lines of the thirteen-line model). This is to say that the openings of cross-rhyming quatrains are preferred by the poet for openers of dialogue, and by far his favorite position is the opening of a stanza.

Yet, despite this preference for obvious places of juncture, the Wakefield playwright is a master in the use of enjambment, both within lines and across stanzas. What he does with consummate artistry is to mask the metrical unit within which he chooses to work and to invest his long, ungainly stanza, which has every opportunity of being a burden of rhythmic monotony, with such a variety of juncture and stress patterns that it easily takes on the character of natural speech. Consequently it is not the use of a brilliantly designed dramatic stanza, as is usually assumed, but ironically the breaking of stanzaic form into natural phrasing that contributes so importantly to his success as a playwright. The first line of his stanza, which of course would be used by a lesser craftsman often as a place to begin

149

speeches, serves well to illustrate my point.[58] While it is still the most frequent place for change of dialogue in the corpus of the five plays, over three-quarters of all his stanzas remarkably do not begin with new speeches. In fact, we can expect as a fairly natural pattern for stanzas to enjamb. Frequently, a speech in the Wakefield stanza will begin with the bob or one of the lines in the *cauda* and carry over into the *frons* of the next stanza. Thus stanza endings are by no means marked out as special boundaries. Very few stanzas, relatively speaking, serve as units of dialogue wherein the beginning and endings of stanza and speech coincide. I count only twenty-five such instances in the five plays, and of these, fourteen occur in situations where a regular alternation of speakers is dramatically and aesthetically justified for reasons of balance, as in the appearance of the Angel and the responses, in turn, by each of the Shepherds in the *Prima Pastorum* (Caw. 37–38/296–332).[59] Moreover, long speeches (those which extend beyond the boundaries of the single stanza) often either begin or end in the middle of a stanza (I count twenty-one such speeches out of a total of twenty-nine).

It is noteworthy that the Wakefield author wrote a good many long speeches (in the sense just defined). He is, of course, a master of dialogue, and yet nearly one-third of all his lines in the five plays are monologues. Clearly long speeches can be quite as dramatic as rapid dialogue, and certainly some plays with dominant characters like Noah and Herod demand more monologues. The *Magnus Herodes* has, in fact, the fewest changes of speakers (75 speeches as compared with 201 in the *Secunda Pastorum*), but that in itself does not make it less effec-

[58] The rime couée plays in the Wakefield cycle provide a good counterexample. A declamational and processional play like the *Processus Prophetarum* has no dialogue at all, and every one of the four long speeches begins at the beginning of stanzas. The *Purificacio Marie*, which likewise is written entirely in rime couée, begins all speeches at the head of stanzas. Even in a lively rime couée play, like the *Oblacio Magorum*, more than half the stanzas (56 out of 105) begin speeches.

[59] The other instances of one-stanza speeches in alternation occur as follows: Caw. 41–42/458–493; 61/674–691; and 62–63/710–745.

tive dramatically. This point needs to be mentioned because several critics have noted an improvement in the Wakefield author's dramatic effectiveness as he progresses toward the end.[60] Such effectiveness is usually characterized by the number and the nature of the breaks in dialogue that occur in individual plays. Obviously a play with long speeches will have fewer such breaks, but that is hardly a measure of its effectiveness. In the case of the Herod play, moreover, the criterion of "improvement" collapses altogether, since it clearly has far less dialogue than its predecessors and yet is one of the later plays in the manuscript. A. C. Cawley points out, as an example of the Master's greater dramatic power in the *Secunda Pastorum* than the *Processus Noe*, that a change of speaker breaks the line less often in the latter than in either of the Shepherds' plays. By his definition, these breaks occur at the beginning of *b*-verses in the conventionally conceived *frons* of a nine-line stanza.[61] Table 1 shows that while the *Processus Noe* makes such breaks only eleven times, the *Prima Pastorum* makes them twenty times to twelve in the *Secunda Pastorum*, four in the *Magnus Herodes*, and twenty-seven in the *Coliphizacio*. Thus, while I call into question the whole notion that the Master's technique improved as he provided more unconventional breaks, the facts do not support the view that he provides more such breaks as he proceeds from the earlier to the later plays in the cycle.

Is the Wakefield stanza a distinctive, even unique, form that lends a special dramatic quality to the work of its author? If I am right that this stanza is, in fact, a two-stress thirteener with a one- or two-stress bob, the answer would have to be a cautious no. While there are few, if any, stanzas in Middle English literature that are exactly the same as that of the Wakefield thir-

[60] See Carey, *Wakefield Group*, p. 228.

[61] When Cawley speaks of the breaking of lines, he cites at first as examples the beginning of speeches in the *b*-lines of the *frons*. He also refers to the division of lines at unnatural points, as the breaking of a *c*-verse into two parts. This type of division does occur with greater frequency in later plays, but the beginning of speeches with *b*-lines shows no such progression. For Cawley's discussion, see *Wakefield Pageants*, p. 128.

teener, there are a good many that are quite similar. Some with the same rhyme scheme conventionally have longer lines, as for example the stanzas of *The Castle of Perseverance* and the Proclamation stanzas of the N-Town cycle. Others have similar short lines but a slightly different rhyme scheme, such as the metrical romance verse of *Sir Tristrem* in the Auchinleck Manuscript or the thirteen-line stanza of Towneley Play 15, the *Fugacio Iosep et Marie in Egiptum*. Certainly the stanza of the York *Mortificacio*, and perhaps the *Conspiracio*, as Gayley has pointed out, could have influenced the form of the Wakefield stanza. The point is that there are many forms of the thirteener, many models of two-stress lines, and many stanzas with bob-lines in Middle English. The Wakefield stanza does not especially stand out when it is seen as a thirteener. In contrast, there is not another stanza similar to the nine-line version by which we have come to know it in its modern editions.

If there is structurally any metrical distinction in the Wakefield stanza, I think that it is in the use of the bob. Without the long *frons*, as represented in the nine-line model, we come to recognize that the one significant formal variation within the stanza is in the ninth or bob-line. Of course, as we have seen, the bob is not by any means unique to the Wakefield poet. Chaucer satirized its uninspired use for all time in *Sir Thopas*. The Wakefield Master shows how a first-rate poet can convert this conventional minstrel device into highly varied and functional dialogue. In the hands of the Master, the one-stress line is put to a wide variety of uses. Let us look at some of them from the *Coliphizacio*, a play marked by an abundance of dialogue and therefore potentially a rich store for good functional use of one-foot lines. Here as elsewhere, the bob most often does not stand in isolation as a tag (see Chaucer's use of it in *Sir Thopas*—"in towne"; 7.793). It can be a self-standing asseveration (Caw. 78/14); it can stand medially to modify the same verb that both precedes and follows (Caw. 80/77); it can emphasize by exclamation (Caw. 81/140, 85/257) and by characterizing its own measure as "At onys" (Caw. 90/437); it can end a sentence with adverbial modifiers (Caw. 78/5, 23; 79/41) or the main verb (Caw. 78/32) or postpositional adjectives (Caw. 79/50). It can, of course, be a full exclamatory sentence (Caw. 81/131) or part of a running dialogue (Caw. 83/185; 85/257). And it can give crucial words, as when the First Torturer wants a joint decision from the bickering Annas and Caiaphas and asks for a response "togeder" (Caw. 81/113), or when Annas predicts the demise of Jesus, "to dam" (Caw. 84/248). A study of the Master's technique in his use of the bob would no doubt establish his versatility in adapting a traditional device to his poetic and dramatic needs.

But it is important not to place too much emphasis on ascribing the unique artistry and originality of the Wakefield Master to the metrical form he devised. Arnold Williams is no doubt right in seeking some initial objective criterion by which to isolate the contributions of the Wakefield Master, and, therefore, I continue to hold with Williams that the starting point for any consideration of his canon must be the distinctive stanza, whether written in nine or thirteen lines. But I no longer share the view that we must use only this one "objective" criterion by which to identify his work.[62] Surely a great poet is capable of writing many different lines and verse forms; Chaucer was as much at ease with the octosyllabic couplet as with the decasyllabic (or hendecasyllabic) couplet as with the ballade or rhyme royal. There is no reason to think that the writer of the two-stress thirteen-line stanza I have been examining was incapable of writing other kinds of lines or stanzas. If such other stanzas display his characteristic humor, style, tone, rhythm, diction, and thematic preoccupations, I think we are being too cautious and too narrow in our critical method in not ascribing those

[62] In reviewing A. C. Cawley's excellent edition of *The Wakefield Pageants in the Towneley Cycle* some years ago, I made a point quite similar to Arnold Williams's, criticizing the edition for its method of choosing the "Wakefield Pageants." I emphasized the point that the *Mactacio Abel* could not really be attributed to the Wakefield Master because it contains only one Wakefield stanza. While I still have some difficulty isolating the "Wakefield Pageants" in the cycle, I now consider my earlier objection based on metrical considerations dubious. See my review in *Speculum* 34 (1959): 454–455.

stanzas to him as well. The insistence on totally objective criteria, like the invariable stanza format on which Williams fixes his attention, may blind us at minimum to the fact that even within the fixed canon of the Wakefield Master we can find metrical aberrations. Take, for example, those stanzas which contain only one quatrain in the *frons* (see Caw. 32/127–133; 50/262–268), or stanzas that vary from the norm in rhyme scheme (e.g. *a b a b a b a b c a a a c*, Caw. 71/280–288; or *a b a b c b c b d e e e d*, Caw. 79/55–63), or lines that contain more than two stresses (see Caw. 68/145–153, 70/226–229, 74/373, 379). Must we not agree that he wrote these lines? And if we do, why can we not agree with equal assurance that he wrote the long thirteeners at the opening of the *Flagellacio*, stanzas that share the "tone and style" of the Master's work and that are in Williams's mind "the major contribution to the Towneley characterization of Pilate"?[63] If we look to see why they do not qualify formally as "Wakefield stanzas," it is because they are thirteeners with an unusually heavy *frons* containing four stresses and alliteration. Yet in diction, tone, rhythm, phrasal complexity, thematic orientation—even in rhyme scheme (*a b a b a b a b c d d d c*) and nearly verbatim repetition of previous lines (cf. 244/23–26 about *endytars, quest-gangars, Iurars, and out-rydars* with the phrasing in the *cauda* of a true Wakefield stanza in the *Conspiracio*, 205/24–26)—they are unmistakably the work of the Master. Surely, the requirements of the tyrant's rant, which are fulfilled with an arsenal of special effects by the Master (including macaronic verse, complex images, and long catalogs of outrageous exaggerations), will permit the expansion of the first four lines with the gusto of their raging speaker.

And once we see the logic of assigning him thirteeners with longer *frons* lines, I see no reason, on equally subjective grounds, to feel uncomfortable in attributing to him stanzas with variations in rhyme scheme, as stanza 2 in the *Processus Crucis* (written out by England and Pollard as a thirteener and rhyming *a b a b c b c b d c c c d*), or stanza 57 in the same play

---

[63] Williams, *Characterization of Pilate*, pp. 62–63.

(written as a nine-liner by England and Pollard rhyming *a b a b c b c b d e e e d*). Nor would I hesitate to assign him the truncated last stanza of the *Processus Talentorum* or the section of fourteen-liners rhyming *a b a b a b a b c c c d c d* in the *Lazarus* (390–392/125–173) and countless other revision stanzas sharing the Master's stamp even if not his exact verse form.

Finally, and quite apart from versification altogether, I feel comfortable even in the absence of those clinching objective criteria in attributing to him the characterizations of Cain, Garcio, the Three Torturers in the *Processus Talentorum* (if not most of the other Torturers in the cycle), as well as the consistently evil Pilate identified by Williams. This is not to say that he wrote every line of dialogue spoken by these characters. He surely retained some earlier speeches in couplets, quatrains, and rime couée stanzas. But the persons who emerge from the plays are nevertheless his because as supreme reviser of the cycle he gave them their special dramatic vitality.

Any attribution like the foregoing must finally be made subjectively. We do not know who the Wakefield Master was. We invented him to account for the remarkable poetry that he wrote, usually in the same metrical form, in many parts of the Towneley cycle. When we see him as the author of a thirteen-line stanza rather than the unique nine-liner that is usually attributed to him, we come to recognize that his basic measure was similar to parts that hitherto we might have hesitated in assigning to him. We know him subjectively and sufficiently as the artist who brought a special voice to the Wakefield cycle. He was master of the Yorkshire dialect and gave it a distinct literary dimension. He created a wide assortment of worldly and errant characters with Bruegel-like aspect, and through them he was able to project everyday life into sacred history. He had, above all, a complicated mind and a poetical vocabulary, extending from the rustic to the learned, which gave him the power to write about contemporary life in complex ironic structures. He gave us a panoramic view of human foibles and corrupt social institutions that tried but failed to challenge God's immutable truths. We need no constricting standards of objectivity to grant him his identity. And while I would not argue that it is necessarily wrong to write his stanza in nine rather than thirteen lines—after all we have lived with that form for nearly a hundred years—I would urge that we should see it for what it really is, a scribal and editorial device. When we do that, we will be in a better position to understand both objectively and subjectively what is original and brilliant and real about the Wakefield Master's contributions to the Towneley cycle.

It is precisely for the brilliance and originality of its poetic vision that the Wakefield cycle has been singled out as the most "literary" of all the medieval Corpus Christi plays. As a step toward bringing that literary quality into perspective, I propose now to examine one of its significant thematic strands: its self-conscious interest in literary art as a medium, or to put it in other terms, its concern with the uses and abuses of language. I believe that we owe this focus to the Wakefield author as reviser and compiler of the cycle. We can find this theme not only in all the five full plays traditionally assigned to him, the *Processus Noe cum filii* (Play 2), the *Prima Pastorum* (Play 12), the *Secunda Pastorum* (Play 13), the *Magnus Herodes* (Play 16), and the *Coliphizacio* (Play 21), but also in all the plays that bear evidence of his familiar scansion, whether put into the traditional stanza associated with him or others that resemble them in poetic form and substance by the criteria I have discussed. In all, he clearly had a demonstrable role in editing or revising the following additional plays in the cycle: the *Mactacio Abel* (Play 2), the *Conspiracio [et Capcio]* (Play 20), the *Flagellacio* (Play 22), the *Processus Crucis* (Play 23), the *Processus Talentorum* (Play 24), the *Peregrini* (Play 27), the *Ascencio Domini* (Play 29), the *Iudicium* (Play 30), and the *Lazarus* (Play 31). And since he clearly reworked the plays borrowed from York—witness his major alteration of the York Judgment play to which he added 378 of his characteristic lines out of a total (in the Wakefield version) of 664[64]—I think we can safely assume that he had a hand in

[64] My calculations are based on the Cawley-Stevens transcription of the

compiling if not adapting all the plays in this category. Indeed, one must conclude that, if he was the principal compiler of the cycle, his editorial hand must be present everywhere, even if merely in what was retained and what was rejected in the final version.

The Wakefield author is pervasively concerned with "vayn carpyng," as Abel accusingly calls it (Caw. 3/97), or to put it more fundamentally, with the abuse of language, especially by those who oppose God. The demonstration of that abuse is, ironically, a central feature of the cycle's rich verbal complexity and depth of meaning. We have already seen that the Wakefield author's most immediate interests are centered on humankind—on "natural man" in the terminology of V. A. Kolve[65]—rather than on God, Christ, the angels, and the saintly. In the five plays ascribed to the Wakefield author, God makes but one speech, in the Noah play, and it is straightforward and distinctly colloquial: God begins by reproving man for his wickedness, announces that he will bring forth a Flood, and appears before Noah to give very practical instructions for building the ark and storing provisions (Caw. 16–18/73–181).[66] The Wakefield author is even more sparing in the lines that he gives to Jesus—four in all (Caw. 84–85/251–254)—and these lines in themselves, as I shall show later, are a ringing testament to the eloquence of silence. What interests the Wakefield author is the common man—such types as tyrants, soldiers, shepherds, shrewish wives—the humble and the unregenerate in all their guises. He prefers to focus on middle earth, straying only once into the world of the demonic when he presents Tutivillus and his cohorts in the *Iudicium*. But even these characters are

---

Towneley ms for the forthcoming EETS edition. In this edition, what appear as long couplets with central rhyme in the England-Pollard edition have been expanded into quatrains with alternating rhymes. The result is that the text in the new edition contains many more lines than the old.

[65] See V. A. Kolve, *The Play Called Corpus Christi* (Stanford: Stanford University Press, 1966), esp. chap. 9.

[66] Millicent Carey has noted the straightforwardness of this scene by comparing it with the speeches of God in other Noah plays; see *Wakefield Group*, p. 83.

seen in worldly shape as if they were tax collectors or summoners rather than gatherers of the damned. As a reviser in his own peculiar format and language, he carefully chooses only those subjects which emphasize his interests, as in his characterization of Pilate in the *Processus Talentorum* or the Torturers in the *Flagellacio*. His contributions do not appear in the more solemn and sacred settings in the cycle, such as the *Annunciacio* or the play about John the Baptist. If indeed he was overall reviser of the cycle, as I argue here, he let such passages stand in their original language. His direct contributions, then, stand in marked contrast to the rest of the cycle; indeed, it is largely from the "counter-language" he provides for his natural man that the rest of the cycle, and particularly the lyrical passages in couplets and rimes couées, take on their eloquence.

The essential premise of the Towneley cycle as a whole about language is that simplicity and artlessness mark the speech of the virtuous. There is a homely eloquence about God's opening in the Creation play:

> Ego sum alpha et o,
> I am the first, the last also,
> Oone god in mageste;
> Meruelus, of myght most,
> ffader, & son, & holy goost,
> On god in trinyte.
>
> (1/1–6)

One is tempted to take literally the opening line in the play from the Apocalypse (1:8). For God and his votaries speak everywhere with alphabetic clarity and concision. Their speeches are made largely in the simplest of stanzaic forms—couplets, quatrains, octaves, and rimes couées—and their diction is plain, direct, and uncomplicated. The rhythm of their language is even and free of the harsh alliterative dissonances that characterize the speech of errant men. E. Catherine Dunn has pointed out that there is a basic lyric voice in the Towneley cycle that she calls "the voice of the Church" ("la voix de l'église"), a voice that is highly subjective and that speaks or even chants characteristically in patterned sound structures.[67] This is the voice of which I speak here, though I would expand its scope to extend far beyond its occurrence in the *Processus Prophetarum* play from which she takes her paradigm illustrations. It is, of course, first and foremost a prophetic voice—even God's speech at the outset is prophetic, drawing for its basic text on the Apocalypse and Isaiah (see especially 41:4 and 48:12)—and its lyricism is often expressed directly in hymns and chants, the only occasions except for straightforward prophecy when the playwright veers from the vernacular approvingly. Music (as part of the quadrivium) was, of course, one of the four highest subjects of learning, and in the form of *musica ecclesiastica*, it was the essential expression, among the arts, of cosmic harmony. The frequent appearance of hymns in the Towneley cycle,[68] therefore, is by no means an unimportant thematic consideration in its own right, particularly when a pointed contrast is made several times between *musica ecclesiastica* and *musica vulgaris*. Even more dramatic is the contrast between the composite voice of the church, as expressed in various harmonic forms throughout the cycle, and the cacophony of demonic voices that rings forth from devils and the unregenerate. At its most extreme, this contrast is expressed throughout the medieval popular religious drama on the one hand by divine music, the language of the spirit, and on the other by obscenity (with emphasis on the excremental), or body language. The Devil who comes on stage "cracking wind," as in *The Castle of Perseverance*, is thus the perfect antithesis to the angelic choir.[69] The Wakefield plays, while virtually confining their scatological references to one play, the *Mactacio Abel*,

[67] Dunn, "Style of the Towneley Plays," pp. 483–485.

[68] For a complete classification of the music in the Towneley cycle, see JoAnna Dutka, "The Use of Music in the English Mystery Plays" (Ph.D. diss., University of Toronto, 1972), appendix 1.

[69] For the literary use of scatology, especially in Chaucer though also in the mystery plays, see Roy P. Clark, "Chaucer and Medieval Scatology" (Ph.D. diss., State University of New York at Stony Brook, 1974).

nevertheless make the contrast of music and noise a crucial consideration.

Before looking more specifically into the Wakefield author's concern with language as theme, I want to make a brief observation about stanzaic forms in general as used in the Wakefield cycle. While a good deal of attention was given by the early critics to the various metrical forms as strata within the cycle, little was done, then or later, to discover the function of the various metrical forms in the cycle. It is interesting to note, for example, that the Wakefield Creation play contains what is manifestly a patterned use of stanza forms. Thus, God speaks only in a six-line rime couée stanza, and Lucifer, who parodies God's speech, declaims to the multitude in five- and seven-line corruptions of that stanza demonstrating in the very form of his speech his incapacity to imitate God (see 3–4/77–103). Couplets, which may in the context be regarded as the lowest poetic form, are spoken regularly by the Fallen Angels and by man. While I do not wish to claim that this pattern holds in all the plays that follow, it does seem to suggest that stanza forms are not used indiscriminately by the Towneley playwright(s). The Wakefield stanza has its own tonality—one that is best suited to the speech of common men, a quality that comes through even in its most devout and solemn usages, such as God's speech in the passage already noted within the Noah play (Caw. 16–18/73–81) and the "hayll"-lyrics that Dunn so admires in the *Secunda Pastorum* (Caw. 62/710–736).[70] We have already seen how flexible the Wakefield stanza is in its potential for rhythmic variation, for end-stopping and for enjambment. It clearly is a vehicle to reduce the patterned tempo of the more conventional stanzas in the cycle, and the effect it achieves, therefore, is to represent in its rhythm the characteristic tempo of spoken discourse. The remarkable achievement of the Wakefield author is the dual effect that he allows his stanza to create: It simultaneously communicates the disordered and unstructured and reminds the listener or reader to heed its disciplined form.

[70] Dunn, "Style of the Towneley Plays," pp. 501–504.

The Wakefield author's interest in language asserts itself everywhere, as much in the style as in the subject matter of his plays. Given his worldly perspective, he is, of course, responsible for much that is crude and ignoble and profane in the dramatic action of the cycle. But there is also something grandly paradoxical about his work. For it is in the very excess of language—the racy humor, the crackling alliterations, the earthy proverbs, the shrill tyrants' rants, the trumpet-tongued catalogs, the salty and resourceful dialectalisms—that the Wakefield plays are most dazzling and most engaging to the reader. It seems that the Wakefield author willfully provided a caution against the very fiber of his own art, as if to warn that the voice of poetry in the context of the highest verities can beguile its auditors. There is, in the Wakefield plays, a strong, implicit argument against the enchantment of art, and an equally strong affirmation of the artless. In yielding its most memorable scenes and its most flamboyant verbal art to rustics, scoundrels, miscreants, and demons, the Wakefield cycle is in a class with such works as *Henry IV, Part 1* and *Paradise Lost.* Many great artists have endowed their least hallowed characters with their own versatility and their own highest verbal gifts. It is in this sense that Mak and Herod and Tutivillus are precursors of Falstaff, Satan, Mr. Micawber, and even Humbert Humbert.

The extent to which language occupies a central place in the drama of the Wakefield author can quickly be established by an overview of his work. He is, of course, the foremost linguist among the contributors to the cycle. Two recently completed computer concordances show the extent of the Wakefield author's vocabulary.[71] All told, there are over a thousand words

[71] The first of these is as yet unpublished. It was prepared from the transcription of the Cawley-Stevens text for the forthcoming edition. I wish to express my gratitude to Professor Peter Trower of the Physics Department of the Virginia Polytechnic Institute and State University for his work in developing this concordance. The information here gathered comes from that concordance, which restricts its count of the Wakefield author's language to the five plays written exclusively in his stanza. The second concordance, which I am sure will confirm the conclusions offered here, was compiled by Michael J. Preston and Jean

that appear as single citations in the Wakefield stanzas, or slightly fewer than a third of all such words in the Towneley cycle. Moreover, the Wakefield author is not only the most persistent and colorful user of dialectalisms and local references, but he also makes conscious allusion to dialect as a tool of deception when he has Mak address the Shepherds in his "Sothren tothe," which is, after all, the dialect of the ruling class. The same can be said of his use of Latin and French—languages that appear consistently in the rants of tyrants for the purpose of intimidating their listeners. In fact, it is almost exclusively in the Wakefield stanzas that macaronic verse in Latin and English occurs in the Wakefield cycle; for example, the long opening rant in the *Processus Talentorum* (279–280/1–46) and the Latin proverbs spoken by Caiaphas and Annas in the *Flagellacio* (Caw. 82/143–144; Caw. 83/214–215). When the Wakefield Herod, perhaps the most torrential ranter in the cycle, ends his play with a winded "I can no more Franch" (Caw. 77/513), the Wakefield author in characteristic fashion looks to the language of the upper class to identify for Yorkshiremen the bombast and fustian of tyrants. The Wakefield author is an adept linguist, but finally he distrusts all foreign languages and dialects. Yorkshire speech in itself may not often serve as a vehicle for the highest truths, but it is at least an authentic medium for the homespun wisdom of the earthy characters who make up the play and, we presume, the audience.

The Wakefield author more than any other writer in the medieval drama is aware of literary terms and traditions. He refers directly to "Vyrgyll" and "Homere," makes allusion, as already mentioned, to the learned languages of *Franch* (Caw. 77/

D. Pfleiderer, *A KWIC Concordance to the Plays of the Wakefield Master* (New York: Garland Publishing, 1982). Since this concordance is based on the Cawley text, it also includes the *Mactacio Abel* in its corpus of citations. While that play may well have been written in its entirety by the Wakefield author, for purposes of a concordance, it probably should not have been included in the volume. If we are to have a reasonably objective criterion for testing the special properties of the language and the diction of the Wakefield author, we should confine ourselves to those stanzas which can be definitely attributed to him.

513) and *Laton* (Caw. 39/391), knows technical musical language (see especially 384/537–540), and uses a wide variety of
literary terms such as *pystyls* (Caw. 69/205), *verse* (Caw. 34/386),
legende (Caw. 64/203), *poetré* (Caw. 39/386) *poecé-tayllys* (Caw. 69/
204), *glose* (Caw. 54/413), *gendere* (372/161), *gospell* (376/302),
grales (i.e. graduals; Caw. 69/205), and *gramere* (Caw. 39/387,
Caw. 242/242; 375/253). In addition, he directs his scorn especially against the misusers of language. One of his favorite devices, the catalog of agent nouns, names, among other offenders, the following: *wryers, bollars, hullars, extorcyonars,
carpers, slanderars, kyrkchaterars, swerars, iurars, writars, bakbyttars,
quest-dytars, indytars, flytars, lyars, flyars, cryars, byllhagers, bragers,
wragers, quest-mangers, bewshers, runkers,* and *rowners.* Like
Dante, he regards fraud—at base a verbal offense—as among
the most heinous of crimes. His attack on the misuse of language, his strong preference for the vernacular and especially
the local, and his open slurs on such masters of verbal manipulation as friars (see Caw. 37/286, Caw. 39/389) suggest that he
may have been a parish priest and possibly even a Wycliffite.[72]
Most important the Wakefield author chooses to end the cycle
by introducing in the *Iudicium,* which was borrowed in its basic
form from York, the devil Tutivillus, whose whole concern was
to collect those offenders who had spoken out of turn in
church. What emerges from this summary is a playwright who
in his subject matter and his very language demonstrated an
overriding concern with the falsity of man's word as contrasted
with the Word. It is this contrast that constitutes a major theme
and an artistic focus for the Wakefield cycle.

LET us now look somewhat more closely at a few of the crucial
passages of the Wakefield author's work that concern them-

---

[72] G. R. Owst makes the point that the vernacular was used by antimendicant
preachers as a matter of principle. In the north, there was a close affinity between such preachers and Wycliffites; see *Preaching in Medieval England* (Cambridge: Cambridge University Press, 1926), p. 229. The word "lollar" is used
disparagingly by Tutivillus (374/213), but, given the source, that may indeed be
high praise.

selves with this theme. I shall begin with an examination of the *Iudicium* because it serves as dramatic summary to the cycle and highlights the doom of those who abuse language (the "kyrk-chaterars" of their time), among whom, ironically, we also find their oppressors, the devils. Because the abuse of language centrally involves the law (with "parlement" and "debate" as its vehicle), the rantings of tyrants, and the contrast of cacophony and music, I shall move on to a consideration of these topics in the plays of the Doctors in the Temple, Noah, the Buffeting, and the two versions of the Shepherds, all of which are essential for an understanding of this theme in the cycle.

First, then, the Judgment play. Its principal character is the demon Tutivillus. From several allusions to his short stature, one would deduce that he was conceived as a sprite, and it would seem logical that he was played by a boy actor (see the references in 374/232 and 375/245, and his self-representation as one who sits atop the shoulder pads of dandies, 376/290). He is, therefore, not the usual devil figure of the mystery plays, and he certainly does not partake of the scatological humor so characteristic of the type. From the very outset, he announces his interest in language:

> · Mi name is tutiuillus,
> my horne is blawen;
> ffragmina verborum / tutiullus colligit horum,
> Belzabub algorum / belial belium doliorum.
>
> (375/249–252)

The Latin here is barely coherent, but it does tell us that Tutivillus collects "fragments of words" in contrast to Beelzebub who seemingly collects "the cold" (?) and Belial "the sorrows of war." I suspect that the Latin passage serves as something of a diabolic litany here, reflecting Tutivillus's verbal agility without calling for any particular literal sense (there is an oral gamesmanship in conjoining "belial" with "belium," and that may be the only justification for the line besides the rhyme on *-orum*).[73]

---

[73] Cawley has suggested to me that if *algorum* be interpreted as "of colds, fe-

There is even a possibility that the Latin words were chanted, as is commonly the case with lines that are not part of the rhyme scheme. All this comes, of course, in response to the First Demon's saying "with wordes will thou fill vs," a perfectly calibrated rhyme with Tutivillus. Ironically, this loquacious devil is the very agent who traditionally gathers up in sacks the words mumbled or dropped by clergymen and those spoken idly by parishioners during church service ("kyrkchaterars"; 376/296).[74] To the extent that Tutivillus at once practices the abuse that he is designed to guard against—that is, the incoherent and excessive utterance of words—he is a most interesting reflection of the Wakefield author himself.

The two most basic sins against which the energies of Tutivillus and the demons seem to be directed are excessive adornment (especially in apparel) and the frauds practiced by men of the law. Tutivillus reserves some of his best verbal showmanship in cataloging the latest excesses of fashion. With a chorus of approval from the demons who take delight in his "gramory" (learning; 253), Tutivillus describes the extravagant dress of the dandies and the women of fashion, obviously ready subjects for damnation, with a zest matched only by the extravagance of his own words. Indeed, there seems to be, in the mind of the playwright, a correspondence between sartorial and linguistic extravagance. With all the emphasis in the play on misusers of language—from "kyrkchaterars" (296) to "runkers" and "rowners" (298), and with the identification of excessive adornment with pride, the deadliest of sins (305–313), one cannot but recognize in passages like the following a lack of restraint in language, with the flamboyant alliterations, the double rhymes, and the eccentric diction, which resembles the very offense it describes:

---

vers," then *belium doliorum* could mean "of belly aches" (with *-um* stuck onto the English *belly*, and with a comic play on the *beli* of *belial* and *belium*).

[74] For a characterization of Tutivillus, see Arthur Brandeis, ed., *Jacob's Well* (London: Oxford University Press, 1900), pp. 114–115; and G. R. Owst, *Literature and Pulpit in Medieval England* (Oxford: Basil Blackwell, 1961), pp. 512–515.

His luddokkys thai lowke / like walk-mylne cloggys,
his hede is like a stowke / hurlyd as hoggys,
a woll blawen bowke / thise fryggys as froggys,
This Ielian Iowke / dryfys he no doggys
    To felter;
Bot with youre yolow lokkys,
ffor all youre many mokkys
ye shall clym on hell crokkys
    With a halpeny heltere.

                (377/314–322)

Shortly thereafter, Tutivillus describes the drunkards who sit all night imbibing "with hawvell and Iawvell, syngyng of law-vell" (378/337–338: with wailing and jabbering and singing of lowbell, i.e. of drinking songs; *MED*, s.v. "lavel") until the bells of the church deafen them in the morning (378/341–345). It is so also with the demons who, in the tour de force language of the Wakefield Master, create their own "hawvell and Iawvell" to be chastened by the straightforward and direct words of Christ (in the version of the source play from York). The point to be remembered is that sinners and demons alike will be climbing "on hell crokkys." The demons betray their lust for power, much like earthly tyrants, in their language. The severest ironies in the play finally lie in linguistic self-condemnations.

    Just as important as the issue of excessive adornment is the interest of the Wakefield playwright in the law as metaphor at the Last Judgment. The whole play, as indeed the cycle also, is structured to contrast the true law against the false—which is to say, the true word against the false. The very trumpet of the Judgment, which at the outset of the play gives such a "sturdy . . . showte" (370/91), is parodied by Tutivillus at his entrance ("my horne is blawen," 375/250). To the extent that the clarion call is to gather sinners from everywhere, it calls as much for the demons as it does for their prey. But the demons do not recognize the true significance of God's call despite the fact that it releases them from the bonds of Hell (370/89–116).

While Christ is waiting to render the great Last Judgment, they still use the idiom of the manorial economy:

> Bot fast take oure rentals / hy, let vs go hence!
> ffor as this fals / the great sentence.
>
> (371/134–135)

They set out to go to "this dome / vp Watlyn strete" (126), but for them it undoubtedly meant the Roman road that actually crossed the parish of Wakefield,[75] rather than the Milky Way, as, in the context, it must have been known to others (*OED*, s.v. "Watling Street," ¶2). The confusion here as elsewhere is between the civil and divine law. And the spokesmen of the civil law, who are ironically demons, invariably expatiate at length about the evil in the world, which they will expose and punish. Thus, the Second Demon reminds his compeers:

> It sittys you to tente / in this mater to mell,
> As a pere in a parlamente / what case so befell.
>
> (371/118–119)

The fact is that the demons never cease to talk; they continue their "parlement" all the while that they are on stage. Their frantic catalogs and their extended, colorful descriptions of mostly venial rather than mortal sins are the only aspects of their scene that provide movement, for physically nothing happens through the major portions of the Judgment play. In contrast to the Devil's "parlement" is Christ's straightforward speech. The demons themselves tell us, "ffor wysely / he spekys on trete" (371/129–130). In perfect balance, he addresses the good souls and the bad souls, delivering his judgment fairly and succinctly. When his speech is all over, the good souls go to the right, the bad souls to the left, and the demons remain the only speakers on stage. The Highest Judge has spoken, and the petty civil judges make their way to their eternal doom, leading the whole company of sinners to the tune of their unceasing chatter:

---

[75] See Cawley, *Wakefield Pageants*, p. xiv, n. 8.

Hyte hyder warde, ho / harry ruskyne!
War oute!
The meyn shall ye nebyll,
And I shall syng the trebill
A revant the devill
Till all this hole rowte.
(384/535–540)

The judges are finally judged, and they all "go . . . sam" (386/610) to their eternal damnation while the good souls sing the Te Deum Laudamus. At the very last, the divine law triumphs ringingly over the false civil law, and silence triumphs over loquacity and chatter. In the *Iudicium*, which we know to be a borrowed play from York, we can observe to greatest advantage the skill of the Wakefield author as reviser. He adds those passages which emphasize the abuse of language in his characteristic stanza, diction, and meter. The rest he lets stand as a way of highlighting the contrast between the excess of language in substance and style and the quiet dignity of simple locution.

A word should be said about the frequently cited thematic contrast between the Old Law and the New in the Wakefield cycle. It is, of course, true that a major concern of the cycle as a whole is to show how the retributive justice of the Old Testament gives way to the mercy of the New Testament. This issue is brought into direct enactment in the Doctors' pageant, another of the plays that depend almost entirely for their dramatic interest on debate. The Doctors continuously refer to what they characterize as "oure lawes" (the word in its various forms appears seven times in the pageant) and what specifically at one point the Tercius Magister calls "Moyses lay." But interestingly, when challenged by the Doctors, Christ brings forth a perfect recitation of the Ten Commandments, the kernel of their own law, as living evidence that he has come to fulfill and not to destroy the Old Testament. The body of the divine law itself, whether Old or New, is thus not ever a matter of controversy in the Wakefield cycle, only the way that the laws are carried out. The Doctors are haughty and self-serving men who,

168

in sending Jesus away, fail to honor their God and their neighbor, the very laws they say they espouse:

> yei, lett hym furth on his wayes,
> for if he dwell, withoutten drede
> The pepyll will ful soyn hym prayse
> well more then vs, for all oure dede.
> (192/185–188)

Jesus, who is the real Magister of the sequence, is, however, the embodiment of his own teaching—mild and generous to all men—and by his example he brings out the best even in the Doctors as he parts from them (see 194/261–268). While the play is, by the canon generally accepted, not the work of the Wakefield author, it does present the background on which he built his major thematic concentration. (And it is of course one of the York plays on which he made major revisions elsewhere.) The divine law, Old and New, is never out of harmony. It is only the faulty perception of its interpreters (and of impostors) that brings with it the resonance of chaos.

The real conflict, then, is between the divine law and the civil, a conflict central to the Wakefield author's dramatic vision. This contrast stands at the core of the dramatic action throughout the cycle; it exists literally from the beginning, with Lucifer proclaiming to all Creation "master ye shall me call" (4/98), to the very end when Jesus calmly presides at the highest doom. The civil law is constantly exposed for its abuses, and primary among these is the tyranny of temporal rulers, the characteristic ranters of the cycle drama in whom the Wakefield author took a special interest. It is usually the arrogant, self-aggrandizing, and loquacious tyrant figure who disturbs God's stillness with his ear-piercing harangues. In a sense, the Noah pageant, which by conventional standards is the first of the Wakefield author's full-length plays in the cycle, is a microdrama in which the central issue of the Wakefield cycle is given a humorous first airing. The reason for the Flood is familiar to all; God complains

169

> I repente full sore that euer maide I man;
> Bi me he settys no store, and I am his soferan.
> (Caw. 16/91–92)

The divine law is therefore entrusted to Noah, who in the familiar form of the *figura* becomes a type of Christ on stage. Opposed to him, at least in the process of his building the ark (or, as familiarly interpreted, the church) is his *uxor*, who thus becomes the first, if unlikely, tyrant figure in the Towneley cycle. She has all the attributes: She challenges right order (by opposing her "syre"; Caw. 24/396); she boasts and rants (sometimes addressing the audience directly, as in Caw. 19/208–209); and she freely uses her cudgel in the form of a distaff (see Cawley note to 200). For a time at least she holds sway, much as Herod will later even as the Christ Child is born. What is particularly noteworthy about Noah's wife is her garrulousness. Her husband entreats her over and over again to hold her tongue, and much of his humor is in his characterization of her as a shrew. He describes her perfectly when he tells first her and then the audience:

> Thou can both byte and whyne
> With a rerd;
> For all if she stryke,
> Yit fast will she skryke.
> (Caw. 20/229–232)

And, at one point, he admonishes men who have wives "whyls thay ar yong" to "chastice thare tong" (Caw. 24/397–398). The whole of the action in the pageant is to bring harmony out of discord, a process for which the silencing of Noah's *uxor* is the central dramatic metaphor. In effect, Noah tells us as much when, in the beginning of their conflict, he says to her: "We! hold thi tong, ram-skyt, or I shall the still" (Caw. 19/217), or again later, "I shall make þe still as stone" (Caw. 24/406). And of course, he succeeds entirely in stilling her and thus reestablishing order and harmony in the human family. Most significantly, at the very end, even the ark is brought to calmness: "As still as a stone oure ship is stold" (Caw. 28/525). Thus physical and verbal storms abate, and if we bear in mind the figural interpretation of Noah and the ark, then the stillness and stability at the end of the play tell us something about the role of the church in a world too much obsessed with the discord of words.

Stillness, as was observed in the York cycle as well, characterizes the stability of God. The silence of Jesus dominates the Wakefield author's play of the Buffeting. Here as elsewhere in the cycle, notably the Herod pageant, tyrants by contrast virtually expire from their overuse of words. Where in other cycles, such as the N-Town, the tyrants are generally brought to violent deaths, in the Wakefield author's pageants they simply fade out; they seemingly suspire. Herod boasts himself to oblivion with his "I can no more Franch." Caiaphas, Annas, and Pilate, after their virtuoso performances as speechmakers and ranters, disappear from sight in the onset of calmness and harmony. The central issue of the Buffeting is once more the law. Jesus is accused by one of the Torturers, ironically, for teaching the people "a new law" (Caw. 80/66), and Caiaphas and Annas are implored, in turn, to "defende all oure law" (Caw. 81/115). The civil law is thus made the instrument by which the divine law—the whole spirit of the New Testament— is to be measured and judged. All through the accusation scene, Jesus stands in glorious silence while his temporal, ecclesiastical judges, Caiaphas and Annas, let go a stream of oaths and imprecations to make him "speke on oone word" (Caw. 82/145). Never has flamboyant and biting language been undercut more eloquently by silence than the point in the Buffeting at which Caiaphas ends his long tirade literally crying and shouting in frustration for Jesus to speak one syllable "be it hole worde or brokyn" (Caw. 82/174). The more subdued and cunning Annas recognizes that the force of Jesus' stillness is infinitely more potent than all the words he can summon. He asks, almost plaintively, "Why standys thou so styll when men thus accuse the?" (Caw. 84/246). In the end, neither the verbal nor the physical assaults on Jesus break his silence or discredit his law. The play with its emphasis on "vayn carpyng"—a fault for which, ironically, Jesus is directly accused as he proceeds on the Via Crucis in the *Flagellacio* (243/346)—is a brilliant poetic attack on the limits of rhetoric.

Much as the law is one topic of great thematic concern to the Wakefield author, so music is another. Both serve him to make implicit statements about the uses and misuses of language, and, even more narrowly, about the function of poetry. I have already shown how *musica ecclesiastica*, usually in the form of hymns, inheres in all those parts of the Wakefield cycle which give direct expression to the voice of God. I now wish to suggest that it is the contrast of *musica vulgaris* and *musica ecclesiastica*, and even more pointedly the eventual merging of the two, that becomes the most significant feature in the Wakefield author's revision from the First to the Second Shepherds' plays. I will maintain that, in the view of the Wakefield author, the solemn angelic song, the Gloria in Excelsis Deo, is the highest expression that common man can perceive and emulate. The shift from discord to harmony, both in speech and music, can be seen as the fundamental concern of the Wakefield author's masterpiece—the Second Shepherds' play—which in its Adoration scene is the yardstick for the eloquence of simple reverence. (Although the applications differ, it is worth noting the common concern of both York and Towneley with stillness as a state in which the presence of God is manifest.)

The nucleus of all the Shepherds' plays, including the two in the Wakefield cycle, is clearly the appearance of the Angel announcing the Nativity and the angelic choir singing the Gloria in Excelsis Deo. The contrast of the divine messenger and the earthly listeners is the frequent subject of parodic humor, as note the response to the angelic singing in the Chester cycle by the three Shepherds:

> PRIMUS PASTOR. Fellowes in feare,
> may yee not here
> this mutinge on highe?

172

SECUNDUS PASTOR: In 'glore' and in 'glere'?
                  Yett noe man was nere
                  within our sight.

TERTIUS PASTOR. Naye, yt was a 'glorye.'
                 Nowe am I sorye
                 bowt more songe.
                 (141/358–366)

The point here, as also in *The Holkham Bible Picture Book*,[76] is to bring the sacred into the context of the profane and thus to universalize the significance of the Nativity. But whereas the musical burlesque is simply a humorous excursion in the Chester plays, the whole subject of *musica vulgaris*, in its varying forms, becomes a matter of thematic importance in the Wakefield Shepherds' plays and of central significance in the *Secunda Pastorum*.

To make this point clear, I must make some observations about the essential differences in subject matter between the two Shepherds' pageants in the Wakefield cycle and about the apparent process of revision to which the Wakefield author subjected the first version. It is, of course, well known that the two plays share many situations. In both, we have three Shepherds who come on stage remarking about the hardships of life; in both a fourth character (Iak Garcio and Mak) joins the Shepherds; in both, there is festive singing first among the Shepherds themselves, then by the angelic choir; in both, the Shepherds depart singing. There is, as well, a hint that the Wakefield author already had at least one of the main ingredients of the Mak plot in mind when he has Iak Garcio respond to the Shepherds' concern over gathering up the imaginary contents of an empty sack with the following remark:

[76] The inscription "Glum glo ceo ne est rien. Allums la, nous la severums bien" appears in the upper panel of folio 13 of *The Holkham Bible Picture Book*. Below, in English, there is the following observation: "Songen alle wide one steuene, Also be angel song þat cam fro heuene"; see Hassell, *Holkham Bible Picture Book*.

173

Sagh I neuer none so fare bot the foles of Gotham.
Wo is hir that yow bare! Youre syre and youre dam,
Had she broght furth an hare, a shepe, or a lam,
Had bene well.

(Caw. 34/180–183; and cf. 101/182n)

The similarities of plot in the two Shepherds' plays are perhaps less noticeable than the differences. First among the latter
is certainly the inclusion of the Mak episode in the *Secunda Pastorum*. On quick glance one is, in fact, tempted to say that the
Wakefield author simply revised the first play by including this
plot[77] and making otherwise minor revisions. But closer examination will not sustain this view and will lead to the conclusion that the revision from the first to the second version was a
major one in subject matter as well as theme and approach.
The first play is, to begin with, much less obviously unified.
The Wakefield author makes no attempt here to link the first
half of the play focusing on the discussion and merrymaking of
the Shepherds with the second part involving the Nativity. Implicitly, of course, one can view the physical hardships of the
world cited in the soliloquies of the First and Second Shepherds as preparation for the advent of Christ and the spiritual
balm offered at the end of the pageant. There is even some direct pleading with God that he come to bring "a better way" for
the souls of sinners, that he "send theym good mendyng /
with a short endyng" (Caw. 31/79–79). In this sense, one can perceive the games of the first part—all concerned with the imaginary—as a statement about the inconsequential nature of the
material in contrast with the centrality of the spiritual. It is not
the physical presence of sheep but the idea of sheep that causes
the territorial dispute between shepherds One and Two. It is
not a full sack of meal but rather an empty one, and not a real
feast but an imaginary one, which provides the sustenance of

[77] Arnold Williams makes the interesting observation that the Second Shepherds' play is the only "play in the entire corpus of cycle plays [that] has something like a formal plot"; see "The Comic in the Cycles," in *Medieval Drama*, ed.
Neville Denny, Stratford-upon-Avon Studies, no. 16 (1973): 112.

the Shepherds and the substance of their games. The emphasis throughout this early scene seems to be deliberately on the unseeable, perhaps to prepare emotionally for the Incarnation that occurs at the end. The play thus deals with a set of intellectual reversals: In the first part substance becomes shadow in a farcical setting, while in the second spirit becomes flesh in a profoundly serious setting. But it must be emphasized that whatever is here as a unifying thought must be supplied by the insight of the reader or performer; the Wakefield author provides neither direct explanation nor an easily discernable coherence.

It is quite different in the Second Shepherds' play. First, as is well known, there is an obvious situational and even verbal coherence between the parodic and the serious nativities. It takes little effort to connect the "credyll" in Mak's cottage (see 334, 432, 538, 600) with the "cryb" of the Holy Family (see 645, 689) or to recognize that both the sheep and the Christ Child are referred to as that "lytyll day-starne" (577, 727). In contrast, the words "cryb" and "mangere" as well as "mangyng" are used in the First Shepherds' play only in the farcical first part and always with reference to "eating" (see 201, 232), thus implying a much subtler unity that may well be meant to suggest the concept of the Eucharist by linking the feast of Part One with the celebration of the Christ Child in Part Two. The revision, therefore, is very much in the direction of the more explicit. This tendency is especially noticeable in what the two plays have to say about the function of music. The Wakefield author seems to make no special effort to integrate the Gloria with what has preceded in the First Shepherds' play. It is true that the Shepherds engage in a singing contest to see who gets the first drink (Caw. 36/265–266). But even though this event occurs shortly before the outburst of angelic song, with which it no doubt contrasted sharply, the Wakefield author fails to draw attention to this interesting juxtaposition. While song is clearly of great significance to the remainder of the play—thus establishing a tone of reverence and peace—no special mention is made of its place in the overall scheme of the play.

In the Second Shepherds' play, the role of music is much more prominent; indeed, the contrast between noise and music (or cacophony and harmony) is of central thematic importance to the outcome of the play. R. W. Ingram has already pointed out that there is a special significance to the uses of music in the play:

> The music as a whole not only acquires more meaning in the context of the play but is neatly varied and patterned: The cheerful song of the shepherds leads to the creaking voice of Mak's wife, to the sweet singing of the angel and so back again to the shepherds' singing on their way to the manger.[78]

I would like to propose that there is much more here than random patterning and variation. In the first place, the Second Shepherds' play does much from the outset to associate unrest and noise with the profane, and peace and harmony with the sacred. In this respect, it shares of course with the rest of the Wakefield cycle an interest in volatile and often shrill language as an instrument for the portrayal of the lewd and the secular. It also presents the Wakefield author with the rare opportunity of using his stanza, which so characteristically fits the rhythms of the colloquial, to dramatize the solemn, if simple, dignity of the Nativity scene. It is in the Second Shepherds' play where the versatility of his stanza is most fully realized and where he seems most pointedly concerned with its artistic range. In the second place, the play seems to present a deliberate progression from discord to harmony, suggesting that in their imitation of the Angels's song, the Shepherds learn a new tranquillity of discourse with which to address the sacred. The most profound of the Wakefield pageants always are concerned with bringing awareness of the sacred to the profane. In the larger perspective, such common people as the Shepherds or old Jo-

---

[78] R. W. Ingram, "The Use of Music in English Miracle Plays," *Anglia* 75 (1957): 63.

seph or even Noah's *uxor*, drawn anachronistically to Yorkshire specifications, become representatives of the audience. Consequently, whatever they learn stands empathetically for what the Corpus Christi spectator must also learn in the course of the dramatic performance. It is thus that the concept of the sacred is made most directly meaningful by the playwright.

The Second Shepherds' play opens, both in its language and its subject matter, on a note of discord that is sustained and even intensified until the Angel makes his appearance some six hundred lines later. At the very outset the First Shepherd speaks of "stormes and tempest" from which no one has rest (Caw. 43/6–9), while the Second Shepherd complains of the woe caused to wedmen by cackling wives who do nothing but "crok" and "groyne" and "clok" (Caw. 45/69–70). Mak enters upon the scene after the three Shepherds have broken out into a song of mirth, which they discuss with some apparent knowledge of the technical parts that constituted polyphonic singing:

1. PASTOR: Lett me syng the tenory.
2. PASTOR: And I the tryble so hye.
3. PASTOR: Then the meyne fallys to me.
                    (Caw. 48/186–188)

Thereupon Mak interrupts their song with an incantation to God and the exclamation that he is "all vneuen" (Caw. 48/192), and the First Shepherd greets him with the question "Who is that pypys so poore?" (Caw. 48/195). Thus, from the very first, the language of Mak is associated with bad singing. He is consistently characterized as a noisemaker, one who "makys sich dyn" (Caw. 51/297) or "sich a bere" (i.e. noise; Caw. 54/405) or who "commys with a lote" (another word for "noise"; Caw. 54/409). In turn, he makes the Shepherds break out in "a fowll noyse" and causes them to "cry out apon" him when they discover the loss of their sheep (Caw. 54/429–430). On their arrival at the cottage, they are greeted by Mak singing a "lullay" while Gyll groans and cries "outt by the wall on Mary and Iohn" (Caw. 55/442–443), to which the Shepherds respond as follows:

3. PASTOR: Will ye here how they hak? Oure syre lyst croyne.
1. PASTOR: Hard I neuer none crak so clere out of toyne.

(Caw. 56/476–477)

There can be little doubt that the farcical plot of the Second Shepherds' play was deliberately meant to emphasize the dissonances of everyday life. The Wakefield author clearly revised the first version of his play to stress disharmony, as is attested alone by the much more diversified onomatopoetic vocabulary for noise. Thus the limited list of such words in the first play (*blast, brall, brayde, crak, rafys,* and *yelp*) is expanded to include the following: *cry, crok, croyne, grone, mone, bark, blast, blawes, blete, crak, crakyd, ianglyng, kakyls, knakt, pypys, raue, skawde, stamerd,* and *whystyll,* and some of these words are used more than once. Likewise the vocabulary for music is also much expanded in the second play. Where in the first we encounter only such rather common words as *syng, song, sang, tonyd,* and *voce,* in the second we find a much richer mix: *syng, lullay, note, song, stevyn, pypys, tenory, tryble, meyne, chauntt, brefes, long* (note), and *whystyll.* It is evident that the Wakefield author chose in his second version to emphasize the contrastive languages of noise and music.

With the appearance of the Angel and the singing of the Gloria in Excelsis Deo, a new peaceful tone suggesting solemnity and harmony is struck. The First Shepherd is immediately awed by the beauty of the song: "This was a qwant stevyn that euer yit I hard" (Caw. 60/647). In fact, as JoAnna Dutka has already pointed out, the Shepherds of the *Secunda Pastorum,* unlike those of the *Prima Pastorum,* are impressed especially by the musical complexity of the angelic song; they comment specifically on the division of long notes into notes of smaller value[79] when they observe how the Angel "crakyt it, / Thre brefes to a long" (Caw. 60/656–657), a technical description of a perfect relation between *longa* and *brevis.* As I have already

[79] JoAnna Dutka, *Music in the English Mystery Plays,* Early Drama, Art and Music (EDAM) Reference Series, no. 2 (Kalamazoo: Medieval Institute Publications, 1980), p. 96.

observed, the Shepherds in the *Secunda Pastorum* are themselves musicians capable of rendering polyphonic song. It is thus very much in character for them to try to imitate the Angel and to sing a song likewise "of myrth . . . withoutt noyse" (Caw. 61/667–669). That they ultimately fail—they can only "bark at the mone" (Caw. 61/662)—is of course simply acknowledgment of their human limitation. But in their act of imitation, they raise to a simple dignity and beauty their own language. The highest secular expression comes at the very end of the play when each of the three Shepherds recites (perhaps even chants) a perfect "hayll"-lyric (710–736). Manfred F. Bukozer reminds us in his chapter, "Popular and Secular Music in England," that there were such things as "popular" sacred compositions.[80] If any verse ever so qualified, it was surely the "hayll"-lyrics of the *Secunda Pastorum*. What has happened then in the overall progress of the Second Shepherds' play is a wholesale elevation of tone. The most dissonant voices of the secular world have been stilled, and the singers of popular song have been inspired by angelic example to raise their voices in sacred harmony to celebrate the birth of Christ. For the Wakefield author the ultimate interest in the Second Shepherds' play is to elevate the language of his rustics in order that they might find the right tone in which to hail God.

I have attempted to show in this analysis that, largely because of the special slant provided by the Wakefield author as reviser, the Wakefield plays make an important statement about the limits of art. Ironically, when viewed from this angle, the contributions of the Wakefield author must be accepted as deliberately flawed: The very virtuosity of language that gives his stanzas their special flair and distinction hinders communication on the highest level of intercourse. In a sense, the Wakefield stanza is to the simple couplet and quatrain what the Devil is to God: It is at once adversary and servant to the total design. It constantly brings static into the harmony of the cosmos; it

---

[80] See Don Anselm Hughes and Gerald Abraham, eds., *Ars Nova and the Renaissance, 1300–1540* (London: Oxford University Press, 1960), p. 108.

cannot refrain from injecting dissonances into the most solemn of occasions. Its liveliness is also its greatest peril. The artist at his best has always been a rival of God; the Wakefield author knows that fact and fights to suppress his awesome challenge. His greatest moment of achievement is to make his stanza subservient to God at the end of the Second Shepherds' play. And yet he comes back again and again in his more accustomed dissident voice, until finally, in the play of the Great Doom he empirically passes judgment upon himself and leaves us to ponder the resonances of eternal salvation and damnation.

THREE

The N-Town Cycle: Dramatic Structure, Typology, and the Multiple Plot

AMONG the extant cycles, the one ascribed in its Proclamation to N-Town (and now known generally by that name)[1] presents us with the least evidence of provenance, genesis, and performance history. Unlike the other extant cycles, it is totally devoid of references to its place of performance, within either rubrics or text, and there are no extant records that have been positively identified as linked to it. We do have an *a quo* date for the manuscript—1468—which is affixed to the Purification play (see f. 119v), but that date may refer to the play rather than the cycle as a whole.[2] Moreover, unlike the other cycles, N-Town contains no references of any kind to trade guilds, and it is therefore impossible to know whether in fact this cycle was sponsored or performed by them. With all of these very substantial problems in mind, we can be positive about one point:

[1] In line with prevailing practice, I refer to the cycle as *N-Town* throughout. While scholars concerned with the cycle seem to have agreed that N-Town is the most acceptable name for it, the MLA annual bibliography, at this writing, still refers to the cycle by the erroneous name of *Ludus Coventriae*. Some scholars prefer to use the name Hegge because it refers to an ascertainable fact about the ownership of the manuscript (i.e. Robert Hegge, the first known owner whose name appears on the title page of the manuscript). The name Hegge is thus parallel to the usage of Towneley. N-Town, of course, refers to the apparent location, though there is disagreement still about the meaning of *N* (does it refer to *nomen*, hence "any town," or to a city whose name begins with *N*, like Norwich?). In actual fact, however, N-Town is associated only with the Proclamation, and I will argue in this chapter that the Proclamation and the play are really quite distinct entities.

[2] For a discussion of this date, see Peter Meredith and Stanley J. Kahrl, eds., *The N-Town Plays: A Facsimile of British Library MS Cotton Vespasian D VIII* (Leeds: University of Leeds, 1977), p. xiii.

Historical study of this cycle is fraught with difficulty and uncertainty.

So is a study of the text. In general scholars agree that the cycle is a patchwork, one that grew as a result of various editings and revisions. Among the more vexing problems presented by the manuscript is the inclusion of a Proclamation spanning nine leaves of the manuscript and preserving evidently an announcement or advertisement of a performance that was to take place on "sunday next . . . at vi of þe belle" (16/ 525–526).[3] The contents of this Proclamation, unhappily, do not closely correspond to large segments of the text that follows, even though an attempt is made, apparently by the rubricator,[4] to match the numbering of the pageants mentioned in the Proclamation with the episodes in the plays themselves.

Most scholars conclude that the Proclamation describes a performance that took place some time before the extant manuscript was put together and that the numbers in the margin are an attempt to "square" the text with that performance, wherever or whenever it might have taken place. This is not the place to review in any detail the theories that have been advanced to explain the genesis of the manuscript, though it is worth mentioning that most have been based on inferences concerning the variety of stanzaic forms in the cycle and the Proclamation, with the attempt to define layers or strata of composition or compilation. Of these studies by far the most ambitious has been that of Stephen Spector, who, beginning with the "proclamation" stanza, has isolated seventeen stanza forms in the cycle. It is his view that prosodic forms "provide the best evidence as to the strata of the cycle with each prosodic

[3] All references are to the edition by K. S. Block, *Ludus Coventriae: or, The Plaie Called Corpus Christi* (1922; reprint ed., London: Oxford University Press, 1960). Citations, placed within the text, are to page and line numbers.

[4] K. S. Block has shown that the rubricator who was responsible for the decorative writing in the manuscript, particularly on f. 212, the beginning of the Pentecost play, also wrote the play numbers in the margins throughout; see ibid., p. xxvii.

form representing a stage in the development of the cycle."[5]
Spector concludes sensibly that plays sharing the Proclamation
stanzas and matching in content, language, and theme the
Proclamation description were part of the same stratum. He
believes that this stratum was the original layer of the cycle,
which was then retouched and edited at various times by the
writers of the other stanza forms. While there is no hard evidence to show that the Proclamation stanza is, indeed, the
"original" stanzaic form rather than a revision stanza, the uniformity of its use in the Proclamation strongly supports the
Spector thesis. On the other hand, there is reason to doubt that
each of the sixteen other stanzaic forms was the work of a separate editing by a new contributor, a point on which Spector
himself is cautious, though he cites, in support of his conclusion regarding multiple authorship, the following statement by
W. W. Greg:

> Although there is no reason why more than one stanza
> should not have been used in the original composition of
> a single play, an author would not change from one to an-
> other without some rational cause. It follows that wher-
> ever a change of stanza occurs without discoverable rea-
> son we are justified in supposing that we have not got the
> play in its original form.[6]

I believe that there could, indeed, have been good reason for
an author to shift from one to another stanza form, as I have
tried to show in my discussion of the versification by the Wakefield playwright (see p. 160), but perhaps even more important, I believe that stanzas are not in themselves signatures.
Chaucer has shown convincingly that the same poet could
write brilliantly in various meters and stanzaic forms. And
surely a writer who used a thirteen-line Proclamation stanza

[5] See Spector, "The Genesis of the N-Town Cycle" (Ph.D. diss., Yale University, 1973), p. 18.

[6] See W. W. Greg, *Bibliographic and Textual Problems of the English Miracle Plays*
(London: Alexander Moring, 1914), p. 113; and Spector, "Genesis of N-Town,"
p. 18.

that rhymed *a b a b a b a b c d d d c* would not have had to strain very hard to use another stanza rhyming *a b a b b a b a c d d d c*, which Spector makes into a separate and discrete form. Good poets, among whom I place the final reviser of the N-Town manuscript, are surely capable of diversity of expression, and they are just as surely inclined to experiment with verse forms.[7]

I mention my objections to the stanzaic stratification theory because it does not sufficiently account for the genius that I perceive in the N-Town compiler. I mention it also because the Spector theory (together with various others that preceded it) puts far too much emphasis on the patchwork quality of the N-Town cycle—after all, how much artistic control can we expect in a work of art that is the sum product of seventeen revisers?—and not nearly enough emphasis upon its remarkable unity. It is, of course, true that the cycle has been assembled from various sources and also that at least three major parts of the manuscript seem to have been inserted into the codex as part of a late editing (these are the Marian, or Contemplacio, plays; the first Passion sequence; and the Assumption play, which is the only full pageant not written in the main hand of the codex).[8] Yet, the focus in most discussions of the cycle as a whole seems to be on the manner of its growth rather than the nature or quality of its artistic coherence. I will argue, as I did for Wakefield, that we should regard the cycle as product rather than process. I see it as the outcome of a very careful and literate editing that likely took place at the turn of the sixteenth century.[9]

[7] R. M. Lumiansky and David Mills take up the point about stanzaic variation in discussing the so-called Chester stanza. There are many variations in rhyme scheme and length among the Chester stanzas in the cycle, and Lumiansky and Mills come to the conclusion that they are "the result of a single revision." They also come to the following conclusion: "We attach little significance to variations within the 'Chester stanza-form.' We believe that stylistic considerations could have been the dominant reason for the employment of other stanza-forms." See *The Chester Mystery Cycle: Essays and Documents* (Chapel Hill: University of North Carolina Press, 1983), p. 318.

[8] See Meredith and Kahrl, *N-Town Plays*, p. vii.

[9] Malcolm Parkes has dated the main hand "in the last decade of the fifteenth century at the earliest"; see ibid., p. xxvii.

There is no way of knowing what sort of a cycle existed before the time of the present manuscript, if indeed a full cycle existed at all. The Proclamation does indicate that some kind of performance, possibly no more than a series of tableaux vivants, took place in the prehistory of the cycle, but the manuscript provides very little help in establishing how that performance related to the material retained in the extant cycle. What does seem to be clear is that the Proclamation is a performance document, while the play proper is an effort to provide a full literary text of a cycle only parts of which may have been performed after its compilation.[10]

To a large extent, the patchwork nature of the extant cycle is emphasized by its appearance in the Block edition (as indeed it was also in the only other full edition of the manuscript by J. O. Halliwell, published by the Shakespeare Society in 1841). I refer especially to the division of the cycle into pageants. As I have already mentioned, the numbering of the pageants within the manuscript was inspired by the rubricator's apparent desire to match the play texts with the Proclamation account. In fact, however, the manuscript as a whole does not correspond closely with the Proclamation, and it contains very few titles of individual pageants. Among true titles, I count only the following eight, and these are set forth in phrasing that lacks uniformity:

hic intrabit pagetum de purgacione marie & joseph (f. 75)

Modo de doctoribus disputantibus cum jhesu in templo (f. 106)

[10] Apart from the Proclamation, virtually the only performance details in the manuscript occur in the hand of the man identified by Meredith and Kahrl as Reviser B (see *N-Town Plays*, p. 24). It is not possible to know how much of the N-Town cycle was enacted after its compilation, but it does seem likely that if any performance took place it consisted of only a part of its contents, possibly the segments marked by K. S. Block as "Passion Play I" and "Passion Play II." The only textual justification for these titles is the line spoken by Contemplacio at the beginning of the Trial scene, "We intendyn to procede þe matere þat we lefte þe last ȝere" (271/6). This line could, of course, have been copied from a source manuscript that referred to an unrelated performance.

Hic Incipyt Johannes Baptysta (f. 111v, but separated from the beginning of the play by three leaves)

Hic de muliere in adulterio deprehensa (f. 121)

hic incipit de suscitacione lazari (f. 127v)

hic incipit aparicio cleophe & luce (f. 202)

hic incipit Ascencio domini nostri (f. 210)

Modo de die pentecostes (f. 212)

While Block treats all but one of these eight as titles (the first quoted is printed in standard italic, her convention for a stage direction), she adds bold titles for what she calls "The Passion Play I" (p. 225) and "The Passion Play II" (p. 271), and she provides running titles at the top of pages throughout the manuscript. In addition she reproduces the rubricator's large numbers to mark the beginning of pageants throughout the volume. The result is that the reader who does not know the appearance of the manuscript is hard put to know its true organization, and he is likely to make divisions where none actually exists.

I think that we must disregard the rubricator's well-intentioned attempt to match the numbering of the Proclamation with episodes in the cycle. If we follow him, as Block did, we get the wrong perception that the N-Town manuscript is set up as a succession of pageants and that it consequently embodies the performance text that the Proclamation advertises. Nothing could be further from the truth. Let me cite two major illustrations of how the numbering can mislead us.

The first occurs at the beginning of the play text. The rubricator inserted his large Arabic numeral at the beginning of the first play (f. 10) and continued the practice on folios 11v, 17, and 20v to mark off respectively the plays entitled by Block the Creation of Heaven and the Angels and the Fall of Lucifer (presumably a combined pageant), the Creation of the World and Man and the Fall of Man (another combined pageant), Cain and Abel, and Noah. Now the fact is that the action in these so-called pageants is continuous, and except for the intrusion of the marginal numbers there is nothing at all, at least up to the Noah "pageant" (before which the scribe leaves a space of approximately a half folio), to mark the beginning or ending of the pageants. Note that Block could not easily find a comprehensive title for the first two "pageants" because in fact they present a quick succession of scenes, and the only significant separation between them seems to be the marginal numbering by the rubricator. Moreover, the playwright makes a deliberate effort to interweave his episodes. For example, Adam reappears in the Cain and Abel play (30/32–44), and the death of Cain, a unique episode in the English Corpus Christi drama, occurs in the midst of the Noah action (40/174–177). This interweaving is a quite deliberate attempt by the playwright to make us think of the action as evolving and enlarging with the unfolding of salvation history. Adam's appearance in the Cain play gives edge to Cain's limited perception of fatherhood, and Cain's death in the midst of the Noah story suggests a developing genealogy of evil. We lose sight of these facts, and many more, if we allow ourselves to be misguided into a pageant-by-pageant reading of the cycle, a habit that surely grows out of Block's treatment of the early plays. I believe that the manuscript of N-Town was never meant to be read as a collection of pageants. From the very beginning we have a rich tapestry of scenes that are designed to merge into one another on an ever-expanding multiple stage.

The second example comes from the heart of the cycle—the Passion sequence. Here, suddenly, Block provides an alternate format: two organizational schemes within which to read this part of the cycle. The first is the division of the action into two large clusters called Passion Play I and Passion Play II. While these titles do not appear in the manuscript, they are legitimate divisions based on an internal reference by the narrator, Contemplacio, who begins the second of these sections by stating the intention "to procede þe matere þat we lefte þe last ȝere" (271/6) and then outlines the subject of "last year's" play:

The last ȝere we shewyd here how oure Lord for love
    of man
Cam to þe cety of Jherusalem mekely his deth to take,
And how he made his mawnde his body ȝevyng þan
to his Apostelys evyr with us to abydyn for mannys sake.

In þat mawnde he was betrayd of Judas þat hym solde
to þe Jewys for xxx^{ti} platys to delyver hym þat nyth;
With swerdys and gleyvys [to] Jhesu they come with þe
    tretour bolde
And toke hym amonges his Apostelys about myd-nyth.
                              (271/9–16)

Translated into the text of N-Town, this division would embrace the episodes beginning with the Prologue of the Demon
(f. 136) and ending with the Lament of the Virgin (f. 163), and
it would include the Council of the Jews, the Entry into Jerusalem, the Last Supper, the Conspiracy, and the Betrayal.
(These episodes are identified by Block exclusively in running
page titles.) The text in this segment is continuous in the manuscript, and Block accommodates to this fact (for the first time
in the volume) by numbering the lines in one continuous sequence. Notably, the only attempt to break the continuity is
once more that of the rubricator, who inserts three pageant
numbers into the margins coinciding with the beginning of the
Prologue of the Demon (f. 136), the Last Supper (f. 146), and
the Betrayal (f. 158). As elsewhere in her edition, Block faithfully reproduces these numbers even though they serve no
clear purpose and they fail, at this point, to match both the
numbering and the content of the Proclamation. Their sublim-
inal effect, however, continues, for they make the unwary
reader assume that there are divisions where none occurs in
the manuscript. Passion Play II, which covers the remainder of
the action, from the Trial scenes to the Visit of the Three
Marys to the Tomb,[11] presents the same problem for the

---

[11] The end of the second Passion Play is not clearly marked. Block implies in
her introduction that it comes with the beginning of Senturyo's speech on f.

reader, though with additional complication because the action is more extended and the setting more elaborate.

If the action in the Old Testament plays is already inter-woven from episode to episode, it becomes entirely inter-meshed in the Passion plays. Here, the stage itself is a large *pla-tea*, and with extensive stage directions (written at this point entirely in English and carrying much of the action of the play), we become aware that various *sedes* repeatedly become en-gaged and disengaged as the focuses of the action. Indeed, at least two of the *sedes* are curtained, as the stage directions tell us: the council house where all the rulers and judges gather— "a lytil oratory with stolys and cusshonys clenly be-seyn lych as it were a cownsel hous" (235/124f.)—and Simon's house with large table and chairs where the Last Supper will be played (254/669f.). Both have curtains that "sodeynly onclose" (see 245/397f. and 254/669f.), and with their use the spectator is treated to the first recorded "discovery scenes" in the English drama. Altogether the stage seems to require a large *platea* (often referred to in the stage directions as "the place") and the following *sedes*: scaffolds for Annas and Caiaphas; the "cownsel hous" in "þe myd place"; Simon's house; a place "lych to a park" (262/908f.) representing the Garden of Gethsemane; probably a hill, the Mount of Olives (262/916f.); a heaven scaf-fold from which an angel can descend (263/944f. and 264/956f.); and possibly an abode for Mary (see 267/1041f.). The action in the place is elaborate and varied; it includes the jour-neying back and forth of the messenger summoning Caiaphas for Annas and the gathering of bishops, clerks, and Pharisees (235/124f.); an enclosure for the ass and the foal furnished for the Entry into Jerusalem; the riding about of Jesus, the preach-ing of John and Peter, the greeting of Jesus in Jerusalem, where Jesus walks upon the cloths spread by the citizens; the

---

186v (see 308/143 and her remarks on pp. xiv–xv), though her consecutive numbering would bring the play to a close at 327/1647 prior to the entrance of the three Marys on their way to the tomb. The fact that the demarcation is so blurry is further evidence of the attempt made by the main editor of the cycle to integrate his material.

journeying of Peter and John to Simon's house, followed eventually by Jesus; Judas's crisscrossing between Simon's house and the council house (and his return to both places twice); the walk of Jesus and the disciples to the Garden of Gethsemane; the arrest of Jesus by ten soldiers; and the exit of Jesus in captivity. This enumeration shows how extensive the interweaving of the plot has become. After Jesus and John and Peter enter the stage, there is never a time when only one group or the other is on stage alone, and episodes like the Entry into Jerusalem, the Last Supper, and the Agony in the Garden take place entirely in the context of the evil rulers who all along are conspiring to capture Jesus. The flow of the dramatic action thus requires a large stage, and that stage provides a counterpoint that would be impossible to achieve in a pageant-wagon performance, which necessarily must be episodic.

Since I will save until later a full structural analysis of the Passion sequences in the N-Town cycle, I will forgo a discussion here of the unified dramatic action in the part of the cycle called the Passion Play II. Suffice it to say for now that if the rubricator's pageant numbers are misleading and confusing in the first play, they are even more so in the second. Here they intrude in the middle of scenes (see 307/1021), and they suggest a chopping up of the action that is wholly unjustified by the dramatic structure (for example, the demarcation of two plays set in Hell—the Descent and the Harrowing—when clearly the action is continuous, even while the Burial and the Guarding of the Sepulcher are presented on another part of the stage). One has to conclude that the rubricator's numbers are vestigial and that the cycle as a whole moves forward in a single main action, made up of countless scenes that are joined overtly or implicitly.

In the absence of documentary evidence to the contrary, I will argue that the N-Town compiler, much like the Wakefield Master, was the "author" of the N-Town cycle, that he put that cycle together from disparate parts with an eye toward providing the whole of the cycle with a highly developed structure and a close-knit unity.[12] In so arguing, I will disregard what the text of N-Town might have been like when it was performed as described in the Proclamation, if, in fact, there ever was a full text for that performance. Nor will I assume that N-Town, in the form that it survives, was ever performed in its entirety. What we have entire is a literary text—one that deserves to be read for its extraordinary dramatic power and intelligence.

To facilitate such study we must have better headings of major parts than the manuscript furnishes. We have seen that neither stanzaic forms nor the rubricator's pageant numbers really provide us with very useful tools for an examination of the dramatic structure of the cycle. While it is risky to "invent" headings with which to divide the text of a manuscript, the N-Town cycle invites the reader constantly to perceive its coherence inferentially, as we shall have occasion to see in the study of its typological cues. I therefore suggest that a set of major headings be silently superimposed on the text as a way of perceiving its progressions and its balances.[13] The headings I have devised are prompted essentially by narrative content, more or less to reflect major divisions in sacred history.

Corpus Christi plays, though not often enough seen in that content, really belong to the broad medieval genre of Lives of

[12] Rosemary Woolf suggests similarly that the author and reviser of the cycle could easily have been the same person. For a fuller discussion of this point, see below, p. 211. See also Woolf, *The English Mystery Plays* (London: Routledge and Kegan Paul, 1972), pp. 309–310.

[13] While my divisions are admittedly arbitrary, I see great advantage in the use of major headings and the de-emphasis of pageant numbers in any future editions of the cycle. The only time that the Block edition gives a true impression of the sweep and complexity of the action is in its separately numbered Passion Plays. Major headings clearly demand continuous line numbering, a practice that will also facilitate citations. The Block edition does not allow easy reference to individual plays, as noted by Meredith and Kahrl (see *N-Town Plays*, p. viii). It should be borne in mind, further, that even the clumsy divisions in Block are largely editorial. We should recall that there are very few headings in the manuscript. The question then becomes, Should divisions and titles be created in accordance with the order and content of the Proclamation or should they be fitted to the manuscript? I intentionally beg the question.

Christ. As such they share with numbers of works (especially from the fifteenth century) a well-established though certainly not a fixed narrative ordo. Ultimately, of course, these Lives go back to the first Gospel harmonies and, more directly, to Biblical histories such as Peter Comestor's *Historia Scholastica*. The immediate context of N-Town includes a particular Life of Christ that is known to be one of the cycle's sources: Nicholas Love's *Mirrour of the Blessed Lyf of Jesu Christ*, a somewhat loose translation of the Pseudo-Bonaventuran *Meditationes Vitae Christi* (Love reduces the 161 chapters of the original to 65 in the *Mirrour*).[14] Love's translation, which was written in the early fifteenth century, was essentially a meditational guide for the uneducated, and it purports "to sette in mynde the ymage of cristes incarnacioun / passioun / and resurreccioun so that a symple soul that kan not thenke bot bodies or bodily thinges mowe haue somwhat vnto his affeccioun wherwith he may fede and stire his deuocioun."[15] For our purposes, it is instructive to examine Love's table of contents, which is arranged as a daily meditational guide from Monday to Sunday, with each day of the week as a major heading. Monday begins with the Council in Heaven (parts of which were borrowed directly by N-Town), and includes among other episodes the Annunciation, the Visit to Elizabeth, Joseph's Doubt, the Nativity, and the Purification. Tuesday extends from the Flight into Egypt to the Baptism; Wednesday from the Temptation to the Conversion of Mary Magdalene; Thursday from events in the Ministry to the Last Supper; Friday from the Capture to the Burial; Saturday con-

---

[14] For the text of Nicholas Love's translation, see *The Mirrour of the Blessed Lyf of Jesu Christ*, ed. Lawrence F. Powell (Oxford: Oxford University Press, 1908). For an excellent translation of the *Meditationes*, see I. Ragusa and R. B. Green, trans., *Meditations on the Life of Christ* (Princeton: Princeton University Press, 1961). For an analytical and critical survey of medieval Lives of Christ including, centrally, a discussion of Love's *Mirrour*, see Elizabeth Salter, *Nicholas Love's "Mirrour of the Blessed Lyf of Jesu Christ,"* Analecta Cartusiana 10 (Universität Salzburg: Institut für Englische Sprache und Literatur, 1974). Block discusses the specific influence of Love's *Mirrour* on the N-town cycle (*Ludus Coventriae*, pp. lvii–ix).

[15] Powell, *Mirrour*, pp. 8–9.

centrates on "what oure lady and othere with her deden"; and Sunday includes the Resurrection, Appearances, and Descent of the Holy Ghost. This plan shows clearly that the Life of Christ as narrative was presented in segments that were arranged in a manner suitable to the purpose of the work.[16] As I see it, the N-Town cycle allows for a mode of perception that similarly encourages the reader to think in terms of large narrative divisions, of "acts" rather than "scenes."

In fact, at times the N-Town author / reviser makes a deliberate effort to divide his narrative. The Old Testament plays, for example, do not merely form a narrative segment based on source material; their end heralds a new beginning, a radical turn in salvation history that is signaled directly by the narrator, Contemplacio, who at the outset, in what Block calls a "prologue," prepares us for the contents of the plays that form his segment, a small cycle of plays about Mary:

> This matere here mad is of þe modyr of mercy,
> How be Joachym and Anne was here concepcion,
> Sythe offred into þe temple compiled breffly,
> Than maryed to Joseph and so folwyng þe salutacion,
> Metyng with Elyzabeth and þer with a conclusyon.
>
> (62/9–13)

This preview turns out to be entirely accurate except that an additional playlet intrudes, the one named "Joseph's Return" by Block—a playlet that may, however, be regarded by the

---

[16] Salter calls attention to a manuscript, Trinity College Cambridge MS B.2.18, which includes yet another fifteenth-century translation of the *Meditationes*. This manuscript resembles N-Town even more closely than does Love's *Mirrour*. It divides into three parts: "First comes an account of the Creation and Fall, the Conception, and the Birth and early life of the Virgin, for most of which the writer draws on the Apocryphal Gospels. Then follows an independent translation of the *Meditationes*, from the episode of the Council in Heaven to the raising of Lazarus . . . The third part of the work consists simply of Love's translation of the *Meditationes* from the raising of Lazarus to the coming of the Holy Ghost to the disciples" (see E. Salter, *Love's "Mirrour,"* p. 105). My own examination of this manuscript leads me to conclude that it was not a direct source of N-Town, but it is an interesting analogue.

Contemplacio author as being embraced in the Salutation, as indeed that action is in the Wakefield cycle where clearly the Annunciation and the Joseph play are one and the same and are so treated by the scribe. The promised conclusion announced in the prologue does materialize and precisely at the place indicated: the end of the meeting with Elizabeth, where Contemplacio makes his final appearance in the segment (he has had a prologue to introduce every playlet with the exception of the aforementioned Return of Joseph episode). Here then is a true unit within the manuscript as signaled by the internal device of a narrator.

Apart from traditional divisions of narrative and the use of narrators (a recurrent device in the cycle), there are also less direct ways of bridging episodes and creating larger units in the cycle. One is structural parallelism, a device that can be well illustrated by the conjoining of the adjacent episodes of the Woman Taken in Adultery and the Raising of Lazarus. Here there are two playlets similar in style and tone, similar even in conventions (e.g. the incipits, the Latin stage directions, and the dominant use of octaves with the unusual rhyme scheme *a b a b b c b c*,)[17] and similar, most significantly, in defining the complementary roles of Jesus as minister (who preaches mercy) and as healer (who performs miracles). In addition, both plays deal with legend that has attached to Mary Magdalene: the "mulier" in the adultery scene is often associated with her;[18] and the sister of Martha, who in the Gospels is of course Mary of Bethany, here is named "Magdalen." The two plays

[17] Spector calls the stanza of this play a "short octave," and he identifies seven plays that use it—Abraham, Moses, Cleophas and Luke, Three Marys, and Mary Magdalene—in addition to the two under consideration, as linked by common authorship. While he may well be right in this ascription, I am less interested here in the growth of the cycle and its "prehistoric" layers than I am in the deliberate juxtaposing and conjoining of scenes and acts. When he discusses the two plays specifically, he finds much common ground between them; see Spector, "Genesis of N-Town," pp. 72, 76.

[18] The Demon in the Prologue to Passion Play I speaks of "Mawdelyn's playne remyssyon," an episode that in its function as plot review can refer only to the Woman Taken in Adultery; see 226/40.

are unmistakably companion pieces that resonate with each other. And the same devices of linkage that serve to hinge these plays operate in larger frames to connect full segments within the cycle.

The following proposed division of the manuscript excludes the Proclamation, which is of course a distinct part in its own right. I would exclude it from consideration here, however, because I consider it separate in function and design from the cycle proper. In my view, proclamations and banns should properly be considered extratextual material—they are external records not parts of the dramatic text—and they should either be considered by editors as prefaces or be placed in an appendix. The divisions that follow have been defined as much as possible by the criteria I have just outlined; they take into account what I believe to be the major junctures of the manuscript.

The Old Testament Play: folios 10 through 37, including the following episodes as identified by Block:

> The Creation of Heaven and the Angels
> The Fall of Lucifer
> The Creation of the World and Man
> The Fall of Man
> Cain and Abel
> Noah
> Abraham and Isaac
> Moses
> The Prophets

Numbered consecutively, this part of the cycle would come to 1,456 lines. Its junctures are the beginning of the text proper and the first appearance of Contemplacio, who as narrator introduces Part 2. The narrative continuity is of course defined by the Old Testament subject matter, which ends at this point. Marginalia in the manuscript in the form of genealogies, writ-

ten in red and in a large *textura quadrata* script,[19] occurs on folios 16v through 18, 21 through 22v, and 37 through 37v.
These genealogies, which link Adam to Noah, Noah to Lot,
and end at the conclusion of the Old Testament Play with Anne
and her sister Emeria, clearly have the purpose of underscor-
ing the "begats" of the Old Testament as a preparation for the
birth of Christ. Whether inserted by the scribe or a separate rubricator, they reveal the perception of at least one of the major
designers of the manuscript that an important juncture occurred at folio 37.

They also highlight an important thematic concern of the
Old Testament Play, and for that matter of the cycle as a whole.
The issue of fatherhood is here, as in some other cycles as
well,[20] a point of central importance. The Old Testament Play
is perforce the play in which the role of God the Father dominates (by contrast, the next play explores the issue of the moth-
erhood of Mary, the following three the sonship of Jesus, and
the last the presence of the Holy Spirit). And God the Father,
who by virtue of his first speech is both prologue to and primary narrator of the cycle, is actively engaged throughout the
segment in defining the limits of earthly fatherhood in the light
of his celestial presence. I have already noted how Adam as father reappears in the Cain and Abel episode (prepared by
Cain's ironic remark, "I kan be mery so moty the / thow my fadyr I nevyr se"; 29/20–21). Noah calls himself "þe secunde fadyr" after Adam (35/17), and with the unique episode, embedded in the Noah play, of the killing of Cain by the blind
Lamech, the playwright shows dramatically how the failure to
"see" the father, figuratively if not literally, is carried forward
by the race of Cain. On the other hand there are the obedient
sons—precursors to Christ—such as Abel, Shem, Ham, Ja-
pheth, and, of course, notably Isaac. Abraham identifies himself as "patryarke of Age ful olde" (43/10), and Moses, his suc-

---

[19] For a description, see Meredith and Kahrl, *N-Town Plays*, p. xxiii.

[20] See my discussion of this point in relation to the Wakefield plays, "The Theatre of the World: A Study in Medieval Dramatic Form," *Chaucer Review* 7
(1973): 246.

cessor, sees God as a bright flame in the burning bush (recalling the blindness of the race of Cain); when he rehearses the Ten Commandments, he makes a special point of adding to the honoring of father and mother "þi gostly fadyr" and "þi gostly modyr," that is, God and the holy church (55/127–28). The issue of fatherhood is, of course, carried forward to its resolution with the Prophets play, which in this cycle is a dramatized representation of what artists depicted as the Tree of Jesse. Fatherhood is the prominent issue from beginning to end; the Old Testament Play is thematically and theatrically the play of God the Father.

The Marriage Play: folios 37v through 74, including the following episodes:

> The Conception of Mary
> Mary in the Temple
> The Betrothal of Mary
> The Parliament of Heaven
> The Salutation and Conception
> Joseph's Return
> The Visit to Elizabeth

Consecutively numbered, this section of the cycle comes to 1,926 lines. It derives its unity most directly from the presence of Contemplacio, who introduces the whole of the section with the enumeration of episodes already cited (see p. 193); provides prologues for each of the episodes (except for Joseph's Return, but as already explained, that playlet may have been construed by the N-Town reviser as properly part of the Salutation and Conception); and ends with an epilogue ("with Aue we be-gunne and Aue is oure conclusyon / 'Ave regina celorum' to oure lady we synge"; see 122/35–36).[21] This segment of

---

[21] The Plays in this unit are sometimes referred to collectively as the Saint Anne's Day Plays; see especially the valuable articles by M. Patricia Forrest, "The Role of the Expositor Contemplacio in the St. Anne's Day Plays of the Hegge Cycle," *Mediaeval Studies* 28 (1966): 60–76; and "Apocryphal Sources of the St.

the N-Town plays is marked by a shift in tone and, less directly, in style. Contemplacio addresses not only the learned but also the "lewd," thus reflecting the meditative purpose and the popular piety of Love's *Mirrour*. While stanzaic form and prosody are far from uniform, the diction is distinct from the preceding section in its frequent use of aureate language (especially in the speeches of Contemplacio). The section also introduces elaborate English stage directions (e.g. 65/72, 71/17, 80/227f., 81/259f., 107/292f.) that are interspersed with the more frequently occurring short Latin directions and that anticipate the remarkable stage directions of the two Passion Plays. In subject matter, the section restricts itself to the early life of Mary, based in large part on Love's *Mirrour* and the apocryphal *Book of James* (the *Protevangelium*). Because the plays in this section are widely acknowledged as constituting a unit within the cycle, I will forgo a discussion at this point of the thematic unity within this grouping.

The Infancy Play: folios 74v through 111, including the following episodes:

> The Trial of Joseph and Mary
> The Birth of Christ
> The Adoration of the Shepherds
> The Adoration of the Magi
> The Purification
> The Massacre of the Innocents
> The Death of Herod
> Christ and the Doctors

If numbered consecutively, this segment would total 1,958 lines. In terms of narrative coverage, it is the most variegated and extended "infancy play" in the English mystery cycles. The junctures of this segment are probably the least distinct in the cycle. The opening follows, of course, on the conclusion of the

Anne's Day Plays in the Hegge Cycle," *Medievalia et Humanistica* 17 (1966): 38–50.

preceding section. It is also marked by an interesting opening narration of Den, the Summoner, who stands in significant contrast with Contemplacio—a contrast that signals an important new tone and perspective. (I shall note that the N-Town cycle shifts back and forth in its voices of narration between the good and the evil, a contrast that becomes noticeable when one reads the cycle in large segments as suggested here.) The end of the segment has no clear mark of juncture, but there is a large gap (for this manuscript) between the ending of the Doctors and the beginning of the Baptism plays, a total of one and a half leaves. Moreover, the first leaf (recto and verso) of the Baptism play is an interpolation and is written by the man identified by Meredith and Kahrl as "Reviser B." While this spacing and irregularity in the manuscript do not definitely establish the fact that a section comes to an end here, it is an indication that the conclusion of the Doctors play does not naturally flow into the next episode. The Infancy Play is, however, very clearly a patchwork, which has less consistency of tone, style, convention, and source indebtedness than other segments in the cycle.

Yet, in thematic content and in perspective it certainly is of a piece. Its main concern is to put the idea of the Virgin Birth and the reality of the Christ Child into the world of man. If before, in the episode of Joseph's Return, we saw a wary and profane Joseph respond to Mary's pregnancy in the voice of the cuckolded *senex amans*, the scene was nevertheless private and the joke good-natured (especially since enlightenment and reverence come to Joseph very quickly). Now, in the unique and fascinating playlet of the Trial of Joseph and Mary, the idea of Mary's infidelity becomes a matter of public, lowbrow response. The events of the previous scenes are here transformed into story—into fabliau to be exact—and the dialogue is filled with sexual innuendo and carried to the outermost limits of the socially permissible (for example, it is said of the Holy Virgin that "sum fresch ȝonge galaunt . . . his leggys to here hath leyd"; 125/54–55). A trial by ordeal, with magic intervention, brings public exoneration to Mary and Joseph and at the same time condemnation and shame upon the heads of their accusers, the two "detractors." These results anticipate the action of the other major episodes in the Infancy Play: the Holy Family is threatened by the power of temporal social forces, and it survives with greater strength while its enemies are diminished or destroyed. The climax comes when Herod dies while gorging himself at a mock-Eucharistic feast in the self-delusion that after the Slaughter of the Innocents he is now "kynge ovyr All kyngys" (174/171). And the play ends when Jesus overcomes the smug Doctors with his powerful learning and reason. It is not accidental that the Infancy Play borrows so widely in its method from the moral play (see the two detractors named Reyse Sclaunder and Bakbyter, Mors in the Death of Herod episode, and the quasi-allegorical struggle between *wysdam* and *cunnyng* in the Doctors play). The dramatic conflict has the dimension of a psychomachy: the forces of good confront and subdue the forces of evil. The Infancy Play thus foreshadows in overall structure and in resolution the victory of Christ over Lucifer.

The Ministry Play: folios 111v through 135v, including the following episodes:

> The Baptism
> The Temptation
> The Woman Taken in Adultery
> The Raising of Lazarus

I have already noted the juncture in the manuscript at the beginning of this play. However the blank space and the interpolation of Reviser B are to be interpreted, the gap does give a sense of transition to another phase of the life of Jesus (though it must be noted that blank pages alone do not seem to signal significant junctures in this manuscript). The ending of the Ministry Play, while not highlighted physically, is marked by the beginning of what Block calls the Passion Play I with its Prologue of the Demon. The Ministry is, of course, an important narrative unit, and it conventionally begins with the Baptism and ends with the Conspiracy and the Entry into Jerusalem.

It can be said that the four episodes of this play divide into two main narrative segments: the Baptism and Temptation on the one hand, and the Woman Taken in Adultery and Lazarus on the other. I have already shown that the latter are natural companion pieces in that they reveal two of Jesus' most important ministerial missions: his work as teacher and as healer. The play as a whole is notable because its purpose is to portray Jesus at work and thus to show us, by example, the meaning and significance of his teaching. The first two episodes dramatize Jesus as he partakes of his own sacraments: he is himself baptized by John as an example of meekness (Jesus comments, "þe vertu of mekenes here tawth xal be / Euery man to lere / And take ensawmple here by me"; 190/73–75); and he goes to the wilderness to do penance (192/136), fasting for forty days and nights and then resisting the three temptations of the Devil. Both episodes mix dramatization with straight sermonizing, thus not only enacting the way to salvation but also exhorting it. The N-Town cycle has been noted for depicting a suffering Christ whose dramatic example was designed to bring to the audience an affective response of sympathy and piety. In the Baptism and Temptation plays, where the audience first meets the adult Jesus, he emerges as one among the multitude (here the audience) who will lead mankind by the example of his agony and virtue. And it is against the background of his own involvement in the sacramental life that he then proceeds to minister to the fallen and the sick. The Temptation, which brings Lucifer back to the stage, introduces a dramatic plot that is to be repeated in the subsequent two episodes of the Woman Taken in Adultery and the Raising of Lazarus. All three plays, in varying degrees show Jesus performing tasks that his onlookers *doubt* he can accomplish: the Devil tests Jesus out of his "grett dowte" (the noun is repeated seven times within the first thirty lines of the play) that he is the Son of God; the Pharisees set up a dilemma to "assay his lore" (202/62); and Mary Magdalene knowing that "no whith may helpe" her dead brother (215/179) has no hope that Jesus can bring him back to life. What we witness, then, is Jesus overcoming the doubt of foe and friend alike. And with his success, his Ministry has become manifest.

Passion Play I: folios 136 through 163v, including the following episodes:

Prologue of the Demon
Prologue of John the Baptist
The Council of the Jews
The Entry into Jerusalem
The Last Supper (in two parts, continued after Conspiracy)
The Betrayal
The Lament of the Virgin

This play comes to a total of 1,325 lines, including prologues and epilogues, which are numbered separately by Block. Although not set off in the manuscript by a title or in itself identified as a unit, Passion Play I is clearly a separate, or more accurately, a separable part of the cycle. As already indicated (see p. 188), we know this fact from the introduction of the unit that follows, Passion Play II. Moreover, Passion Play I occupies four consecutive gatherings that share a distinct watermark.[22] This may mean that at an earlier stage in the composition of N-Town, Passion Play I replaced material that was then in the cycle. If so, Passion Play I in its "prehistoric" shape might have been a self-standing play, which the N-Town reviser adapted for inclusion into his cycle. Unlike the beginning, the end of Passion Play I is quite clearly marked. It ends with what seems to be a coda, spoken by two Doctors, and although its content is not entirely appropriate to the play (it gives praise to the Apostles), the last stanza is an apostrophe to John the Baptist, who appropriately spoke the prologue of the play. The coda is

[22] See Meredith and Kahrl, *N-Town Plays*, p. xv. The gatherings in question are N, P, Q, and R with a single folio, 143, grafted on as gathering O; see Block *Ludus Coventriae*, p. xiii.

followed by a blank page. The junctures of Passion Play I are thus clearly defined, and, as a part of the cycle, it is widely recognized as a semi-independent play.[23]

The title Passion Play I is not sufficiently specific to describe the central dramatic action, and it implies that the play is really the first part of a two-part play, similar perhaps to Shakespeare's two plays of *Henry IV*. Actually, as in Shakespeare's plays, the action of the two parts is quite distinct, and, except for the cycle's need to dramatize the life of Christ, Passion Play I could easily stand as a complete play. In effect, the plot takes in the major events from the Conspiracy to the Arrest, and thus includes among its major episodes the Entry into Jerusalem, the Last Supper (which is here conflated with Jesus' visit to Simon of Bethany), the Betrayal, and the Agony in the Garden. It is noteworthy that the play interweaves without break the action of the conspirators and of Jesus and his disciples. Judas serves as the link between the two main *sedes* on the stage, crossing from Simon's house to the "cownsel hous." It is therefore impossible to separate the action of either the Last Supper or the Conspiracy into one distinct episode. The Last Supper actually consists of three scenes, the approach (322–397), Mary Magdalene's anointing of Jesus' feet and the gathering of the disciples around the table (462–589), and the meal proper (670–892). In turn, the Conspiracy progresses on another part of the stage simultaneously, and we cannot be conscious of the progress of one without noting in the periphery of our attention the presence of the other (even if for some of the action the curtain to the scaffold is drawn). The significant point is that the traditionally conjectured pageant performance vir-

[23] See, for example, the article by Daniel P. Poteet, "Time, Eternity, and Dramatic Form in *Ludus Coventriae* Passion Play I," in *The Drama of the Middle Ages*, ed. Clifford Davidson, G. J. Gianakaris, and John H. Stroupe (New York: AMS Press, 1982), pp. 232–248. Noteworthy also is the discussion by Eleanor Prosser in an appendix entitled "The Reviser of the Hegge *Passion Play*, Part I" in *Drama and Religion in the English Mystery Plays* (Stanford: Stanford University Press, 1961), pp. 201–205. Prosser believes, as I do, that the play is the work of one person. She also challenges the use of stanzaic tests for determining authorship.

tually demands a linear progression of episodes, and that sort of performance is ruled out by the structure of this play. Moreover, the play has a skillfully enclosed plot, one that allows independent performance without the need for an enactment of what precedes or follows. It has an elaborately balanced prologue—the Devil speaks first, followed by John the Baptist, calling to mind, in reverse order, the actions that open the preceding segment of the cycle, the Baptism and the Temptation. That balance foreshadows the dual threading of the plot. At the center of the play is the enactment of the Last Supper, which is done elaborately in the form of a Mass and thereby gives emphasis to the sacramental core of the whole cycle. The action of the Conspiracy and the Arrest frames the play—with Jesus in the center of the performance and the conspirators at its ragged and bustling edges. Slowly the antagonistic forces are closing in; the sphere of evil expands until, at the inevitable climax of the arrest, it envelops the stage. The drama concludes in a lament by the two Marys and an epilogue of the Doctors. The formal design of the play is unmistakable.

The Passion Play II: folios 165 through 201, including the following episodes:

> Prologue by Contemplacio
> Prologue by Herod
> The Trial before Annas and Caiaphas
> Peter's Denial
> The Death of Judas
> The Trial before Pilate
> The Trial before Herod
> The Dream of Pilate's Wife
> The Second Trial before Pilate
> The Scourging
> The Crown of Thorns
> The Procession to Calvary
> The Crucifixion
> The Descent into Hell

The Burial
The Guarding of the Sepulcher
The Harrowing of Hell
The Resurrection
The Announcement to the Three Marys
The Appearance to Mary Magdalene

This play is considerably longer than the first Passion; it comes to a total of 1,934 lines, including the proem by Contemplacio and the Mary plays (which are numbered separately in Block's edition). The break between the two Passion plays is clearly marked in several ways in the manuscript even though again no explicits or titles are used. The clearest and most direct signal that a new play follows is, of course, in the text itself. Contemplacio, who reappears for the first time since the Marriage Play, welcomes the audience, reviews the contents of last year's play, and then previews this year's:

> Now wold we procede how he was browth þan
> Beforn Annas and Cayphas and syth beforn Pylate,
> And so forth in his passyon how mekely he toke
>   it for man,
> Besekyng ȝou for mede of ȝour soulys to take good
>   hede þeratte.
>
> (271/17–20)

What follows is, then, truly a "passion" play.

A further indication in the manuscript that a break occurs between the two Passion plays is the occurrence of a blank leaf that at the top of the page includes the words, "In nomjne Dei Amen," typically an opening title (the Towneley manuscript, as noted, opens with these words). Block believes that this folio may "have been an outside leaf at some time" (see p. 270), though it is difficult to know when and under what circumstances that might have been the case.[24]

---

[24] An interesting suggestion has been made by Richard Daniels that the N-Town MS was originally divided into two volumes, which were identified as Cotton Vespasian D.viii and D.ix. This would explain the reference by William

The ending of the second Passion Play is not so clearly marked. Unlike Passion Play I, which occupies four full quires, this play is not a manuscript unit as such. Block has attempted to explain how one might be able to accommodate the material to quires S and T, speculating in the process about the kinds of adaptations that the reviser would have had to make, but her argument sheds little light on where the extant text of Passion Play II would end most logically in terms of manuscript evidence. In fact, she seems to offer three possible endings, and the one upon which she settles in the text proper she fails to justify altogether. That ending occurs at the point where her numbering sequence ends, namely after the so-called Resurrection play (in the middle of folio 196 and also in the middle of a gathering). This division is in conflict with her view that "the action is continuous until the end of the Appearance to Mary Magdalen play on f. 201, the middle of quire U." But in contradiction with that view is her strenuous argument that the most significant break comes at the end of quire T at a point where the four soldiers leave Pilate to guard the sepulcher, a scene that in narrative terms is surely in the middle, and not at the end, of the dramatic action (see Block, esp. pp. 14–15, but also passim). While the demarcation of the end of the play must remain a puzzle, I feel most confident about placing it at the end of the Appearance to Mary Magdalen. Here, as Block notes, there is truly a break in the action, and though the juncture comes in the middle of a gathering, it is followed by one of the very few explicits in the manuscript (which in turn is followed by an almost equally rare incipit on the next leaf, where the Cleophas and Luke play begins). There is, in fact, a manuscript gap of practically all of folio 201 (which is filled with what appears to be an actor's speech written in another hand and

---

Dugdale in his *Antiquities of Warwickshire* (1656) to exclusively New Testament plays in a volume that he identifies in the Cotton library as "sub effigie Vesp. D. 9." And if Dugdale was right in this ascription, Daniels speculates, both he and Richard James, who is responsible for the title *Ludus Coventriae*, might also have been right in their ascription. See Daniels, "A Study of the Formal and Literary Unity of the N-Town Mystery Cycle" (Ph.D. diss., Ohio State University, 1972), pp. 160–165.

summarizing the preceding speech by Mary Magdalene) and of the entire folio 201v. My numbering would bring the Passion play to an end at this point.

In narrative terms the action of Passion Play II, if that play ends with the Mary Magdalene episode, is very similar in structure to Passion Play I. Again, the center of our interest is Jesus, and the center of the play, almost exactly, is the Crucifixion. The play opens, once more, with two prologues, the first by a "good" character, Contemplacio, who exhorts his audience to "kepe þe passyon in ȝour mende þat xal be shewyd here" (271/8), and the second by the tyrannical King Herod, who tells us that he takes special delight in torturing and killing Christians (as he did John the Baptist for baptizing Jesus and so many others). Just as the preceding play began with a council, the object of which was to capture Jesus, so does this play begin with Herod's announcement to his soldiers that he will "seke jhesus with my dew dilygens" (273/55). Herod, of course, does not know that Jesus is already taken, and since this is the second of two plays, a messenger comes forth at this point to tell us that fact and in the process to review the details of the arrest (274/78–93) as portrayed in Passion Play I. There follows a series of trial scenes that give the audience an incremental characterization of the enemies of Christ, ending with the visit of Satan to Pilate's wife and reminding us of the role that he has played since the Temptation as the central antagonist in the cycle. The N-Town cycle makes a good deal of the fact that Satan is the self-deluded "prince of the werd" (see 237/182), the offense that ironically enough Jesus' earthly enemies perceive to be *his* (see 282/303–314). Dramatically, Passion Play II affords the same opportunity for the interweaving of action on a multiple stage as did Passion Play I. Among the trial scenes, we once more have the intrusion of Judas, who again seeks out Annas and Caiaphas, this time to give back the money. The Crucifixion, somewhat as did the Arrest, brings to center stage all the participants on both sides, leading of course to more lamentation, recalling the ending of Passion Play I where the Virgin Mary, in the company of Mary Magdalene, delivers a long *planctus.* Here, however, the action moves beyond lament, as the appearance of Jesus, first to his mother and then to Mary Magdalene, leads to a joyful ending. Structurally the second Passion Play is at once a reflection of and an extension upon the first.

The Appearances and the Last days: folios 202 through 225v, including the following episodes:

> The Appearance to Cleophas and Luke
> The Appearance to Thomas
> The Ascension
> The Choice of Matthias
> The Day of Pentecost
> The Assumption of the Virgin
> Doomsday

If consecutively numbered, this last section of the N-Town cycle would total 1,157 lines. It should be noted, however, that the final play, Doomsday, is incomplete, and the Assumption, which is the longest episode in this segment, is the work of another scribe and seems to have been incorporated wholesale into the N-Town manuscript. It has been suggested that this latter play represents, "as it stands, an earlier stage in the history of this collection of plays, and may be thought of as typical of the material in its most usable form, from which the main scribe was working."[25] Thus, while we have in the Assumption play an episode that is integrally part of the cycle—and an important part as I hope to show later—the last segment is relatively less consistent in design than the other parts I have examined.

The main action of this last part of the cycle is, of course, the reappearance of Christ in various settings. And the episodes, as is true of other parts in the cycle, seem to blend into one another without significant breaks. Of special note is the merging of the scenes in which Jesus appears before Cleophas and Luke

[25] Meredith and Kahrl, *N-Town Plays*, p. xiii.

and before Thomas. Here for once even the scribe is drawn in since he fails to insert the pageant number at the point where it would be expected (on f. 207, halfway down the page), and Block in turn makes no attempt to separate the two scenes, even though the Proclamation lists them as separate pageants. The fact is that the action is clearly continuous, in stanza form as well as narrative line. After Jesus rises, Cleophas and Luke decide to seek out their "bretheren" to tell them the news (344/234). They walk for a time until they come upon Peter and Thomas and probably also the other disciples (see 345/269, a passage in Block's edition that requires an editorial stage direction, or at very least, annotation). They tell their story, and directly Thomas doubts it, and Christ comes back yet again. Cleophas and Luke never exit. Although at this point the Appearance play ends, we learn from a stage direction attached to the incipit of the next play, the Ascension (see p. 349), that the eleven disciples never leave the stage. At the opening of this play, Christ appears in an alb with two angels by his side, and after the Ascension, the eleven remain on stage for yet two more scenes, the Choice of Matthias and the Descent of the Holy Ghost. Even the Assumption play, intrusive though it is, brings the Apostles back on stage, and the impression that we are witnessing a play centering upon the expanding awareness of the Apostles is reinforced. In the process, of course, the play reiterates the truth of the Resurrection, and it builds ineluctably to the climactic doom in the final episode.

I have attempted in this section to demonstrate that the N-Town cycle is organized into "acts" rather than scenes. While some of these acts, at least as they now stand in the manuscript, may never have been staged, they are carefully designed and elaborated, and it is clear that at least two of them in the course of their history were self-standing dramas. But they were also part of a larger whole—the cycle itself—which was put together by an author/reviser who gave each act the special imprint of his vision and his remarkable sense of dramatic structure. With the acts in mind, then, I want now to look more closely at the feature of the N-Town cycle that I consider the mark of its peculiar genius: its formal organization.

THE opinion that the N-Town cycle is a unified work of art worthy of consideration as a single drama has not had wide acceptance in published scholarship. Indeed the opposite view, expressed most forcefully by Eleanor Prosser, namely that "an entire mystery cycle should not be considered as one play,"[26] has dominated the critical consideration of the N-Town cycle. For example, in her discussion of the Saint Anne's Day plays, Patricia Forrest extends upon Prosser's statement by observing:

> Certainly the Hegge plays, a compilation of independent units produced in different years, should not be considered as a structural unit. The St. Anne's Day plays, apparently presented without a break by one cast and unified by the recurring appearance of Contemplacio, are structurally independent.[27]

This opinion is based on hypothetical performance considerations, for which no evidence exists. While we do know that N-Town is a compilation, that fact alone does not rule out the structural unity of the cycle. Wakefield is also a compilation—we know that it borrowed plays from the York cycle—and yet no one has argued that it lacks unity on that account. Moreover, the fact that a segment of a cycle could be independently produced does not rule out its integration with the rest of the play when it stands in context. Surely, no one would argue that G. B. Shaw's *Man and Superman* lacks unity because the "Don Juan in Hell" segment is sometimes extrapolated from it and acted independently.

Scholars may well have shied away from undertaking interpretations of whole cycles because they have focused too much on the growth of the manuscripts, which as we have seen for N-

---

[26] Prosser, *Drama and Religion*, p. 54.
[27] Forrest, "The Role of Contemplacio," p. 70, n. 30.

Town has meant the positing of strata of composition and multiple authorship. The fact is, however, that the manuscripts we have all represent a very late stage in the growth of the cycle—indeed, the last stage, since any further growth was obviously left unrecorded. Hence, what we have is not a record of the process of composition but rather the final product in the creative enterprise. In this respect the cycle manuscripts are not so different from the prime manuscripts of *The Canterbury Tales*. Each no doubt reflects many layers of composition, but that does not preclude the presence of a final editor or group of editors who added their perceptions and insights to those of the author(s). In the case of N-Town, final editor and author may have been one and the same person, as Rosemary Woolf has suggested. Certainly once we recognize that possibility we must agree with Woolf that it is not difficult to explain "why the cycle gives such a strong impression of a single controlling mind and individual sensibility and yet contains sections at least partially detachable."[28] When we recall, moreover, that the extant manuscript was not compiled as a script for performance, indeed seems clearly to have been intended for the private reader,[29] the argument for an interpretation of the cycle as a whole work of art becomes even more compelling.

Despite the disposition by scholars to regard the N-Town cycle as a patchwork, a number of recent studies have called attention to its overall organization and design. Of particular interest is the fact that in the last twenty years no fewer than six dissertations specifically devoted to N-Town have based their argument on the underlying assumption that the cycle must be read as a whole work of art.[30] (And this figure does not include

[28] Woolf, *English Mystery Plays*, pp. 309–310.

[29] See Greg, *Bibliographic and Textual Problems*, p. 143.

[30] My search turned up the following entries: Robert Leonard, "Patterns of Dramatic Unity in the N-Town Cycle" (Ph.D. diss., State University of New York at Stony Brook, 1984); Sandra Robertson Nelson, " 'Goddys Worlde': Revelation and Its Transmission in the N-Town Cycle," *DAI* 37 (1977): 4344A; Sidney Jerry Vance, "Unifying Patterns of Reconciliation in the Ludus Coventriae," *DAI* 36 (1976): 4472A–4473A; Richard J. Daniels, "A Study of the Formal and

the numerous dissertations that have developed the same premise in the wider context of all the medieval Corpus Christi cycles.) The disposition, then, to find structural unity in the cycle is clearly evident in the emerging scholarship of our time, and perhaps on that ground alone one need no longer engage in a lengthy defense of the approach.

Among published studies, several have put forward thematic interpretations of the cycle as a whole. Of these the most influential and widely quoted has been that of Timothy Fry under the revealing title of "The Unity of the *Ludus Coventriae*," published as long ago as 1951. Fry, finding an "architectonic plan" in the cycle, argues that the "dramatist" (of whom he speaks consistently in the singular) deliberately developed a central thesis—the abuse-of-power theory of the Redemption—in putting together the cycle. This theory holds that

> when Adam and Eve fell into original sin, Satan was permitted to inflict death on them and all mankind and hold them captive in hell. Christ born of the Immaculate Virgin Mary, was not subject to that law of death. Satan, however, was deceived by the human nature of Christ, and, in bringing about His death, abused his power, and lost the souls in hell.[31]

He goes on to show meticulously how the dramatist used this theory to develop the central conflict of the cycle between Satan and Christ—how, for example, the abuse-of-power concept justifies the Marian plays by which means the Devil is "deceived" into believing that Christ was born into an ordinary hu-

---

Literary Unity of the N-Town Mystery Cycle," *DAI* 33 (1973): 6304A–6305A; Mary L. Tobin, "A Study of the Formation and Auspices of the Ludus Coventriae," *DAI* 34 (1973): 1258A–1259A; and Daniel P. Poteet 2d, "The *Hegge Plays*: An Approach to the Aesthetics of Medieval Drama," *DAI* 30 (1970): 3020A–3021A. I have not included in this list dissertations devoted to textual, linguistic, or staging problems. Interestingly, not a single critical dissertation I have seen argues in favor of multiple authorship.

[31] Timothy Fry, "The Unity of the *Ludus Coventriae*," *Studies in Philology* 48 (1951): 529.

man family only to discover at the height of the Passion that Christ is not, in fact, an ordinary human and therefore does not fall under his sway. The Fry study still stands as a landmark in medieval drama criticism, for it was the first disciplined study of a cycle based on the "doctrinal content of the plays." And even today it provides a highly useful analysis of a unifying strand in the cycle that undeniably binds together the major sections and strata.

More recently, in an illuminating article, Kathleen Ashley constructs what is essentially an exercise to discover whether the N-Town cycle, as one among several, offers the reader/ viewer aesthetic coherence rather than simply "an assortment of disparate plays." She observes that each of the cycles has been noted as being "unified by a dominant mode or tone" and that N-Town in particular has been characterized as being the most learned of the English cycles. While she attributes this perception *partly* to the influence of Fry's interpretation, I believe that it derives *entirely* from it. Fry's study stands alone among those claiming structural unity in focusing on the doctrinal content of a cycle, and consequently the perception that N-Town is the "learned" cycle quickly grew into a commonplace. Ashley shows that there is both less and more to this characterization of N-Town than has previously been noted: less, in the sense that N-Town is neither erudite nor abstruse; more, because its very subject seems to be "learning" itself. She goes on to demonstrate that in many segments of the cycle, though especially in the episodes of Christ and the Doctors and the Parliament of Heaven, Christ is singled out for his wisdom and that the central action of the play focuses on the uses and abuses of "wysdam," "wyt," and "cunnyng." She concludes that this emphasis "permeates the cycle and is not confined to one group which has been identified as having a separate existence."[32] The centrality of learning—that is, the whole question of where wisdom resides, how it is acquired, and who should

[32] Ashley, " 'Wyt' and 'Wysdam' in the N-Town Cycle," *Philological Quarterly* 58 (1979): 127.

have access to it—is an important theme of the N-Town cycle, one that surfaces at the very beginning of the Old Testament Play (see 20/120) and one that, as Ashley shows convincingly, can leave little room for the notion that the cycle is the unassimilated product of multiple authorship. Whoever finally put the N-Town cycle together was concerned that it be perceived as an extended play with an integrated interpretation of the place held by knowledge and wisdom in God's plan of salvation.

It is important for a full understanding of the thematic unity of the N-Town cycle that we examine more fully and particularly the place that learning occupies in its dramatic plan and in its interpretation of salvation history. While Ashley has given a sound interpretation of the place of "wyt" and "wysdam" in the cycle, she does not show how ultimately these terms relate to learning and to the larger question of the relationship between learning and faith. Nor does her article finally offer a developed insight into the nature of the "learned tone" that most scholars have found in the cycle.

The essential argument of the cycle is that Christ as the Second Person of the Trinity has as his special quality the power of wisdom. He volunteers in the Parliament of Heaven to redeem man, an act that can only be accomplished through wisdom because it was in the quest for wisdom that man fell. God the Father speaking to the Son puts it as follows:

> In ȝour wysdam, son, man was mad thore,
> And in wysdam was his temptacion;
> þerfor, sone, sapyens ȝe must ordeyn herefore,
> and se how of man may be salvacion.
>
> (103/173–176)

Throughout the cycle, man is seen as perverse and impious whenever he pursues learning and when, in effect, he seeks for his own ends the wisdom that is Christ's. Satan, by extension, is evil incarnate because he uses deceit in bringing down the kingdom of God. The word that best describes Satan's *modus operandi* is "sotylte," which means "acuteness of mind" or "sagacity" but also, when brought to its most pejorative extension,

"craftiness," "guile," and "treachery" (*OED.*, s.v. "Subtlety,"
¶1.3). He tells us in his prologue, which serves as the introduction of Passion Play I, that he will avenge "be sotylte al my ma-
lycious grevauns" (227/59), and he clearly has his own plan
("myn intent" 226/30) with which he will confront the "intent"
of Jesus (226/46):

> But whan þe tyme xal neyth of his persecucion,
> I xal arere new engynes of malycious conspiracy,
> Plente of reprevys I xal provide to his confusyon;
> þus xal I false þe wordys þat his pepyl doth testefy,
> His discipulis xal forsake hym and here mayster denye,
> Innovmberabyl xal his woundys be of woful grevauns,
> A tretowre xal countyrfe his deth to fortyfye,
> þe rebukys þat he gyf me xal turne to his displesauns.
>
> (226/49–56)

With this master plan announced at the outset of the Passion,
we become aware that the betrayal, torture, and death of Christ
are implemented entirely through Satan. Interestingly, the
agents themselves employ subtlety in carrying out the evil design of Satan; see Annas (245/402), Caiaphas (246/419), and especially Judas (253/654).

Satan's first subtlety is, of course, the Temptation, when he
bids Eve to bite into the apple and implants in her, and by extension in Adam, the notion that they can be as wise as God in
all respects:

> Of þis appyl yf ȝe wyl byte,
> Evyn as god is so xal ȝe be,
> Wys of Connyng, as I ȝow plyte,
> Lyke on to God in al degre.
>
> (22/181–185)

"Cunnyng" is the key word in the Fall (see 22/196, 23/232, 24/
244), and it is also the word that characterizes the learning of
the Doctors: "of all cunnynge we bere þe maystrye" (179/28).
They begin their play with the boast that they bear the prize of
all learning; they are self-professed masters or "redynge,"

"wrytynge," "trewe ortografye" (a skill that regrettably the N-Town scribe never learned!), "gramer," "cadens," "prosodye," "musyke," "dyaletyk," "sophestrye," "logyk," "phylosophye," "metaphesyk," "astronomye," "calculacion," "negremauncye," "augrym," "asmatryk," "lynyacion," "jematrye," "phesyk," and "retoryke" in which they have attained "þe hyest degre" (see 178/5–24). These are medieval men who have mastered all the "science" of their day as taught in the trivium and the quadrivium, and they are deluded into thinking that this knowledge gives them the power of God. Their learning, however, is mere "science," as opposed to "sapience," and as a result, like the postlapsarian Adam (24/276), they are unable to see God when they confront him. The play of Christ and the Doctors, unlike those of the other mystery cycles, is a true disputation (in the others, the central scene is the young Jesus' recitation of the Decalogue), and what it finally proves is that for all their learning the Doctors fail to understand the highest truth.

The play goes yet a step further, for in Jesus' argument proper it also gives a living demonstration of the meaning of wisdom. Jesus asks the Doctors:

> Can ȝe owth tellyn how þis werde was wrought,
> How longe xal it laste can ȝe devyse,
> With all þe cunnyge þat ȝe han sought?
>
> (179/50–52)

And they reply that no "erthely" clerk has an answer to those questions. Jesus goes on to explain what no earthly mind can grasp by itself: how one God can live in three Persons; how a clean maid gave birth; and why Jesus was chosen to be incarnated (repeating in much greater detail what God had already announced in the Parliament of Heaven; see 182/115–132). The Doctors play thus exposes the inadequacy of science and imparts wisdom in the person of Christ. It is worth noting that disputation is an important element in the N-Town cycle. The Parliament of Heaven, the Doctors play, the Temptation (which first presents a Parliament of Devils, see 193–195/1–65 and then a debate between Jesus and Satan), the Council of the

Jews at the outset of the Passion—all are structured as debates, and each reminds us of the power that wisdom holds over mortal men.

The N-Town cycle says that mortal man may have acquired worldly knowledge but his only access to wisdom is through faith, for wisdom itself resides in Christ, who at the very end, in the interpolated Assumption play, is identified for the reader as "Sapientia" when he appears for the first time in that play (358/81). Truth, in the person of Veritas, resides with God alongside her sisters Mercy, Justice, and Peace. The way to discover her is to believe in Jesus and to shun doubt, for it was his "grett dowte" (193/4) that caused Satan not to believe in the divinity of Christ. The doubt of the Apostles in this cycle is therefore a deviation that must not be taken lightly. Those who saw Christ and who served him were in direct touch with the truth, and through them the good news ("glad tydyngys," 346/294; "gode Novell," 346/298) of his Resurrection and hence his divinity must be spread. Access to truth is thus through the wisdom of Christ, who appears most memorably in the N-Town cycle as the archetypal priest administering his own Eucharist at the Last Supper.[33] This sacerdotal function is highlighted throughout the cycle, and those who are true priests, including the commanding figure of Contemplacio (the narrator who imparts the truth), are seen to speak in the image of Christ, giving access to wisdom.

There is yet one other way in which learning plays an important role in the N-Town cycle, namely in the life of Mary. She is characterized from the time of her Presentation in the Temple as an extraordinary scholar. Her rehearsal of the fifteen Psalms in Latin and English when she is a mere babe of three

---

[33] For a discussion of this scene, see Woolf, *English Mystery Plays*, p. 234; and especially the enlightening article by Theresa Coletti, "Sacrament and Sacrifice in the N-Town Passion," *Mediaevalia* 7 (1981): 239–264. Coletti argues that among all the extant cycles, "the most sustained emphasis on the sacramental meaning of Christ's body occurs in the N-Town Passion, in which the sacrament and sacrifice of *corpus christi* figure as a dramatic and devotional theme" (see p. 239).

barely able to ascend the fifteen steps is unique in the English drama. Note that the second Psalm, following directly upon the "holy desyre with god to be" (75/85), advocates

> stody with meke inquysissyon veryly:
> How I xal haue knowynge of Godys wylle
> To þe mownteynes of hefne I haue lyfte myn ey
> From qwens xal comyn helpe me tylle.
>
> (75/88–91)

Mary is put in the cloister to worship God and to learn "þe lyberary of oure lordys lawe" (80/234). She is at home in the Temple, where she was brought up and to which she retreats after the Crucifixion with the announcement, "Here in þis temple my lyff I lede" (305/963). And, indeed, she apparently remains there until her death, for we discover her "in templo" at the beginning of the Assumption play (357/67f.). Her favorite reading is the Book of Psalms, which, as we have already seen, she seems to know by heart (she again recites Psalms in Latin and English on her visit to Elizabeth; see pp. 118–120). When Joseph leaves her in the play of the Betrothal, she tells him

> And I xal here abyde ȝour aȝen-comynge,
> And on my sawtere book I xal rede.
>
> (95/423–424)

The Psalter is the sacred book that she uses in particular to praise God (95/432), and she tells us in an eloquent passage what the Psalter means to her:

> þe song of psalmus is goddys dete,
> Synne is put awey þerby;
> It lernyth a man vertuysful to be,
> It feryth mannys herte gostly
> Who þat it vsyth custommably,
> It claryfieth þe herte and charyte makyth cowthe;
> He may not faylen of Goddys mercy
> þat hath þe preysenge of God evyr in his mowthe.

O holy psalmys, O holy book,
Swetter to say than any ony.
þou lernyst hem love, Lord, þat on þe look
And makyst hem desyre thyngys celestly.

(96/437–448)

This passage, perhaps more than any other in the cycle, reveals what true learning is and how it must be used. Clearly, whatever intimations of wisdom may be available to man must come from Scripture, which is the book of God. And what man learns from the Psalms, Mary tells us, is how to be virtuous and how to love. As the paradigmatic human being committed to a life of learning, that is what she has gathered from her own assiduous reading of the Psalter.

Hers then is truly the contemplative life. As mother of God, she has access to God's wisdom, a fact that we are meant to perceive in the aureate language to which she returns throughout the cycle and which stands in obvious contrast to the simple, unsophisticated language of Joseph. Here is an example:

Farewell Gabryel specyalye,
Farewell Goddys masangere expresse,
I thank 30w for 30ur traveyl hye,
Gramercy of 30ur grett goodnes.

And namely of 30ur comfortabyl massage,
For I vndyrstande by inspyracion,
þat 3e knowe by singulere preuylage
Most of my sonys incarnacion.
I pray 30w take it in to vsage,
Be a custom ocupacion
To vesyte me ofte be mene passage;
30ur presence is my comfortacion.

(108/317–328)

Her language, with its obtrusive Latinisms, here and elsewhere, is meant to project the register of a well-spoken, enlightened person. She shares this register with Contemplacio

219

and other priestly voices. The N-town cycle thereby reflects, especially in the Marian plays, not only an interest in learning but a demonstration of its presence in the rhetoric of the educated.

The ultimate effect of the emphasis on the wisdom of God is an affirmation of his will and power. The cycle repeatedly makes us aware that the conflict between God and Satan is preordained and that, indeed, true wisdom and wit allow us to discover that plan. We are told again and again about the *intent* of God and Satan, and we know, of course, that the former must prevail. The Angel tells Jesus directly:

> He bad þat þou xuldyst not drede
> But fulfylle his intent,
> As þe parlement of hefne hath ment.
> (264/947–949)

Against this carefully ordained purpose, which we have watched unfold, the Devil's declaration is noticeably feeble: "þis werd at þis tyme to myn intent is browth" (228/96). It cannot be brought "to his intent" because he fails to recognize the truth, that Jesus is the Son of God. Indeed, finally the conflict is between *true* and *false* intent, as we are told in Jesus' exhortation on the meaning of the Eucharist:

> Takys þese chalys of þe newe testament,
> And kepyth þis evyr in ʒour mende:
> As oftyn as ʒe do þis with trewe intent,
> It xal defende ʒow fro þe fende.
> (259/807–810)

The strongest evidence that the N-Town cycle's perspective upon salvation history emphasizes learning is its concentration on God's intent. Throughout, one is aware that the drama depicts a grand design of providential wisdom.

I have tried to show in the foregoing discussion that the N-Town cycle is thematically unified. No doubt there are many other strands that can be found to show that a deliberate effort was made in this cycle to bind together its various parts or strata.[34] Studies of this type can provide deeper insights into the meaning of the cycle as a whole; yet they are not the only nor necessarily the best means by which we can arrive at a coherent overview of the work. The N-Town cycle, in particular, provides yet another way of discovering its carefully planned coherence—one that is imbedded in its structure. I refer specifically to the playwright's deliberate and multifaceted use of figural interpretation and the typological design that results from it. To understand this accomplishment, we need first to review the place of figural interpretation in the mystery cycles.

THE use of typology in the medieval drama is a subject of wide interest, one that was opened for critical consideration by Erich Auerbach in *Mimesis*, first published in Europe in 1946 and in America in 1953. Concentrating on the Anglo-Norman *Le Jeu d'Adam*, Auerbach sets out to show how the use of the *figura* or *type* in that liturgical play creates a wholly integrated style in which the sublime is mixed with the everyday and in which time is universalized. God is not merely lawgiver; he is identified as "Figura" and he is already the Redeemer. Adam, in turn, "has advance knowledge of all of Christian world history, or at least of Christ's coming and the redemption from that original sin which he, Adam, has just committed."[35] For Auerbach, *Le Jeu d'Adam* is primarily of stylistic interest; it vividly illustrates the way in which the universal truths of Scripture could be integrated with everyday life. Adam and Eve are con-

---

[34] Of particular interest is the work of Patrick Collins on the relationship of the N-Town cycle to the visual arts of its day. His monograph, *The N-Town Plays and Medieval Picture Cycles* (Kalamazoo: Medieval Institute Publications, 1979), traces three motifs through the cycle—the "symbolic fruit," "fraud and disguise," and "worldly chaos and heavenly calm"—and shows their parallel uses in contemporary works of the visual arts. While unity is not a topic he considers per se, it clearly inheres as a given in his approach.

[35] Auerbach, *Mimesis: The Representation of Reality in Western Literature*, trans. Willard R. Trask (Garden City, N.Y.: Doubleday, 1957), pp. 136–137. See also his classic essay on "Figura," perhaps the most enlightening explanation and discussion of typology available, in *Scenes from the Drama of European Literature*, trans. Ralph Manheim (New York: Meridian, 1959), pp. 11–76.

temporary rustics, speaking in the vernacular, and what happens in the Genesis story is thereby transmuted into contemporary life with the effect of universalizing the experience of the Temptation and the Fall. While Auerbach's discussion centers on the Anglo-Norman play, he singles out scenes from the mysteries to which he attributes the initiation of "a particularly striking development of realism."[36]

Much has been written since Auerbach's pioneering study on the subject of typology as applied to the mystery cycles, but here for the sake of economy only a few studies can be singled out. Probably of greatest influence and importance to our understanding of the application of typology to the vernacular English drama has been V. A. Kolve's *Play Called Corpus Christi*. Kolve enlarges upon Auerbach's interpretation essentially to do two things: first, to use typology as a way of justifying the inclusion of various Old Testament episodes in what he calls the "protocyle" of the English Corpus Christi plays; and second, to provide the reader with a deeper understanding of "certain patterns of language and action" in the plays.[37] While his justification of specific Old Testament episodes is open to criticism (one constantly asks why, if figura was the basis of selection, certain Biblical episodes that are missing from all English cycles, like Joseph's captivity or the death of Jonah, are not included), Kolve nevertheless introduced a whole new critical method of explaining the presence and significance of the Old Testament plays in the English cycles.

Walter Meyers in his book, *A Figure Given: Typology in the Wakefield Cycle*, gave, several years later, a typological interpretation of an entire cycle of plays. Apart from demonstrating the wide applicability of the typological method as a key to interpretation, Meyers expanded upon the strict definition of the Biblical type and allowed it to explain dramatic action that by purist standards did not apply to the method. A type, when

[36] Auerbach, *Mimesis*, p. 139.

[37] V. A. Kolve, *The Play Called Corpus Christi* (Stanford: Stanford University Press, 1966), pp. 65–66.

considered in the context of hermeneutics rather than literary criticism, requires several attributes. First, it must be an Old Testament figure, event, action, or place that foreshadows a parallel (or *antitype*) in the New Testament. Second, a type as well as its antitype is a historical fact in context, and therefore the correspondence is metaphysical not metaphoric or allegorical. Third, the antitype always fulfills the type, and for that reason the antitype is *forma perfectior*, a more complete or perfect form than the type. What Meyers introduced was a larger application of type to the drama; instead of confining himself to the traditional Old Testament *figurae*, he included a chapter on "diabolical typology," accounting for the tyrants and villains of the Old and New Testaments as types based on Lucifer much as the patriarchs are types of Christ. This scheme violates, among other rules, that which insists that the antitype must be *forma perfectior*, and it thus reverses the outcome of the process because in the correspondence from Lucifer to Herod and Pilate, the process is degenerative (in oxymoronic terms, from the perfect type to the imperfect antitype). It leads to the interesting result of highlighting the redemption as an ascending dramatic action while representing the diabolic as a descending action. As Meyers puts it, "The culmination of this diabolical typology, Pilate, will stand as a living symbol of the city of man against the City of God in Christ."[38]

The next major attempt to link typology with the English Corpus Christi cycles (and for that matter the liturgical drama as well) was Theo Stemmler's book-length study *Liturgische Feiern und geistliche Spiele*. Stemmler is concerned with the linkage between the hermeneutic use of the type and its literary applications; he attempts in effect to come to terms with the problem found in Meyers's approach. Stemmler suggests a new term by which to understand the application of typology: "typologische Übertragung" or, in his own English rendering,

---

[38] Walter E. Meyers, *A Figure Given: Typology in the Wakefield Plays* (Pittsburgh: Duquesne University Press, 1970), p. 55.

"typological transfer."[39] What he advocates is the acceptance of a certain kind of "typological thinking" wherein one scene was "transferred" into another of the same type. He sees, for example, the relationship of the liturgical *Visitatio Sepulchri* and the *Officium Stellae* as one of "typological transfer." Here we have two very similar situations: three visitors (the Marys and the Kings) arriving at a site (the sepulcher, the manger) bringing gifts in honor of Christ. Since we know the historical priority of the visit to the sepulcher scene, we can accept the visit to the manger as the transfer scene. In other words, the drama grew out of the exploitation by the dramatists of successful scenes or characters into new scenes or characters that were similar. In the mystery cycles, Stemmler finds a great many examples of typological transfer—for example the extension of the life of Christ to the life of Mary, as one finds the two dramatized in the Crucifixion and the Assumption, respectively (e.g. in the York and N-Town cycles). Stemmler's study is useful especially for those who wish to move out of the realm of hermeneutics and into dramatic criticism. I shall have occasion to return to the term "typological transfer" in my consideration of typology in the N-Town cycle.

Rosemary Woolf has brought attention to typology in the drama in yet another context, the relative success with which the type can be rendered dramatically. Her interest is specifically in types and their potential for dramatic interpretation. She first dealt with this subject in her enlightening article on the Abraham and Isaac plays in the English drama as early as 1957 and no doubt helped to fan the interest already ignited by Auerbach.[40] She carried the argument forward in her book, *The English Mystery Plays*, where it became the informing method of analysis of her chapter on the Old Testament plays

---

[39] See Stemmler, *Liturgische Feiern und geistliche Spiele* (Tübingen: Max Niemeyer Verlag, 1970), pp. 17–18; and an English summary of ibid., "Typological Transfer in Liturgical Offices and Religious Plays of the Middle Ages," *Studies in the Literary Imagination* 8 (1975): 123–143.

[40] Woolf, "The Effect of Typology on the English Mediaeval Plays of Abraham and Isaac," *Speculum* 32 (1957): 805–825.

of Noah, Abraham and Isaac, and Moses and the Prophets. In essence she asked which of the versions of these plays does the best job dramaturgically with each of the types without damaging its doctrinal meaning. Is it effective dramatically to have Isaac, as in the Towneley cycle, plead pathetically for his life and to persuade his father not to strike him? Yes, says Woolf. Is it effective doctrinally? No, since that interpretation does violence to the relation of type to antitype. Is it effective doctrinally to have Isaac be a grown man of thirty? Yes, of course, since it facilitates the identification of Christ. In turn, is it effective dramatically? No, not at all, for the pathetic element so necessary in conveying the feelings engendered by the hardness of God's command is seriously diminished when Isaac is not an innocent child. In this manner, Woolf uses typology as a method of critical appraisal that addresses both doctrine and drama. Her approach has proved to be a valuable tool in the critical examination of dramatic types. It has no doubt influenced a great many studies of individual episodes.

The studies mentioned in the foregoing sketch, and a host of others devoted to individual plays and themes,[41] have contributed profoundly to our understanding of the uses of typology in the Corpus Christi drama, and they have done much to enrich the quality of drama criticism. Indeed, they have sparked

[41] Among the more important studies are John R. Elliott, Jr., "The Sacrifice of Isaac as Comedy and Tragedy," *Studies in Philology* 66 (1969): 36–59; John Gardner, "Theme and Irony in the Wakefield *Mactacio Abel*," *PMLA* 80 (1965): 515–521; idem, 'Imagery and Allusion in the Wakefield Noah Play," *Papers in Language and Literature* 4 (1968): 3–12; John Dennis Hurrell, "The Figural Approach to Medieval Drama" *College English* 26 (1965): 598–604; Louis H. Leiter, "Typology, Paradigm, Metaphor, and Image in the York *Creation of Adam and Eve*," *Drama Survey* 7 (1968–1969): 113–132; W. M. Manley, "Shepherds and Prophets: Religious Unity in the Towneley *Secunda Pastorum*," *PMLA* 78 (1963): 151–153; Linda E. Marshall, " 'Sacral Parody' in the *Secunda Pastorum*," *Speculum* 47 (1972): 720–736; Leslie H. Martin, "Comic Eschatology in the Chester *Coming of AntiChrist*," *Comparative Drama* 5 (1971): 163–176; William F. Munson, "Typology and the Towneley Isaac," *Research Opportunities in Renaissance Drama* 11 (1968): 129–139; and Michael Paull, "The Figure of Mohamet in the Towneley Cycle," *Comparative Drama* 6 (1972): 187–204.

serious consideration of the methodology itself with the publication of several articles questioning applications of the approach. Among the objections raised, two have been especially prominent; they argue, first, that typology is not amenable to dramatic representation, and second, that Biblical typology is misapplied and misunderstood in much modern criticism.

The first of these objections was raised by Arnold Williams, who argued that close typological "scrutiny of the text detects features that would escape recognition in a casual reading and certainly a one-time viewing of the acted play."[42] Objecting that the method first arose elsewhere, Williams claims that it is not congenial to understanding the drama. For it to be effective, he insists that typology must be obvious and simple, or the popular audiences of the Middle Ages would not have grasped it. While various scholars have refuted these assumptions, Walter Meyers devoted an entire article to challenging the Williams argument (because he felt Williams is too important a critic to be ignored). The main point Meyers makes is that typology does not require the erudition that Williams claims for its successful treatment, maintaining that popular audiences did not need to know Tertullian or Saint Augustine to understand the function and meaning of a type. He says that the plays are clear enough about introducing types and explaining their meaning, and he shows how the Chester cycle in its treatment of Abel and Abraham makes these meanings explicit.[43] As a former student and a great admirer of Arnold Williams, I must admit with reluctance to the misgivings voiced by Meyers. I would add that if exegesis is valid only if it can be perceived by the least enlightened, much drama criticism, including a vast body of Shakespeare interpretation, would have to be discarded. In our time, the text must finally be judged on whatever meaning can validly be found in it by its best readers. Moreover, we must be aware that what we discover through

---

[42] Williams, "Typology and the Cycle Plays: Some Criteria," *Speculum* 43 (1968): 678.

[43] Meyers, "Typology and the Audience of the English Cycle Plays," *Studies in the Literary Imagination* 8 (1975): 145–158.

erudite scholarship would often have been available in the perceptual set of the most ordinary medieval spectator.

The antidramatic argument is extended upon by Patrick Collins, who believes that typological interpretation is more congenial to the plastic arts than to the drama. He takes this view for two reasons. First, he believes the sequential and linear narrative of the cycle drama is not nearly so conducive to the exposition of types as the "match scenes" that juxtapose Old Testament types and New Testament antitypes in the plastic arts. And second, he finds that true types occur only sporadically in the drama, that the ones that are most often cited are "a function of their importance in the overall divine plan," and that, in sum, "it is invalid to assume that an underlying typological system controls the subject matter and form of the dramatic cycles."[44] These are large claims to which I will have occasion to return in my discussion of typological applications in the N-Town cycle. Suffice it to say here that they are based on the dubious assumption that types exist only when they reveal "the clear and direct intention of the writer"; by implication, when they are not clearly revealed, they do not exist and become "hidden nuggets of meaning" for rummagers. (Such an argument, one supposes, could as well be made of Biblical exegesis, wherein the types were discovered by Saint Matthew and Saint Paul, and enlarged upon by the patristic commentators, and where, incidentally, the original text is as linear and sequential as the drama without the benefit of "match scenes.") There is in Collins's argument an underlying distrust of the drama as an intellectual medium. He offers, for example, the following statement about the drama: "The playwrights' primary concern is to produce a coherent and meaningful *story*. Understanding the art of narrative story-telling is the best way to unlock the meaning of the Corpus Christi drama."[45] These views provide an interesting clue to the real reasons for the dis-

[44] Collins, "Typology, Criticism, and Medieval Drama: Some Observations on Method" *Comparative Drama* 10 (1976–1977): 298.

[45] Ibid., p. 306.

trust of typological interpretation: It is thought suspect not because the method is deemed faulty but because the detractor is
inclined to underrate or misconstrue the Corpus Christi drama
as a serious art form. (Imagine applying Collins's statement to
Shakespeare, Shaw, or Beckett.)

The second major objection is that typological criticism is
often misapplied or misunderstood. That, of course, is more of
an objection to the quality of the criticism than to the system
itself. In the use of typology as a critical implement, there is a
risk that *type* and *antitype* can be used incorrectly as terms.
When, for example, a critic speaks of Adam as both a type and
an antitype of Christ,[46] he misuses the language of typology
egregiously, for there is no authority, either in the Bible or by
its responsible commentators—or by the logic of the method—
that would allow Adam to be his own antitype. The confusion
in this example implies a total misapplication of typology as a
system of Biblical interpretations. And while many such examples can be found in recent criticism, one must also be careful not to insist on an application of hermeneutics so rigorous
that it rules out what may well be valid extensions of typological
interpretation. Is it right, for example, to object to the identification of an old Testament person like Job as a type simply
because no New Testament writer so regarded him?[47] If that
were to be a principle of evaluation, much of patristic commentary would have to be discarded as methodologically invalid. It
is clear that typological criticism developed in post-Biblical
times into an elaborate system, and its definitions varied from
one commentator to another. What was the relationship between *type* and *allegory*? Were there two or three or four levels
of meaning? Was it legitimate to extend typology to secular literature? These questions suggest that the application of typological criticism has been unsettled since its inception, and to

[46] This example is cited by David S. Berkeley in an article that takes a broad
critical look at the uses of typology in recent criticism; see "Some Misapprehensions of Christian Typology in Recent Literary Scholarship," *Studies in English
Literature* 18 (1978): 1–12.

[47] Berkeley makes this objection; see ibid., p. 8.

insist on a rigor of application beyond the identification of obvious errors is to curtail the use of the method as a key to understanding. The New Testament does not warrant the perception that Satan and Herod stand in inverse typological relationship, nor does it sanction the parallelism one can find in the lives of Jesus and Mary in the drama, and yet the typological model would lead us to think that the playwrights very clearly saw some fundamental relationships in these instances. To object to them as valid illustrations of what Stemmler would call "typological transfer" is to make a straightjacket out of too-rigid standards applied by purists.

The mystery cycles, because they are enactments of sacred history, provide a particularly rich field for the exploration of the typological method in a secular genre. Because they must link Old Testament episodes to the narrative of the New Testament, it is natural for them to rely on typology as a structural principle. And once they do that, they have come upon a whole new method of unified representation. Let me cite an illustration. If the Old Testament patriarchs—Adam, Noah, Abraham, Moses—are played as types, they become in a dramatic representation (as indeed also in pictorial cycles) manifestations of Christ. *The Holkham Bible Picture Book* has often been noted as an especially close analogue, even though it is a fourteenth-century work, to the Corpus Christi cycles. It has been linked particularly to the N-Town cycle because the two works share an East Anglican provenance. In it, the types are made visually clear by the fact that they have the same face as Christ. Not only that, God and Jesus are identical, and thereby make manifest the concept of oneness among the separate Persons of the Trinity. Note, for example, the Creation scene on folio 3 in which, by extension, the faces of God and Adam are identical (see figure 13). This principle of representation was clearly available to the playwright, the director, and the reader, and it would not be unreasonable to say that Christ was, in fact, the central character of the play. Doctrinally, we must see him in God as well as in his types. A dramatic script that opened the way toward this perception strengthened the play's impact and

FIGURE 13. The Holkham Bible Picture Book, f. 3 recto, Additional
Ms. 47682. (Courtesy the British Library)

gave a new dimension of unity to the dramatic representation of sacred history (to say nothing of the concept of the Trinity). Typology, therefore, is important not only as a method of interpretation but also as a dramaturgic structuring device.

In the mystery plays, because they are enactments of Biblical scenes, typology also enforces a new way of linking the play with the audience. Anachronism, as Auerbach showed in his essay on the *Jeu d'Adam*, is an outgrowth of typology, wherein human history is seen from the timeless perspective of God. Two events that in human time are far removed are, as Auerbach has noted, temporally undifferentiated in God's eyes. This simultaneity allows a further extension, one that was by the very nature of the medium invoked by the playwrights. If they were to write a vernacular version of the Creation or the Passion, they had to do it from the vantage point of the here and now. As Kolve has shown in his brilliant chapter, "Medieval Time and English Place,"[48] this perspective made the Biblical narrative immediately relevant to contemporary life in England. In this fashion, the Old Testament was not only Christianized but, through typology, modernized, and the whole play thus allowed the ready identification of audience with characters. The point is important because the drama enhanced a habit of thought that is fostered by typology—identification of the everyday lives of Christian people with the life of Christ. Just as the Mass "rememorates" (to use Hardison's word) the Last Supper, so does it enable the participant (as well as the celebrant) to experience the death and Resurrection. D. W. Robertson, in an enlightening article on the Wakefield *Mactacio Abel*, calls this phenomenon "tropological versimilitude" as it pertains to the drama and puts it in the form of an example: "The burden of Isaac seen as the burden of the Cross is a forceful reminder that every Christian must also engage in self-sacrifice." This way of seeing the drama permits us to enter into it with much greater appreciation for its deepest meaning,

[48] Kolve, *Play Called Corpus Christi*, pp. 101–123.

as Robertson shows with the following example from the Second Shepherds' play.

> When the Shepherds, under the inspiration of the "youth" among them who shows from the outset glimmerings of wisdom, and whose charitable impulse leads to the discovery of the sheep, are led to perform an act of mercy, substituting a toss in a blanket for the legal death penalty for stealing sheep after Mak has shown repentance (ll.622–623), they have, in effect, implemented the New Law and are thus in a position to discover Christ.[49]

Typology, as we have seen, must by its nature "match" two events, scenes, characters, or institutions. It promotes a binary perception: relating the Old and New Testaments, and relating the whole of Scripture to present life. Transferred to the popular religious cycles, it encourages the playwright to envisage one scene or character in terms of another, and it invites the reader/spectator to discover the "matches." The result is a whole new dramatic form in which scenes, characters, and even plots are linked implicitly as a fundamental structuring plan. The playwright counts on this structure to hold together the disparate parts of his play and to encourage the spectators or readers to make the connection for themselves—to see, for example, that Lucifer, Pharoah, Caesar, Herod, and Pilate are basically the same person, and thereby to bind together the evil of the fallen angel with that of fallen man and to provide a nexus for the cycle in which the basic conflict between Satan and God is renewed again and again until it is finally resolved. It is the same principle that structures the Second Shepherds' play, linking the quest for Mak's stolen sheep with the quest for the Christ Child. The drama that is created by this form is the expansive drama of the native tradition—a drama that operates on principles exactly opposed to the application of the clas-

[49] Robertson, "The Question of 'Typology' and the Wakefield *Mactacio Abel*," in *Essays in Medieval Culture* (Princeton: Princeton University Press, 1980), p. 225.

sical unities. This is so because the form created by typology is neither time bound nor space bound, but is additive; its success rests on the possibility of expansion in all dimensions: time, place, and dramatic action. Moreover, it is expansive because though its coverage is linear, it opens options of discovery that match established scenes with new ones. If a debate is an effective way to reveal the "intent" of God in the N-Town Parliament of Heaven, it will be equally effective as a device later in the cycle to reveal the "intent" of Satan, and later yet the "intent" of the Jews. The distance between this kind of dramatic structuring and that found in Shakespeare's major tetralogy is not very great. King Henry's "Once more unto the breach" becomes Bardolph's "On, on, on, on, on. To the breach" becomes Fluellen's "Up to the breach, you dogs," and in the process of silently matching these scenes the audience obtains the sweeping view that Shakespeare asked of them in the Prologue as well as a critical comment upon all segments of the English army on the battlefield. Here, as in the mystery cycle, the additive style allows us to build a macrocosm out of matched microcosmic events, and the result, as I have shown elsewhere,[50] is antithetical to the single setting in neoclassical drama—a true *theatrum mundi*. Typology is not only a key to the meaning of the Corpus Christi cycles, it is the essential dramatic structuring device upon which the native English dramatic tradition is built.

N-TOWN stands out among the English Corpus Christi cycles for its pervasive and sophisticated use of typology as a unifying structuring device. We shall see that the concept of figuration is built consciously into the cycle in virtually all aspects of its dramatic design. It exists in the development of Old Testament episodes, in its complex usage of metaphoric language, and most important in its multiple plot. N-Town is the cycle in which Jesus and Mary have parallel roles, and if we view the cycle whole, as its typology and typological transfers encourage

[50] M. Stevens, "Theatre of the World," pp. 234–249.

us to do, it will be seen as the first "double-plot" play on the English stage. This makes the N-Town cycle a true example of what Dryden calls "a play in the *English* fashion," for which he sets the following requirements:

> As in a Play of the *English* fashion . . . there is to be but one main design; and tho' there be an Under-plot, or Second Walk of Comical Characters and Adventures, yet they are subservient to the chief Fable, carry'd along under it and helping to it.[51]

The Mary plot, as we shall see, is the "Under-plot" of N-Town. When seen in terms of its dramatic function, it does indeed become subservient to and supportive of the main design.

First, then, for the development of types in the Old Testament plays. The N-Town episode of Abraham and Isaac is the first developed illustration of standard typology in the cycle, and consequently it conditions the expectations of the reader/ spectator to apply "typological thinking" to the text and the performance. The N-Town Isaac is noteworthy for his compliance to Abraham's will. Rosemary Woolf has singled out this aspect of his portrayal as the significant feature that, in her eyes, makes the N-Town version the most effective of all the Abraham plays in the cycles judged from an aesthetic as well as typological vantage point.[52] Though we are not told how old the N-Town Isaac is, he is "a chylde full bolde" (43/12), one whom we admire through his father's worshipful gaze:

> Amonges all chylderyn þat walkyn on wolde
> A louelyer chylde is non trewly.
>
> (44/15–16)

It is, of course, a commonplace that the playwright is here introducing us to Jesus indirectly, as we consequently have in this scene the first bifocal view of Isaac/Christ the obedient son.

---

[51] John Dryden, "A Discourse concerning the Original and Progress of Satire," in *Essays of John Dryden*, ed. W. P. Ker, 2 vols. (Oxford: Clarendon Press, 1926).

[52] Woolf, *English Mystery Plays*, pp. 149–150.

Even with allowance made for impersonation on stage, Isaac *is* Christ, and the strongest typological representations bring this point home as forcefully as possible. Thus, for example, we have an authentic series of typological images in the play when Abraham says:

> Now must þe fadyr his suete son schende
> (46/99)

or

> Now, son, in þi necke this fagot þou take
> (46/113)

or

> Thyn owyn fadyr þi deth must be
> (47/139)

or when Isaac responds:

> All redy, fadyr, evyn at ȝour wyll
> And at ȝour byddyng I am ȝow by,
> With ȝow to walk ovyr dale and hill,
> At ȝoure callyng I am redy.
> To þe, fadyr, evyr most comly
> It ovyth þe childe evyr buxom to be.
> I wyl obey ful hertyly
> To all thyng þat ȝe bydde me.
> (46/105–112)

In terms of dramatic structure, the event of Isaac's impending self-sacrifice is of course powerful because we are allowed, in our foreknowledge, to see it as not only a self-sacrifice but also as the tearful sacrifice of a son by a father and ultimately of the sacrifice of *the* Son by *the* Father. It *foreshadows*, a term that dramatic criticism has taken directly (if unconsciously) from typology. As readers or spectators, we therefore constantly project how the "other" scene—the one that will fulfill—will vary from this one. If this Isaac is compliant and obedient, how much more will be the next? And how much greater the agony for us

when we add to the simple humanity of the child the full suffering divinity of God himself?

The dramatic power of the type lies as much in its difference
from as in its similarity to the antitype. In this scene, we have a
double exposure of obedience—for the role of Abraham allows
us inferentially to understand the emotional meaning of the
sacrifice made by the father as well as the son. The Passion will
never allow us that private insight into God the Father. The
type scene has humanized and grounded that grief for us, so
that it remains in our consciousness throughout. The type
scene also prepares us for a deeper understanding of the antitype. It elevates the motivation of self-sacrifice, from the mere
impulse to obey, to the larger purpose of making a gift of one-
self for the benefit of the other. (In that sense, Jesus' act is an
exemplary act for grown men; Isaac's is an exemplary act for
children.) Moreover, the antitype converts the self-sacrifice
from an act of sheer pathos into one of tragic fulfillment and
eventual comic resolution. With Isaac, we anticipate death as final; with Jesus, we see it as a necessary step in the journey to
Resurrection. Finally, the antitype elevates the sacrifice from
the arbitrary to the purposeful. In the type scene, the death has
no meaning beyond the satisfaction of God's will. It thus dram-
atizes God as the authoritarian figure of the Old Testament by
whom the death itself is not construed as his sacrifice, or gift,
for mankind. In the antitype scene, it is God himself who surrenders his Son. He makes the sacrifice for man, thus exempli-
fying the power of divine love and illuminating the relation of
two of the Persons of God in the Trinity.

N-Town is a web of such connections. The playwright makes
every effort to bind his dramatic action together and to show
us that no single part of his drama can be separated from the
whole. He is, moreover, fully conscious of the meaning of "fyg-
ure" and "signifure," that is of figura and sign, as a way of explaining the underlying unity of God within his created universe and the significance of Christ as the Word. Thus, for
example, in a revealing self-reflexive scene, Jesus admonishes
Cleophas and Luke for their doubt about the Resurrection:

> A, ȝe fonnys and slought-of-herte,
> For to beleve in holy scrypture
> Haue not prophetys with wurdys smerte
> Spoke be tokenys in *signifure*
> That Cryste xuld deye for ȝour valure
> And syth entre his joye and blys?
> Why be ȝe of herte so dure
> And trust not in God þat myghtful is?
>> (340/89–96; italics added)

Here Jesus reminds Cleophas and Luke that Prophets found through "signs" in Holy Scripture the truth of the Resurrection. The audience is reminded of an earlier play, that of the Prophets, in which Jonas explicated the "figure" of Jonah:

> I, Jonas, sey þat on þe iij morn
> Fro deth he xal ryse—þis is a trew tall
> *fyguryd* in me, þe which longe beforn
> Lay iij days beryed within þe qwall.
>> (59–60/66–69; italics added)

The Old Testament plays are, in fact, full of allusions to typology, most of which forecast the advent of Mary. For example, Moses after looking with wonder upon the burning bush that stays "grene . . . as fyre doth flame" (a very popular medieval figure of the Virgin Birth) muses in puzzlement:

> It *fyguryth* sum thynge of ryght gret fame
> I kan not seyn what it may be.
>> (52/21–22; italics added)

The playwright does not bother to explicate the figure, for unlike Moses, the medieval audience understood its referent without the need of a gloss. In much the same way as the figure is introduced in the Old Testament plays, so is the idea of fulfillment in the New Testament plays. Here, for example, the Angel explains to the Apostles (and reminds the audience):

> O, ȝe bretheryn attendyth to me,
> And takyth good hede what I xal seyn:

237

It behovyth *þe scripture fulfyllyd to be.*
(351/56–58; italics added)

So also does Jesus extend upon his earlier explanation to Cleophas and Luke by showing how Scripture reveals the Resurrection and admonishing them for their lack of faith:

> Bothe Moyses and Aaron and othyr mo,
> In holy scrypture ȝe may rede it,
> Of Crystis deth thei spak also,
> And how he xuld ryse out of his pitt.
> Owt of feyth than why do ȝe flitte,
> Whan holy prophetys ȝow teche so pleyne?
> Turne ȝoure thought and chaunge ȝour witte
> And truste wele þat Cryst doth leve ageyn.
> (340/97–104)

Jesus is disguised as a pilgrim in this scene, but Cleophas and Luke will discover his true identity, and we understand (as they will) that in this manifestation he is his own commentator, explicating the real meaning of the Old Testament and tying its meaning to the bewildering events they have witnessed but have not understood. To drive home his point, he now returns to the story of Jonah as type, interpreting it from the point of view of reality rather than shadow (as we had heard it formerly in the words of Jonah himself):

> þat was in a whallys body iij nyghtis and iij day,
> So longe Cryst in his grave lay;
> As Jonas was withinne þe se,
> His grave is brokyn þat was of clay,
> To lyff resyn aȝen now is he.
> (340/116–120)

Cleophas and Luke, however, are not convinced. The "example" (an interesting substitution for "figure"), they say, is "sumdele good" (341/122), but it is not quite accurate:

> For Jonas on lyve evyr more was he,
> And Cryst was slayn vpon a rood.
>   (341/123–124)

The N-Town playwright thus allows the characters themselves not only to question the truth of Scripture but also the truth of the play, and by making Jesus the explicator, he provides what is the most persuasive and authentic affirmation of the Resurrection in both the play and in real life. Jesus responds to the two skeptics by presenting yet another sign of something dead made live again:

> Take hede at Aaron and his dede styk,
> Which was ded of his nature;
> And ʒit he floryschyd with flowrys ful thyk
> And bare almaundys of grett valure.
> The dede styk was *signifure*
> How Cryst þat shamfully was deed and slayn.
> As þat dede styk bare frute ful pure,
> So Cryst xuld ryse to lyve ageyn.
>   (341/129–136; italics added)

Still, Cleophas and Luke are not convinced: "That was a mere dead stick, and bringing it back to life is not the same as bringing back a human body that bled to death." Jesus tries once more, this time calling on the ultimate figure, because he himself created it, the raising of Lazarus (an episode that we have witnessed amid much foreshadowing earlier in the cycle).[53] If he had the power to raise Lazarus, why could he not have raised himself out of the grave? But no amount of interpreta-

---

[53] Stemmler shows that the scene involving the large stone was transferred directly from the *Visitatio Sepulchrum* plays, not from the Gospels. Its clear intent is to foreshadow the Resurrection, yet the playwright deftly provides a logical explanation for the stone—to keep the body from being eaten by "ravenous bestys" (215/164). In this fashion, he gives a narrative as well as typological justification for the scene (see Stemmler, *Liturgische Feiern*, pp. 248–253). Here we can observe an instance in which the N-Town playwright shows an interest in the writing, not just the reading, of type scenes.

tion will ultimately convince the two well-meaning travelers.
They drop the subject and implore the stranger to stay with
them and break bread and then to resume their discussion "of
Cryst, oure maystyr, þat is now ded" (343/208). It is only after
Jesus blesses the bread and, in fact, celebrates the Eucharist,
and ascends that the two believe in the Resurrection. The N-
Town playwright uses the encounter and the elaborate discourse as a way of proving the truth of Scripture not through
words but through the living Sacrament. It is finally Jesus' own
Eucharist that attests for his skeptical audience (inside and outside the play) to the truth of typological interpretation.

In addition to the dramatic enactment of figures, the N-
Town cycle also presents its typological interpretation through
the development of metaphor or analogy. One such has to do
with the fruit (or flower) of the garden, a figure that occurs
widely in medieval commentary and iconography. In keeping
with the traditional concept, N-Town shows how the plucking
and eating of the fruit in the Garden of Eden leads to a universal barrenness—a loss of God's grace that will not return until
the fruit is replaced. The replacement, of course, is in the form
of Jesus, who throughout the cycle is referred to as flower or
fruit (thus echoing the words in the traditional Hail Mary,
"blessed be the fruit of thy womb," as originally spoken by Elizabeth; see N-Town, 117/59); for example, the First Shepherd
calls him "þat fayr fresch flowre" (148/68) and "floure of
flourys" (149/90), and Mary, upon finding her son among the
Doctors in the Temple, hails him as "my frute" (185/227). In a
complicated way, the apple in the Garden of Eden is thus a figure for Christ. The N-Town cycle brings us to an understanding of that fact by showing the dramatic development of the
new seed after Adam and Eve have eaten God's first fruit in the
Garden. The idea is captured for us in the prophecy of Daniel:

> I, Prophete Danyel, am well apayed,
> In fygure of þis I saw a tre;
> All þe fendys of hell xall ben affrayd,

Whan maydenys frute þeron þei se.
(59/59–62)

The image that Daniel calls forth here is the Tree of Life whose fruit is Jesus (the Tree, in turn, becomes the Cross where the fruit is a sign of the redemption),[54] and it of course brings to mind the replacement of the fruit plucked at the instigation of Satan from the Tree of Knowledge. The fiends of Hell are right to be afraid of the "new" fruit, for that is the retributive signal to them that God has made the Tree intact again. In this instance, the fruit becomes a symbol of the "abuse of power" theory.

The progression from the first tree and fruit to the second is highlighted in N-Town. When we first meet Adam, he is a "good gardenere" (21/151), tending to the rich array of flowers and fruits in the luxuriant garden of Paradise. As soon as Eve and he have succumbed to the Temptation, the garden imagery is transformed: fruitfulness and plenty give way to death. Adam laments,

> þat sory Appyl þat we han sokyn
> To deth hath brouth my spouse and me.
> (24/266–267)

He observes that the "flourys do fade" (24/275), and the vocabulary of the play becomes stark and grim (words like "dethe," "werm," "spille," "nought," "schrowde," "peyne," "brokyn," "velony," "wreth," and "hate" set the tone). It is not long thereafter that Adam instructs his sons to offer God "the fyrst frute of kendely engendrure" (30/33), where, for the first time, we connect the fruit of Paradise with offspring, and the play, of course, develops the irony of Adam himself losing his "first fruit" as one part of the price that he pays for his trangression.

"Engendrure" is a preoccupation of the N-Town Old Testament plays. Flashed before us is the lineage of the patriarchs

---

[54] For a discussion of this image in medieval art and in the N-Town cycle, see the discussion by Collins, *Medieval Picture Cycles*, pp. 3–9.

and that lineage is spoken of consistently in the metaphor of the tree and the fruit. Isaac is, in Abraham's eyes, "þis fayr frute" (reinforcing his role as type); Abraham's "seed," we are told, will multiply. The Prophets play is a dramatic parallel to the iconographic Tree of Jesse; the idea is, of course, traceable to the messianic prophecies of Isaiah, who not only declared "Ecce virgo concipiet, et pariet filium" (see Isaiah 7:14 and N-Town 58/9–10) but also, "Et egrediatur virga de radice Iesse, et flos de radice eius ascendet" ("And a shoot shall sprout from the stump of Jesse, and from his roots a bud shall blossom"; see Isaiah 11:1–2 and N-Town 58/17–18), associating *virga* and *virgo*, the tree with the Virgin. The N-Town Prophets play, unique in form and substance, then prepares the way for the Virgin Birth, summoning as its structural metaphor the growth of the tree from Jesse's root upward to each of the Kings following in succession and speaking in alternation with the Prophets who comment on the advent of Christ in fact and figure. When the thirteenth King has spoken in this "sacerdotale lynage" (58/13), as Isaiah, the first speaker, calls it, the substance of the play merges with the form of the manuscript, for here text and marginalia come together, and the scribe brings the family tree to its conclusion as Joachim and Anne beget Mary the mother of Jesus, Mary Cleophas, and Mary the mother of John the Evangelist and James.

With the genealogy brought up to date, Contemplacio introduces the Mary plays. Here the tree-and-fruit metaphor is carried forward in terms of a paradox that dominates the cycle: the capacity of the barren tree to be fruitful. We recall Jesus' own reference to "Aaron and his dede styk" that though dead by nature "floryschyd with flowrys ful thyk" (341/129–131), which recalls the story in Numbers (17:16) where Aaron's rod is left in the Tabernacle to yield flowers and bud with almonds the next morning. This popular figure for the Virgin Birth also suggests another flowering rod, the one by which Joseph is selected as Mary's husband—an episode that is portrayed in the N-Town play of the Betrothal (the Bishop anticipates the language of Jesus when he pronounces in awe, "a ded stok beryth flourys fre," 90/262).

The birth of Mary reflects this metaphor. She is born of a mother and father that are "barrany and bare" and that "frute-ful nevyr yett ware" (65/76–77). Only by the miraculous in-tercession of God do they conceive. The Angel who brings this word to Joachim, Mary's father, shows that it has been God's way, when he wished to show his might, to make barren women fruitful, as indeed he had done before Anne with Sarah, the mother of Isaac, and Rachel, the mother of Joseph (68/155–158), both sons of course being types of Christ. Now as he fore-tells of the birth of Mary he observes:

> And as sche xal be bore of a barrany body,
> So of here xal be bore without nature Jhesus.
> (69/169–170)

The birth of a child to a barren mother, so important to the parallelism of the lives of Anne and Mary, and to the structural balance of the Mary plays, is of course finally the fulfillment of the fruit-in-Paradise figure. As that first fruit was plucked from a living tree, so now the second fruit will grow on a dead tree. God has brought forth the image of the Resurrection. The fruit of Mary represents life; it will not die as the first did. As final symbol of this fulfillment, when Mary and Joseph are on their way to Bethlehem, they pass by a blooming cherry tree. She asks him to pluck some cherries for her, in a charming reversal of the original sin. Joseph tries to comply but he is not strong or tall enough to reach them. So he says, "lete hym pluk ʒow cheryes begatt ʒow with childe" (136/38), and, lo and be-hold, the tree bends down and Mary helps herself. There is no better evidence in the cycle of the fact that "here þis name Eva is turnyd Aue" (104/219).[55] By tracing the fruit-and-tree im-

[55] For an excellent discussion of the association of the cherry with the Christ Child, see Lawrence J. Ross, "Symbol and Structure in the *Secunda Pastorum*," *Comparative Drama* 1 (1967): 122–149; reprinted in *Medieval English Drama: Es-says Critical and Contextual*, ed. Jerome Taylor and Alan H. Nelson (Chicago: University of Chicago Press, 1972), see esp. pp. 192–196.

ages through the plays, we see yet another application of typology to bind together the pageants and the larger sections of the cycle.

Let us now return to the idea that typology is important as a dramatic structuring device, particularly in its capacity to engender multiple plots. We have seen in our examination of the Isaac/Christ juxtaposition how typology adds meaning and dramatic significance to its paired scenes. It also provides a "binding" power to the play as a whole so that its scenes are brought into harmony and the dramatic world is synthesized. This "binding" quality, I believe, is a fundamental feature of the medieval way of seeing in its attraction to juxtaposition and its quest for similitudes. Paired scenes occur as much in non-Biblical texts as in the plays. Chaucer's *Troilus*, as I have shown elsewhere,[56] presents as its main structural challenge the ability of the reader to match the scenes of the "double sorwe." Full interpretations of *Sir Gawain and the Green Knight* depends in large measure upon "matching" the three hunting scenes and juxtaposing them with the three temptation scenes. The meaning of *Beowulf* depends similarly on our perception of such paired scenes as the two Grendel fights and the dragon fight.

In the N-Town cycles, the multiple plot matches the life of Jesus with the life of Mary. As a unique feature in the English Corpus Christi cycles, this pairing is the result of typological transfer. At an early point in the development of the legendary life of Mary, two important segments were added in the Pseudepigrapha to the Gospel narratives that contain the life of Mary from the Annunciation to the Resurrection. These were the Infancy years and the Death and Assumption. As we encounter them in the early apocryphal books they no doubt were modeled after the corresponding segments in the life of Jesus.[57] In the N-Town cycle, these narrative sections are di-

---

[56] M. Stevens, "The Double Structure of Chaucer's *Troilus and Criseyde*," in *The CUNY English Forum*, vol. 1 (New York: AMS Press, 1985), pp. 155–174.

[57] The Infancy years stem from the *Protevangelium* and the Gospel of Thomas of the second century; the Death and Assumption are traceable to various sources of which one prominent form is the Latin Narrative of Pseudo-Melito.

rectly indebted to Nicholas Love's *Mirrour of the Blessed Lyf of Jesu Christ* and to the *Legenda Aurea*. They represent the effort by the playwright to broaden the emphasis on affective piety in the cycle, as we shall see shortly.

By adding the early and late years to the life of Mary, the playwright provides a second plot that, in many details, shadows the main plot of the life of Christ. Mary is born, as was Jesus, to parents who are barren. While her birth is not a Virgin Birth, it is nevertheless miraculous, and it happens, as does the Virgin Birth by the intercession of God in the person of an Angel (it was, of course, not pronounced the "Immaculate Conception" until the First Vatican Council proclaimed it such in the nineteenth century). As a toddler of three she is taken to the Temple, foreshadowing, first, the scene of the Purification and, second, the scene of Christ with the Doctors. Significantly, both children are shown as being precociously learned. Like Jesus, Mary, together with Joseph, is brought to trial before hostile judges. Her death, again like that of Jesus, is ordained by God, but not until she has visited the sites of the major events in his life—where he was baptized, tempted, buried, and from which he ascended into heaven (these are recounted, not dramatized; see 354/14–21). She dies, like Jesus, in the presence of John, though unlike Jesus also in the presence of all the Apostles. She is buried in a sepulcher, watched by her maids-in-waiting instead of the soldiers, and she ascends from the grave after three days.

The addition of these details from the early and late life of Mary thus creates a double plot for the N-Town cycle. To my knowledge, this is the first consciously developed double main plot in the English drama, and as such it is decidedly a precursor to the form as we frequently encounter it in Renaissance drama. The fact that the English tradition owes its reliance on multiple plots to typological transfer has not been heretofore

---

The nucleus of this story belongs to the third century. For text and discussion, see M. R. James, trans. *The Apocryphal New Testament* (Oxford: Clarendon Press, 1924).

recognized; indeed, the most exhaustive treatment of the subject, by Richard Levin, makes no attempt to trace its origins. Instead, Levin undertakes to describe the various forms and permutations of the multiple plot, using Aristotle's four causes as the basis for the classification of his "modes."[58] Of these, the one identified as the third mode, based on Aristotle's formal cause, seems to me to describe the double plot that issues from typological transfer. Levin defines this mode as "based on the comparison of two or more persons, events, or concepts in one plot with an equivalent set in the other." He considers such plots essentially analogic because they "are all reducible to the two fundamental relations of parallelism and contrast (or positive and negative analogy)."[59] Using the famous double plot of *King Lear* as an example, Levin shows that both of these "relations" must be perceived by the reader for an appreciation of the formal structure of the play. Critics, of course, have had little difficulty finding the parallelism of the Lear and Gloucester plots, but few have focused on the contrast that these plots develop. For a full understanding of the play's structure, we need to note, for example, that Lear's demise is self-generated while Gloucester's is imposed upon him by the evil deeds of Edmund; that Lear's suffering is climaxed by loss of reason while Gloucester's is by loss of sight; that Lear's regeneration is sparked by Cordelia's forgiveness in contrast to Gloucester's, which is occasioned by a staged physical fall from a spurious cliff; that Lear finally dies of inconsolable grief for the loss of Cordelia while Gloucester dies as his heart "burst smilingly" over the joy of his reunion with Edgar. The contrasts in the play work to emphasize the depth of Lear's tragedy; it gains in significance by showing how a much more ordinary man, who is not proudly responsible for the events that befall him, responds to similar circumstances. This kind of contrast is generated by formal analogy, which ultimately, in Levin's view, lies at the heart of the multiple-structure play of the Renaissance

[58] Levin, *The Multiple Plot in English Renaissance Drama* (Chicago: University of Chicago Press, 1971), esp. pp. 1–20.

[59] Ibid., pp. 11–12.

and which serves as the basis for his chapter divisions in the book.[60] "Formal analogy" is merely a descriptive, neo-Aristotelian term for "typological transfer."

In the double main plot of the N-Town cycle, contrast operates to enlarge the dramatic power of Jesus' role and to put it more fully into its central place in Christian sacramental history. By providing the expanded parallel plot of Mary's life, the playwright not only gives emphasis to Mary's presence in the life of Jesus but also to the special role that she plays as his most devoted disciple. She is the model anchorite whose full satisfaction lies in affective meditation, usually within the shelter of the Temple, where she longs to be. We see her thus in contrast to her son, whose life is spent in the dialectic of his Ministry.

The parallel Temple scenes in the Presentation of Mary and in Christ with the Doctors furnish a good example. In the Mary scene, the playwright gives us the model child, totally devoted to her parents and the bishops, and wholly dedicated to God and the Bible, which she interprets with the innocence and wisdom of the pure. Her very first speech, responding to her mother's question whether she would be a pure maid and God's wife, affirms this role:

> Fadyr and modyr, if it plesyng to ʒow be,
> ʒe han mad ʒour avow, so sothly wol I
> To be Goddys chast seruaunt whil lyff is in me.
> But to be Goddys wyff, I was nevyr wurthy;
> I am þe sympelest þat evyr was born of body.
>
> (72/17–21)

Her aureate speech translates the fifteen Gradual Psalms (120–134) and prepares the way for her larger role as mother of God in the cycle, for as she recites these Psalms she ascends the fifteen steps that lead to the altar and allegorically to participation in the life of Christ. In essence the ascent is designed to teach directly the application of the Old Testament to the spirit of the New. Tropologically, we see Mary in this scene symbol-

[60] Ibid., p. 20.

izing the church (a figure commonly expressed in the Middle
Ages since the time of Saint Ambrose)[61] and glossed for us in
the N-Town cycle by Solomon Rex in the Prophets play:

> I am Salamon þe secunde kynge,
> And þat wurthy temple for sothe made I
> Which þat is fygure of that mayde ӡynge
> þat xal be modyr of grett messy.
>
> (59/39–42)

Anagogically, Mary is, of course, Queen of Heaven, and her ascent of the steps foreshadows the higher ascent that will take
place in her Assumption and Coronation.

The Doctors play directly parallels and contrasts with the
Mary in the Temple scene. Jesus, like Mary, is a mere child.
The First Doctor says to him,

> þyselfe art but a chylde al men may wel se,
> late camst out of cradyl as it semyth be þi vesage.
>
> (183/155–156)

Like Mary, Jesus ascends to a higher level, in this instance to
the presbyter's seat symbolic of God's throne within the
church, as a stage direction tells us: "hic adducunt ihesum inter
ipsos et in scanno altiori ipsum sedere faciunt ipsis in inferio-
ribus scannis sedentibus" (182/144f.; "Here they lead Jesus
among themselves, and they make his seat on the higher stage,
and they seat themselves on the lower stage"). Jesus himself indirectly glosses the significance of the "higher stage," when he
tells us shortly after that as God is endless "in his hyӡ stage"
(183/159) so shall he be without end. Here, then, as in the Mary
scene, we have an inspired child among elders, raised to the position of honor in the Temple. The difference in the two scenes
lies in their tone and meaning. Jesus disputes with the Doctors;
he is not the submissive child we encountered in Mary. We are
prepared for Jesus' role by the title: "Modo de doctoribus disputantibus cum jhesu in templo" (p. 178). Because his role is to

---

[61] See the *Expositio Evangelii Secundum Lucam*, book 2, in Migne, *PL*, 11:1555.

create the New Law, he must be more than an obedient child. He must challenge authority, and so, unlike Mary, he makes his own way to the Temple in a way that might seem to the unenlightened an act of rebellion against his earthly parents. (When called to account for his "disobedience" by his mother, he quickly affirms "I am 3our sone and subjecte childe"; 187/ 275.) Mary, we recall, was the model daughter. She came with her parents and submitted entirely to their authority. There is no similar conflict built into her role.

As we have already seen, this play is the theological center of the cycle, and in it Jesus gives a self-characterization of wisdom to contrast with the *sciencia* of the Doctors. In formal contrast with the Presentation play, we have the perfect relationship between Jesus and Mary. She is the devoutly submissive persona of the church; he is the Redeemer who works within the Ministry and the Passion to create the New Law. He is active; she is contemplative. He is priest; she is disciple. He preaches; she prays. She prepares; he fulfills. It is impossible for us not to bear in mind the earlier scene as we read the later. By formal analogy, then, the Doctors play defines the relationship of Jesus and Mary, and by extension, of Christ and his church.

Yet another part of the double main plot is the Trial of Joseph and Mary, which foreshadows the whole of Passion Play I and part of Passion Play II. Here, the relationship of the two dramatic segments is parodic: The type scene anticipates in broad comic outline the high tragic drama of the accusation, Arrest, and Trial of Jesus. The Joseph and Mary scene is put squarely in the setting of an ecclesiastical court where the quasi-Morality characters of Reyse Sclaunder and Bakbyter (who are also Primus and Secundus Detractores, respectively) accuse Mary of cuckolding Joseph:

> That olde cokolde was evyl begylyd,
> To þat fresche wench whan he was wedde,
> Now muste he faderyn anothyr mannys chylde,
> And with his swynke he xal be fedde.
>
> (126/65–68)

249

This scene forshadows the accusation by Caiaphas and Annas that Jesus is a worker of false witchcraft (232/64) and false miracles (235/131). The early scene suggests that the conception occurred in what can best be pictured as a fabliau plot, and indeed it reduces the Virgin Birth to the most vulgar possible interpretation, expressing vividly all the most dangerous taboo thoughts that the subject could occasion. For example, Reyse Sclaunder dares to portray the Holy Virgin as follows:

> Such a ӡonge damesel of bewte bryght,
> And of schap so comely also,
> Of hire tayle ofte tyme be lyght
> And rygh[t] tekyl vndyr þe too.
>
> (126/61–64)

To bring the culprits before the Episcopus, who is a type of Christ's judges, the playwright introduces the character of Den, a summoner. Den is in the employ of the bishop and, as is customary of medieval summoners, he uses his office as a means to work his scams. He admonished the audience directly:

> But ӡit sum mede and ӡe me take,
> I wyl withdrawe my gret rough toth.
> Gold or sylvyr I wol not forsake
> Bot evyn as all somnorys doth.
>
> (128/125–128)

The role clearly foreshadows Judas and puts him into a new, parodic light. The summoner is traditionally a Devil figure, as we see in Chaucer's Friar's Tale, and here that association is also highlighted. Den makes the customary scatological observations (see 127/124) that are associated with the Devil of the mystery plays (the only other character in N-Town who uses scatology). He also introduces the play in a short prologue that prefigures the Demon's Prologue of Passion Play I. The association of Den with both Judas and the Devil prepares us for their close association in Passion Play I (see the Devil's encomium to Judas, 258/787–798).

In the trial proper, Joseph and Mary defend themselves against the charge that they have been promiscuous. They speak in their own defense, and they, of course, submit to the trial by ordeal, by taking a swallow of the "drynge of vengeawnce" (130/200), which seems to be a parodic variation of the Christian rite of trial where the accused was challenged to confess before taking the Sacrament.[62] Both Joseph and Mary freely partake of the potion, and neither shows the telltale spot on the face. In turn, Reyse Sclaunder is given the potion in response to his false accusation, and he instantly suffers from a severe pain and fire in the head. When he repents, Mary asks God for his forgiveness and the pain goes away. The resolution is thus a demonstration of poetic justice, toward which all forces—pagan and Christian—contribute. It its noteworthy that Mary and Joseph cooperate entirely with their accusers in proving their innocence. Thus the miracle of the Virgin Birth is affirmed.

In contrast, Jesus refuses to cooperate with his accusers because he will not submit to any law other than God's. The simple operation of poetic justice, which is the standard resolution of the fabliau plot, cannot be applied in his case, partly because his case is far from cut and dried, as is the case of Joseph and Mary. They insist, in the face of accusation, that they are pure—an indisputable fact that we have known all along and that is attested by their easy survival of the ordeal. But Jesus is guilty of the accusation that is raised against him. He is, indeed, the King of Kings. Jesus' trial is not the accustomed test of the accused but a weighing of the law itself. He is innocent of breaking the law because he is above the law that is used to judge him. The contrast thus shifts the emphasis: At the second trial it is not the accused but the law itself that is being tried. The matched scenes make us aware of the heightening in tone and conflict as the play progresses. The contrast estab-

[62] See Dorothy Whitelock, *The Beginnings of English Society* (London: Penguin Books, 1952), p. 142.

lished how severe was the burden and the suffering of Jesus among men.

In N-Town, unlike any other cycle, the Virgin Mary has a prominent role in the Resurrection appearances. Here, no doubt, the playwright was following Love's *Mirrour* in an effort to enlarge Mary's role in the overall dramatic plot. The Appearance of Jesus to Mary is unique to the N-Town cycle. It occurs as the first appearance immediately after the Resurrection and thereby puts Mary in the center of our attention. In this scene, typology works somewhat more indirectly than is true of the other scenes, principally because the typological match is primarily compositional and inferential rather than verbal. Nevertheless, there is a match—specifically with the Annunciation scene.[63] As Mary was the first to be informed of the Incarnation, so also is she the first to be told about the Resurrection. The contrast is, of course, in the person who brings the revelation. Where in the earlier scene, it is the Archangel Gabriel who brings word, now it is Jesus himself, testifying not only to the power of the Incarnation for all posterity but also elevating the role of his mother, Mary, as a mediator in man's Redemption. It is, moreover, through the Virgin Mary that the tragedy of Jesus' death is converted into the joy of the Resurrection (the

[63] This typological match occurs in various works of art during the fifteenth century, most notably in Roger van der Weyden's *Christ Appearing to the Virgin*, and it is traceable to a long tradition, as far back as the second century. Like many depictions of the Annunciation, the setting of the van der Weyden painting is in an arched Gothic chamber with a landscape visible through a window in the background. Jesus comes upon Mary from her right side; she is seated with a book by her side. In various German woodcuts, Jesus appears from behind Mary, with the implication that he comes upon her unaware, a point that would relate the scene to the Annunciation. A Flemish miniature (contained in Huntington HL 1149), roughly contemporary with the N-Town cycle, shows Jesus approaching his mother from behind in a similar setting and heads a passage based on the Saint Luke version of the Annunciation, with no reference at all in the text to the Appearance scene. This curious juxtaposition would indicate that the two scenes were clearly taken to interact upon each other. For a discussion of the iconography and the history of the Appearance scene, see James D. Breckenridge, " 'Et Prima Vidit': The Iconography of the Appearance of Christ to His Mother," *Art Bulletin* 39 (1957): 9–32.

word *mirth* is repeated with great frequency in the Appearance plays). She becomes the presiding spirit of comic resolution, as is fitting.

The Appearance scene strengthens the role of Mary in the latter part of the N-Town cycle, and it leads naturally to the eventual inclusion of the Assumption play. While N-Town is not unique in containing that episode (it appears in York and was once part of Wakefield),[64] the Assumption scene in N-Town rounds out the life of Mary, which is here more organically justifed than it is in the other cycles. Typology clearly contributes to this effect. Among the more important scenes in the play is the gathering of the Apostles, whose presence at her death she prays for, and who appear miraculously at the appointed time (364/259). Her special companion is of course John the Apostle (misnamed "Euangelista" in a stage direction, as a result of a long standing confusion, see 360/161f), who is swept back to her on a white cloud from his ministry in Ephesus. The presence of the Apostles directly recalls the last days of Jesus, and an effort is made in the play to show how much they have grown in belief since that time. Not only are they no longer afflicted with doubt about the forthcoming Assumption of Mary, but they are by her side throughout the ordeal and they bear the body together to the sepulcher. A scene of Mary's last hours vividly contrasts with the episode in the Garden of Gethsemane. This time Peter bids each of his brothers to take a candle and to sit at vigil over her so

> That when oure Lord comyth in his spoused pure,
> He may fynde vs wakyng and redy wyth oure lithtis.
> (365/278–279)

The development of faith in the Apostles is a good example of the turn that is taken by typology in the eschatological plays. The promise has been fulfilled, and the sapient know that it has. Now the type scene is connected with the life of Jesus and

---

[64] See Martin Stevens, "The Missing Parts of the Towneley Cycle," *Speculum* 45 (1970): 254–265.

the antitype with those who follow. Typological transfer works here to show the gradual establishment of faith in those who are true followers of Christ. That we should witness this transformation in a play concerned with the Virgin Mary is altogether fitting since she is, as noted before, a figure for the church—she is to reign over the "hefnely temple" (372/483). In that way, the playwright returns to the central emphasis in the double plot, of portraying Mary as the spirit of quiet faith and hope who epitomizes the perfect life of devotion that is expected of all followers of Christ for all time.

Generally speaking, the N-Town Assumption is not a complicated play; it has, in fact been called "easy to dismiss . . . as the work of an inferior writer."[65] I will therefore refrain from lingering over it for a full explication of its uses of typology. Suffice it to say that there are countless obvious scenes of typological transfer: the announcement by the Angel of Mary's death; the burial in the sepulcher; the resurrection on the third day; the presence of the two handmaidens at Mary's grave to anoint her body; the ascension. These are too self-evident in their parallelism and their contrasts to warrant discussion. But one episode perhaps is worthy of notation. It involves the Episcopus and his soldiers who are intent on burning the body of Mary because they fear another resurrection (they are still troubled with the disturbing rumor that Christ is alive). Later in the play, they attack the funeral procession in hope of carrying off Mary's body, but they are thwarted by miraculous intervention. One of them who leaps upon the bier finds that his hands have become attached to it and have withered. He pleads for help, and Peter releases him upon his profession of faith and his willingness to convert his fellows. This incident is clearly reminiscent of an earlier miraculous scene, the one of the unbelieving midwife in the Nativity play whose hand has withered after she probed Mary's body (see 147–292). On that occasion it is the Christ Child who effects the cure after the midwife has confessed her sin. The antitype scene in the As-

---

[65] Woolf, *English Mystery Plays*, p. 287.

sumption shows by implication that the Ministry has taken effect. Peter now carries on the work of Christ, and the typological linkage between the birth of Jesus and the death of Mary is complete.

As a way of concluding this discussion of typology in the N-Town cycle—and, more generally, the examination of typology as a dramatic structuring device—I want finally to turn to a triplet of scenes within the earlier Mary plays. Until now, I have focused on the binary character of typological structuring essentially as a means of linkage within a double main plot. There is, however, a much broader use of typology that has pervasive influence on the structure of the native English drama. This is the practice of building a dramatic plot by the matching of multiple scenes or situations. Here typology, while clearly the original cause of the structural pattern, may no longer be in evidence. The two segments of the Wakefield Second Shepherds' play are a good example. It is not typology but a secularized and generalized structural analogy that provides the linkage in the play. Mak may be seen as an Antichrist figure, but that is the interpreter's allegorism; the point is that beyond being a putative father, he does not really match with the idea of Joseph in the second part (we sometimes forget that Joseph has no lines at all in the play). The same can be said of the pairing of Gyll and Mary, even though the parallelism in this instance is slightly more viable. The resemblance of the plots lies in the two manger scenes and the spiritual progression that issues from them. In a general sense, what typology has done is to train the playwright to construct analogic plots or situations. Shakespeare's use of Prince Hal, Falstaff, and Hotspur as dramatic foils is a palpable outgrowth of the method.

The triplet set of scenes from N-Town on which I wish to focus is that involving Joachim and Anne, Joseph and Mary, and Zachary and Elizabeth. The parallelism of the three plots is, of course, manifest: All three involve miraculous births occasioned by the barrenness of the mother and by the advanced age of at least the father. We have already seen how important in figural terms the concept of barrenness and fruitfulness is to the playwright. Here it is the focal point of the multiple plot-ting. The playwright relies constantly on our perception of likenesses and differences as we concentrate on each of the plots. The Joachim and Anne plot is the starting point. It anti-cipates by virtue of our familiarity with the Joseph and Mary story, and it is clearly seen or read in that extended context. Joachim and Anne are foils for Joseph and Mary in that they are both barren but also both eager for progeny. Joachim's de-parture to join the shepherds comes after he and Anne are evicted from the Temple because of their barrenness. It clearly foreshadows Joseph's two departures from Mary: the first to go out and make a living (during which the Annunciation oc-curs at home), and the second in angry response to Mary's pregnancy. The most notable contrast in the two situations is the harmony that exists between husband and wife in the first situation and the potential discord in the second. The union of the *senex* Joseph, who despite his age is still fruitful, and the young Mary who vows to remain chaste, has all the earmarks of a bad marriage. But with Joachim and Anne in the periphery, and especially with our recollection of their divine mission—to be agents in the generation of Christ—we have a standard against which to dismiss the insipient discord of a couple who, under normal circumstances, would rather be barren.

What then of the third of the matched scenes—that of Zach-ary and Elizabeth? Here we return to the situation of Joachim and Anne brought into the present for Joseph and Mary. Eliz-abeth is also barren, and she will also conceive a son by divine intervention (she is six months pregnant at the time of the Vis-itation). The primary purpose of the scene is, of course, to pro-vide a parallel in the lives of John the Baptist and Jesus as prep-aration for the eventual baptism of Jesus. In actual fact, the N-Town playwright—and for that matter, the other Corpus Christi playwrights—does very little with this potentially strong typological and dramatic association. The rather droll scene in which the unborn John the Baptist bows to the unborn Jesus as the two mothers meet (one wonders how that scene was staged!) is about as far as the N-Town playwright takes that association in the play of the Visitation. But he does seem to use the parallelism for an effective contrast of the two sets of parents, within the context already established by Joachim and Anne. If Anne and Joachim stand as the norm of marital harmony, then Elizabeth and Zachary provide a means by which to elevate the roles of Mary and Joseph above the low comic resonance that their discord might occasion. Joseph as *senex* is not as feeble or as frail as the benign Zachary who is so afflicted with the palsy (a "vesytacion of God," 120/122) that he cannot even speak. And Mary, who might have seemed too cloistered until now, is brought into the sphere of domestic life by Elizabeth, who shares her condition and who brings out Mary's impulse to help and give comfort. In all, the three scenes provide an expanded setting for the miraculous birth of Jesus, and they help the playwright to create a throughly engaging and immediate drama.

We have seen that the N-Town cycle, despite its apparently fragmented manuscript, demands a reading that focuses on its overall textual and dramatic unity. With the likelihood that it was never performed in its entirety, we must entertain the possibility that if it was not aimed to serve as a script for a production it at least was designed to be read thematically and structurally as a dramatized life of Jesus within the yet larger framework of salvation history. Its playwright, no matter how he might have assembled and revised the extant text, took great care to present an artfully wrought dramatic whole. He gave us the Corpus Christi cycle in which typology is brought to its full power as a dramatic structuring device.

FOUR

The Chester Cycle:
The Sense of an Ending

THE HISTORY of the Chester cycle has undergone a substantial revision in recent years. It used to be fashionable to think of the Chester plays as the oldest surviving Middle English cycle, a conclusion that was derived from E. K. Chambers's interpretation of the Chester records. While Chambers himself was puzzled by various inconsistencies in these documents, he offered the years 1327–1329 as the date when the cycle was inaugurated. And while the evidence from the records did not really provide acceptable proof for such an early date, Chambers developed a series of interpretations that would vaguely justify it. His reason for seeking an early date was to support the unwritten premise, as noted so cogently by O. B. Hardison, Jr.,[1] that the drama was part of an evolutionary process. Chambers himself puts it as follows:

> The English miracle-play reaches its full development with the formation of the great processional cycles almost immediately after the establishment of the Corpus Christi festival in 1311. The local tradition of Chester, stripped of a certain confusion between the names of two distinct mayors of that city which has clung about it, is found to fix the foundation of the Chester plays in 1328. The date has the authority of an official municipal document, forms part of a quite consistent story, several points in which can

[1] Hardison, *Christian Rite and Christian Drama in the Middle Ages* (Baltimore: Johns Hopkins University Press, 1965), pp. 5–18.

be independently corroborated, and is on *a priori* grounds extremely plausible.[2]

Chambers's date was widely accepted thereafter with the result that the Chester cycle came to be regarded not only as the oldest among those extant but also the dullest,[3] no doubt on the scale of values that equates excellence (or at least, complexity) with the most highly evolved and simplicity with the least. Happily the cycle has been rescued by the lively mind of F. M. Salter and by the meticulous historical research of Lawrence M. Clopper. Salter was the first to look closely at the documentation on the basis of which the early-fourteenth-century date was assigned to the Chester cycle. The early date, he shows, results from a series of misstatements and myths in a Proclamation written in 1531/1532, fully two hundred years after the putative inauguration of the cycle. Yet another document, written sometime before 1575, connects the Chester plays with Randall Higden, the author of the *Polichronicon* and Chester's most famous man of letters. Tradition also ascribes the cycle to the mayoralty of Sir John Arneway, a famous Chester mayor who died in 1278. By a series of steps too complicated to review here, Salter shows that civic pride was more than likely responsible for the association of the cycle with Chester's auspicious past. His review of the documentary evidence leads him to date the cycle at approximately 1375, a date that Salter, with tongue in cheek, prefers over the more logical 1385 in order to pre-

[2] Chambers, *The Mediaeval Stage*, 2 vols. (Oxford: Clarendon Press, 1903), 2:108–109.

[3] Arnold Williams, for example, finds Chester lacking in "the spectacle, the fervor, and the naturalism which fifteenth century revisers introduced into the other cycles"; see *The Drama of Medieval England* (East Lansing: Michigan State University Press, 1961), p. 57. Rosemary Woolf, similarly, dismisses Chester as the "least imaginatively exciting" among those extant; see *The English Mystery Plays* (London: Routledge and Kegan Paul, 1972), p. 306. While neither of these critics directly attributes the lack of quality in Chester to its early date, their assessment echoes a perception that has dominated Chester criticism.

serve Chester's "pride of priority in which she has gloried for four centuries."[4]

The most recent scholarship, especially that of Lawrence Clopper, would move the date of inception—at least of the version of the plays in the surviving manuscripts—to the first quarter of the sixteenth century. Noting, with Salter, that the earliest record of a Chester performance dates to 1422, and noting also that the remaining fifteenth-century records are extremely sparse, Clopper set out to make a systematic reexamination of all of the Chester documents, including the Early and Late Banns, the so-called Newhall Proclamation of 1531/ 1532, and the Harley List of Guilds. His most important conclusions are: (1) The fifteenth-century cycle was essentially a Passion play performed in one location (outside Saint John's church). (2) The cycle in the form that survives is basically the product of revision and addition within the period from 1505 to 1532. (3) Two significant events occurred in the period from 1521 to 1532—the cycle was expanded into a three-day performance, and it was shifted from Corpus Christi Day to Whitsuntide with the result that it was thereafter referred to as the Whitsun play or plays (with the plural form applicable to the version that emerged in 1532). At least the second and third of these conclusions are based on documented facts and strike me as incontrovertible.[5]

What emerges from this revaluation is a Chester cycle that is Tudor in origin. It is still very much a medieval play in content and style, and in the course of its sixteenth-century history it became on that account a controversial text that seems to have been censored several times before its last performance in 1575. (The cycle, as is well known, once contained an Assumption play performed by the Wives of Chester, but that play was apparently suppressed after 1548 in response to the Reforma-

[4] F. M. Salter, *Mediaeval Drama in Chester* (Toronto: University of Toronto Press, 1955), pp. 29–42.

[5] Clopper, "The History and Development of the Chester Cycle," *Modern Philology* 75 (1978): 219–246.

tion.)[6] The most recent book-length study of the Chester plays, that by Peter W. Travis, builds upon the Clopper conclusions and goes one step further in attributing a sixteenth-century origin to the surviving texts of the cycle. Travis believes that the long-recognized influence of the *Stanzaic Life of Christ* as a source for certain of the Chester plays was in fact not a product of the early history of the text, as has usually been maintained, but is rather the result of a revision that took place at the time when the cycle was shifted to Whitsuntide.[7] The argument he presents shows in close detail that the *Stanzaic Life of Christ* passages are in essence amplifications upon the basic narrative focusing especially on the marvelous. The Travis thesis, which derives in part from an article published by Robert Wilson in 1931, is persuasive. It is clear that the *Stanzaic Life* material in the cycle must have been the contribution of a single reviser or author, and since that material does not advance the plot but rather embroiders upon it, it must have been inserted later rather than earlier in the cycle's history. Travis argues that this amplification was occasioned by the shift and expansion of the cycle from a single-day Corpus Christi performance to the three-day play at Whitsuntide. This argument is plausible, and it adds an ironic twist to the evolutionary conception of the growth of the English drama, for it would make latest some of the elements that organicists have always regarded as the simplest (read: dullest) and earliest parts of the cycle. In fact, Travis recognizes this reversal and elaborates upon its critical significance:

[6] Ibid., pp. 226–227. It is well to note that the cycle as a whole is incontestably and maybe even assertively Catholic in tone and substance. The Antichrist plays in particular go out of their way to present a medieval Christian interpretation of the Last Days, a viewpoint that clashed significantly with the Protestant version in which Antichrist is a figure who symbolizes the pope. For a full discussion of the two Antichrists, see the useful differentiation in Richard Emmerson, *Antichrist in the Middle Ages: A Study of Medieval Apocalypticism, Art, and Literature* (Seattle: University of Washington Press, 1981), pp. 211–221.

[7] Travis, *Dramatic Design in the Chester Cycle* (Chicago: University of Chicago Press, 1982), pp. 44–61.

This would of course effectively reverse certain standard assumptions about how the aesthetics of the cycles developed: rather than progressing from the "stolid" and "didactic" to the "playful" and "realistic," Chester may have developed a "naive" and "presentational" dramatic form in its early years, which in later years became more "self-conscious" and "self-interpretive."[8]

While the progress that Travis pictures is still Darwinian in its implications (note the early form is described as "naive"), it does allow, rightly I believe, for the appreciation of the Expositor, a relatively sophisticated dramatic voice in the cycle.

The historiography pertaining to the Chester cycle has thus run the gamut in our times. From the estimate by Chambers at the turn of the century that Chester is the earliest of the extant Middle English Corpus Christi cycles (dating to 1328), we now have come to the perception, based on a careful reinterpretation of the evidence, that its text is in fact among the latest, with an *ad quem* date of 1532. It is important to understand what is embraced by this two-hundred-years' shift. The 1532 date refers to the text, not the performance, of the Chester cycle. We know, in fact, that the Chester plays were performed as early as 1422, when they seem already to have been an established fact. And while evidence is lacking, I would expect the performance history of the cycle to go back at least as far as that of the York cycle, which was already in existence as early as 1376. While the

---

[8] Ibid., p. 48. For the article by Robert H. Wilson, see "The *Stanzaic Life of Christ* and the Chester Plays," *North Carolina Studies in Philology* 28 (1931): 413–432. Wilson wrote his article in response to Frances Foster's argument in her edition of *A Stanzaic Life of Christ* (London: Oxford University Press, 1926), maintaining that this poem, which clearly was a source for numbers of tail–rhyme passages in the Chester cycle, was wrtten in the fourteenth century. Her only evidence for this early dating of the poem, as Travis points out, was based on the assumption that the text of the Chester plays was of fourteenth-century origin. In fact, the manuscripts of *A Stanzaic Life of Christ* are all from the fifteenth century. Travis, thus, would revise the date of origin for the *Stanzaic Life* from the fourteenth to the fifteenth century, a conclusion that strikes me as entirely sensible and one that corrects the sort of mistaken chain reaction that is possible with the misdating of an important literary text.

Chester mythology cannot be accepted as historical fact, there is in the documents a clear sense of a long historical tradition, which may or may not have included the association of the plays with Randall Higden and other Chester luminaries, but which does not, on the other hand, rule out a processional, quasi-dramatic performance of pageants dating at least to the mid-fourteenth century that became the nucleus of the cycle that has come down to us. By the fifteenth century, as Clopper has shown through his study of the Early Banns and the Harley List, a Corpus Christi cycle that was largely a Passion play seems to have been in existence, but no one knows whether even that cycle was recorded in a complete text.

I must disagree for a moment to explain this latter point. The fact is, as I have already shown in my discussion of the York plays, that it is difficult for us to know how the extant manuscript(s) of complete cycles related to the performances or, for that matter, to other manuscripts (especially those held by guilds) of individual plays. Scholars have assumed, with no supporting evidence, that some kind of composite book that contained an entire cycle existed prior to the generation of those cycle manuscripts which survive. In fact, there may not have been a composite book for the fifteenth-century Corpus Christi play that Clopper has posited for Chester. There are references in the Chester records to *regynalls*, but this term is consistently used to describe copies of individual plays that were in the hands of the guilds. When, therefore, there is a reference to the regynall in the entry of 1422 referring to the Coopers, we should not automatically assume that it denote a composite book. Indeed, it much more likely refers to the Coopers' copy of their own play. The term *regynall* has simply not been taken at face value to mean "original," and as I have already shown in my survey of other manuscripts, it has consistently been interpreted, even by the most enlightened scholars, to stand as a synonym for "register." Thus, for example, Clopper describes the regynall as a "master text which included more scenes than were normally performed," and Lumiansky and Mills consistently use the term to describe the "master copy" of the Chester plays.[9] If, however, the regynall is precisely what in the context it seems to refer to—the original text of an individual guild play—then it may well have been true that there never existed a composite early text from which the present manuscripts have been copied. At Chester, the regenalls might then have been a reference text for whatever was performed by the guilds in the fifteenth-century Corpus Christi play, which in itself could have been a dramatic procession attached in some fashion to the religious procession, with enactments of one or more scenes each along the way, similar to the model I have envisioned for the early performance at York. The Late Banns may hint at this type of performance in their observation: "and everye playe of the matter gave but a taste."[10]

The implications of the sort of genesis I have been proposing are, I think, significant. If I am right that the regynalls were truly the original texts and that no composite register existed as the cycle grew from semidramatic religious ridings into full-blown plays, then the first true Chester manuscript was likely to have been generated from the establishment of the three-day performance at Whitsuntide, when there was time enough

[9] Clopper, "History of the Chester Cycle," p. 241; Robert M. Lumiansky and David Mills, eds. *The Chester Mystery Cycle: Essays and Documents* (Chapel Hill: University of North Carolina Press, 1983), pp. 170, 188, 194. It is worth recalling that the terms "regynall" and "originall" occur in the titles of the Fullers' and Glovers' pageants in the York register. They clearly refer here to the individual pageants and were undoubtedly copied from the titles of the guild copies. In York, the copying into the register of individual pageant texts from guild copies, like the one still extant of the Scriveners, seems to have been the norm. If guild copies of pageants rather than the register were used as the reference texts for performances, then one could make good sense out of such citations as the Smiths' at Chester "for paper to Coppy out the parcells of the book" (BL Harl. 2054, f. 16v) which would clearly refer to actors' parts being copied out of the Smiths' regynall. Clopper believes that this reference together with others (e.g. the Smiths' entry of 1572, "for parchment to make a new originall booke," f. 19v) proves that the register itself was copied several times in the later years of the Chester performances. However, it seems much more likely that the entries in question refer to the making of new guild copies or of actors' parts.

[10] Lumiansky and Mills, *Chester Mystery Cycle*, p. 285.

for the extant versions of the plays to have been fully performed. In that case, an effort might have been made by the city to collect a register and to coordinate the performance. It is at this point that a single redactor would have assembled the regynalls from the several guilds and given them continuity. This redactor could well have used the *Stanzaic Life of Christ* as a unifying source, as Travis has suggested, and he could also have put the plays into the reasonably uniform stanzaic form that we discover in the extant copies of the Chester plays. I shall try to show in the discussion that follows that Chester, much like the other three cycles, is a carefully unified play and that, undoubtedly, it is the product of a single intelligence.

The Chester cycle is unique among English Corpus Christi manuscripts in that it survives in five complete manuscripts, all of which were copied from a now-lost exemplar virtually a generation later than its last recorded performance. Lumiansky and Mills believe that the

> five were prepared from the Regenall [*sic*, for Register?] remaining in the Pentice after the final performance in 1575. The Regenall may have reflected some of the shifts of the cycle's final years, and it may also have retained at some points evidence of the cycle's previous states. Thus perhaps the scribes for the cyclic texts at times made choices between alternative materials available in the Regenall.[11]

Whatever the reason for the differences in the manuscripts (e.g. the choice of the Cappers' play about Balaam in MSS H and Hm), all five are reasonably close to what must have been the exemplar, and while we must be aware of the choices that the manuscripts offer at various junctures, we can also be satisfied that we have a composite text—Lumiansky and Mills call it a "cycle of cycles"—of the play, or more accurately plays, that came into being between 1521 and 1532 for performance at Whitsuntide.

[11] Ibid., p. 194.

If then we have in the extant manuscripts a relatively faithful composite version of the contents of the exemplar, we are in a position to note what is unique in the format and style of the Chester "Whitsun" cycle. Certainly one unusual feature is its uniformity of style. The Chester stanza, rhyming $a\ a\ a\ b\ c\ c\ c\ b$ or $a\ a\ a\ b\ a\ a\ a\ b$—an expanded form of the rime couée or tail-rhyme stanza—appears throughout the cycle as overwhelmingly the majority form. No other English cycle is so "regular" or consistent in its format. Indeed, when the cycle veers from the Chester stanza, the effect becomes as a consequence extremely noticeable—as, for example, the rhyme-royal stanzas in the middle of the Vintners' play of the Magi (167/269–171/345) or the opening of the Glovers' play of Chelidonius and Lazarus (230/1–231/39). In these two instances, the plays comment upon Latin quotations, and the royal stanza with its elevated demeanor is used to raise the tone.[12] On the other hand, the clipped short stanza, with its variety of rhyme schemes, used by the Shepherds immediately after the appearance of the star, serves to introduce the parody of the Gloria in Excelsis that is carried off in the Chester cycle with particular verve and playfulness. The customary Chester stanza is, however, not a very flexible dramatic tool. Usually speeches break at the natural division of the stanza (that is, after the fourth or the eighth line), and the result is a set pattern that intrudes even into the most lively pageants, for example, that of Noah's Flood. At his best, the playwright manages to use the stanza to maximum effect as a tool for conveying natural conversation, as in the touching scene between Abraham and Isaac (see pp. 67–77). But if readers find the Chester cycle unexciting, as Rosemary Woolf did, it is probably because the Chester stanza can become tedious in its steady application.

Another unique feature in the format of the Chester cycle is the figure of the narrator, variously called Expositor, Doctor,

[12] For a discussion of the tone of the rhyme royal stanza in Middle English poetry, see my article, "The Royal Stanza in Early English Literature," *PMLA* 94 (1979): 62–76.

Preco, or Nuntius. While we have seen a narrator before, specifically in the figure of Contemplacio in the N-Town cycle, narration in the Chester cycle is considerably more complex in its function as a theatrical device. Contemplacio is fundamentally a prologue and epilogue for several segments and pageants in the N-Town cycle. He guides us, as an extradramatic voice, essentially to know what is happening on stage and what to expect next. The Chester narrators do that, too—for example, the Doctor at the end of the Balaam play

> Now, worthye syrs both great and smale,
> here have wee shewed this storye before;
> and yf hit bee pleasinge to you all,
> tomorrowe nexte yee shall have more.
> Prayenge you all, both east and west
> where that yee goe, to speake the best.
> The byrth of Christe, feare and honest,
> here shall yee see; and fare yee well.
> (97/448–455)

But the Chester narrators do much more: they are commentators and true impresarios. Take, for example, the Expositor in his first appearance, commenting on the symbolic exchange between Abraham and Melchizedek. He comes on stage in stately fashion, riding a horse, and he explicates the meaning of the scene to the audience:

> Lordinges, what may this signifye
> I will expound yt appertly—
> the unlearned standinge herebye
> maye knowe what this may bee.
> This present, I saye veramente,
> signifieth the newe testamente
> that nowe is used with good intente
> throughout all Christianitye.
> (62/113–120)

He goes on to show how the Old and New Law differ, how "signification" (i.e. typology) works, and how to interpret Abraham and Melchizedek in this context. The Expositor is constantly concerned to do just what his name implies: to explain what is going on to a lay audience. And unlike the Contemplacio figure, he is likely to appear at any time in the play, not just the beginning or the end. In fact, in his final appearance, as explicator of the Prophets of Antichrist (Play 22), he has the main part in the play and provides a memorable resonance to his role.

In his function as impresario and commentator on playcraft, the Expositor (or at times his alter ego, the Doctor) actually advances the plot. We shall have occasion to examine more fully his role as "miracle maker" later in the chapter. But it is the narrator/explicator who links miracle making with playcraft, and at important junctures he recites miraculous narratives that have not been enacted, consequently providing those miracles that have been played with greater and more far-reaching importance. Here, for example, is his introduction to a lengthy speech in the Nativity pageant:

> Loe, lordings all, of this miracle here
> freere Bartholemewe in good mannere
> beareth wytnes, withowten were,
> as played is you beforne.
> And other myracles, yf I maye,
> I shall rehearse or I goe awaye,
> that befell that ilke daye
> that Jesus Christ was borne.
>
> (119/564–571)

The miracle in this instance was the withering of Salome's hand, but, of course, the "grand miracle," as C. S. Lewis calls it,[13] is the Incarnation itself. To give this central miracle its proper dramatic emphasis and to call attention to it as miracle, the Chester playwright deftly uses his narrator to paint for his audiences a canvas of the whole miraculous event.

---

[13] Lewis, *Miracles: A Preliminary Study* (London: Geoffrey Bles, Centenary Press, 1947), pp. 131–158.

The Expositor is a unifying device in the cycle, and he gives Chester a very special tone. Through him, we gain the impression that the Chester playwright seeks a direct relation with his audience. The Expositor is there as a reminder not only of the serious purpose of what I will throughout this chapter call "miracle playing" but also as a way of connecting the play with the here and now. True, he breaks the dramatic illusion whenever he appears; in Brechtian terms, he is an alienation device,[14] but precisely because he serves that function, he is not, as some have seen him, an undramatic character or a throwback to primitivism. The Chester cycle has had bad press from the critics to the effect that it is didactic, a feature that was once attributed to its early date of composition when playwrights allegedly were still groping for the best way to put their ideas on stage. No doubt that sense of the didactic comes from the use of the Expositor. But a closer look at his function, as I hope I have shown, will make clear that he is not there simply to explicate the play to the simple-minded. He is a very important voice in the cycle, and most readers remember his presence out of all proportion to the frequency of his stage appearances (ironically, the narrator has a part in only five plays: 4, 5, 6, 12, and 22). His may finally be the most important and memorable voice in the cycle. He is clearly a binding force, a figure who helps significantly to give unity to the cycle.

Unlike the N-Town cycle, Chester maintains clear demarcations among its twenty-four pageants. In the manuscripts, each pageant carries the title of its sponsoring guild, followed by the pageant number, and in some, the title of the episode proper. Yet, while the individual pageants are independent units, they nevertheless join together into an integrated and carefully unified design. We thus perceive two interlocking narrative configurations: the microstructure of the pageant and the macrostructure of the cycle. The pageants usually

---

[14] I have discussed the application of a Brechtian aesthetic to the Corpus Christi plays elsewhere; see "Illusion and Reality in the Medieval Drama," *College English* 32 (1971): 448–464.

present a well-defined episodic plot, and they emphasize closure. They conclude typically with a formal leave-taking as, for example, in the following speech by Garcio at the end of the Shepherds' play

> Well for to fare, eych frend,
> God of his might graunt you;
> for here now we make an ende.
> Farewell, for wee from you goe nowe.
>   (156/693–696)

Departure of the characters from one another and from the audience signals closure. Endings seem to work that way throughout the cycle. The impression we gain is that the Chester cycle does not so much link scenes into acts, as N-Town and to some extent York and Wakefield do, but rather that it advances by an accretion of units.

Clopper has discovered that the shift from the Corpus Christi performance at Chester to the Whitsun show also prompted the change from the use of the singular "play" as a descriptive word for the cycle to the plural "plays."[15] This shift recognizes the self-standing nature of the individual pageants, and it suggests that the cycle should be viewed essentially as a construct in which the whole is the sum of its parts. The unitary structure is basic to the organization of the cycle; it even occurs within pageants, where formal transitions between episodes are often omitted. Take, for example, the curious collocation of the Blacksmiths' play—the conjoining of the Purification and the Doctors. Nowhere does the playwright tell us that Jesus is an infant in the first and a twelve-year-old in the second. The only linkage we have occurs within a short scene in which Mary laments to Joseph that Jesus has strayed away from home and that she wishes to seek him—a scene that comes as a stark and abrupt departure immediately after the closure of the Purification scene. Yet there is a logic in the combination of the two episodes, for they represent the growth of Jesus in the Infancy

---

[15] Clopper, "History of the Chester Cycle," p. 230.

270

FIGURE 14. Hans Memlinc's Passion, ca. 1470.
(Courtesy Galleria Sabauda, Torino)

period. One has to read the cycle in blocks of episodes; the narrative advances by collocation.

One might compare the Chester framework to a cathedral window picturing salvation history in a series of twenty-four panels. In contrast, N-Town and York are more nearly akin in framework to the famous panoramic view of the Passion by Hans Memlinc (see figure 14), wherein all the action is temporally and causally connected on a single plane.[16] The overall effect is the same—a grand design of salvation history—but the sense of narrative progression is distinctly different. In Chester, closure itself seems to be an important structural fact. Endings accrue; they give a foretaste of completion. Each unit at once forwards the plan, and foreshadows the structure, of the

---

[16] I am indebted for the analogy to frames in the visual arts to my student, Sylvia Tomasch, who devotes a chapter to the "framing" of the Chester plays in her dissertation; see "The Unwritten *Dispositio*: Principles of Order and the Structures of Late Middle English Literature" (Ph.D. diss., City University of New York, 1985).

grand design. The narrative pattern thus depends essentially on its frames for its overall meaning.

I have tried to show in the foregoing discussion that the text of the Chester cycle is quite likely the original work of one playwright who wrote in the early sixteenth century and that the cycle is carefully unified in terms of its stylistic and formal devices. Let us now see how the unity of the cycle is enhanced by various prominent and unique thematic strands that integrate its dramatic action.

THE content and dramatic impact of the Chester plays seem to be the product of a number of governing ideas. Among these, no doubt the primary is the depiction of a powerful God whose image dominates the cycle from its outset. This representation of God the Father leads in turn to an emphasis upon Jesus' divinity rather than his humanity,[17] and further to a neglect of

---

[17] Kathleen Ashley has made this point in an influential article that relates what she regards as the primary theme of the cycle, the concern with showing God's omnipotence, to the nominalist argument of the fourteenth and fifteenth centuries; see "Divine Power in Chester Cycle and Late Medieval Thought," *Journal of the History of Ideas* 39 (1978): 387–404. Ashley does an excellent job in demonstrating the Chester concentration on an all-powerful God, but there is some question in my mind that this emphasis necessarily reflects a conscious attempt by the playwright to espouse late-medieval nominalist doctrine. The same objection was raised in a reply to the article by James R. Royce, who observes that the Chester playwright probably obtained his inspiration about the power of God directly from the New Testament and not from the nominalists; see "Nominalism and Divine Power in the Chester Cycle," *Journal of the History of Ideas* 40 (1979): 475–477. In her reply to Royce, Ashley agrees that the Bible is, of course, the chief primary, though perhaps not direct, source of the playwright's theology. She argues that he probably worked within the context of the pastoral theology of the nominalists, which she feels was likely to have affected a much larger body of fifteenth-century literature than we are now aware; see "Chester Cycle and Nominalist Thought," *Journal of the History of Ideas* 40 (1979): 477. While I agree that such a context might well have influenced the Chester playwright, I hope to show that the primary and direct influence on his theology was the Gospel of St. John. It seems likely to me that a single Gospel could well be the most important direct primary source for a cycle of plays, especially if, as I have argued, a single author/reviser was at work to give shape to a cycle as a full dramatic text. A modern example is the use that the Italian di-

Mary as a leading dramatic figure. Finally, it puts the emphasis on God's works with the result that the cycle has the most developed Ministry section among English Corpus Christi cycles and it enacts, in line with that focus, the greatest number of miracles. The latter in themselves become, in consequence, a subject of sustained interest to the playwright.

God's very first speech in the Chester cycle sets the tone for his austere role. The emphasis is on solemnity, distance, power.

> Ego sum alpha et oo,
> primus et novissimus.
> It is my will it shoulde be soe;
> hit is, yt was, it shalbe thus.
>
> I ame greate God gracious,
> which never had begyninge.
> The wholl foode of parente is sett
> in my essention.
> I ame the tryall of the Trenitye
> which never shalbe be twyninge,
> pearles patron ymperiall,
> and Patris sapiencia.
> My beames be all beawtitude;
> all blisse is in my buyldinge.
> All meirth lyeth in mansuetude,
> cum Dei potentia,
> bouth viscible and inviscible.
> As God greatest and glorious
> all is in mea licencill.
> For all the meirth of the majestye
> is magnifyed in me.
> Prince principall, proved
> in my perpetuall provydence,
> I was never but one
> and ever one in three,

---

rector Franco Zeffirelli made of St. John in representing the Passion in his fine television film, "Jesus of Nazareth."

set in substanciall southnes
within selestiall sapience.
The three tryalls in a throne
and true Trenitie
be grounded in my godhead,
exalted by my exelencie.
The might of my makeinge
is marked in mee,
dissolved under a deadem
by my devyne experience.
(1/1–2/35)

This is an awesome speech. The God we meet here speaks mostly of his great power: he is "pearles patron ymperiall," "prince principall," "majestye" endowed with "selestiall sapience"; he sits Three Personed on his throne wearing the heavy diadem of perpetual providence. His Latinate diction distances him from the common folk who are his audience. He creates a vocabulary of power that will cause his feckless human imitators—all those ranting tyrants—to be bereft of an authentic language by which to proclaim their authority. In fact, he sets a tone by which all subsequent attempts to claim power, including Lucifer's, will be reduced to parody.

It is instructive to compare this self-portrait with the one that opens the York plays. Here, too, God pictures himself as omnipotent. The first-person pronouns predominate as much in York as in Chester. There is no question that the York God is any less "formaste and fyrste," to use his own language, than the Chester God. But what is different about him is his emphasis on preparing a world of "bliss" by which his beneficence can enrich his own creation. He is busily engaged in making "a place full of plente" (1/12); and his first task is to bid "a blys albeledande abowte me" (1/21). He quotes his own reassuring language to mankind: "I am lyfe and way vnto welth wynnyng" (1/3), and his vocabulary, even in this first traditional assertive speech, includes the word "louyng" (1/24), a term for which one looks in vain in the opening speech of Chester (my count shows that it occurs but once in all of God's speeches—in his address to Lucifer, 5/89, where it prepares, of course, for the heinousness of the Fall).

The Chester God is stern and ominous. He puts emphasis on what he forbids, and prepares for his grievous disappointment with his own creation. Even as he speaks to Lucifer, the first of his creation, the emphasis is on admonishing: "exsalte you not to exelente into high exaltation" (4/71), he commands. He makes Lucifer aware that "the world . . . is bouth voyde and vayne" (4/73) and that it contains "a dongion of darkenes which never shall have endinge" (4/74). When he decides to survey his realm, he forbids the angels to move from their places (5/106). In the manner of the stern Old Testament God, he virtually leads his subjects into temptation (the Fall of Adam is, in this respect, a replica of the Fall of Lucifer). His vengeance is swift and personal: Upon his discovery of Lucifer's disobedience, he speaks his sentence of doom directly and presides magisterially over the Fall ("I charge you to fall till I byd 'Whoo' "; 10/228). This scene, like that of God's warning, is repeated in the Fall from Paradise: God confronts Adam and Eve directly, metes out his awful justice, and ultimately expels the two from Paradise personally. In the other cycles, it is the Archangel Michael who drives them out of Eden. The punishment is thereby distanced from God, and it seems less formidable in consequence.

In the first three pageants, the Chester God is at once creator and destroyer. In his most fear-inspiring speech, at the opening of the Noah pageant, he says, "Man that I made will I distroye" (42/9), and he laments openly that he created man in the first place. While God, of course, conventionally utters these thoughts, the emphasis in the other cycles is on the "saving remnant," on Noah and his family who are spared by their loving Father, and N-Town in particular stresses that "thei xul not drede be flodys fflowe" (38/112). In Towneley, the conversation between God and Noah is personal, a loving interchange between Father and son, with emphasis on the "frendship" (26/118, 121) between them and the rewards that will come to those who love God. As in most other scenes involving God and his creatures, the Chester cycle is sparse in dramatizing acts of love and reward. Noah is, of course, singled out as God's exception, but God speaks virtually no personal words to him (he limits his praise to calling Noah "righteous," 42/18, 47/115), and he waits until the Flood is over to speak his benediction as he accepts Noah's sacrifice, almost as if the Flood was brought down as a trial imposed on Noah. The final speech in the pageant is a resolution by God to bring bounty to the earth and never again to destroy mankind with flood waters. Yet, despite this new beginning, the role of God as destroyer, as the all-powerful judge of mankind, lingers and sets the tone of the entire action that follows.

The portrayal of a stern God in the Old Testament plays influences two important roles in the cycle: It leads at once to a diminution—one might almost say a neglect—of Mary[18] and to the characterization of Jesus as *Christus triumphans*. Traditionally, Mary is the embodiment and purveyor of divine love. She is the mediatrix, the entirely human link between God and mankind. Her presence as mother endows the life of Jesus with its humanity—through her nurture and her love, the Christ Child grows into gentle and true manhood, and it is in her experience that the rest of mankind knows best how to feel the pain and joy of the Incarnation. When she is a background figure, as she clearly is in Chester, the life of Christ is deprived of its most human dimension. We see Mary in only six of the pageants; she speaks 18 times for a total of 192 lines in the whole cycle. Of these, only one substantial speech comes after the Infancy period, a conventional *planctus* of 24 lines delivered at the foot of the Cross as Pilate affixes his infamous sign. Except for the *planctus*, she makes not a single memorable contribution to the play. Her speeches are almost all responses; they register a worshipful and devout but colorless person who is often overshadowed by a consistently drawn, affectionate, so-

---

[18] In line with the argument I shall be developing in this chapter, I wish to note that the Chester cycle shares with the Gospel of St. John a neglect of her role. She appears but twice in St. John; see 2:5 and 19:25–27.

licitous, and very compassionate Joseph, who forever recalls the visitation of the angel to him with the message that the Christ Child was conceived without sin (see 148/516–517, 183/216–217, 209/143–144). Of the two, Joseph is without doubt the more memorable character.[19]

The emphasis on a powerful God in the Chester cycle seems also to inspire the persistent elevation of man above woman. In fact, the Chester playwright is almost virulently antifeminist. The adder, we recall, has a maiden's face (21/195), and Lucifer will use this shape to inspire the temptation of Eve, for, he explains, "wemen they be full licourouse" (21/199). The cause of the Fall, in Adam's eyes, is the combination of his voluptuous wife and the Great Deceiver, whom he sees as her relative:

[19] A word should be said about the Assumption play, widely recognized because it was apparently played by the Wives of Chester. Since Mary would, of course, have been the subject of that play, her role in the cycle might at one stage in its development have been much larger. However, there is some reason to question the actual existence of an Assumption play in the Whitsun cycle. All the references to the play (as apart from the "company" of the Wives) are to a separate play that seems to have been performed for honored guests at various times of the year; see Clopper, *Chester: Records of the Early English Drama* (Toronto: University of Toronto Press, 1979); pp. 20, 21–22, 23. The only actual association of the Assumption play with the Chester cycle per se occurs in the Early Banns, but there is no definite date for the origin of these Banns and the section in which the description of the Assumption play appears was apparently copied as late as the seventeenth century by a certain Randle Holme. Reference to the Wives' "Assumpcion" is included in the Harley (2104) List of Guilds, assigned by Clopper a date of 1499–1500, but that list may simply be an accounting of all the pageant wagons then in the possession of guilds, and it may consequently not describe a cycle per se. The later list, which accompanies the Early Banns, no longer includes reference to the Wives' Assumption. Clopper assumes that the Wives' play of the Assumption actually was once part of the cycle but that, on the basis of the dates of external documents, it must have been dropped before 1548; see "History of the Chester Cycle," p. 226. While it is clear that the Wives did perform some kind of Assumption plays as an independent pageant, its association with the Corpus Christi cycle is at best nebulous. Possibly at any early time when there might have been a dramatic procession rather than a complete dramatic cycle, Chester included an Assumption tableau. In any case, no matter what the nature and the history of this play, it likely was already out of the cycle at the time when the Whitsun text was put together.

277

> My licourouse wyfe hath bynne my foe,
> the devylls envye shente mee alsoe.
> These too together well may goe,
> the suster and the brother.
>
> (28/353–356)

This shift of blame—it continues in Noah's wife's complaint
"women bynne weake to underfoe / any great travell" (44/67–
68)—very nearly exculpates Adam. But more important, no effort is made in Chester to reverse the traditional role of Eve as
the instigator of the Fall. In Wakefield, God announces that

> Angell must to mary go
> ffor the feynd was eue fo
>
> (87/61–62)

implying the classical reversal in which EVA is turned in meaning as well as form into AVE. For the Chester playwright this
reversal is impossible; Eva is unredeemed, and Mary's role is of
little consequence in the redemption of mankind. God's words
to Eve, and no doubt to women in general, resonate in the absence of any important sympathetic female characters in the
cycle: "man shall master thee alwaye" (26/318).

The character of Jesus is influenced by the playwright's atti-
tude toward God as the Trinity. In this cycle as in at least two
of the others, Wakefield and N-Town, God emphasizes his
threefold nature in his opening speech. It is instructive to note,
however, that the N-Town God, in particular, differentiates
the roles of the Three Persons. He says,

> I am þe trewe trenyte,
> here walkyng in þis wone;
> Thre personys myself I se
> lokyn in me God alone.
> I am þe Fadyr of powste,
> My sone with me gynnyth gon,
> My gost is grace in mageste,
> Weldyth welthe up in hevyn tron.
> O God thre, I calle:

278

I am Fadyr of myth,
My sone kepyth ryth,
My gost hath lyth,
and grace with-alle.

(17/14–26)

As we saw in the preceding chapter, the N-Town Christ has a carefully planned role that is quite distinct—even if inseparable—from that of the Father. He is "Sapientia," or "Ryth," as he is called by the Father in the opening speech. The Chester God, in contrast, tells us from the outset that he is the "tryall of the Trenitye / which never shalbe twyninge" (1/9–10). He never names the other two Persons of the Trinity.[20] The result is that Jesus is truly inseparable from God; he is seen as the triumphant incarnation of God among mankind, and we are asked to respond to him in wonder and awe more than in fellowship and sympathy for his suffering. The emphasis on miracles, which, of course, is the central subject of the Ministry plays, is a reflection of God as "maker," much in keeping with the focus on God's creation in the opening of the Drapers' play. The words of Caecus in the fascinating play of the Glovers, which combines the stories of the Man Born Blind and Lazarus, attest to the sheer wonder and awesomeness of Christ in his role as miracle maker:

there is noe man that ever could
restore a creature to his sight
that was blynd borne and never sawe light.
If he of God were not, iwis,
hee could never worke such thinges as this.

(239/220–224)

I am not the first to suggest that the Chester Christ differs from his counterparts in the other cycles because of his consis-

---

[20] Lynette Muir has shown that no distinctions are made in the Chester cycle among the three Persons of the Trinity, and she concludes that "the same actor could well have played God throughout"; see "The Trinity in Medieval Drama," *Comparative Drama* 10 (1976): 122–123.

tent characterization as the powerful and just King who has come into the world to exercise God's will. We have seen that this interpretation was offered by Kathleen Ashley in support of the view that the Chester cycle develops a nominalist theology. Peter Travis expands upon this perception, and while he attributes the idea of power to a basic anti-scholastic bias in the Chester playwright (a bias that, he believes, was part of a neo-Romanesque context that influenced the cycle), he demonstrates in an excellent chapter how the Ministry plays in particular develop a Christocentric focus the purpose of which is to represent Jesus' "victorious reign on earth."[21] Noting that Chester offers more Ministry episodes than any of the other cycles—he counts eight—Travis shows that in each of these episodes the central point is consistently the demonstration of Christ's power: "Every character and every action gain definition exclusively through their subordinate relationship to Christ" (p. 144). The Ministry section in the Chester cycle includes the scene of the Temptation combined with the Woman Taken in Adultery (Play 12, the Butchers' pageant), the episode of the Blind Chelidonian combined with the Raising of Lazarus (Play 13, the Glovers' pageant), and the scene in the house of Simon the Leper together with the Entry into Jerusalem and the Destruction of the Temple (Play 14, the Corvisors' pageant). As a group, these plays put emphasis on what Travis calls "Christ's suprahuman accomplishments," "his transcendent divinity" (p. 156); they are true "miracle plays" in which the center of our attention is constantly on Christ as minister. Thus, for example, where the other cycles give much attention to the redemption of those who are healed or liberated, these plays focus on the power in the act itself. The conversion of the adulteress, to cite one of Travis's examples, has much more to do with her perception of Christ's divinity than with the recognition of her own sin (p. 155). In the Entry play, "we are presented with the awesome image of *Christus Rex* in the most glorious hour of his ministry" (p. 165). In the unique

[21] Travis, *Dramatic Design*, pp. 142–173.

scene with the moneylenders, Christ enters "cum flagello" as stern judge who very much resembles the all-powerful Father of the Genesis plays.

The dominant source of the entire Chester cycle, not merely as generally acknowledged the Ministry plays, seems to be the Gospel of Saint John. This influence is reflected not only in the selection of episodes, most of which derive directly from John, but also in the emphasis and the tone. If "Johannine" means emphasis on faith (the association of Saint John with Gnosticism is widely made), on spirituality, and on the Word of God, then Chester is the Johannine cycle among those which survive. We can see that influence best perhaps in the brilliant play of the Man Born Blind and Lazarus (Pageant 13). The conjunction of the two episodes, which are not usually treated together, is no doubt the direct result of their proximity to each other in Saint John. Here, literally at the center of the Chester cycle, the playwright provides a single, carefully integrated dramatic adaptation of four chapters from Saint John (8 through 11) with the clear purpose of representing the Ministry and, more broadly, the Incarnation itself, from a Johannine perspective.

An examination of the singular rhyme-royal speech by Jesus at the beginning of the pageant will demonstrate this point. I have already observed that rhyme royal in Middle English poetry is usually reserved for elevated and ceremonial occasions; it was originally spoken either by or to royalty. In this five-stanza speech, introduced by and concluded with Latin quotations from the Gospel of Saint John, Jesus speaks for the first time in the cycle to his disciples and, I believe, directly to the audience. He sets forth here in formal terms, either by paraphrasing or directly quoting the text of Saint John, not only the purpose of the pageant that is being introduced, but also the significance of his role in the cycle. Jesus characterizes himself as "revealer" who brings God's Word (a Johannine leitmotif) to lead believers into the light of day and away from the darkness of night. He brings "signs" by which the "glory" of God's universe can be discovered, and these signs are the miracles that he is about to work. The Gospel of Saint John, which concentrates on interpreting rather than, as do the synoptics, narrating the life of Christ, is often divided into two major parts: chapters 1–12, known as the "The Book of Signs," and chapters 13–21, called the "Book of Glory."[22] The material in the Chester pageant is taken from the latter chapters of the Book of Signs and thus deals specifically with miracles and their meaning. Miracles are a direct sign of the essential truth that Jesus is the Son of God, and it is this point that is made by the Raising of Lazarus. As Mary of Bethany tells Jesus (and us),

> By verey *signe* nowe men maye see
> that thou arte Godes Sonne.
> (250/476–477; italics added)

With knowledge of this essential truth (see John 8:32), God's "glory" is set forth (see 232/56). The break that comes between the end of chapter 12 and the beginning of chapter 13 is thus a crucial demarcation, for before that break Jesus manifests the power of God by revealing it through "signs"; after it the power is established and he moves resolutely toward his destiny. As George W. MacRae puts it, "the Johannine story accentuates the autonomy of Jesus in the passion. He lays down his life; it is not just taken from him. In fact, he behaves throughout almost as the architect of the passion, not its victim."[23] The Chester interpretation is exactly the same, and the pageant of the Man Born Blind and Lazarus highlights that understanding.

The opening rhyme-royal speech establishes the identity of Jesus and spells out his mission. He is at once "lux mundi" and "Filius Dei" (230/1; cf. John 8:12); he and the Father "are all on," or as Jesus put it "Ego et Pater unum sumus" (230/8; cf.

---

[22] We owe the title of the "Book of Signs" to C. H. Dodd, *The Johannine Epistles* (New York: Harper, 1946). The terms are used as basic divisions by R. E. Brown in his edition, "The Gospel according to John," in *The Anchor Bible*, 2 vols. (Garden City, N.Y.: Doubleday, 1966, 1970).

[23] MacRae, *Invitation to John: A Commentary on the Gospel of John with Complete Text from "The Jerusalem Bible"* (Garden City, N.Y.: Doubleday, 1978), p. 164.

John 10:30); he is, moreover, the "good sheppard," as "scripture beareth wytnes: 'bonus pastor ponit animam suam pro [ovibus] suis' " (230/18, 231/20–21; cf. John 10:11). His purpose is ordained by the Father: "to preach and declare" (230/10). He is on earth to do his "Fathers workes . . . to heale the sicke and restore the blynd" (231/23–24), and he charges his disciples to imprint and even memorize his word (231/28–31) because "Si vos manseritis in sermone meo, veri discipuli mei eritis, et cognoscetis veritatem, et veritas liberabit vos" ("If you abide in my word, you shall be my disciples indeed, and you shall know the truth, and the truth shall make you free"; 230/35–36; cf. John 8:31–32). In this eloquent self-revelation, the Chester Jesus quotes the heart of the Ministry Gospel in Saint John, and he puts before his audience no less than a full interpretation of his role in the cycle.

It is, in fact, in this speech, rather than the Narrator's voice, that the cycle really becomes the didactic vehicle that critics have so often vaguely characterized. For Jesus here speaks not merely to his disciples but, as does Saint John, to all the world. He will prove with "miracles" (which he calls "works") the truth of his divinity, and using the shepherd metaphor he declares that he is not speaking alone to the flock that is already his,

> For other sheepe I have which are to me commytted.
> They be not of this flocke, yet will I them regard,
> that there may be one flocke and one sheppard.
>
> (231/26–28)

What happens, therefore, is the dramatic conversion of Jesus' speech into a sermon to all who are listening. It is, of course, addressed to the Apostles who must surround him as he delivers these words, and it may be addressed as well (depending on how the play is performed) to the actors of the play that follows—the Blind Man, his parents, the two Neighbors, the Jews, the Pharisees, Mary and Martha–but it also speaks to the Chester audience. Seen in this light, the cycle takes upon itself the Christological function of the Gospel of Saint John. It reaffirms the purpose of the Incarnation and the Resurrection. Its miracles are no mere theatrical legerdemain—they are enactments of divine mystery.

We can see directly how this process works by examining the play of the Man Born Blind and Lazarus. In it, at the very outset, Jesus tells us that he will bring sight to the blind man "to sett forth Goddes great *glorye*" (232/56; italics added). The miracle is not performed for the benevolence of the act itself nor as a way of applying mercy to a sinner, for the fact that the man was born blind has nothing to do with his or his parents' morality. Jesus says,

> Hit was neither for his offence,
> neither the synne of his parentes,
> or other fault or negligence
> that hee was blynd borne.
>
> (232/51–54)

The reason, plain and simple, was for God

> his power to shewe manifestlye
> this mans sight to reforme.
>
> (232/57–58)

The identical reason is given by Jesus later in the play for the sickness that has visited Lazarus. Jesus does not come to his rescue because he loved him so "tenderlye" (the reason used by Martha in her appeal; 243/310) but rather because he needed to manifest himself as God's Son (243/315–316). In both episodes, moreover, Jesus employs the light/darkness contrast that is so prominent in the Gospel of Saint John. Ironically, it is not applied to the bringing of sight to the blind man. Rather, it is used throughout to show that Jesus himself, as he has announced in the opening speech, is "lux mundi." He must work his miracles while "the daye is fayre and bright" (232/59), and his light that shines in the sun will appear to those who believe (232/65–66). Later, in the introduction to the Lazarus episode, he identifies himself as the "worldes light" and likens himself to the day and his followers to the twelve hours "that lightened be through followinge mee" (245/351; cf. John 11:9). Extending the metaphor to all humanity, he says,

284

Hee offendeth not that goeth in light;
but whosoever walketh abowte in night,
hee tresspasseth all agaynst the right,
and light in him is non.

(244/341–344)

Of course, both the persons rescued—the Blind Man and Lazarus—come out of darkness to light, and thus the metaphoric sense is that they are truly followers of Christ.

The foregoing analysis makes clear that the pageant is not *about* miracles; it is about the mission of Jesus. The use of miracles simply "beareth wytnes" (another favorite Johannine theme) to the power of God (240/242). And thus, the dramatic focus is much more on the effect of the miracles than the miracles themselves (though every theater person knows how dramatic "miracle playing" in itself can be on stage, a point to which I shall return). The play focuses on those who are witness to the miracle, ourselves as readers/spectators included. What is the "truth," a word that is constantly repeated in the play? How did Caecus gain his sight? The neighbors and the Pharisees puzzle about this question, and while Primus Pharaseus is consistently hostile to Jesus in his interpretation, Secundus wavers—he cannot get himself to believe that "hee which hath thys marveyle wrought should be a synner" (235/136–137). Even the Blind Man's parents are "uncertayne" (237/182), and they want to inquire of him what is the "trueth" (237/184). The "truth," of course, rests in the word (and the sign) of Jesus. Those who see it, like Mary of Bethany, the play's paradigmatic convert, are made free. The play, thus, was written, very much like the Gospel of Saint John, to promote belief. And also like the Gospel, it was concerned with the persistent "misunderstanding" of God's word. Its underlying purpose, as that widely attributed to the Gospel itself, was "to remove the misunderstandings which persisted in an age when authentic understanding had become possible."[24]

It is now time to see the pageant in its full context: the cycle. In effect, it brings into realization the plan laid down by God

[24] See John Painter, *John: Witness and Theologian* (London: SPCK, 1975), p. 9.

the Father at the very first. I would argue that the Johannine emphasis was there from the beginning. In direct contrast to N-Town, Chester makes very little attempt to differentiate the Persons of the Trinity. This view of God is in accord with the Gospel of Saint John, where the Son is simply seen as the "Revealer." He is a Second "Person" but he also is in all respects indistinguishable from the Father. Here is how Painter describes the relationship:

> Jesus' dignity is wholly dependent on his obedience to the Father's will. For John, Father and Son are used in the sense of the two persons who are both divine, but where the relationship between the two is that of the dependence of the Son on the Father. Because of this, the Son's words and actions really do come from the Father.[25]

If, as I have argued, the Chester playwright was guided throughout in his theology by the Gospel of Saint John, then he clearly had no other option than to give a consistent and single characterization to the Father and the Son, with the result that Jesus manifestly needed to be portrayed as *Christus Rex*. The indication that the playwright chose this deliberate plan for the cycle is not only in his treatment of the Trinity but also in his early emphasis on light and darkness and on "signs."

While, of course, light is usually associated with the divine and while darkness, even more emphatically, is equated with the satanic, Chester stands out among the English cycles as the one to make the contrast of light and darkness a pivotal theological point from the outset. For the York playwright the light of day was to be differentiated only in intensity from that of the night. In his creation both were deemed good:

> Two lyghtis, one more and one lesse,
> to be fest in þe firmament;
> The more light to the day
> fully suthely sall be sent,

[25] Ibid., p. 63.

þe lesse lyght allway
to þe nyght sall take entent.

(56/95–100)

This interpretation of light veers sharply from the Johannine. The Chester view is much more in accord, with its emphasis on stark contrast and on the persistent equation of darkness and evil. The Chester God says:

At my byddynge made be light.
Light is good, I see in sight.
Twynned shalbe through my might
the light from thestearnes.
Light "day" I wilbe called aye,
and thestearnes "night," as I saye.

(14/9–14)

By calling himself "day," the Chester God clearly anticipates the Johannine role of Jesus—we recall Jesus' words, "to the daye myselfe may likened be" (245/349). And darkness for the Chester God is always representative of his absence; it informs the dungeon "which never shall have endinge" (4/74). There can be little doubt that in his treatment of light and darkness as basic metaphors, the Chester playwright gives a consistent Johannine interpretation from the outset.

The same is true of signs. The best illustrations in the Old Testament plays come from the plays of Noah and Moses, where the works of God—his saving of Noah and his family and his passing down the commandments—are presented as "tokens" of his covenant with mankind. At the conclusion of the Flood, Deus promises Noah that he will never bring the floodwaters again, and he says:

My bowe betwene you and mee
in the fyrmamente shalbe,
by *verey tokeninge* that you may see
that such vengeance shall cease.

(55/309–312; italics added)

287

True, the reference to the rainbow as token of the Covenant comes directly from Genesis. But its occurrences here, much as the reference to the tablets that Moses brings down as "token" of God's "pearles . . . postee" (80/38–39), is of exceptional interest in the context of the Johannine emphasis in the cycle. In a recent article, John J. McGavin has commented on the recurring use of "signe" and "tokeninge" in the Chester cycle to "display . . . Christ's identity as God's Son and his intentions for Man." Focusing on the Purification play as a particular instance, McGavin finds in the use of signs (e.g. Simeon's prophecy "Manye signes hee shall shewe / in which untrewe shall non trowe"; 211/183–184) the thematic linkage between the Purification and the Doctors episodes in Pageant 11.[26] In effect, then, the signs of God are in our consciousness long before Jesus begins his Ministry. And they remain there throughout the cycle; indeed, Philippus in the Ascension play presents a terse and dramatic summary of the matter:

> For knowe we mone by sygne vereye
> that hee ys Godes Sonne, sooth to saye.
> (377/173–174)

We have seen in the foregoing discussion that the Chester characterization of God is theologically of a piece throughout the cycle. This thematic design, based uniquely among English cycles on the Gospel of Saint John, is crucial for our understanding of what I regard as the most significant unity in the cycle: its remarkable dramatic strategy, which, from the outset provides a sense of its ending. To understand how this strategy functions, we must now explore the overall dimensions of the cycle as a dramatic form.

SINCE the nineteenth century, the term *cycle* has been widely applied to the major Corpus Christi plays that survive from the late Middle Ages in England. This usage is a curious one,

---

[26] McGavin, "Sign and Tradition: The *Purification* Play in Chester," *Leeds Studies in English*, n.s. 11 (1979): 90–101.

which, though it lacks historical authority, has taken firm root in our critical vocabularly, probably because it reveals something notable in our perception of the Corpus Christi plays when they are read whole as literary works dealing with salvation history. The *OED* lists the first occurrence of "cycle" in its literary sense in 1835 (referring to "the epic cycle") and it provides the following definition:

> A series of poems or prose romances, collected round or relating to a central event or epoch of mythic history and forming a continuous narrative; as the *Arthurian Cycle*.
>
> (s.v. "Cycle," ¶6)

While this definition is an adequate beginning for understanding the term in its literary context, I believe it to be partial. *Cycle* clearly implies "a circle or a round of events" (see W. W. Skeat's definition in his *Etymological Dictionary of the English Language*), and it is exactly that notion—"a round of events"—which I conceive as crucial when it is applied to the Corpus Christi collections or to the Arthurian romances. The obvious fact that each of these works is centrally concerned with the "second coming" of its principal figure makes it *cyclic*. Endings thus superimpose over beginnings, with the suggestion that as one round of narrative ends, a new one, based on the former design yet also improved or perfected, begins. The Corpus Christi plays, in their overall structure, surely exemplify this cyclic nature. They set up our expectations for patterned repetition and for incremental and infinite recurrence. God as expositor in the Wakefield Annunciation provides a paradigmatic list of ingredients by which to view the full play cyclically:

> A man, a madyn, and a tre:
> Man for man, tre for tre,
> Madyn for madyn; thus shal it be
> (87/32–34)

When these words are said, we have already experienced the postlapsarian, typological recurrence of Christ in the figures of Abel, Noah, Isaac, Jacob, and Moses, and now we look forward not only to the Incarnation of Christ but also to his death, to the Resurrection, to several dramatic ascensions and reappearances, up to doomsday, which is at once the end of time and the beginning of eternal life—the substance of a new illusory play that is meant to be enacted in the imagination of the spectators when they leave the performance and one that builds on our quest for the perfectability of Paradise, even as Adam and Eve are led for a third time to a new realm. Dante's circles, aspiring ever upward beyond the paradisal summit of Purgatory, provide a perfect image for this structural design.

As a preliminary to an examination of the dramatic plan of the Chester plays, we need to recognize the cycle structure in its general configuration and its dramatic limits. That structure, of course, derives ultimately from the liturgy, and most particularly from the festival year that provided the occasions for the enactment of "rememorative" liturgical plays. This cyclic structure, with its open-endedness, presents an artistic problem to the secular dramatist—one that is most successfully solved in the extant cycles by the Chester playwright. If we accept the premise that the Corpus Christi cycles are the work of single redactors whose purpose it was to shape material of diverse origin—in combination with their own literary contributions—into an artistic whole, then the problem of devising beginnings, middles, and endings becomes an important critical consideration. In narrative terms, of course, these divisions are quite clearly defined as applied to salvation history. Whatever framework the redactor might choose—say, the Seven Ages, or the design used by many Continental plays of matching Old Testament type with New Testament antitype—he must begin with the Creation and end with the Day of Judgment. This straight linear narrative simply defines the outer limits and the chronological zones within the work. It tells us nothing very subtle or satisfying about the rise and fall of dramatic conflicts. In fact, the linear narrative is really at odds with the liturgical calendar about the complexities of initiation and closure. The Chester cycle confronts this aesthetic problem head-on, and it provides among the Corpus Christi cycles the most satisfactory solution to it.

I have said that the "cyclic" structure that is characteristic of the Corpus Christi play as a generic feature derives ultimately from the liturgy. It is irrelevant for my immediate purposes to reopen the question concerning direct development, a point that remains at issue among historians of the drama.[27] Suffice it to recognize the influence of the liturgical drama on the cycle plays; there are, of course, direct echoes, as in the iteration in every one of the cycles of the "quem quaeritis" question, and there is also a coincidence of central episodes, both in the Christmas and the Easter segments, as well as a similarity in the conventions and the modes of play that we encounter in the two forms. The time frame, both in its macroscopic and its microscopic dimensions, is also a shared feature of the liturgy and the drama. As we know, the Mass is the core of the liturgy. As O. B. Hardison has pointed out, it is a comic form in its ritual commemoration of the Last Supper. (Hardison would say it is a dramatic peripeteia from "*tristia to gaudium*").[28] As such the Mass and the episodes of dramatic action that have sprung from it to form the liturgical drama are linear in their representation of time. But there is also the macrostructure of the liturgical year, and that structure is cyclical. In Hardison's words, "Each Mass is related to every other Mass through its connection with the larger structure of the Church year. Thus each Mass is an episode in a cycle that repeats itself every 365 days."[29] The Corpus Christi play, as it were, is an image of this macrostructure. It may have been planned, as V. A. Kolve has maintained, for performance on Corpus Christi Day because during the feast, which is devoted to a celebration of the Sacrament, the proper subject for enactment is "the whole story, from man's fall to the salvation of the blessed at the Judgment,

---

[27] A useful critical summary appears in Alan H. Nelson, *The Medieval English Stage: Corpus Christi Pageants and Plays* (Chicago: University of Chicago Press, 1974), pp. 1–14.

[28] Hardison, *Christian Rite and Drama*, p. 83.

[29] Ibid.

to reveal the central episode—the Passion—as joyful in meaning."[30] Corpus Christi occurs on the Thursday after Trinity Sunday, and it marks at once the end of *Quinquagesima*, the Easter season, and the beginning of ordinary time. Thematically, its significance is to conclude the sequential commemoration of sacred history and "to apply to the Christian life the lessons of the first half of the year."[31]

The linear segments of the liturgical year—the Christmas and the Easter seasons—are thus embedded in a timeless, recurrent cycle. And while their internal chronologies are entirely sequential, they nevertheless present an ambiguous view of beginning and endings. The celebrations of Advent and *Septuagesima*, the two formal occasions of beginning within the liturgical year, curiously begin with endings. The traditional Epistle and Gospel readings of the first Sunday in Advent demonstrate this overlapping: The Lesson of the Epistle from Romans 13 celebrates the coming of Christ, "it is now the hour for us to rise from sleep," while the Gospel passage from Matthew 25 foretells the signs of Doomsday and Christ's Second Coming. In fact, that first Sunday, which marks at least one beginning in the liturgical year, is devoted principally to the recog-

---

[30] Kolve, *The Play Called Corpus Christi* (Stanford: Stanford University Press, 1966), p. 49. Jerome Taylor, in an extended argument, has attempted to show that the cycles derive their unity from the purpose of the Corpus Christi Feast. Showing that the text of the feast stresses the "comprehensive commemoration of all of God's wonders in the Eucharist," he maintains that the cycles reflect this objective and that their purpose is to show "the history of God's wonders, that is, of his responses, specifically, to man's defections from the divine Monarchy and Law and to man's consequent social, familial, and personal disintegrity." While the cycles do examine these defections, I doubt that any of them except Chester puts central emphasis on God's monarchy. The difficulty with Taylor's discussion is its failure to discriminate among the cycles. He offers, toward the end of the article, a homogenization of the "Corpus Christi cycle" plot and, in so doing, he overlooks the differences that make each cycle a distinct work of art. See "Dramatic Structure of the Corpus Christi, or Cycle, Plays," in *Medieval English Drama: Essays Critical and Contextual*, ed. Jerome Taylor and Alan H. Nelson (Chicago: University of Chicago Press, 1972); pp. 148–156.

[31] For a useful review of the facts, see Edward T. Horn, *The Christian Year* (Philadelphia: Muhlenberg Press, 1957), pp. 150–153.

nition of the Last Judgment. *Septuagesima*, likewise, marks a point of departure, the beginning of the Easter cycle. While this day commemorates the seven days of Creation, the first words of the Introit speak plaintively of death:

> The groans of death surrounded me, the sorrows of hell encompassed me:
> And in my affliction I called upon the Lord, and he heard my voice, from his holy temple.
>
> (Psalms 17:5–7)

Endings are enveloped in beginnings, and the cyclic structure of the liturgical year is thus, experientially, one that is infinitely repeatable without clear points of demarcation. The beginning of the year could be reckoned at various times. Technically, of course, it occurred in the Old Style calendar on 25 March, the traditional date of the Annunciation. But ceremonially, particularly in the context of commemorative feasts, it could as easily be marked by the first Sunday in Advent, as by Christmas, as well as many other dates. As we know from the world of romance, feast days were set aside not only for the telling of tales but for their beginnings and endings. The *Roman de Lancelot* tells us that Arthur held court five times a year—at Easter, Ascension, Pentecost, All Saints' and Noel—and that any of those feasts could thus begin and end romances. So, too, there was wide variation in the civic calendar and the demarcation of the fiscal year. In the Chester records, for example, the Churchwardens' Accounts begin at Easter, the List of Mayors in November, the accounts of the Drawers of Dee on 30 June, of the Painters on 18 October, of the Glovers on 5 January, of the Mercers in May.[32] The absence of a definitive date marking the start or end of a new ecclesiastical or legal year is no doubt influenced by the cyclical nature of the liturgical year.

Since the liturgy was historically the core of the drama, it left the Corpus Christi playwrights with an overall structure that was indeed cyclical. It also left them with the aesthetic problem

---

[32] See Clopper, *Chester: REED*, p. lxii.

of how to provide a satisfactory sense of an ending for the play at large. Not only was the play of Corpus Christi cyclical in its narrative structure and comic in its movement—the ending recapitulated and reengendered the beginning—but it also was an annual, seasonal event, suggesting in its very performance that the cycle would be renewed in the subsequent year. This is, of course, not to say that the play lacked an ending. The Doomsday play (it was rarely called the Last Judgment) provided a grand curtain scene for all of the performers except, significantly, Satan. In narrative terms, the coming of Doomsday is fully expected, and there is nothing abrupt about its occurrence. What is lacking in most of the cycles and, for that matter, in much of the secular literature, is the Aristotelian cohesion among beginnings, middles, and endings, a cohesion that results from the playwright's craft to justify the inevitability of his ending in the structure of his narrative design. The cyclical model created a problem in aesthetics for the writer. He had to find a satisfactory structural plan by which he could at once anticipate comic recurrence and formal closure. It is not that he failed to provide an ending, but rather that he lacked an aesthetic of closure.

Let me illustrate this point with the works of Chaucer, who was also perplexed by closure. His endings are troublesome to us, as they no doubt were to him. Was the *House of Fame* left deliberately unfinished? Did he ever really plan to bring the pilgrims back to the Tabard Inn? What is the real ending of the *Troilus*, and where does it begin? Is it coincidental that the ending of the *Book of the Duchess* with the dreamer waking up recapitulates the beginning of the poem's central episode? Puzzling as these endings may be, they nevertheless do not leave us wondering about their finality. Good arguments have been made that the *House of Fame*, the *Squire's Tale*, and the *Monk's Tale* are left deliberately unfinished. Certainly, *The Canterbury Tales* as a whole has a very emphatic finality about it (so strong a finality that a return trip is, for most readers, an aesthetic impossibility). Like the *Troilus*, *The Canterbury Tales*, far from lacking an ending, has too many endings; the Manciple symbolically silences the teller of frivolous tales; the Parson casts fable and jest aside entirely, preaches a penitential homily, and "knits up" the festivities to "make an end"; finally, Chaucer speaks his Retraction as a coda to all his works.[33] In all this, we have emphatically an ending; what we lack is the *sense* of an ending and particularly the expectation of the endings we are given.

The problem in the cycle plays, while literally not the same, is similar. They begin by setting up a conflict—that between God and Satan, the archetypal protagonist and antagonist. Yet this conflict is, in dramatic terms, only of peripheral interest. One expects that the Corpus Christi play, which begins so clearly by focusing on that conflict, would concentrate on it as often and as variously as tradition and the substance of myth would allow. And one expects, by the same logic, that the play will come to an end shortly after that conflict is resolved. Yet, most of the cycles keep Satan off stage for lengthy intervals, and they resolve the conflict long before the formal ending. The Doomsday play is thus, in its largest setting, something of a dramatic anticlimax. I will argue that among the English cycles, only the Chester playwright directly confronts this problem. He solves it by building into his text a pervasive sense of an ending.

In designating the Chester cycle as the Corpus Christi play with the best planned and most dramatically emphatic sense of an ending, I have in mind what Barbara Herrnstein Smith has said about the imperatives of satisfactory closure: "We take particular delight, not in all endings, but in those that are designed." Successful endings are the result of deliberately shaped expectations; they must, in Smith's words, tease "our tensions" and defer "the immediate fulfillment of our appetites." When such endings occur they "confirm retrospectively,

---

[33] For an enlightening view of these "endings" to *The Canterbury Tales*, see James Dean, "The Ending of the *Canterbury Tales*," *Texas Studies in Language and Literature*, 21 (1979): 17–33.

as if with a final stamp of approval, the valued qualities of the entire experience we have just sustained."[34]

With a story as familiar as salvation history, one might conclude that since the outcome is already so well known a deliberately shaped ending is gratuitous. We know, after all, that Adam will be redeemed, that he will ultimately be brought to Heaven with the saints, and for the playwright to belabor this point is to disclose the obvious. The issue, however, is not disclosure; it is the containment within an aesthetically defined shape of the artist's purpose and vision. The anticipation of the ending allows the playwright to reveal his control over the cycle—to show that he is not simply chronicling the story of God's Creation but that he is, in fact, imitating the very process of creation and putting his own stamp on the work. The Chester playwright, as can be seen from his rendering of Adam, does that from the very outset. No other cycle gives us a glimpse into Adam's domestic life as father to his sons, thus personalizing the love of fatherhood that had been muted by the characterization of Chester's magisterial God. A very human Adam tells his sons about his experience in Paradise, warning them by confessing his error:

> To make you ware of comberouse case
> and lett your doinge from trespasse.
> (31/445–446)

He recounts the remarkable dream he had while Eve was taken from his side. It is worth quoting the passage in full:

> I wott by things that I there see
> that God will come from heaven on hie,
> to overcome the devill soe slee
> and light into my kynde;
> and my blood that hee will wyne
> that I soe lost for my synne;

[34] Barbara Herrnstein Smith, *Poetic Closure: A Study of How Poems End* (Chicago: University of Chicago Press, 1968), pp. 1, 3, 4.

a new lawe ther shall begine
and soe men shall them sure.

Water or fyer also witterlye
all this world shall distroye,
for men shall synne soe horryblye
and doe full much amysse.
Therfore that yee may escape that nye,
doe well and be ware me bye.
I tell you heare in prophecye
that this will fall ywisse.

Alsoe I see, as I shall saye,
that God will come the laste daye
to deeme mankynde in fleshe verey,
and flame of fyer burninge,
the good to heaven, the evell to hell.
Your childrenn this tale yee may tell.
This sight saw I in paradyce or I fell,
as laye there sleepinge.

(32/449–472)

The Chester Adam had foreknowledge of his destiny from the
very beginning. And through his act of revelation he imparts
to all who follow the same knowledge. He wants his progeny to
share that sense of an ending, as indeed the playwright wishes
his audience to share his own sense of an ending. In Chester we
know the outcome of the cosmic struggle as part of the artistic
design from the very beginning. It is in this fashion that the
playwright dominates the cyclic structure and allows it to move
toward closure. His play is designed to end even in the face of
the endlessness of the eternal.

Adam has defined for us the central conflict of the drama
that will ensue: "God will come from heaven on hie / to over-
come the devill. . . ." We have seen that the Chester cycle has
one protagonist: the trinitarian God. Viewed as a composite,
this protagonist is represented on stage by God the Father, Je-

sus, and indirectly by such characters as Enoch and Elias and the Archangel Michael. Like the other Corpus Christi plays, Chester also has one antagonist—Satan—but unlike them, here Satan is transfigured into Antichrist, with the effect that the force of evil is compounded, and the essential conflict is sustained to the very end. In this respect the structure of the Chester cycle is unique. In the other cycles, the climactic encounter occurs when Christ, or *Anima Christi* as he is usually called in the episode, confronts Satan at the gates of Hell.[35] It is at the conclusion of this pageant that a triumphant Christ binds Satan to his throne, who, as in Wakefield and York, then speaks the last words we hear from him, "I synk into hell pyt" (W. 304/360 and Y. 392/348). Thereafter, with the archenemy vanquished, we encounter his forces once more, on Doomsday, in the form of grotesque and subdued demons, who act (ironically) as subordinates of God, carrying the sinners to eternal damnation.

The lineage linking the Chester Satan and Antichrist is based on tradition, and it is clearly built into the structure of the cycle. Although no direct sources are known for the Chester Antichrist play, all medieval accounts are traceable to Abbot Adso's *Essay on Antichrist* (the *Libellus de Antichristo*) of the tenth century, which explains the birth of Antichrist as follows:

> At the very beginning of his conception, the devil will enter with him [Antichrist's father] into his mother's womb, and by the devil's strength he will be fostered and protected in his mother's womb, and the devil's strength will be with him always. And just as the Holy Ghost came into the womb of the Mother of our Lord Jesus Christ and covered her with divinity, so that she conceived from the Holy Ghost and what was born was divine and holy; so also the devil will go down into the womb of Antichrist's mother and fill her completely, possess her completely inside and out, so that she will conceive by man with the devil's assist-

[35] See Peter Stuart Macaulay, "The Play of the Harrowing of Hell as Climax in the English Mystery Cycles," *Studia Germania Gadensia* 8 (1966): 115–134.

ance, and what is born will be completely foul, completely evil, completely ruined.[36]

Other traditions maintain that Antichrist was born of a union of the Devil and a prostitute (often the Whore of Babylon) or of the incestuous relationship between father and daughter (recalling the births of Pilate and Judas). The Chester cycle does not go into detail about Antichrist's birth, but after Michael has vanquished him, Primus Demon comes on stage to fetch the body, and he tells us

> This bodye was gotten by myne assent
> in cleane whooredome, verament.
> Of mother wombe or that he went,
> I was him within
> and taught him aye with myne intent
> synne, by which hee shalbe shent.
> For hee dyd my commaundement,
> his soule shall never blynne.
>
> (435/667–674)

This story is obviously a conflation of several myths. He is finally carted off to Hell, with one devil carrying him by his "toppe" and the other by his "tayle" (436/693). Perhaps this latter anatomical reference suggests that he was costumed with a token of his satanic ancestry, and that when he imitated Christ, no doubt made up to resemble him, he nevertheless reminded us of his real nature. But no matter how he was costumed (and the play is otherwise silent on this point), we are clearly asked to picture Antichrist either as progeny or as reincarnation of Satan. Both Elias and Enoch, the traditional adversaries of Antichrist, refer to him as the "devylls lymme" (420/313, 421/341), that is, an agent or scion of Satan (see *OED*. s.v."Limb," ¶3.b), but more directly as "that false feynde" (421/337) and explicitly

---

[36] *The Play of Antichrist*, ed. and trans. John Wright (Toronto: Pontifical Institute of Medieval Studies, 1967), p. 103.

as "the devyll" (420/299) and the "fals fyend common from
hell" (424/395).[37]

The coming of Antichrist is clearly built into the cycle. It is
foretold not only in the immediately preceding play of Antichrist's Prophets but also at the crucial moment when Christ
vanquishes Satan during the Harrowing of Hell. Immediately
after Michael has led the patriarchs out of Limbo, and after Satan has lamented "I am so stretlye tyed" (334/224), the prophets Enoch and Elias appear, identifying themselves and explaining that they were ordained to remain "here" (i.e. in the
"holye cittye" of Paradise; 335/250) until "Antechriste come"
(335/248). Thus, at the very moment when, in all the other
cycles, the central conflict is over, Chester suspends its ending
and allows us to anticipate yet another, even more climactic encounter. Indeed, even prior to the Harrowing, Satan had already been diminished as a force of opposition, and the playwright had prepared for his demise. Echoing the very words of
Adam's prophecy, the Doctor tells us at the conclusion of the
Temptation that "Christ hasse overcommen the devill" (224/
176). Thereafter, Satan is never again a force of contention; in
fact, he does not reappear until the Harrowing, and even there
he surrenders without so much as a single fliting. His power
now is dominion over a solitary tapster. The force of evil thus
lies dormant for the time, but we know that it will rise again in
a last powerful thrust. When, finally, the Antichrist play is performed, we expect an incremental repetition of the action we
had witnessed in the Harrowing. And we realize at that point
that the real ending of the cycle is at hand.

There is yet another way in which the playwright builds a

[37] It is important, however, to remember that the Devil and Antichrist were
not interchangeable. Antichrist is an eschatological figure who is the last manifestation of evil in the world. It is precisely his power to imitate the human form
of Christ that makes him different from the Devil. He is, foremost, a parodist,
and thus his human form, as differentiated from Satan's grotesque form, is an
important attribute, at least as he appears in the Chester cycle. For a discussion
of the need to distinguish between Antichrist and the Devil, see Emmerson, *Antichrist in the Middle Ages*, p. 147.

sense of an ending into the very first play of the cycle. As in all the other cycles, this play in Chester begins with an enactment of Lucifer's usurpation, which typically involves his vainglorious act of sitting in God's throne. This scene foreshadows the elemental conflict that is enacted throughout the cycle. The central prop in the cycle, and the most significant dramatic metaphor, is the throne. This archetypal *sedes* is the place of power and the focus of aspiration for all the pretenders. When Lucifer assumes the throne (while God surveys the towers of Heaven), the dramatist creates parody. And when God ultimately topples Lucifer, the comic pretender begins his "parlous playe," as the Dominacions call his act of usurpation. They warn him and his followers:

> Goe too your seates and wynde you hense.
> You have begone a *parlous playe*.
> Ye shall well witt the subsequence—
> this daunce will torne to teene and traye.
> (9/206–209; italics added)

"Parlous playe" is a perfect characterization of Lucifer's dramatic action, which is both "perilous" and "awful" (see *OED*, s.v."Parlous," ¶1, 2).[38] In the corresponding scene of the Wakefield cycle, Lucifer is instantly thrown into Hell, and he emerges after his fall black as coal and "tatyrd as a foyll" (5/137),[39] the first recorded appearance of the raggedly clad fool on the English stage. The devil as fool thus emerges as one model of the prime antagonist in the Corpus Christi drama. In Chester, while not manifestly a fool, he is primarily a pretender and shape shifter. The next time we see him after the Fall, he

[38] The word *perlouse (perrelous)*, occurs twice more in the cycle; see 95/395 and 311/168. In both instances it describes the perils of playcraft. In the first citation, it is used by the Doctor in the Balaam play to describe the conjuring up of the fair women by Balaam to entice the young Hebrew men to adopt Balaak's gods. In the second instance, it is used by Primus Judeus to describe the contest of nailing Jesus to the Cross.

[39] The word is wrongly glossed in England and Pollard's edition as "foal"; see *The Towneley Plays* (London: Oxford University Press, 1897), p. 401.

appears to Eve with "feete as an edder" and "a maydens face" (21/195). And he inspires all those pretenders who follow him. Others before me have noted the genealogy of evil in Chester. As Leslie Howard Martin has put it, Satan, Herod, and Antichrist form a "ludicrous triangle of bombast and deceit" within the play.[40] But it is not simply in their attitudes and their speech that they resemble one another. Each is an extension, almost an embodiment, of the other. Herod and Antichrist are to Satan as the figurae are to Christ—only with the parodic antagonists, as we saw in our consideration of N-Town, the order is reversed: the antitype in the demonic world preceding the type. Each is a pretender, and each occupies that ubiquitous place of power, the throne. In each case, therefore, we have a reenactment of the primal "parlous playe." Herod is discovered on stage, with minstrels playing, "crowned in gould" (the traditional makeup of God onstage) and "sittinge on hye" (162/146). Like Lucifer, he proclaims sovereignty: he is "kinge of kinges" (163/169). When his plan to kill the infant Jesus is foiled, he withers before our eyes and announces in his farewell speech:

> I bequeath here in this place
> my soule to be with Sathanas.
> (201/430–431)

Satan, having failed to vanquish Christ in the role of Herod, tries once more—this time in his own person. In the play of the Temptation, he attempts by subtlety to topple Jesus from the high seat just as God had toppled him. Leading Jesus to the Temple, he places him on the pinnacle ("statuat Jesus super pinnaculum templi") and tempts him as follows:

> Say thou nowe that syttes so high:
> if thou be Goddes Sonne, by sleight
> come downe.
> (221/113–115)

[40] Martin, "Comic Eschatology in the Chester *Coming of Antichrist*," *Comparative Drama* 5 (1971): 169.

But Jesus refuses to relinquish his high seat. We are reminded by dramatic action that the real seat of power, throughout the play, is occupied by God. The use of the throne, often called *cathedra* in the cycle, is highlighted again in the Coopers' pageant of the Trial and Flagellation. Here Jesus is made to sit first on a stool for the buffeting (287/69f.) and then on another seat, "possibly a panelled chair with boxed-in seat"[41] for the mocking (cf. 299/322f. and variant reading in Harley 2124: "cum purpura sedentem in cath[edram]").[42] The second of these seats is clearly a reminder of God's throne in the opening pageant, and it thus serves as a cruel reenforcement to the mockery, with God being ridiculed by those who serve the Devil. The next reference to a *cathedra* occurs in Hell as Satan confronts the triumphant Jesus ("Tunc Sathan sedens in cathedra," 329/96f.). It is appropriate to look back at this point, as Satan sits for a final time in his seat of power, to his expulsion from the other seat that he occupied. The throne as stage metaphor underlines the just power of God.

The most spectacular satanic figure and usurper is, of course, Antichrist, and his play is, no doubt, the ultimate parody, the most "parlous" enactment of the opening scene.[43] It is, in any case, impossible not to recall the whole course of God's incarnation as we watch the archsimulator and deceiver descend from his throne, imitate the death and Resurrection of Jesus, and assume his high seat once more (Primus Rex begs

[41] For a full discussion of these two seats, see John Marshall, "The Chester Coopers' Pageant: 'Selles' and 'Cathedra,'" *Leeds Studies in English*, n.s. 8 (1975): 120–128.

[42] See Lumiansky and Mills, *Chester Mystery Cycle*, p. 299, note to SD after 322.

[43] For a discussion of Antichrist's parodic imitation of the life of Christ in the Chester cycle, see Emmerson, *Antichrist in the Middle Ages*, pp. 182–183. In the visual arts as well, especially in the late Middle Ages, Emmerson tells us, "the human Antichrist comes increasingly to resemble Christ." The Velislav Bible (ca. 1350) is a particularly good example of this emphasis, with twenty-two illustrations devoted to parodying the life of Christ; see ibid., p. 124. These illustrations, together with those from fifteenth-century block books, should be studied as possible models for the costuming and representation of the Antichrist character in the Chester plays.

him to "goe sytt up in thy see," 415/171), where *ex cathedra*, to paraphrase the stage direction, he gives a perfect imitation of God's opening speech:

> I am verey God of might.
> All thinges I made through my might.
> sonne and moone, daye and night.
> To blysse I may you bringe.
>
> (417/221–224)

Later he adds:

> I made the daye and eke the night
> and all thinges that are on yearth growinge—
> flowes fayre that freshe can springe;
> also I made all other thinge—
> the starres that be so bright.
>
> (426/457–461)

The central plot of the Antichrist play shows what would have happened had Lucifer been allowed to stay for a time in God's seat. It is a parodic reprise of the Creation and of the life of Christ enacted by that familiar figure from the Midsummer Show, the Lord of Misrule. (There is evidence that the Chester Midsummer show, which alternated with the Corpus Christi play, included characters from the cycle, so that Antichrist might well have ridden as a mock king.)[44] But just as the Antichrist play gives us a parodic reenactment of the usurpation and of the Passion and Resurrection, so does it put a conclusive end to the conflict, when finally, in a recapitulation of the defeat of Satan, the Archangel Michael kills Antichrist ("Tunc

---

[44] See Clopper, *Chester: REED*, p. liii. The Puritan writer Phillip Stubbs, writing in 1583, comments as follows: "Against May, Whitsunday, or other time all the young men and maids, old men and wives, run gadding over nights to the woods, groves, hills, and mountains, where they spend all the night in pleasant pastimes. . . . And no marvel, for there is a great Lord amongst them, as superintendent and Lord over their pastimes and sports, namely Satan, prince of hell"; see *The Anatomie of Abuses . . . in the Country of Aligna*, ed. F. V. Furnival (London, 1877–1882), p. 149.

Michael occidet Antechristum," 434/644f.), and he is carted off by two demons into Hell. The mock king is dead, and the play can close.

It is important to observe that the Chester cycle is centrally concerned with "parlous playe." Some years ago, Robert Hanning published an important article with the descriptive title " 'You Have Begun a Parlous Pleye': The Nature and Limits of Dramatic Mimesis as a Theme in Four Middle English 'Fall of Lucifer' Cycle Plays." Hanning argues persuasively that the scene in which God vacates his throne is, on a deeper level of interpretation, "about the origin and nature of drama" because it opens the possibility for impersonation.[45] I believe that this self-conscious purpose is very much imbedded in the Chester cycle, yet I take issue with Hanning's thesis, which is based on V. A. Kolve's discussion about the nature of play, that the cycle dramatists introduced the scene of the vacated throne in order to make a statement about "the limits of their art" (p. 23). The problem with this view, I believe, is the equation of play simply with low-mimetic action, when in actuality, everything that happens in the cycle is play. Hanning, though recognizing the broader meaning of game and play, nevertheless characterizes the stage representation of God as "non-dramatic (i.e. declarative, audience-directed, and acclamatory)" (p. 27), and he regards the rather solemn opening of the Lucifer pageant as one that extends "far in the direction of a liturgical celebration, both in medium and in content" (p. 28). At the base of this view is the notion that the dramatic imitation of God is blasphemous and that the purpose of the vacated throne was to allow the playwright to escape the charge of sacrilege by making all of the play and game focus on the low mimetic.

This view is not in accord with contemporary definitions of *play* or *game*. It presupposes that *play* and *earnest* are always mutually exclusive terms, when in actuality they are often used together. The storytelling contest in *The Canterbury Tales* is called

[45] Hanning, " 'You Have Begun a Parlous Pleye,' " *Comparative Drama* 7 (1973): 28.

a "game" (1.853) but it also includes much that Chaucer himself considered "ernest," including the Melibeus and the Parson's Tale, which for all their solemnity were yet part of the sto-
ryteller game. Harry Baillie surely echoes Chaucer when he
says to the Monk:

> But be not wrooth, my lord, though that I pleye
> Ful ofte in game a sooth I have herd seye.
>
> (VII. 1963–1964)

It was Kolve who first called attention to "the polarity of 'play'
and 'ernest,' "[46] but that opposition was basically a tenet of cler-
ics who attacked the drama, like the Wycliffite preacher who
wrote the infamous "Sermon against Miracle Plays," and not
the opinion of the church in general. In fact, there is much evidence that the church, both regular and secular, supported
plays. An excellent example comes from an entry in the York
A/Y Memorandum Book, which mentions a certain Friar William
Melton,

> a professor of scripture and a most famous preacher of
> the word of God . . . [who] commended the said play to the
> people in several of his sermons, by affirming that it was
> good in itself and most laudable.[47]

Somewhat later in the same entry, the city clerk, William Burton, calls the York Corpus Christi play "ludus ille solempnis"
(p. 44). Surely, this "solemn play" was not perceived as blasphemous because it included an impersonation of God.

The Chester cycle makes an important statement about the
nature of play in its pervasive contrast between that action
which can properly be called *ludus solempnis* and that which, by
its own definition, is "parlous playe." The former begins with
the first appearance of God on stage. It embodies all impersonation of the divine, and it embraces the various mimetic forms

---

[46] Kolve, *Play Called Corpus Christi*, p. 17.

[47] Alexandra F. Johnston and Margaret Dorrell (Rogerson), *York: Records of
the Early English Drama*, 2 vols. (Toronto: University of Toronto Press, 1979), 2:
728.

that are characterized by the *imitatio Dei*. While the very play is an impersonation, it is also about impersonation. We are aware that an actor plays the role of God, but at the same time we know that the central action in the play is about the dramatic transformation of God, the Father, into the several figurae and eventually into the suffering Jesus and the resurrected Christ who bears the stigmata of his earthly suffering. The Corpus Christi play—and not just the one at Chester—is by definition concerned with the ubiquitous presence of the body of Christ in all of his shapes. It is this many-faceted Christ who is indeed the protagonist and the focus of the play.

In direct contrast stands the role of the Devil. As part of his "parlous playe," he too impersonates God, but his role from the beginning is that of the impostor and usurper. From the moment that he apes God by assuming his throne, he becomes the *simia Christi*, a figure that we recognize as a deliberate parodic impersonation. The playwright thus makes the very nature of impersonation, whether true or false, the pivotal aesthetic and moral concern of his play. His question, simply put, is, What is the proper form of *imitatio Dei*? The Chester cycle, alone of those Corpus Christi plays which survive, undertakes to expose "parlous playe," and it does so by bringing on stage the ultimate false imitation of God in the figure of Antichrist. This look-alike, this stage sorcerer, this "bad" actor—and he has to be bad at impersonation because it is essential that he not be mistaken for the "real" God—is allowed a final romp on stage that will show dramatically what kind of impersonation of God is altogether improper. By destroying Antichrist, the playwright, ipso facto, destroys false art. When the *simia Christi* perishes before our eyes, the Chester playwright has not only brought the dramatic conflict to a resounding close, but he has also exposed the craft of "parlous playe" for the stage sham that it is. By putting an end to false play, he creates a new reverence for *ludus solempnis*, which in Chester alone of all extant cycles ends ceremonially in a dance of death.

I want to return in a moment to an examination of play and game as formal devices of closure in the Chester cycle. First, however, I need to call attention to a tradition that seems to lie behind the Chester theme of the demolition of false play. It appears that from the time of the earliest criticism of the drama by the church, there has been a curious association of Antichrist with drama itself. Given the extreme position of reformers that all impersonation of God is evil, this association is a natural one, for is Antichrist not the ultimate impersonator? In his *De Investigatione Antichristi*, dated at about 1161, Gerhoh von Reichersberg puts forward an argument "that clergy who turn the churches into theatres are doing the work of that very Antichrist of whom they make a show."[48] The fourteenth-century "Sermon against Miracle Plays" makes a similar point by characterizing "thise myraclis pleyinge" three times within a short paragraph as the "gynnys of the devvel to cacchen men to byleve of Anti-Christ."[49] The Lollard preacher goes on to call those who enact plays for the worship of God liars because they "feign" miracles and therefore beguile themselves and despise God. Drama in the eyes of its clerical critics is thus the work of Antichrist, who is seen as the crafty actor, the maker of false illusion. The incorporation of "parlous playe" with the climactic appearance of Antichrist the maker of false miracles at the end of the Chester cycle may, in consequence, be read as a subtle and forceful refutation to the critics of "miracle playing." Such an ironic purpose would underline my argument that the Chester cycle is concerned at its aesthetic core with the efficacy of dramatic play. Indeed, in presenting various forms of play and game, it becomes a showcase of its own craft, and it allows us to discriminate between good and bad art. It validates the play of Corpus Christi by exposing the sham play of Antichrist.

It follows that the Chester cycle itself may have been written as a defense not only of playcraft but of the mystery cycles as a legitimate expression of the Catholic religion at a time when reform was in the air. It has been argued, persuasively I believe,

[48] Chambers, *Mediaeval Stage*, pp. ii, 98.
[49] *Selections from English Wycliffite Writings*, ed. Anne Hudson (Cambridge: Cambridge University Press, 1978), pp. 100–101, lines 147, 153, 157.

that the Chester plays were written by a monk from Saint Werburgh Abbey, "the dominant force politically, socially, economically, culturally, and spiritually in Chester from its founding in 1093 until its dissolution in 1540." Such authorship, the argument goes, would account both for the apocalyptic emphasis of the cycle and for its performance at Whitsuntide rather than the Feast of Corpus Christi.[50] If, as I have argued, the cycle was first given a composite text in the early 1530s, then it seems likely that its redactor was intent on building into it a defense of orthodoxy and on taking as one of his purposes the demonstration of the efficacy and the desirability of mystery cycles as a way of buttressing the established faith. We must recall that the period of the shift to Whitsuntide and the writing of the cycle exactly coincided with the establishment of the Church of England. Political considerations aside, this was a time of challenge to religious practices and to prevailing thought. Luther's ideas gained prominence quickly in England where the Lollard tradition was still alive and receptive to his thought,[51] and as we have seen, "miracle playing" was lumped with images and pilgrimages, among other practices, for widespread condemnation (because "God comaundid þat no man shulde make ony ymage or lickenesse of hym").[52] Most often it was the performance of miracles themselves that was the basis for objection; as Keith Thomas, the foremost historian of the subject, puts it, "Catholic miracles were confidently attributed to witchcraft," and such witchcraft was seen not only in the lives of saints but in the basic ritual of the Catholic church.[53] The Chester cycle, as we shall see shortly, is centrally concerned with a defense of miracles and with discriminating between

[50] See John Harty, "The Unity and Structure of *The Chester Mystery Cycle*," *Mediaevalia* 2 (1976): 138–140.

[51] See John R. H. Moorman, *A History of the Church of England*, 3d ed. (London: Adam and Charles Black, 1973), p. 163.

[52] "Images and Pilgrimages," in Hudson, *Wycliffite Writings*, p. 83.

[53] Thomas, *Religion and the Decline of Magic: Studies in Popular Belief in Sixteenth and Seventeenth Century England* (London: Weidenfeld and Nicolson, 1971), pp. 68–69.

true miracles (that is, revelations of God in the Johannine sense) and false magic (which always emanates from Satan and especially Antichrist). To help understand the function of miracle in the Chester cycle and also to complete the study of closure, we need now to examine the unique last segment of the cycle, the eschatological plays of the Prophets before the Day of Doom,[54] the Coming of Antichrist, and Doomsday.

APART from providing a dramatic ending to playcraft, the Chester playwright also uses formal devices of closure to effect finality. The final three plays function as a formal coda to the cycle; they recapitulate in microcosm the structure of the whole play. Beginning with a procession of Prophets recapitulating the traditional Old Testament Prophets play (see the latter part of the Cappers' play preserved in the H MS),[55] they provide a parodic reenactment of the Incarnation and the Resurrection, and they bring the satanic usurpation to a final defeat, recalling the moment of Christ's victory during the Harrowing of Hell. At the very end, they present in the shape of a morality play the judgment upon all mankind, with Christ in his conventional Corpus Christi play role delivering his powerful Last Judgment Complaint in which he reviews the seven works of mercy and shows how the saved and the damned responded to his needs. The Chester Judgment play ends with the four Evangelists each bearing witness that in their Gospels, as Matthew puts it, they "expresse / this that my lord of his goodnesse / hath rehearsed here" (462/678–680). Significantly, the last voice in the cycle is that of Saint John:

> And I, John the Evangeliste,
> beare wytnes of thinges that I wyste
> to which they might full well have truste
> and not have donne amysse.

---

[54] I choose this title in favor of Lumiansky and Mills's "Antichrist's Prophets" because it is more accurate and also because it was used by the Early Banns; see Clopper, *Chester: REED*, p. 32.

[55] See Lumiansky and Mills, *Chester Mystery Cycle*, appendix 1b, pp. 466–481.

And all that ever my lord sayth here,
I wrote yt in my mannere.
Therfore, excuse you, withowten were,
I may not well, iwysse.

(463/701–708)

Here is the wrapping up of the major emphasis in the cycle:
Saint John himself attesting to his witness of the miracles that
speak the incontestable truth, and Saint John telling his audience, as a final reminder, that everything God spoke in the
cycle came from the Gospel of Saint John.

By providing this formally designed three-pageant ending,
the Chester playwright gives the audience a new time perspective. The emphasis in this formal ending is such that eschatological time—the time of the future—becomes an important
dramatic dimension. We are deliberately distanced from historical time, and the "moralizing" Expositor (398/73) now prepares us, with proper didactic guidance, for the coming of the
end-of-the-world prophecies. The actors from here on are no
longer historical figures. They are persons from the world of
the audience—popes, emperors, kings, judges, merchants—
morality figures, abstracted from reality.[56] The Chester cycle is
unique in incorporating into its Doomsday play a dance-of-
death sequence, which generically injects the contemporane-
ous into the consideration of death and which depicts a panorama of medieval social types. It can be argued that the Dance
of Death as depicted in art is in reality a kind of estate satire,
with all the foibles of the age brought to exposure. Clearly,
while only a few "estates" have speaking roles in the Chester
Judgment, the stage would have been occupied by every social
type, from pope to beggar. By including this contemporary
emphasis in its last plays, the Chester cycle strengthens its di-
dacticism, for it now projects its outcome into the world of its
audience—a world with which its spectators can identify. If evil

[56] David Leigh has written about the nonhistorical setting of all the doomsday
plays; see "The Doomsday Mystery Play: An Eschatological Morality," *Modern
Philology* 67 (1969): 211–223.

has loomed large in the historical plays, it was nevertheless removed; it was distanced by myth and made alien by its grotesque otherworldliness. Antichrist is an all-too-human adversary (despite what the Expositor makes of his beastly origin, see 404/236–237). The preachers of the age regularly told their parishes that the time of Antichrist is now and that he could be right in their midst and not be recognized.[57] Because of that threat of imminence, the Chester playwright gives a vivid insight into deceit, into false miracle making.

Unlike the other cycles, Chester not only has an elaborate ending, but it also prepares the audience step by step to anticipate its closing scenes. It allows the spectator to perceive dramatic closure from the moment that the Prophets Ezekiel, Zacharias, Daniel, and Saint John, significantly called the Evangelist though here clearly also the author of the Apocalypse, process on stage. The Prophets foretell while the Expositor comments, all so that the audience will know how to respond to the action that follows. The spectators learn in singular detail everything that will transpire so that there can be no mistake that the impersonator of Christ they are about to see is, indeed, Antichrist. And what they learn is by no means restricted to the Coming of Antichrist. The Prophets really serve to announce all of the Last Days, including the fifteen signs of Judgment. The Expositor states this function directly:

> Nowe that you shall expresselye knowe
> these prophettes wordes upon a rowe . . .
> By them understand may I
> the daye of doome skyllfullye.
>
> (397/25–26, 29–30)

He performs as chorus and narrator to introduce the last act on stage, a mini-cycle in a form that mirrors the Corpus Christi play of which it is a vital part.

---

[57] See the fine chapter by Richard Emmerson, "Antichrist in Medieval Literature," in *Antichrist in the Middle Ages*, especially the discussion of didactic works, pp. 146–203.

Each of the individual pageants in this elaborate conclusion incorporates a recognizable form of play. And it is by this range of forms that the playwright imparts a tone of theatrical finality to his work. The first of the three final plays is a procession. It recalls the celebration of the feast out of which the cycle arose. The second, the Coming of Antichrist, is almost entirely a play-within-a-play. To my knowledge, it is the only extended true play-within-a-play in the Corpus Christi drama (the Mak and Gyll scene played for the shepherds would qualify in a lesser sense). Unlike any other pageant that I am aware of, it has a stage audience (the four kings) and its main action is a dramatic performance (the magic show of Antichrist). The playwright depends entirely on dramatic irony to make the play work, for he has carefully prepared the real audience to know the truth—Antichrist is an illusionist, a stage magician—while the stage audience slowly becomes enlightened. This ironic perspective is important to notice, for it prepares us to perceive Antichrist as a comic, even a farcical, character.[58] The play gives the real audience a distorted image of Antichrist's craft. It shows vividly that the whole action is equivalent to the stage trickery of a magic show. The real spectators *know* from the outset who Antichrist is; they are made aware of his deceptions by the Expositor (404/221–244), and only the stage audience is pulled into the illusion. For those who might object that the interpretation of the play as farce trivializes Antichrist, I respond that to the contrary it makes him the more powerful because the more elusive. The warning is that his miracles are phony stage magic. If the magician is good enough, we might

---

[58] Scholars have disagreed about the characterization of Antichrist. Emmerson argues that "he is not primarily a 'comic' character" (ibid., p. 186); while Kolve has characterized him as a "buffoon, a confidence man" (*Play Called Corpus Christi*, p. 140); and Leslie Howard Martin regards the whole play as "farcical" ("Comic Eschatology," p. 164), a view with which I am in substantial agreement. Peter Travis, who offers a splendid discussion of the play, at first finds Antichrist "quasi-comic" (*Dramatic Design*, p. 231), but later comes to a view of the play that is very much like my own; he says, "the show-within-the-show of Antichrist's career may just as easily be construed as a burlesque of the cycle itself" (ibid., p. 236).

all, like the kings in the stage audience, be pulled inside the illusion. It was the Chester playwright's objective to let us observe the process so that we might be armed not to be duped by it ourselves. In any case, when Antichrist is unmasked as a sham, the play-within-a-play disintegrates. The magic show is over, and so is the false illusion of playcraft. It is by this formal design that the Chester playwright demolishes "parlous playe."

The final play in the triad, the Judgment pageant, resembles a traditional morality play by incorporating the dance of death. Mankind in the shapes of the saved (Papa, Imperator, Rex, Regina) and of the damned (Papa, Imperator, Rex, Regina, Justiciarius, Mercator) is brought for final judgment from the grave. The morality play in its pure form is the quintessential eschatological drama of the Middle Ages. In Chester, it takes the interesting form (unique in all England) of a matched set of so-called dances—the Dance of the Blessed and the *danse macabre*. Most likely, as the blessed and the damned climb out of their graves in a Bosch-like scene and as they approach, respectively, stage right and stage left, they line up for a grand musical processional as the cycle comes to an end with the words of the Evangelists. The two traditional forms of dance have a long connection with music,[59] and, indeed, the text of the play itself tells us that the Angels lead the blessed to heaven singing ("Tunc angeli ibunt ac cantabunt euntes"; 456/508f.). The formality and finality of ending are thus powerfully reinforced.

Within this larger context of the forms of play with which the cycle ends, we need to be aware of the cycle's thematic concern with magic and miracle, which comes to fruition here. In its pervasive concern with this contrast, Chester is, again, unique among the extant English cycles. In effect, the dramatic action sets out to demonstrate that the miracle of the Incarnation of Christ—his miraculous birth and Resurrection—is not mere stage trickery or mere playcraft but a mystery that defies rational understanding and one that is finally incapable of dem-

---

[59] See the discussion by Kathi Meyer-Baer, *Music of the Spheres and the Dance of Death* (Princeton: Princeton University Press, 1970), p. 5.

onstration by stage performance. The playwright of the Corpus Christi drama was, no doubt, vexed by the problem of enacting Christ's miracles without running the risk of having them appear as mere sleight of hand. After all, it is not difficult to enact a miraculous resurrection from death; stage magicians with their elaborate devices have developed all sorts of intricate acts by which at first they perform a putative dismemberment of their "victims" and then put them back together again. The "sawing in half" act is always the core of the magician's show. The genius of the Chester cycle is that it puts stage magic forward as a Devil's trick to validate those actions which are truly miraculous. The devils, of course, do not believe in God's mysteries. They are the rationalists who ask for the performance of stage magic and for whom the Virgin Birth or the Resurrection is nothing more, or less, than "contyse" or "cunninge" or "sorcerye," three words that are used often to cast disbelief on the miracles of God. The play that we witness is essentially concerned with the Corpus Christi. To succeed it must refute the concept advanced by the Lollard that its subject is "myraclis pleyinge," and it must reaffirm for its audience that the Eucharist is the highest form of truth, one that finally must be grasped at a spiritual level and that can be only intimated by stage enactment. The contrast of miracle and magic brings this perception to the spectator, and when, at last, magic is exposed as mere stage trickery—as nothing more than what is repeatedly called the fiend's or "the devylls phantasie" (see 120/595, 121/635, 429/526)—he recognizes that play has indeed come to an end. On the deepest thematic level, therefore, the coming of Antichrist signals the end of the dramatic enactment.

The direct contrast between magic and miracle is appropriately introduced in the Nativity play. It comes with the traditional incredulity of the Midwife, the one named Salome, who insists that there was no miraculous birth:

> Was never woman cleane maye
> and chyld withowt man.
> (117/535–536)

Thereafter, as the stage direction tells us, "Salome tentabit tangere Mariam in sexu secreto," and she suffers the usual consequence: "My handes bee dryed up in this place" (118/542). An Angel appears and asks her to beseech the Child for forgiveness, which she does, and her hands instantly become whole again. The Angel says to her, referring to the Virgin Birth:

> This miracle that now thow seest here
> is of Godes owne powere.
>
> (118/552–553)

This stage action then prompts the Expositor to rehearse other "myracles" for us, and particularly he tells the story of the Roman temple, as reported by "cronicles," which was so rich and marvelous that it was worth the "thryd parte the worlde" (119/578). In this temple there were statues of the gods of all the provinces, and each of them had a silver bell hanging about the neck and the name of the country inscribed upon the breast. In their midst was the god of Rome, "right as a kinge," and above there was a man on horse, made of brass, bearing a spear and moving around the temple. If ever any nation resolved to attack Rome, the statue of its god would instantly ring its bell and turn its face "dispituously" toward the god of Rome, while the "image" above would turn in the direction of the attack and point its spear. The Expositor explains that this elaborate structure was named the "Temple of Peace," and it was made "by arte of neagromancye" (120/613) so that all nations would bow to Rome. He reports further that when the builder asked the Devil how long this monument should stand, the devil answered "suttillye"

> and sayd yt should last sickerlye
> untyll a mayden wemmostlye
> had conceyved a chylde.
>
> (121/625–627)

Everyone, of course, believed (shades of *Macbeth*) that therefore the temple should endure forever. And—of course—at the time when Christ was born, "hit fell downe soone in hye" (121/631). The Expositor leaves by promising

> moe miracles, as wee have ment
> to playe right here anon.
> (121/642–643)

The rehearsal of this story makes a significant statement to confirm the miraculous birth of Christ. It tells us instantly that the King of Kings was born, that the power of all other kings, of whom the god of Rome was foremost in earthly renown, would crumble. And it tells us further that this power, established subtly by necromancy, was endowed by the Devil. With the elaborate machines that we know to have been used on pageant wagons and in royal entries, especially in sixteenth-century Europe, the legerdemain described by the Chester Expositor could easily be perceived as a theatrical device, though Chester clearly was incapable of enacting it. The point, however, is that trickery, on stage or otherwise, from the outset is seen as the Devil's craft, and it is invalidated by the miracle of Christ's birth.

Thereafter the Chester play associates all sorts of miracles with Christ, and it continues to pose questions, raised by ordinary men and by devils, ultimately to verify their truth. Simeon is made to be such a doubter. He is, of course, a priest in Jerusalem, and we see him in the Temple reading from his book the prophecy of Isaiah: "Ecce virgo concipiet et pariet filium." The Chester Simeon cannot get himself to believe this prophecy. "It is wronge written" (205/31), he says, and he decides he will "scrape . . . awaye" the words "a virgin" and write "a good woman" in their stead (interesting testimony to creative reading and the despoiling of manuscripts in the Middle Ages). An elaborate stage direction tells how he performs this act and how an angel comes subsequently to recorrect the book. To his surprise Simeon, when he looks again at his book, finds the words "a virgin" written in red—a "miracle" (206/61) he tells us. So he tries a second time, and the routine is repeated, only this time the words "a virgin" appear in "goulden letters" (207/

84). Simeon is made a true believer, ready now to behold the infant Jesus in the Temple.

Unlike Simeon, in a subsequent scene, the Devil is not won over. The Temptation in the Chester cycle serves to inquire into the Virgin Birth from the Devil's point of view. He tells us that nowadays there is a "dosebeard" (a dullard) walking abroad everywhere who seems to have been born of a mother who "did never amisse" (217/11) and a father who is nowhere to be found. He will test this strange man's craft, and tempt him to perform a few "stage" tricks—like making bread of stone. Jesus will not be coerced into the Devil's game playing, and the Doctor, commenting on what was "playd in this place" explains that "Christ hasse overcommen the devill" (224/176). He has refused to make a stage show out of his miraculous power. What we perceive, as well, is that the Devil is incapable of grasping the truth of miracle.

We have observed that during the Ministry plays, the Chester Christ performs a variety of miracles, including the traditional restoration of sight to the blind man and the raising of Lazarus. The Jews, like the Devil, are unbelieving, but Jesus, rather than ignoring their disbelief as he does Satan's, makes a dramatic show of his miraculous power. After he restored the sight of the blind man, the Jews ask him whether he is the Christ. He chides them because they will not believe him even having witnessed his good works (240/239–242). And though they desist from stoning him as a heathen, Jesus will teach them a lesson by "staging" a disappearance ("et statim evanescit Jesus"; 242/284f.). The peformance of this miracle is designed, as is the raising of Lazarus, to prepare for the Resurrection and to dispel the doubt with which ordinary mortals, as distinct from the devils, perceive Christ. The dramatic momentum of the mystery cycles is maintained by the constant doubt that humans, even the most devout, express toward the divinity of Christ. But because unlike the devils they have the potential of conversion, there must be a continuing demonstration, through miraculous appearances among other proofs, of this central mystery. On a dramatic level, staged miracles are thus intended to reinvigorate the belief of the audience. Chester, of all the English cycles, is the most intent on this sort of dramatic demonstration. A brilliant example comes from the Crucifixion play, when Centurio returns to Caiaphas converted by Jesus' death cry, "Consummatum est." But Caiaphas will prove to him that Jesus was a man after all. He orders the blind Longinus to pierce the body of Christ with a spear so that Centurio can see "his hart bleede" (320/370). Of course when Longinus does as he is told, it is not blood but water that runs out of Christ's wound—water that will also restore Longinus's sight. This "trick" is dangerously close to stage magic, and the sort of dramatic spectacle that the Lollards found ungodly. It is this sort of play that the dramatist wished to counteract in the penultimate pageant of the cycle, the Coming of Antichrist.

The pageant begins with Antichrist posing to the four Kings the very same question that Christ asked of the Jews: Do you not believe "that I am Christe omnipotent?" (410/59). And they express the same doubt: "Christ ys not common yett" (410/62). But, unlike the Jews and very much like the Devil, they ask for a demonstration of his "maystrie." As the Third King puts it,

> Then will I leeve that yt ys soe.
> Yf thou do wonders or thou goe.
> (410/69–70)

Unlike the real Christ who refuses to do a "magic act" for Satan, Antichrist responds with a show demonstrating to the four Kings, who sit as audience on the stage, the magic power with which he can regenerate life. First he pulls trees up from the ground to show that fruit is growing on their roots—a traditional scene made into an interesting stage metaphor for the upside-down nature of his "magic" (and also testimony to the triviality of his power). Then, in anticipation of the rising of the dead from their graves, which the Prophets play had already forecast as the scene of Judgment Day, he asks the dead to rise and honor him, a clear parody accomplished by elementary stage manipulation. Resurrection becomes a false game, especially when Antichrist stages his own putative death, allows himself to be placed in a tomb by the Kings, and then rises. It is after this charade has taken place that Antichrist ascends "ad cathedram" to dole out the spoils of his power to the Kings. With the appearance of Enoch and Elias, the Devil's power (which we have seen as simplistic stage magic) is finally tested, this time before a knowing and sophisticated stage audience. He is challenged by Enoch to bring forth those men whom he has raised from the graves and to make them eat and drink. Antichrist will oblige, and the dead agree to eat and drink, but Elias intervenes, and before they can follow Antichrist's order, he performs the Eucharistic rite on stage, blessing the bread "in nomine Patris . . . et Filii virginis . . . et Spiritus Sancti" (431/ 569–576). The practice of testing the veracity of one's word by the use of the Mass is referred to as a "poison ordeal"; it was commonly used in Tudor times and was part of the magical power of the church to which the reformers objected.[60] Here it is used to apply the final discredit of Antichrist. With their inability to partake of the bread and wine, the four Kings are converted from their heresy. It is the Mass that has defeated the Devil's magic. And significantly in keeping with the meaning of Corpus Christi Day, the festival that has given rise to the popular outdoor drama, the perilous play of Satan and his kin has been demolished as "fantasye . . . sorcerye, wytchcraft, and nygromancye" (432/597–598). Antichrist has only the power to feign and to destroy; he cannot conquer death. In a last act of bravado he kills Enoch and Elias, but the power of God prevails when they experience a true resurrection at the end of the play. The death of Antichrist signifies the end of the magic show, and we are prepared to experience the miracle of the Judgment.

In the foregoing discussion we have seen that the Chester plays are unique among the surviving cycles in their treatment of the Satan-Antichrist conflict as a parodic plot. Their injection of "parlous playe" as a pervasive challenge to the main plot is as

[60] Thomas, *Religion and the Decline of Magic*, pp. 44–45.

interesting and innovative as the N-Town device of the double plot. Both types of plot set important precedents for the English drama, and indirectly at least they provide a paradigm for the development of the native tradition.

In a sense, "parlous playe" as parodic plot is another option for mirroring the main plot. As Levin has put it, all analogic plots are "reducible to the two fundamental relations of parallelism and contrast."[61] In N-Town, the analogic plot is parallel: We see a mirroring of the main plot, the life of Jesus, in a subordinate plot, the life of Mary. In Chester, the analogic plot is contrastive: Here the main plot, the course of God's salvation, is distorted in the image of a counterplot, the challenge of God's order by Satan/Antichrist (hence, the first extended use of the "foil" in English drama). The difference is mainly that Chester uses the multiplication of the main plot as a way of structuring its central conflict. N-Town, in contrast, uses it as a device to reinforce the main action. Both, of course, are ways of expanding the dramatic action into large patterns that are built on incremental repetition, and thus both implicitly defy the restrictive conventions that we associate with the neoclassical play. In structural as well as thematic terms, Chester is the antithesis of N-Town. It presents an alternative model for the building of a Corpus Christi cycle.

I have tried to show in this chapter that the Chester cycle is a carefully unified work of dramatic art, the product of a single redactor whose implicit mission it was to defend the mystery play against its detractors by dramatizing the Johannine vision of a triumphant Christ. It is the ultimate example of the art and power of "myraclis pleyinge." From the outset, it gives a perfectly realized whole—a cycle that is stretched into linear form and whose ending is the logical outcome of its beginning. The Chester cycle, of all the Corpus Christi plays, provides a carefully realized plan of closure. It highlights the conflict between God and Satan. By prolonging the climactic encounter between protagonist and antagonist, it gives the audience a the-

---

[61] Levin, *Multiple Plot*, p. 12.

atrical experience that is considerably more heightened in intensity and expanded in interest than that of any other medieval mystery cycle. The sharp dramatic conflict, further, makes possible the discrimination between solemn and "parlous" play, confirming through the exposure of Antichrist's magic the miraculous presence of Christ.

CONCLUSION

I HAVE argued in this book that the English mystery cycles, at least as we see them in the four extant complete examples, are remarkably unified and powerfully developed works of art. They rank with the best that poets, dramatic or nondramatic, wrote in their times, which extended roughly from the last half of the fifteenth to the first quarter of the sixteenth century. Despite this comparatively late date, the cycles are thoroughly medieval in world view and dramaturgy; they reflect a tradition that grew, as we have seen in the example from York, over a long period of performance. We may, therefore, see in the cycles not only what is typical in subject and approach to the Middle Ages but also what is unique in the formation of an emerging native dramatic tradition. The power of their art rests finally in their ability to preserve the ingredients of traditional festive folk celebration within a learned, finely structured, and self-conscious poetic drama of Christian salvation history.

My approach to the mystery cycles throughout this book has been to separate text from performance. While I believe that the text allows, indeed requires, us to reconstruct a potential medieval stage for a full appreciation of its dramatic art, I conclude that it is impossible for us to know what was actually performed in the streets of York, Chester, Wakefield, and countless other English cities and towns. We certainly cannot assume that the extant cycles we read were ever performed in the forms that survive. As we have seen, we have absolutely no external performance history for one of the four cycles (N-Town) and very little documentary evidence for another (Wakefield). In both York and Chester, which do retain ample civic and guild records, we nevertheless have too little descriptive information of what was actually performed. We do not know, for example, how many of the pageants were produced in any given year. We have no idea whether those pageants which were performed were done as entire plays, as ridings of single dramatic scenes, or as tableaux vivants. The sparse information that does exist indicates that, for York at least, during the one year that does yield circumstantial evidence of plays scheduled for performance, some crucial episodes, among them the Annunciation, were not included.

As one looks closely at the surviving manuscripts and the accumulated records, it becomes evident that the text of the plays came into being at a very late stage in the history of the English Corpus Christi cycles. I have tried to show in this book that among the cycles that clearly were first generation—York and Chester—performances were already well established before any kind of composite text was assembled. Prior studies to the contrary, the texts that we do possess yield no evidence that they were accumulated over long years in strata or layers. They do indicate, in every instance, that there were one or more editings of individual "regynalls," which were customarily held by the individual guilds. These editings were the work of what in the context of medieval literature would have to be considered authors.

Not one of the surviving manuscripts can be shown to have been used as a text for a performance. We have seen that the York manuscript, which is the only true register to survive from the Middle Ages, did not contain the text of several plays that we know from the civic records were performed over the years. While it is true that the York Register was used by the city clerk to ascertain what was being played, it was nevertheless not in any way a prompt book. The city clerk checked out the performance at the first station for what appears to be principally an archival purpose. He wanted to make sure that the York book was accurate in what it represented as the substance of the Corpus Christi play. The Chester manuscripts, in turn, had nothing at all to do with the performance of the plays. As we have seen, they came into being a full generation after the Whitsun plays were last performed. The N-Town manuscript, with its banns and allusions to performance of the Passion plays, does seem to record a partial performance, but the manuscript as a whole is, as I have tried to show, a composite book designed for reading—a dramatic rendering of the Pseudo-Bonaventuran *Life of Christ* that was so popular in fifteenth-century lay spirituality. The Wakefield manuscript is no doubt the most handsome of all the surviving texts. Except for some observations by censors in sixteenth-century marginalia, it gives no evidence of any direct relationship to a performance. This vellum volume with its handsome strap-work initials was a coffee-table book in its time.

We do not, of course, know for what specific readership these volumes were written. I believe that they were implicitly addressed to posterity to preserve the full dramatic contents of the civic cycles. It therefore matters little whether the entire contents of a cycle were ever performed, and to use criteria for the evaluation of the plays based on a putative performance is at best the final curve in a self-fulfilling argument. To say, for example, as some critics have, that there is no true dramatic continuity in a cycle—that, in fact, each pageant is an independent, self-standing streetcorner production—is to deny the existence of the only source we have of the plays, the composite manuscripts. These latter documents are the best testament that we have of the playwrights' intentions, and we have seen that, no matter what might or might not have been performed, they attempt to provide us with distinctive and unified interpretations of salvation history. Throughout this book I have insisted that the manuscripts we have are *literary* texts. They therefore deserve to be read as works of literature. If they can also provide the theater historian with insights into how mystery plays were performed, that is of course all to the good. But both the critic and the historian must be cautioned not to see the text as a record of a performance, for the latter existed in some places (as I believe of the Chester plays) some hundred years before there was a composite text. Indeed, the performance history of the civic cycles is best seen as a thing apart from the extensive manuscript plays that survive.

Once we take the manuscript text for what it is (that is, the fully realized Corpus Christi play shaped by a central intelligence), we have what must rank, along with the large outdoor moralities, as the first indigenous vernacular drama of the English stage. The mystery cycles are truly a theater of the world. They embrace all of time and of God's created universe, and their action links the cosmic events in salvation history, so that the Old and New Testaments are a single volume in which types and antitypes provide the binding nexus. What we see in these plays is the emergence of a dramatic genre, one that is to govern what can best be called the native tradition. This tradition is the antithesis in form and substance of the classic drama with its tightly conceived unities and its high poetic style. Its special quality is mixture: of sacred and profane, divine and diabolic, urbane and provincial, old time and new time as refracted through the lens of anachronism. It is a sweeping drama that has its roots in the festive enactment of Carnival.

This book has attempted to treat the Corpus Christi cycles as genre. Its object was to show what variety of dramatic approach, design, and emphasis was achievable within the generic form of the Biblical cycle. While to some extent, of course, there is overlap in all of these categories among the extant cycles, I think it is possible to find significant special emphases in each work. The implicit progression of the chapters in this book has been from a consideration of setting to language to dramatic structure. The York cycle is most notable for the way in which it incorporates the essence of medieval urban life into the dramatized life of Christ. It is a play that gives thematic significance to its setting—indeed, it is possible to say that the setting *is* the play. The Wakefield cycle is notable especially for the versatility of its language, the abuse of which the Wakefield playwright takes as a self-referential measure of his worldly power as a poet. The N-Town cycle presents a carefully crafted double plot, in which the use of typology creates a paradigmatic dramatic structure. The Chester cycle, in turn, with its deliberate defense of Catholic "miracle playing," gives an alternative paradigm by introducing a major parodic subplot in its central action. By placing these interpretations side by side within the covers of one book, I have hoped to demonstrate that, as in all good literature, the generic is enlivened by the individual talent. The Corpus Christi cycles are, indeed, memorable for their shared grand design. But they survive as great art because each one reflects the special accomplishment by gifted dramatic poets of the act of engendering.

BIBLIOGRAPHY

Adams, Joseph Quincy, ed. *Chief Pre-Shakespearean Dramas*. Cambridge, Mass.: Houghton Mifflin, 1924.

Ashley, Kathleen M. "Chester Cycle and Nominalist Thought." *Journal of the History of Ideas* 40 (1979): 477.

———. "Divine Power in Chester Cycle and Late Medieval Thought." *Journal of the History of Ideas* 39 (1978): 387–404.

———. " 'Wyt' and 'Wysdam' in N-Town Cycle." *Philological Quarterly* 58 (1979): 121–135.

Auerbach, Erich. *Mimesis: The Representation of Reality in Western Literature*. Translated by Willard R. Trask. Garden City, N.Y.: Doubleday, 1957.

———. *Scenes from the Drama of European Literature*. Translated by Ralph Manheim. New York: Meridian, 1959.

———. *Typologische Motive in der mittelalterlichen Literatur*. Krefeld: Scherpe Verlag, 1953.

Bakhtin, Mikhail M. *Rabelais and His World*. Translated by Helene Iswolsky. Cambridge: MIT Press, 1968.

Bartlett, J. M. "The Expansion and Decline of York in the Later Middle Ages." *Economic History Review*, 2d ser. 12 (1959): 17–33.

Beadle, Richard, ed. *The York Plays*. London: Edward Arnold, 1982.

———, and Peter Meredith. "Further External Evidence for Dating the York Register (BL Additional MS 35290)." *Leeds Studies in English*, n.s. 11 (1980): 51–55.

———, eds. *The York Play: A Facsimile of British Library MS Additional 35290*. Leeds Texts and Monographs, Medieval Drama Facsimiles, no. 7. Leeds: University of Leeds, 1983.

Benson, Edwin. *Life in a Mediaeval City*. London: SPCK, 1920.

Berkeley, David S. "Some Misapprehensions of Christian Typology in Recent Literary Scholarship." *Studies in English Literature* 18 (1978): 1–12.

Bernbrock, John E. "Notes on the Towneley Cycle *Slaying of Abel*." *Journal of English and Germanic Philology* 62 (1963): 317–322.

Bevington, David, ed. *Medieval Drama*. Boston: Houghton Mifflin, 1975.

Block, K. S., ed. *Ludus Coventriae; or, The Plaie Called Corpus Christi.* Early English Text Society, extra series 120. 1922. Reprint. London: Oxford University Press, 1960.

———. "Some Notes on the Problem of the 'Ludus Coventriae.'" *Modern Language Review* 10 (1915): 47–57.

Brandeis, Arthur, ed. *Jacob's Well.* Early English Text Society, original series 115. London: Oxford University Press, 1900.

Braudel, Fernand. "Pre-Modern Towns." In *The Early Modern Town: A Reader*, edited by Peter Clark, pp. 53–90. London: Longmans and Open University Press, 1976.

Brawer, Robert A. "The Characterization of Pilate in the York Cycle Play." *Studies in Philology* 69 (1972): 289–303.

———. "The Dramatic Function of the Ministry Group in the Towneley Cycle." *Comparative Drama* 4 (1970): 166–176.

Breckenridge, James D. " 'Et Prima Vidit': The Iconography of the Appearance of Christ to His Mother." *Art Bulletin* 39 (1957): 9– 32.

Breitenbach, Edgar. *Speculum Humanae Salvationis: Eine typengeschichtliche Untersuchung.* Strasbourg: J. H. E. Heitz, 1930.

Bristol, Michael D. "Carnival and the Institutions of Theater in Elizabethan England." *ELH* 50 (1983): 637–653.

Brockman, Bennett A. "Cain and Abel in the Chester *Creation*: Narrative Tradition and Dramatic Potential." *Medievalia et Humanistica* 5 (1974): 169–182.

Brown, Arthur, "Some Notes on the Medieval Drama at York." In *Early English and Norse Studies Presented to Hugh Smith*, edited by Arthur Brown and Peter Foote, pp. 1–5. London: Methuen, 1963.

Brown, John Russell, ed. *The Complete Plays of the Wakefield Master, in a New Version for Reading and Performance.* London: Heinemann, 1983.

Bukozer, Manfred F. "Popular and Secular Music in England." In *Ars Nova and the Renaissance, 1300–1540*, edited by Don Anselm Hughes and Gerald Abraham. London and New York: Oxford University Press, 1960.

Bultmann, Rudolf. *The Gospel of St. John: A Commentary.* Translated by G. R. Beasley-Murray, R.W.N. Hoare, and J. K. Riches. Philadelphia: Westminister Press, 1971.

Burke, Peter. *Popular Culture in Early Modern Europe.* New York: New York University Press, 1978.

Burlin, Robert B. *Chaucerian Fiction*. Princeton: Princeton University Press, 1977.

Cady, Frank W. "The Liturgical Basis of the Towneley Plays." *PMLA* 24 (1909): 416–469.

————. "The Wakefield Group in Townley." *Journal of English and German Philology* 11 (1912): 244–262.

Campbell, Thomas P. "Why Do the Shepherds Prophesy?" In *The Drama of the Middle Ages*, edited by Clifford Davidson, G. J. Gianakaris, and John H. Stroupe. New York: AMS Press, 1982.

Cantelupe, E. B., and R. Griffith. "The Gifts of the Shepherds in the Wakefield *Secunda Pastorum*: An Iconographical Interpretation." *Mediaeval Studies* 28 (1966): 328–335.

Carey, Millicent. *The Wakefield Group in the Towneley Cycle*. Baltimore: Johns Hopkins University Press, 1930.

Cargill, Oscar. "The Authorship of the Secunda Pastorum." *PMLA* 41 (1926): 810–831.

Cawley, A. C. *Everyman and Medieval Miracle Plays*. New York: E. P. Dutton and Company, 1959.

————. "The Grotesque Feast in the *Prima Pastorum*." *Speculum* 30 (1955): 213–217.

————. "Iak Garcio of the *Prima Pastorum*." *Modern Language Notes* 68 (1953): 169–172.

————. "Middle English Metrical Versions of the Decalogue with Reference to the English Corpus Christi Cycles." *Leeds Studies in English*, n.s. 8 (1975): 129–145.

————. "The Staging of Medieval Drama." In *The Revels History of Drama in English*. Vol. 1, *Medieval Drama*. London: Methuen, 1983.

————, ed. "The Sykes MS of the York Scriveners' Play." *Leeds Studies in English and Kindred Languages* 7–8 (1952): 45–80.

————. "Thoresby and Later Owners of the Manuscript of the York Plays." *Leeds Studies in English*, n.s. 11 (1980, for 1979): 74–89.

————, ed. "The Wakefield First Shepherds' Play." *Proceedings of the Leeds Philosophical and Literary Society* 7 (1953): 113–122.

————. *The Wakefield Pageants in the Towneley Cycle*. Manchester: Manchester University Press, 1958.

————, and Jean Forrester. "The Corpus Christi Play of Wakefield: A New Look at the Wakefield Burgess Court Records." *Leeds Studies in English*, n.s. 8 (1975): 108–116, with appendixes.

————, and Martin Stevens, eds. *The Towneley Cycle: A Facsimile of Hun-*

tington MS HM 1. Leeds Texts and Monographs, Medieval Drama Facsimiles, no. 2. Leeds: University of Leeds, 1976.

Chambers, E. K. *English Literature at the Close of the Middle Ages*. Oxford: Clarendon Press, 1945.

―――. *The Mediaeval Stage*. 2 vols. Oxford: Clarendon Press, 1903.

Clark, Eleanor G. "The York Plays and the Gospel of Nicodemus." *PMLA* 43 (1928): 153–161.

Clark, Peter, ed. *The Early Modern Town: A Reader*. London: Longmans and Open University Press, 1976.

―――, and Paul Slack, eds. *Crisis and Order in English Towns, 1500–1700: Essays in Urban History*. Toronto: University of Toronto Press, 1972.

Clark, Roy Peter. "Chaucer and Medieval Scatology." Ph.D. dissertation, State University of New York at Stony Brook, 1974.

Clopper, Lawrence M., ed. *Chester: Records of the Early English Drama*. Vol. 3. Toronto: University of Toronto Press, 1979.

―――. "*The Chester Plays*: Frequency of Performance." *Theatre Survey* 14 (1973): 46–58.

―――. "The History and Development of the Chester Cycle." *Modern Philology* 75 (1978): 219–246.

―――. "The Principle of Selection in the Chester Old Testament Plays." *Chaucer Review* 13 (1979): 272–283.

―――. "The Rogers' Description of the Chester Plays." *Leeds Studies in English*, n.s. 7 (1973): 63–94.

―――. "Tyrants and Villains: Characterization in the Passion Sequences of the English Cycle Plays." *Modern Language Quarterly* 41 (1980): 3–20.

Coldewey, John C. "The Last Rise and Final Demise of Essex Town Drama." *Modern Language Quarterly* 36 (1975): 239–260.

Coletti, Theresa. "Devotional Iconography in the N-Town Marian Plays." *Comparative Drama* 11 (1977): 22–44.

―――. "Sacrament and Sacrifice in the N-Town Passion." *Mediaevalia* 7 (1981): 239–264.

Collier, J. P., ed. *Five Miracle Plays, or Scriptural Dramas*. London, 1836.

Collier, Richard J. *Poetry and Drama in the York Corpus Christi Play*. Hamden, Conn.: Archon Books, 1978.

Collins, Patrick J. "Narrative Bible Cycles in Medieval Art and Drama." *Comparative Drama* 9 (1975): 125–146.

―――. *The N-Town Plays and Medieval Picture Cycles*. Early Drama, Art, and Music (EDAM) Monograph Series, no. 2. Kalamazoo: Medieval Institute Publications, 1979.

——. "Typology, Criticism, and Medieval Drama: Some Observations on Method." *Comparative Drama* 10 (1976–1977): 298–313.

Constable, Giles. "Opposition to Pilgrimage in the Middle Ages." *Studia Gratiana* 19 (1976): 123–146.

Cornelius, Luke. *The Role of the Virgin Mary in the Coventry, York, Chester, and Towneley Cycles*. Washington: Catholic University of America Press, 1933.

Cosbey, R. C. "Mak Story and Its Folklore Analogues." *Speculum* 20 (1945): 310–317.

Cowling, Douglas. "The Liturgical Celebration of Corpus Christi in Medieval York." *REED Newsletter* 2 (1976): 5–9.

Craig, Hardin. *English Religious Drama of the Middle Ages*. Oxford: Clarendon Press, 1955.

——, ed. *Two Coventry Corpus Christi Plays*. Early English Text Society, extra series 87. London: Oxford University Press, 1957.

Craiger-Smith, A. *English Medieval Mural Paintings*. Oxford: Clarendon Press, 1963.

Craigie, William A. "The *Gospel of Nicodemus* and the *York Mystery Plays*." In *An English Miscellany Presented to Dr. Furnivall*, pp. 52–61. Oxford: Clarendon Press, 1901.

Danielou, Jean. *The Bible and the Liturgy*. Notre Dame: University of Notre Dame Press, 1956.

——. *From Shadow to Reality: Studies in the Biblical Typology of the Fathers*. Translated by Wulfstan Hibberd. London: Burns and Oates, 1960.

Daniels, Richard J. "A Study of the Formal and Literary Unity of the N-Town Mystery Cycle." Ph.D. dissertation, Ohio State University, 1972.

Davidson, Charles. "Studies in the English Mystery Plays." *Transactions of the Connecticut Academy of Arts and Sciences* 9 (1892): 125–297.

Davidson, Clifford. "After the Fall: Design in the Old Testament Plays in the York Cycle." *Mediaevalia* 1 (1975): 1–24.

——. "Civic Concern and Iconography in the York Passion." *Annuale Mediaevale* 15 (1974): 125–149.

——. *Drama and Art*. Kalamazoo: Medieval Institute, 1977.

——. *From Creation to Doom: The York Cycle of Mystery Plays*. New York: AMS, 1984.

Davidson, Clifford, ed. *A Middle English Treatise on the Playing of Miracles*. Washington: University Press of America, 1981.

———. "The Realism of the York Realist and the York Passion." *Speculum* 50 (1975): 270–283.

Davies, Robert. *Extracts from the Municipal Records of York*. London: J. B. Nichols, 1843.

Davis, Marian. "Nicholas Love and the N-Town Cycle." Ph.D. dissertation, Auburn University, 1979.

Davis, Natalie Zeman. "The Reasons for Misrule: Youth Groups and Charivaris in Sixteenth-Century France." *Past and Present*, no. 50 (1971): 41–75.

———. "The Rites of Violence: Religious Riot in Sixteenth-Century France." *Past and Present*, no. 59 (1973): 51–91.

Davis, Ruth Brant. "The Scheduling of the Chester Plays." *Theatre Notebook* 27 (1972): 49–67.

Dean, James. "The Ending of the *Canterbury Tales*." *Texas Studies in Language and Literature* 21 (1979): 17–33.

Deimling, Hermann, ed. *The Chester Plays*. Part 1. Early English Text Society, extra series 62. London: Oxford University Press, 1892.

Diller, Hans-Jürgen. "The Craftsmanship of the Wakefield Master." *Anglia* 83 (1965): 271–288.

———. "The Composition of the Chester *Adoration of the Shepherds*." *Anglia* 89 (1971): 178–198.

———. *Redeformen des englischen Misterienspiels*. Munich: Wilhelm Fink Verlag, 1973.

Dobson, R. B. "Admission to the Freedom of the City of York in the Later Middle Ages." *Economic History Review*, 2d ser. 26 (1973): 1–22.

Dodd, C. H. *The Johannine Epistles*. New York: Harper, 1946.

Dorrell, Margaret. *See* Rogerson, Margaret Dorrell.

Douce, Francis. *Bibliotheca Townleiana: A Catalogue of the Curious and Extensive Library of the Late John Towneley, Esq*. Part 1. London: R. H. Evans, 1814.

———, ed. *Juditium*. London: Roxburghe Club, 1822.

Dryden, John. "A Discourse concerning the Original and Progress of Satire." In *Essays of John Dryden*, edited by W. P. Ker. 2 vols. Oxford: Clarendon Press, 1926.

Dunn, E. Catherine. "The Literary Style of the Towneley Plays." *American Benedictine Review* 20 (1969): 481–504.

————. "Lyrical Form and the Prophetic Principle in the Towneley Plays." *Mediaeval Studies* 23 (1961): 80–90.

————. "The Medieval 'Cycle' as History Play: An Approach to the Wakefield Plays." *Studies in the Renaissance* 7 (1961): 76–89.

————. "Popular Devotion in the Vernacular Drama of Medieval England." *Medievalia et Humanistica* 4 (1973): 55–68.

————. "The Prophetic Principle in the Towneley *Prima Pastorum*." In *Linguistic and Literary Studies in Honor of Helmut A. Hatzfeld*, edited by Alessandre A. Crisafulli. Washington: Catholic University of America Press, 1964.

Dustoor, P. E. "Some Textual Notes on the English Mystery Plays." *Modern Language Review* 21 (1926): 427–431.

————. "Textual Notes on the Towneley Old Testament Plays." *English Studies* 11 (1929): 220–228.

Dutka, JoAnna. "Music and the English Mystery Plays." *Comparative Drama* 7 (1973): 135–149.

————. *Music in the English Mystery Plays*. Early Drama, Art, and Music (EDAM) Reference Series, no. 2. Kalamazoo: Medieval Institute Publications, 1980.

Elliott, John R., Jr. "The Sacrifice of Isaac as Comedy and Tragedy." *Studies in Philology* 66 (1969): 36–59.

Emerson, Oliver F. "Legends of Cain, Especially in Old and Middle English." *PMLA* 21 (1906): 831–929.

Emmerson, Richard Kenneth. *Antichrist in the Middle Ages: A Study of Medieval Apocalypticism, Art, and Literature*. Seattle: University of Washington Press, 1981.

England, George, and A. W. Pollard, eds. *The Towneley Plays*. Early English Text Society, extra series 71. London: Oxford University Press, 1897.

Everitt, Alan. *Perspectives in English Urban History*. London: Macmillan, 1973.

Faral, Edmond. *Les arts poétiques du XIIe et du XIIIe siècles*. Paris: Librairie H. Champion, 1924.

Flanigan, C. Clifford. "The Roman Rite and the Origins of the Liturgical Drama." *University of Toronto Quarterly* 43 (1974): 263–284.

Fleming, John V. *An Introduction to the Franciscan Literature of the Middle Ages*. Chicago: Franciscan Herald Press, 1977.

Fletcher, Alan J. "The Design of the N-Town Play of Mary's Conception." *Modern Philology* 79 (1981): 166–173.

Forrest, M. Patricia. "Apocryphal Sources of the St. Anne's Day Plays in the Hegge Cycle." *Medievalia et Humanistica* 17 (1966): 38–50.

———. "The Role of the Expositor Contemplacio in the St. Anne's Day Plays of the Hegge Cycle." *Mediaeval Studies* 28 (1966): 60–76.

Forrester, Jean. "Wakefield Mystery Plays and the Burgess Court Records: A New Discovery." Ossett, Yorks.: Harold Speak and Jean Forrester, 1974.

Foster, Frances A. "The Mystery Plays and the Northern Passion." *Modern Language Notes* 26 (1911): 169–171.

———, ed. *The Northern Passion.* Early English Text Society, original series 145, 147. London: Oxford University Press, 1913–1916.

———. *A Stanzaic Life of Christ.* Early English Text Society, original series 166. London: Oxford University Press, 1926.

Frampton, Mendal G. "The Date of the Flourishing of the Wakefield Master." *PMLA* 50 (1935): 631–660.

———. "The Date of the 'Wakefield Master': Bibliographical Evidence." *PMLA* 52 (1938): 86–117.

———. "The Early English Text Society Edition of the Towneley Plays." *Anglia Beiblatt* 48 (1937): 330–333, 366–368; 49 (1938): 3–7.

———. "The Processus Talentorum (Towneley XXIV)." *PMLA* 59 (1944): 646–654.

———. "The Towneley Harrowing of Hell." *PMLA* 56 (1941): 105–119.

———. "Towneley XX: The Conspiracio (et Capcio)." *PMLA* 58 (1943): 920–937.

———. "The York Plays of Christ Led Up to Calvary (Play XXXIV)." *Philological Quarterly* 20 (1941): 198–204.

Frank, Grace. "Revision in the English Mystery Plays." *Modern Philology* 15 (1918): 565–572.

Fry, Timothy. "The Unity of the *Ludus Coventriae.*" *Studies in Philology* 48 (1951): 527–570.

Gardiner, Harold. *Mysteries' End: An Investigation of the Last Days of the Medieval Religious Stage.* New Haven: Yale University Press, 1946.

Gardner, John. *The Construction of the Wakefield Cycle.* Carbondale and Edwardsville: Southern Illinois University Press, 1974.

———. "Imagery and Allusion in the Wakefield Noah Play." *Papers in Language and Literature* 4 (1968): 3–12.

———. "Structure and Tone in the Second Shepherds' Play." *Educational Theatre Journal* 19 (1967): 1–8.

——. "Theme and Irony in the Wakefield *Mactatio Abel.*" *PMLA* 80 (1965): 515–521.

Gayley, Charles Mills. *Plays of Our Forefathers and Some of the Traditions upon Which They Were Founded.* 1907. Reprint. New York: Biblo and Tannen, 1968.

Gibbons, Brian. *Jacobean City Comedy.* 2d ed. London: Methuen, 1980.

Gibson, Gail McMurray. "Bury St. Edmunds, Lydgate, and the N-Town Cycle." *Speculum* 56 (1981): 56–90.

——. " 'Porta haec clausa erit': Comedy, Conception, and Ezekiel's Closed Door in the *Ludus Coventriae* Play of 'Joseph's Return.' " *Journal of Medieval and Renaissance Studies* 8 (1978): 137–156.

Greg, Walter Wilson. *Bibliographic and Textual Problems of the English Mystery Cycles.* London: Alexander Moring, 1914. See also *Library*, 3d ser. 5 (1914).

——. *The Play of Antichrist, from the Chester Cycle.* Oxford: Clarendon Press, 1935.

Hanning, Robert W. " 'You Have Begun a Parlous Pleye': The Nature and Limits of Dramatic Mimesis as a Theme of Four Middle English 'Fall of Lucifer' Plays." *Comparative Drama* 7 (1973): 22–50.

Hardison, O. B., Jr. *Christian Rite and Christian Drama in the Middle Ages: Essays in the Origin and Early History of Modern Drama.* Baltimore: Johns Hopkins University Press, 1965.

Harty, John. "The Unity and Structure of *The Chester Mystery Cycle.*" *Mediaevalia* 2 (1976): 137-158.

Hassall, W. O., ed. *The Holkham Bible Picture Book.* London: Dropmore Press, 1954.

Heaton, Herbert. *The Yorkshire Woolen and Worsted Industries from the Earliest Times up to the Industrial Revolution.* 2d ed. Oxford: Clarendon Press, 1965.

Helterman, Jeffrey. *Symbolic Action in the Plays of the Wakefield Master.* Athens: University of Georgia Press, 1981.

Hohlfeld, A. R. "Die altenglischen Kollektivmisterien unter Berücksichtigung des Verhältnisses der York- und Towneleyspiele." *Anglia Beiblatt* 11 (1889): 219–310.

Holthausen, Ferdinand. "Studien zu den Towneley Plays." *English Studies* 58 (1924): 161–178.

Horn, Edward T. *The Christian Year.* Philadelphia: Muhlenberg Press, 1957.

Hoskins, W. G. "English Provincial Towns in the Early Sixteenth Century." In *The Early Modern Town: A Reader*, edited by Peter Clark. London: Longmans and Open University Press, 1976.

———. *Local History in England*. 2d ed. London: Longmans, 1972.

Howard, Donald R. *The Idea of the Canterbury Tales*. Berkeley and Los Angeles: University of California Press, 1976.

———. *Writers and Pilgrims: Medieval Pilgrimage Narratives and Their Posterity*. Berkeley and Los Angeles: University of California Press, 1980.

Hudson, Anne. *Selections from English Wycliffite Writings*. Cambridge: Cambridge University Press, 1978.

Hughes, Don Anselm, and Gerald Abraham, eds. *Ars Nova and the Renaissance, 1300–1540*. (London: Oxford University Press, 1960).

Hulme, W. H., ed. *The Harrowing of Hell and the Gospel of Nicodemus*. Early English Text Society, extra series 100. London: Oxford University Press, 1907.

Hunter, Joseph, ed. *The Towneley Mysteries*. Publications of the Surtees Society, no. 1. London: J. B. Nichols and Son, 1836.

Hurrell, John Dennis. "The Figural Approach to Medieval Drama." *College English* 26 (1965): 598–604.

Ingram, R. W. "The Use of Music in English Miracle Plays." *Anglia* 75 (1957): 55–76.

Jacob, E. F. *The Fifteenth Century, 1399–1485*. Oxford History of England. Oxford: Oxford University Press, 1961.

James, M. R., trans. *The Apocryphal New Testament*. Oxford: Clarendon Press, 1924.

James, Mervyn. "Ritual, Drama and Social Body in the Late Medieval English Town." *Past and Present*, no. 98 (1983): 3–29.

Jean Marie, Sister. "The Cross in the Towneley Plays." *Traditio* 5 (1947): 331–334.

Jeffrey, David L. "Franciscan Spirituality and the Rise of Early English Drama." *Mosaic* 8 (1975): 17–46.

Johnson, Wallace. "The Origin of the 'Second Shepherds' Play.' " *Quarterly Journal of Speech* 52 (1966): 47–57.

Johnston, Alexandra F. "The Guild of Corpus Christi and the Procession of Corpus Christi in York." *Mediaeval Studies* 38 (1976): 372–384.

———. "The Plays of the Religious Guilds of York: The Creed Play and the Pater Noster Play." *Speculum* 50 (1975): 55–90.

———. "The Procession and the Play of Corpus Christi in York after 1426." *Leeds Studies in English*, n.s. 7 (1973): 55–62.

——. "The York Cycle, 1977." *University of Toronto Quarterly* 48 (1978): 1–9.

——. "Yule in York." *REED Newsletter* 1 (1976): 3–10.

——, and Margaret Dorrell (Rogerson). "The Doomsday Pageant of the York Mercers, 1433." *Leeds Studies in English*, n.s. 5 (1971): 29–34.

——. "The York Mercers and Their Pageant of Doomsday, 1433–1526." *Leeds Studies in English*, n.s. 6 (1972): 11–35.

——, eds. *York: Records of the Early English Drama*. 2 vols. Toronto: University of Toronto Press, 1979.

Jones, Cheslyn, et al. *The Study of Liturgy*. London: SPCK, 1978.

Jones, W. R. "Lollards and Images: The Defense of Religious Art in Later Medieval England." *Journal of the History of Ideas* 34 (1973): 27–50.

Jungmann, Joseph A. *The Mass of the Roman Rite: Its Origin and Development*. Translated by Francis A. Brunner. 2 vols. New York: Benziger, 1950, 1953.

Justice, Alan D. "Trade Symbolism in the York Cycle." *Theatre Journal* 31 (1979): 47–58.

Kahrl, Stanley J. "The Civic Religious Drama of Medieval England: A Review of Recent Scholarship." *Renaissance Drama* 6 (1973): 237–248.

——. *Traditions of Medieval English Drama*. London: Hutchinson University Library, 1974.

Keenan, Hugh T. "A Check-List on Typology and English Medieval Literature through 1972." *Studies in the Literary Imagination* 8 (1975): 159–166.

Kelly, Henry Ansgar. *The Devil, Demonology and Witchcraft: The Development of Christian Beliefs in Evil Spirits*. Garden City, N.Y.: Doubleday, 1968.

Kipling, Gordon. "The London Pageants for Margaret of Anjou: A Medieval Script Restored." *Medieval English Theatre* 4 (1982): 5–27.

Kleinstück, Johannes. "Die mittelalterliche Tragödie in England." *Euphorion* 50 (1956): 177–195.

Kluckert, E. "Die Simultanbilder Memlings, ihre Wurzeln und Wirkungen." *Das Münster* 27 (1974): 284–295.

Knight, Alan E. *Aspects of Genre in Late Medieval French Drama*. Manchester: Manchester University Press, 1983.

Kolve, V. A. *The Play Called Corpus Christi*. Stanford: Stanford University Press, 1966.

Ladurie, Emmanuel Le Roy. *Carnival in Romans*. Translated by Mary Feeney. New York: George Braziller, 1979.

Leggatt, Alexander. *Citizen Comedy in the Age of Shakespeare*. Toronto: University of Toronto Press, 1973.

Leigh, David. "The Doomsday Mystery Play: An Eschatological Morality." *Modern Philology* 67 (1969): 211–223.

Leiter, Louis H. "Typology, Paradigm, Metaphor, and Image in the York *Creation of Adam and Eve*." *Drama Survey* 7 (1968–1969): 113–132.

Levin, Richard. *The Multiple Plot in English Renaissance Drama*. Chicago: University of Chicago Press, 1971.

Lewis, C. S. *Miracles: A Preliminary Study*. London: Geoffrey Bles, Centenary Press, 1947.

Lucken, Linus Urban. *Antichrist and the Prophets of Antichrist in the Chester Cycle*. Washington: Catholic University of America Press, 1940.

Lumiansky, Robert M. "Comedy and Theme in the Chester *Harrowing of Hell*." *Tulane Studies in English* 10 (1960): 5–12.

———, and David Mills, eds. *The Chester Mystery Cycle*. Early English Text Society, supplementary series 3. London: Oxford University Press, 1974.

———. *The Chester Mystery Cycle: Essays and Documents*. Chapel Hill: University of North Carolina Press, 1983.

———. *The Chester Mystery Cycle (MS Bodley 175)*. Leeds Texts and Monographs, Medieval Drama Facsimiles, no. 1. Leeds: University of Leeds, 1973.

———. *The Chester Mystery Cycle: A Reduced Facsimile of Huntington Library MS 2*. Leeds Texts and Monographs, Medieval Drama Facsimiles, no. 6. Leeds: University of Leeds, 1980.

Lyle, Marie. *The Original Identity of the York and Towneley Plays*. Minneapolis: University of Minnesota Press, 1919.

McAlindon, T. "Comedy and Terror in Middle English Literature: The Diabolical Game." *Modern Language Quarterly* 60 (1965): 323–332.

Macaulay, Peter Stuart. "The Play of the Harrowing of Hell as a Climax in the English Mystery Cycles." *Studia Germania Gadensia* 8 (1966): 115–134.

McGavin, John J. "Sign and Tradition: The *Purification* Play in Chester." *Leeds Studies in English*, n.s. 11 (1979): 90-101.

McGinn, Bernard. "Apocalypticism in the Middle Ages: An Historiographical Sketch." *Mediaeval Studies* 37 (1975): 252–286.

McKinnon, Effie. "Notes on the Dramatic Structure of the York Cycle." *Studies in Philology* 28 (1931): 433–449.

MacLean, Sally-Beth. *Chester Art: A Subject List of Extant and Lost Art Including Items Relevant to Early Drama.* Early Art, Drama, and Music (EDAM) Reference Series, no. 3. Kalamazoo: Medieval Institute Publications, 1982.

McNeir, Waldo F. "The Corpus Christi Passion Plays as Dramatic Art." *Studies in Philology* 48 (1951): 601–628.

MacRae, George W. *Invitation to John: A Commentary on the Gospel of John with Complete Text from "The Jerusalem Bible."* Garden City, N.Y.: Doubleday, 1978.

Maltman, Nicholas. "Pilate—*Os Malleatoris.*" *Speculum* 36 (1961): 308–311.

Manly, John M., ed. *Specimens of the Pre-Shakespearean Drama.* 1897. Reprint. 2 vols. New York: Dover Publications, 1967.

Manly, W. M. "Shepherds and Prophets: Religious Unity in the Towneley *Secunda Pastorum.*" *PMLA* 78 (1963): 151–155.

Manning, Robert. *Meditations on the Supper of Our Lord.* Edited by J. Meadows Cooper. Early English Text Society, original series 60. London: Tuebner, 1875.

Marrow, James. *Passion Iconography in Northern European Art of the Late Middle Ages and Early Renaissance.* Kortrijk: Van Ghemmert, 1979.

Marshall, John. "The Chester Coopers' Pageant: 'Selles' and 'Cathedra.' " *Leeds Studies in English*, n.s. 8 (1975): 120–128.

Marshall, Linda E. " 'Sacral Parody' in the *Secunda Pastorum.*" *Speculum* 47 (1972): 720–736.

Marshall, Mary H. "*Theatre* in the Middle Ages: Evidence from Dictionaries and Glosses." *Symposium* 4 (1950): 1–39, 366–389.

Martin, Leslie Howard. "Comic Eschatology in the Chester *Coming of Antichrist.*" *Comparative Drama* 5 (1971): 163–176.

Matthews, J., ed. *The Chester Plays.* Part 2. Early English Text Society, extra series 115. London: Oxford University Press, 1916.

Meredith, Peter. "The Development of the York Mercers' Pageant Waggon." *Medieval English Theatre* 1 (1979): 5–18.

———. " 'Item for a grone—iijd': Records and Performance." In *Proceedings of the First Colloquium, REED*, edited by JoAnna Dutka, pp. 26–60. Toronto: Records of the Early English Drama, 1979.

Meredith, Peter. "John Clerke's Hand in the York Register." *Leeds Studies in English*, n.s. 12 (1981): 245–271.

———. "The *Ordo Paginarum* and the Development of the York Tilemakers' Pageant." *Leeds Studies in English*, n.s. 11 (1980): 59–73.

———, and Stanley J. Kahrl, eds. *The N-Town Plays: A Facsimile of British Library MS Cotton Vespasian D VIII*. Leeds Texts and Monographs, Medieval Drama Facsimiles, no. 4. Leeds: University of Leeds, 1977.

———, and John E. Tailby, eds. *The Staging of Religious Drama in Europe in the Later Middle Ages: Texts and Documents in Translation*. Early Art, Drama, and Music (EDAM) Monograph Series, no. 4. Kalamazoo: Medieval Institute Publications, 1983.

Mayer-Baer, Kathi. *Music of the Spheres and the Dance of Death*. Princeton: Princeton University Press, 1970.

Meyers, Walter E. *A Figure Given: Typology in the Wakefield Plays*. Pittsburgh: Duquesne University Press, 1970.

———. "Typology and the Audience of the English Cycle Plays." *Studies in the Literary Imagination* 8 (1975): 145–158.

Mill, Anna J. "Noah's Wife Again." *PMLA* 56 (1941): 613–626.

———. "The York Bakers' Play of the Last Supper." *Modern Language Review* 30 (1935): 145–158.

Miller, Frances H. "The Northern Passion and the Mysteries." *Modern Language Notes* 34 (1919): 88–92.

Mills, David. "Approaches to the Medieval Drama." *Leeds Studies in English*, n.s. 3 (1969): 47–61.

———. "Religious Drama and Civic Ceremonial." In *The Revels History of Drama in England*. Vol. 1, *Medieval Drama*. London: Methuen, 1983.

———. "Stage Directions in the MSS of the Chester Mystery Cycle." *Medieval English Theatre* 3 (1981): 45–51.

Moore, Arthur K. "Medieval English Literature and the Question of Unity." In *Contestable Concepts of Literary Theory*, pp. 126–154. Baton Rouge: Louisiana State University Press, 1973.

Moorman, John R. H. *A History of the Church of England*. 3d ed. London: Adam and Charles Black, 1973.

Moran, Joann H. "Education and Learning in the City of York, 1300–1560." Borthwick Papers, no. 55. Borthwick Institute of Historical Research, University of York, 1979.

Morgan, Margery H. " 'High Fraud': Paradox and Double-Plot in the English Shepherds' Plays." *Speculum* 39 (1964): 676–689.

Muir, Lynette. "The Trinity in Medieval Drama." *Comparative Drama* 10 (1976): 116–129.

Munson, William F. "Typology and the Towneley Isaac." *Research Opportunities in Renaissance Drama* 11 (1968): 129–139.

Nelson, Alan H. *The Medieval English Stage: Corpus Christi Pageants and Plays.* Chicago: University of Chicago Press, 1974.

———. " 'Sacred' and 'Secular' Currents in the Towneley Play of Noah." *Drama Survey* 3 (1964): 393–401.

Nolan, Barbara. *The Gothic Visionary Perspective.* Princeton: Princeton University Press, 1977.

Owst, Gerald Robert. *Literature and Pulpit in Medieval England.* 2d ed., rev. Oxford: Basil Blackwell, 1961.

———. *Preaching in Medieval England.* Cambridge: Cambridge University Press, 1926.

Painter, John. *John: Witness and Theologian.* Foreword by C. K. Barrett. London: SPCK, 1975.

Palliser, D. M. "The Reformation in York: 1534–1553." Borthwick Papers, no. 40. Borthwick Institute of Historical Research, University of York, 1971.

———. *Tudor York.* Oxford: Oxford University Press, 1979.

———. "The Trade Gilds of Tudor York." In *Crisis and Order in English Towns, 1500–1700: Essays in Urban History,* edited by P. Clark and P. Slack. Toronto: University of Toronto Press, 1972.

Panofsky, Erwin. *Early Netherlandish Painting: Its Origin and Character.* 2 vols. Cambridge: Harvard University Press, 1953.

Patrologiae cursus completus: Patrologia Latina. Edited by J. P. Migne. 221 vols. Paris, 1844–1864.

Patrides, C. A. *The Phoenix and the Ladder: The Rise and Decline of the Christian View of History.* Berkeley and Los Angeles: University of California Press, 1964.

Paull, Michael. "The Figure of Mohamet in the Towneley Cycle." *Comparative Drama* 6 (1972): 187–204.

Peacock, Matthew. "Towneley, Widkirk, or Wakefield Plays?" *Yorkshire Archaeological Journal* 15 (1898–1899): 94–103.

———. "The Wakefield Mysteries: The Place of Representation." *Anglia* 24 (1901–1904): 509–524.

Penninger, Frida Elaine. "The Significance of the Corpus Christi Plays as Drama with Particular Reference to the Towneley Cycle." Ph.D. dissertation, Duke University, 1961.

Peters, Edward. *The Magician, the Witch, and the Law.* Philadelphia: University of Pennsylvania Press, 1978.

Petti, Anthony G. *English Literary Hands from Dryden to Chaucer.* London: Edward Arnold, 1977.

Pfleiderer, Jean D., and Michael J. Preston. *A Complete Concordance to the Chester Mystery Plays.* New York: Garland, 1981.

Phillips, John. *The Reformation of Images.* Berkeley and Los Angeles: University of California Press, 1973.

Phythian-Adams, Charles. "Ceremony and the Citizen: The Communal Year at Coventry, 1450–1550." In *Crisis and Order in English Towns, 1500–1700: Essays in Urban History,* edited by P. Clark and P. Slack, pp. 57–85. Toronto: University of Toronto Press, 1972.

———. *Desolation of a City: Coventry and the Urban Crisis of the Late Middle Ages.* Cambridge: Cambridge University Press, 1979.

Pollard, Alfred W., ed. *English Miracle Plays, Moralities, and Interludes.* Oxford: Clarendon Press, 1890.

Poteet, Daniel P. "Time, Eternity, and Dramatic Form in *Ludus Coventriae* Passion Play I." In *The Drama of the Middle Ages,* edited by Clifford Davidson, G. J. Gianakaris, and John H. Stroupe. New York: AMS Press, 1982.

Powell, Lawrence F., ed. *The Mirrour of the Blessed Lyf of Jesu Christ,* by Nicholas Love. Oxford: Oxford University Press, 1908.

Powicke, F. M. *The Reformation in England.* London: Oxford University Press, 1941.

Preston, Michael J., and Jean D. Pfleiderer. *A KWIC Concordance to the Plays of the Wakefield Master.* New York: Garland, 1982.

Prosser, Eleanor. *Drama and Religion in the English Mystery Plays: A Reevaluation.* Stanford: Stanford University Press, 1961.

Ragusa, Isa, and Rosalie B. Green, trans. *Meditations on the Life of Christ.* Princeton: Princeton University Press, 1961.

Raine, Angelo. *Mediaeval York.* London: John Murray, 1955.

Reau, Louis. *Iconographie de l'art chrétien.* 3 vols. Paris: Presses Universitaires de France, 1955–1959.

Reese, Jesse Byers. "Alliterative Verse in the York Cycle." *Modern Philology* 48 (1951): 639–668.

Rendall, Thomas. "Visual Typology in the Abraham and Isaac Plays." *Modern Philology* 81 (1984): 221–232.

Rimmer, W. G. "The Evolution of Leeds." In *The Early Modern Town: A Reader.* Edited by Peter Clark. London: Longmans and Open University Press, 1976.

Robertson, D. W., Jr. "The Question of 'Typology' and the Wakefield *Mactacio Abel.*" In *Essays in Medieval Culture.* Princeton: Princeton University Press, 1980, pp. 218–232.

Robinson, J. W. "The Art of the York Realist." *Modern Philology* 60 (1963): 241–251.

——. "The Late Medieval Cult of Jesus in the Mystery Plays." *PMLA* 80 (1965): 508–514.

Rogerson, Margaret Dorrell. "The Butchers', Saddlers', and Carpenters' Pageants: Misreadings of the York *Ordo.*" *English Language Notes* 13 (1975): 1–14.

——. "External Evidence for Dating the York Register." *REED Newsletter* 2 (1976): 4–5.

——. "The Mayor of York and the Coronation Pageant." *Leeds Studies in English*, n.s. 5 (1971): 35–45.

——. "Two Studies of the York Corpus Christi Play." *Leeds Studies in English*, n.s. 6 (1972): 63–111.

——. "The York Corpus Christi Play: Some Practical Details." *Leeds Studies in English*, n.s. 10 (1978): 97–106.

Roney, Lois. "The Wakefield First and Second Shepherds Plays as Complements in Psychology and Parody." *Speculum* 58 (1983): 696–723.

Rose, Martial, ed. *The Wakefield Mystery Plays.* 1961. Reprint. New York: Doubleday, 1963.

Ross, Lawrence J. "Symbol and Structure in the *Secunda Pastorum.*" *Comparative Drama* 1 (1967): 122–149. Reprinted in *Medieval English Drama: Essays Critical and Contextual*, edited by Jerome Taylor and Alan H. Nelson. Chicago: University of Chicago Press, 1972.

Rossiter, A. P. *English Drama from Early Times to the Elizabethans: Its Background, Origins and Development.* London: Hutchinson University Library, 1950.

Roston, Murray. *Biblical Drama in England from the Middle Ages to the Present Day.* London: Faber, 1968.

Royce, James R. "Nominalism and Divine Power in the Chester Cycle." *Journal of the History of Ideas* 40 (1979): 475–477.

Salter, Elizabeth. *Nicholas Love's "Mirrour of the Blessed Lyf of Jesu Christ."* Analecta Cartusiana 10. Universität Salzburg, Institut für Englische Sprache und Literatur, 1974.

Salter, F. M. *Mediaeval Drama in Chester.* Toronto: University of Toronto Press, 1955.

——. "The 'Trial and Flagellation.' " In *The Trial and Flagellation with*

Other Studies in the Chester Cycle. London: Oxford University Press, 1935.

Schiller, Gertrud. *Iconography of Christian Art.* Translated by Janet Seligman. 2 vols. Greenwich, Conn.: New York Graphic Society, 1971–1972.

Sellers, Maud, ed. *The York Mercers and Merchant Adventurers, 1356–1917.* Surtees Society Publication no. 129. Durham: Andrews and Company, 1918.

Sheingorn, Pamela. "The Moment of the Resurrection in the Corpus Christi Plays." *Medievalia et Humanistica,* n.s. 11 (1982): 111–129.

———. "On Using Medieval Art in the Study of the Medieval Drama: An Introduction to Methodology." *Studies in Iconography* 22 (1979): 101–107.

Sinangoglou, Leah. "The Christ Child as Sacrifice: A Medieval Tradition and the Corpus Christi Plays." *Speculum* 48 (1973): 491–509.

Skeat, Walter W. "The Locality of 'The Towneley Plays.' " Letter to the editors of *Atheneum,* 2 December 1893, p. 779.

Smith, A. H. "A York Pageant, 1486." *London Mediaeval Studies* 1 (1937–1939): 382–398.

Smith, Barbara Herrnstein. *Poetic Closure: A Study of How Poems End.* Chicago: University of Chicago Press, 1968.

Smith, Lucy Toulmin. *York Plays.* 1885. Reprint. New York: Russell and Russell, 1963.

Spector, Stephen. "The Genesis of the N-Town Cycle." Ph.D. dissertation, Yale University, 1973.

Squires, Lynn. "Law and Disorder in *Ludus Coventriae.*" In *The Drama of the Middle Ages,* edited by Clifford Davidson, G. J. Gianakaris, and John H. Stroupe. New York: AMS Press, 1982.

Stacey, John. *John Wyclif and Reform.* Philadelphia: Westminster Press, 1964.

Stanley, E. G. "The Use of the Bob-Lines in *Sir Thopas.*" *Neuphilologische Mitteilungen* 73 (1972): 417–426.

Stemmler, Theo. *Liturgische Feiern und geistliche Spiele.* Tübingen: Max Niemeyer Verlag, 1970.

———. "Typological Transfer in Liturgical Offices and Religious Plays of the Middle Ages." *Studies in the Literary Imagination* 8 (1975): 123–143.

Stevens, John. "Music in Mediaeval Drama." *Proceedings of the Royal Musical Association* 84 (1958): 81–95.

————. "The Music of Play XLV: The Assumption of the Virgin." In *The York Plays*, edited by Richard Beadle. London: Edward Arnold, 1982.

Stevens, Martin. "The Accuracy of the Towneley Scribe." *Huntington Library Quarterly* 22 (1958): 1–9.

————. "Did the Wakefield Master Write a Nine-Line Stanza?" *Comparative Drama* 15 (1981): 99–119.

————. "The Dramatic Setting of the Wakefield Annunciation." *PMLA* 81 (1966): 193–198.

————. "Illusion and Reality in the Medieval Drama." *College English* 32 (1971): 448–464.

————. "The Johnston-Rogerson Edition of the York Records: An Initial Reading." In *Proceedings of the First Colloqium, REED*, edited by JoAnna Dutka, pp. 160–178. Toronto: Records of the Early English Drama, 1979.

————. "Language as Theme in the Wakefield Plays." *Speculum* 52 (1977): 100–117.

————. "The Manuscript of the Towneley Plays: Its History and Editions." *Publications of the Bibliographical Society of America* 67 (1973): 231–244.

————. "The Missing Parts of the Towneley Cycle." *Speculum* 45 (1970): 254–265.

————. Review of *The Wakefield Pageants in the Towneley Cycle*, edited by A. C. Cawley. *Speculum* 34 (1959): 453–455.

————. "The Royal Stanza in Early English Literature." *PMLA* 94 (1979): 62–76.

————. "The Theatre of the World: A Study in Medieval Dramatic Form." *Chaucer Review* 7 (1973): 234–249.

————. "The York Cycle: From Procession to Play." *Leeds Studies in English*, n.s. 6 (1972): 37–62; "Postscript," pp. 113–115.

————, and Margaret Dorrell (Rogerson), eds. "The *Ordo Paginarum* Gathering of the York *A/Y Memorandum Book.*" *Modern Philology* 72 (1974): 45–59.

Stratman, Carl J. *Bibliography of Medieval Drama.* 2d ed., rev. 2 vols. New York: Frederick Ungar, 1972.

Swanson, Heather. "Building Craftsmen in Late Medieval York." Borthwick Papers, no. 61. Borthwick Institute of Historical Research, University of York, 1983.

Swart, J. "The Insubstantial Pageant." *Neophilologus* 41 (1957): 127–141.

Swenson, Esther Lydia. *An Inquiry into the Composition and Structure of the Ludus Coventriae*. University of Minnesota Studies in Language and Literature 1 (1914).

Taylor, Jerome, and Alan H. Nelson, eds. *Medieval English Drama: Essays Critical and Contextual*. Chicago: University of Chicago Press, 1972.

Thomas, Keith. *Religion and the Decline of Magic: Studies in Popular Beliefs in Sixteenth and Seventeenth Century England*. London: Weidenfeld and Nicolson, 1971.

Thompson, John A. F. *The Later Lollards, 1414–1520*. Oxford: Oxford University Press, 1965.

Tillott, P. M. *The Victoria History of the County of York*. Oxford: Oxford University Press, 1961.

Tomasch, Sylvia. "The Unwritten *Dispositio*: Principles of Order and the Structures of Late Middle English Literature." Ph.D. dissertation, City University of New York, 1985.

Travis, Peter W. *Dramatic Design in the Chester Cycle*. Chicago: University of Chicago Press, 1982.

Tristram, Earnest William. *English Wall Painting of the Fourteenth Century*. London: Routledge and Kegan Paul, 1955.

Trusler, Margaret. "The Language of the Wakefield Playwright." *Studies in Philology* 33 (1936): 15–39.

———. "Some Textual Notes Based on an Examination of the Towneley Manuscript." *Philological Quarterly* 14 (1935): 301–306.

———. *A Study of the Language of the Wakefield Group in Towneley on the Basis of Significant Rime-Words with Comparison of Forms within the Line in Both the Towneley and the York Plays*. Chapel Hill: University of North Carolina Press, 1936.

Turner, Victor, and Edith Turner. *Image and Pilgrimage in Christian Culture*. New York: Columbia University Press, 1978.

Twycross, Meg. " 'Places to Hear the Play': Pageant Stations at York, 1398–1572." *REED Newsletter* 2 (1978): 10–33.

Tydeman, William. *The Theatre in the Middle Ages*. Cambridge: Cambridge University Press, 1978.

Utesch, Hans. *Die Quellen der Chester-Plays*. Inaugural dissertation, Kiel University, 1909.

Vale, M.G.A. "Piety, Charity and Literacy among the Yorkshire Gentry, 1370–1480." Borthwick Papers, no. 50. Borthwick Institute of Historical Research, University of York, 1976.

Vriend, J. *The Blessed Virgin Mary in the Medieval Drama of England*. Purmerend, Neth.: J. Muusses, 1928.

Walker, J. W. "The Burgess Court, Wakefield: 1533, 1554, 1556, and 1579." *Yorkshire Archaeological Society Records Series* 74 (1929): 16–32.

———. *Wakefield: Its History and People*. Wakefield: West Yorkshire Printing Company, 1934.

Wann, Louis. "A New Examination of the Manuscript of the Towneley Plays." *PMLA* 63 (1928): 137–152.

Ward, Benedicta. *Miracles and the Medieval Mind: Theory, Record, and Event, 1200–1215*. Philadelphia: University of Pennsylvania Press, 1982.

Watt, Homer A. "The Dramatic Unity of the 'Secunda Pastorum.' " In *Essays and Studies in Honor of Carleton Brown*. New York: New York University Press, 1940.

Weimann, Robert. *Shakespeare and the Popular Tradition in the Theatre*. Edited by Robert Schwartz. Baltimore: Johns Hopkins University Press, 1978.

———. *Structure and Society in Literary History: Studies in the History and Theory of Historical Criticism*. Charlottesville: University of Virginia Press, 1976.

Whitelock, Dorothy. *The Beginnings of English Society*. London: Penguin Books, 1952.

Wickham, Glynne. *Early English Stages, 1300–1600*. 3 vols. London: Routledge and Kegan Paul, 1959–1981.

———. *The Medieval Theatre*. New York: St. Martin's Press, 1974.

Williams, Arnold. *The Characterization of Pilate in the Towneley Plays*. East Lansing: Michigan State University Press, 1950.

———. "The Comic in the Cycle." In *Medieval Drama*, edited by Neville Denny. Stratford-upon-Avon Studies, no. 16 (1973): 109–124.

———. *The Drama of Medieval England*. East Lansing: Michigan State University Press, 1961.

———. "Middle English *Questmonger*." *Mediaeval Studies* 10 (1948): 200–204.

———. "Typology and the Cycle Plays: Some Criteria." *Speculum* 43 (1968): 677–684.

Wilson, Robert H. "The *Stanzaic Life of Christ* and the Chester Plays." *North Carolina Studies in Philology* 28 (1931): 413–432.

Withington, Robert. *English Pageantry: An Historical Outline*. 2 vols. Cambridge: Harvard University Press, 1918.

Woolf, Rosemary. "The Effect of Typology on the English Mediaeval Plays of Abraham and Isaac." *Speculum* 32 (1957): 805–825.

———. *The English Mystery Plays*. London: Routledge and Kegan Paul, 1972.

Wright, John, ed. and trans. *The Play of Antichrist*. Toronto: Pontifical Institute of Medieval Studies, 1967.

Wright, Thomas, ed. *The Chester Plays*. London: Shakespeare Society Publications, 1843, 1847; reprinted, 1853.

Young, Karl. *The Drama of the Medieval Church*. 2 vols. Oxford: Clarendon Press, 1933.

INDEX

359

Library of Congress Cataloging-in-Publication Data

Stevens, Martin.
  Four Middle English mystery cycles.

  Bibliography: p.
  Includes index.
  1. Mysteries and miracle-plays, English—
History and criticism. 2. English drama—To 1500—
History and criticism. 3. Bible in literature.

I. Title.
PR643.M8S7 1987   822'.0516'09   86-30376
ISBN 0-691-06714-7 (alk. paper)